This book is the first to look at the aristocratic adoption of Roman ideals in eighteenth-century English culture and thought. Philip Ayres shows how, in the century following the Revolution of 1688, the ruling class promoted – by way of its patronage – a classical frame of mind embracing all the arts, on the foundations of 'liberty' and 'civic virtue'. The historical fact of a Roman Britain lent the endeavour an added authenticity, and it was partly out of an attachment to that past that a new 'Roman' present was constructed by Lord Burlington and his circle. Ayres's study shows that the propensity to adopt the self-image of virtuous Romans was the attempt of a newly empowered oligarchy to dignify and vindicate itself by association with an idealised image of republican Rome. This sense of affinity with the ideals of the free Roman Republic gave British classicism an authenticity impossible under the various versions of absolutism on the continent. Its discourse precluded any more thorough-going revolution by suggesting that Britain's liberty had been won by an 'oligarchy of virtue' which now defended, defined and emblematised the nation.

CLASSICAL CULTURE AND THE IDEA OF ROME IN EIGHTEENTH CENTURY ENGLAND

CLASSICAL CULTURE AND THE IDEA OF ROME

IN EIGHTEENTH-CENTURY ENGLAND

Philip Ayres

CAMBRIDGE
UNIVERSITY PRESS

CAMBRIDGE UNIVERSITY PRESS
Cambridge, New York, Melbourne, Madrid, Cape Town, Singapore, São Paulo, Delhi

Cambridge University Press
The Edinburgh Building, Cambridge CB2 8RU, UK

Published in the United States of America by Cambridge University Press, New York

www.cambridge.org
Information on this title: www.cambridge.org/9780521105798

The publisher acknowledges the assistance of the
Monash University Publications Committee

First published 1997
Reprinted 1999
This digitally printed version 2009

A catalogue record for this publication is available from the British Library

Library of Congress Cataloguing in Publication data
Ayres, Philip J.
Classical culture and the idea of Rome in eighteenth-century
England / Philip Ayres.
p. cm.
Includes bibliographical references and index.
ISBN 0 521 58490 6 (hardback)
1. England – Civilization – 18th century. 2. Great Britain – History – Roman period. 55 B.C.–449 A.D. – Historiography. 3. Great Britain – Civilization – Roman influences. 4. English literature – Roman influences. 5. Ethics, Modern – 18th century. 6. Rome – Historiography. 7. Classicism – England. 8. Ethics – England.
I. Title.
DA485.A9 1997
942.07 – dc21 96–45537 CIP

ISBN 978-0-521-58490-6 hardback
ISBN 978-0-521-10579-8 paperback

For Martin Battestin

Contents

Plates

Preface

This study examines the propensity of the English aristocracy and gentry to image themselves as virtuous Romans in the century following the Revolution settlement of 1688–9. It interprets this activity as the conscious effort of a newly empowered oligarchy to dignify and thereby vindicate itself and the recently established principles of constitutional liberty through association with an idealised image of republican Rome. Of course English liberty also had a strong Gothic heritage which many preferred to emphasise and play off against the classical, and which it is not my concern to discount. It is simply not the focus of this book, which is about the use of classical and particularly Roman models, the manner of that use and the reasons for it. It is addressed to history-of-ideas and cultural history scholars in the eighteenth-century area, but I hope it will also be of interest to specialists in the categories it brings within its synthesis.

In the opening chapters the increased use of Roman analogies after 1688 is explained in terms of historical process and political self-interest, including the need to close off, rhetorically and iconographically, the possibility of any more thorough-going revolution. The book thus proposes a strong motivation for the phenomenon it analyses. It brings together for the first time a wide range of material (some of it, within particular categories like the fine arts, previously subjected to analysis by others, though not from this point of view), and reveals its inter-relatedness as a collaborative discourse of philosophy, aesthetics, archaeology, architecture, literature and politics, all referred back to the principles of the Revolution and the self-interest of the oligarchy – an 'oligarchy of virtue'.

The most cursory examination of the material reveals the depth of the British aristocracy's attachment to the values of classical antiquity and especially the pre-Augustan Roman polity (I avoid the contentious term 'Augustan England'). This attachment was not uncritical, and as recent studies have shown, a growing British nationalism liked to stress the superiority of the present political order to that of classical precedents. At the same time, the sense of considerable political affinity with the ideals of the free Roman Republic gives British classicism a cultural authenticity impossible under any of the continental absolutisms – for example in Bourbon France.

It was the aristocracy, Whig and Tory alike, and to a lesser extent the gentry, who were the chief beneficiaries of 1688. As the monarchy's powers and privileges were diminished, theirs proportionately grew. Anxious for legitimacy, they assumed for themselves the defining and safe-keeping of the principles of political liberty and civic virtue more or less as these had been understood by the Roman-republican senatorial oligarchy. In so doing, they clearly distinguished themselves from the more obviously self-indulgent and less self-consciously virtuous aristocracy under Charles II and James II. This entailed a switch in mores as dramatic as that from Regency to Victorian. The British aristocracy of the eighteenth century proclaimed the classical principles of liberty and virtue in their demeanour, their speeches, their busts and statues, houses and gardens. Even Horace Walpole is not altogether immune from the tendency, though he resisted classical analogies and did so much to revive the Gothic.

Nostalgia for antiquity is inseparable from a sense of estrangement from it, and the eighteenth century's identification with the past is subtle and complex in consequence. Moreover we are dealing here not so much with cultural genuflexion as with self-interest. The settlement of 1688 had to be secured from the possibility of a more thorough-going revolution and from Jacobite attempts to restore the old Stuart order. Both were at least rhetorically foreclosed by the claim that the liberty of the entire nation had already been won by those, Whig or Tory, Government or Parliamentary Opposition, who now defended, defined and emblematised the free state – and castigated each other in its name. On the foundation of 'liberty' and 'civic virtue' this class, by way of its patronage, promoted a discourse embracing all the arts. The historical fact of a Roman Britain lent that discourse added authenticity, and it was in large part out of an attachment to Britain's Roman past that a new Roman present was physically constructed by Burlington and his circle. A small minority among the cultural elite came to believe they shared more ground with philosophers like Cicero than with the credal variety of Christianity. Classical nostalgia (supplemented in Shaftesbury by a strong dose of cultural anti-semitism) is the neglected core of English freethinking.

A cynic might see this 'civic' classicism as merely extravagance with a good conscience and on a scale never before witnessed in England, the enjoyment of a social and intellectual exclusivity tighter than ever, all reinforced by an esoteric and privileging frame of mind. It would not be difficult to show that old-fashioned 'hospitality' and mutual-dependency relations, celebrated in seventeenth-century country-house poems like Jonson's or Marvell's, were less evident in eighteenth-century Palladian villas and verse-celebrations of them. In their tighter exclusivity the new villas were akin to their Roman antecedents. Tenants were turned out and villages demolished to create the English landscape garden. The only limits to self-indulgence were those imposed by a very expensive rule of taste which Shaftesbury, in proposing it, had specifically identified with the antique, with political liberty and civic virtue, and necessarily with the rich. What justified 'civic' classicism was its success in anchoring the principle of political liberty deep within the nation's culture and, by way of the plastic arts, in giving civic values visible form.

In its structure the present work follows a logical order. The first chapter describes the historical and political context for Roman self-imaging in eighteenth-century England (some attention is also given here and subsequently to Scotland), underlines the motive of self-interest in the oligarchy as defenders of classically referred liberty and civic virtue, and offers a wide range of examples of the vogue as well as studies in the uses of relevant classical *personae* in Pope, Swift, Johnson, Fielding and, at greater length, in Thomson and Burke. The second chapter then looks at the ways in which the concepts of liberty and civic virtue, classically referred, were given visible form. The third explores the golden age of

Romano-British archaeology and locates this in relation to the themes of the first two chapters. It is the central chapter because the archaeologists turned illusion into reality by uncovering and describing a tangible Roman Britain to complement and 'verify' the frame of mind the book has previously described and analysed. The fourth chapter logically follows from the third, showing how a new 'Roman Britain' was constructed by the oligarchy alongside the remains of the old. The final chapter demonstrates the effect of classical sensibility on freethinking, and it should be stressed that the examples lie beyond the mainstream.

In the course of this study I have enjoyed the help of a variety of individuals and institutions. His Grace the Duke of Devonshire kindly permitted me to consult Burlington's important collection of archaeological works, as well as the rest of the Chiswick Library, in the Library at Chatsworth. I am also grateful to the Keeper of Collections there, Mr Peter Day, for his valued assistance. Giles Worsley encouraged my interest in tracing connections between neo-Palladianism and Romano-British archaeology and shared unpublished insights with me. I owe particularly strong debts to Colin Horne, Harold Love, Clive Probyn, Robert D. Hume and Martin Battestin, all of whom were generous with their deep and extensive knowledge of the period, each reading the manuscript with care and providing many valuable criticisms, as well as factual details I would otherwise have missed. In a work as extensive in focus as this, expertise is something one frequently relies on friends and colleagues to supplement, and I have no doubt many readers will detect what seem to them significant gaps. Each sub-topic is inevitably compromised to some extent by its synthesis within the wider frame, by a finite manuscript and finite time. I am not an art historian and I regret that I met Sir Joseph Burke so late in his life; by the time I began this study he was no longer well enough to discuss it with me, and it would have benefited from his intimate knowledge of eighteenth-century English art.

I am grateful to the Australian Research Council for a grant which enabled me to travel to England to work on Burlington; to the various libraries which provided me with microfilm and photocopies of manuscript materials; to Monash University for periods of leave which enabled me to carry out my research for this book; and to Vassar College, where I began the writing-up during my term as Visiting Professor in 1993. My most recent debts are to Josie Dixon and Leigh Mueller at Cambridge University Press for their help in the production process. In regard to the plates, I acknowledge the kind assistance of J. Douglas Stewart, and the various institutions which provided me with the photographs.

Abbreviations

AA	*Archaeologia Aeliana*
AH	*Architectural History*
AJ	*Antiquaries Journal*
BAR	British Archaeological Reports
BM	British Museum
Bodl.	Bodleian Library
Burl. Mag.	*Burlington Magazine*
CBEL	*New Cambridge Bibliography of English Literature*, 5 vols. (Cambridge, 1969–77)
CJ	*Classical Journal*
CL	*Country Life*
DBA	H. M. Colvin, *A Biographical Dictionary of British Architects 1600–1840* (London, 1978)
DNB	*Dictionary of National Biography*, ed. L. Stephen and S. Lee, 63 vols. (London, 1885–1900), repr. with corrections, 21 vols. (1908–9)
ECS	*Eighteenth-Century Studies*
ES	*English Studies*
Gunnis	Rupert Gunnis, *A Dictionary of British Sculptors 1660–1851* (London, 1953)
HLQ	*Huntington Library Quarterly*
HWC	The Yale edition of Horace Walpole's Correspondence, ed. Wilmarth S. Lewis, 48 vols. (New Haven, 1937–83)
JEGP	*Journal of English and Germanic Philology*
JHI	*Journal of the History of Ideas*

JWCI	*Journal of the Warburg and Courtauld Institutes*
MP	*Modern Philology*
N&Q	*Notes and Queries*
OED	*Oxford English Dictionary on Historical Principles*, 13 vols. (Oxford, 1933)
Parl. Hist.	*William Cobbett's Parliamentary History of England* (London, 1808–20)
PBA	*Proceedings of the British Academy*
PMLA	*Publications of the Modern Language Association*
PQ	*Philological Quarterly*
RES	*Review of English Studies*
RIBA Journal	*Journal of the Royal Institute of British Architects*
SB	*Studies in Bibliography*
SEL	*Studies in English Literature 1500–1900*
TSLL	*Texas Studies in Literature and Language*
Vertue	*The Notebooks of George Vertue*, in *Wal. Soc.*: I (18, 1930), II (20, 1932), III (22, 1934), IV (24, 1936), V (26, 1938), Index (29, 1947), VI (30, 1950)
Wal. Soc.	*Annual Volumes of the Walpole Society*, 1912–

I

Oligarchy of virtue

LIBERTY AND THE ROMAN ANALOGY

As recent historians have shown, the political and social elites of eighteenth-century England were dominated overwhelmingly by the aristocracy and gentry. At least until 1832 the bourgeoisie played little part in affairs of state. The social division that counted was between patrons and clients within a politics of deference. A multi-fronted revisionist assault has fractured the old Whig and Marxist teleologies of English history, which saw the events of the 1640s and 1688 as the achievement and empowerment of new 'bourgeois' forces at the expense of a 'feudal' aristocracy. To reconstruct these teleologies in any form remotely preserving their seductive clarity would seem virtually impossible.[1] In their place we have a better comprehension of the eighteenth century based on close attention to the primary sources and an openness to its values, as opposed to the anachronistic imposition of our own.

The dominant political discourse of the beneficiaries of the Glorious Revolution was appropriate to an oligarchy intent on maintaining power and privileges won at the expense of the crown and the Stuart cause. This discourse, whose key terms were 'liberty' and 'virtue', was not the preserve of the Whigs, though they might think of it as peculiarly theirs, but was current within most of the political tendencies of the first half of the eighteenth century, including Court Whig, dissident Whig (or 'Patriot') Opposition, Tory and even to an extent Jacobite. Because the discourse was so avowedly moral and civic-minded it seemed *ipso facto* self-legitimising;[2] and of course its terms were rich in classical overtones, lending it authority.

It was not the only discourse, and, as the century progressed, nationalism tended increasingly to subordinate the values and achievements of the classical world to the British present and its glorious future. Widely varied cultures of the past, in some of which the concepts of liberty and civic virtue were unexpressed or unheard of, were assessed for their current relevance, including those of the Celts and the ancient Hebrews (the latter culture signally domesticated for England in the music of Handel). As Howard Weinbrot has shown, the 'much deserved and continuing respect for classical literature and values' should not blind us to elements of cultural 'mistrust, suspicion, and outright hostility as well as competition or emulation of the best sort', suggestive of 'a growing British confidence as a maturing nation ready to take her own place in the world, a place superior in some ways to that of the Ancients'.[3] However, for purposes of political self-justification the classical political heritage served too conveniently to be ignored. The achievements of a Julius or an Augustus Caesar might be deprecated, Cicero despised as a time-server, Horace and Virgil castigated for their subservience to political masters, but very few would have denied the continuing validity of the classical ideal of *libertas* or the social virtue obligatory in citizenship or *civitas*.

These concepts were defined in England much as they had been by the strikingly similar oligarchy of late-republican Rome, by Machiavelli and by other Renaissance writers.[4] This is not to say that their use always carries an implicit reference to the classical past, though this is frequently the case. In Rome the concept of *libertas*, before its transformation under the Empire, was inseparable from *civitas* and the constitution of the Republic, for under the *dominatio* of the kings there had been no *libertas*. *Libertas* also distinguished the free citizen from the slave.[5] In England, on the other hand, the concept was accommodated within the framework of monarchy, having long been associated with the unwritten constitution of the common law going back to Anglo-Saxon times. After 1688, however, it was often seen as finally secured by the Revolution settlement, indeed seen by many Whigs as effectively originating with that settlement.[6]

The preferred political analogies after 1688 were more often Roman than Greek or Gothic not merely because of aesthetic inclination, though this was important in the arts, but because, as Reed Browning has put it, 'Republican Rome was marked by struggles between would-be despots and defenders of liberty, by vigorous factional contention, and by a class structure that, without excessive distortion, could be made to appear like Britain's. From the Republic Britons professed to learn the absolute necessity of having good men participate in public life.'[7] The history of the Republic, particularly as analysed by Machiavelli in his *Discourses on the First Ten Books of Livy*, showed how to avoid the errors and corruption that had finally undermined Roman civic virtue and liberty. By analogy with the defence of the Republic by heroes like Cato and Cicero, the English oligarchy could image itself as the classically spirited guarantor of the liberties it had won for all in its fight against Stuart absolutism.

Republican Rome had been celebrated and mined for analogies long before 1688 – the argument of this book is not that the Revolution was causative in this regard but that it was immensely stimulative. Generations had read Sallust, Livy and Tacitus at school and university, assimilating their biases, learning to admire the first Brutus, the Horatii, Cincinnatus, the two Catos and Cicero, rehearsing the arguments for and against Julius Caesar and Octavian/Augustus, Brutus and Cassius. The finest expression of Roman-republican sentiment in English Renaissance literature is Ben Jonson's *Sejanus* (1605), Tacitean in its idealisation of republican principles and in its anti-Tiberian bias.[8] Dryden, defender of Stuart absolutism, casts the English as republican Romans and the Dutch as Carthaginians in his *Annus Mirabilis* (1666), and there are many other examples before the Revolution. Moreover, it was always possible to admire Cicero *and* the best aspects of the reign of an Augustus or a Marcus Aurelius, the principles of the Republic *and* the better *principes* (above all the Antonines) simply by echoing Tacitus: the late Republic proved unworthy of liberty. Jonson makes this point in *Catiline* and *Sejanus*, which extol the principles of the Republic, not its fag-end reality.

It is crucial, however, to note that the struggle of the late-republican Roman senatorial oligarchy was not against regal absolutism, a struggle won by 509 BC, but against a 'democratic' party led by *populares*, politicians and generals like Marius and Julius Caesar who pitched their appeal to the people and sought to diminish the Senate's authority.[9] Not surprisingly, this vital feature of late-republican Roman history receives little overt notice in the England of William and Mary, Anne and the first two Georges. Hardly anyone talks about 'oligarchy'. However, when they associate English liberty with the liberties of Rome as defended for an oligarchic Senate by Cato, Brutus and Cicero, the English oligarchy effectively deny the legitimacy of any more thorough-going, democratising revolution than that already achieved. They needed to do this in a period when some memories reached back to the diggers and levellers. Many at the turn of the century vividly recalled the threat of mob rule during the anti-Popish campaign of 1678–80 and the events of Monmouth's later populist rebellion. Monmouth aspired to be a kind of English Marius, attempting with some success to foment a popular rising in the depressed industrial regions of the west and using a people's army to seize the crown.[10] These events suggested what might lie in store if the limits of revolution were not spelt out. It had to be understood that the propertied, particularly those with considerable landed property, were the appropriate guarantors of liberty and civic virtue.[11] Roman history was supposed to be the proof.

The preference for Roman-republican models, then, had much to do with political convenience and class affinities. The Greek heritage was a less significant ingredient in the political discourse of the early eighteenth century. One exception is Shaftesbury. Half a century before Winckelmann's more scientific neo-classicism established Greek taste above Roman, Shaftesbury reserved his strongest admiration for Greek aesthetic models. He associated freedom with the flourishing of the arts and emphasised the Greek heritage of liberty.[12] However, as James William Johnson has pointed out,

> Although in many ways the Neo-Classicist's obsession with historical authority and his enthusiasm for things Greek complemented each other, in one important way – the formulation of personal codes of conduct – they did not permit a very satisfactory reconciliation. It was partially because of this failure that the [English] Neo-Classical emphasis after 1700 came to be put more strongly on Roman culture than Greek.[13]

The supposedly Gothic source of British liberties in the Saxon assembly or witenagemot, and in the later Magna Carta which confirmed it, also counted strongly for many, of course. There are continuing references, in Bolingbroke and many others, to England's balanced 'Gothic' constitution and its ancient 'Gothic' Parliament, and Cokean respect for the Gothic common law as the foundation of English liberties, with a corresponding resistance to 'Roman' law as codified by Justinian. The 'Patriot' opposition to Walpole invoked this tradition whenever it suited them, as it often did.[14] However, Polybius' praise for the balanced constitutions of Sparta and Rome encouraged many to stress the classical connections when they spoke of England's balanced constitution. Classical republicans in particular cited Aristotle, Polybius and Cicero on constitutional balance and compared England with Sparta, Rome and Venice.[15] The Court Whigs under Walpole, desirous of presenting themselves as the defenders of liberties their party had secured, liked to picture the English as slaves until 1688, and accordingly downplayed England's 'ancient', 'Gothic' constitution and 'Gothic liberties' (as had the Tories, for different reasons, under Charles II,[16] and Bacon – as opposed to Coke – much earlier under James I[17]). Their party, they insisted, had created the balanced constitution with the Glorious Revolution, and their models and analogies were generally classical. Though some, like Blackstone and Burke, might still invoke the 'ancient' medieval constitution, for many the 'Gothic' came increasingly to be associated with tyranny,[18] and in literature with horror. Later in the century, more sophisticated and less glamorised views of the Roman Republic reinforced the tendency of radicals like Joseph Priestley and Richard Price to dissociate themselves from the oligarchic discourse of liberty, reject the Whig thesis of the Glorious Revolution and reinstate the Norman Yoke thesis.[19]

If the Revolution was such a key stimulant to the use of Roman analogies, one may reasonably ask why the official language of that revolution was not itself rich in references to the classical past. Discussions of how the Court Whigs after 1688 'strove to annex the Roman ideal to their own cause'[20] or of the 'controlling importance of Roman models' in the politics of Georgian England[21] beg, but overlook or avoid, this fundamental question. It has to be recognised that the political language of 1688, in the narrow sense of official historical documents, proclamations, accounts of the Parliamentary debates, papers of state generally, was necessarily couched in the language not of classical analogy but of English common law, because the change simply had to be defended and legitimated on that basis. There was no room in that court for metaphor and allusion. An emphasis on the defence of the Protestant religion was also vital.[22] Most of the drier histories of England published in the fifty years after 1688 are similarly concerned to legitimise the outcome of the Revolution in terms of the constitution and the common law, and the danger of popery.

Imaginative literature, on the other hand, frequently insists on the connection between 1688 and the Roman Republic. If one looks through the relevant volumes of *Poems on Affairs of State* and some of the political drama of the period one sees Whigs in particular continually making connections between contemporary political events and ancient Rome, both in the critical years leading up to and immediately after the Revolution. Even when this is merely gestural, an important process of self-imaging is involved. Roman-republican gestures legitimate the ruling class in a cultural–historical court where, because of the universality of classical education, the civic values are generally agreed. As we shall see in the case of Shaftesbury, who continually emphasises the political and cultural analogies between the England of the Revolution settlement and republican Rome, the need for a validating self-imaging gave impetus to the drive for a purer classicism in the arts.

Many Georgian political writers, as well as the occasional historian, viewed the Revolution principles in terms of Roman-republican values. For instance John Oldmixon, in *The History of England* (1730), sees liberty not as a Gothic heritage but as secured at the Revolution. The Whig Government 'has the same Foundation with our *Liberty*' – 1688 and the crises preceding it – 'and the joint Security of both is inseparable' despite Tory attempts to 'blanch' the characters of Stuart kings 'as so many *Patres Patriae*, and to blacken *Your Patriots* and Champions'.[23] Oldmixon is attacking the Tories for describing the Stuarts as *patres patriae*, not directly claiming the title for the Whigs, but the force of his statement is in the suggestion of paradox: the Tories have it around the wrong way, it is they who are morally black and the Whigs the true *patres patriae*. Everyone knew that Cicero had been the first to receive the honorific *pater patriae*, and that Augustus (like the Tories) perversely appropriated it. A writer for the *Gazetteer* blames Augustus Caesar for subverting the mores of Senate and People and destroying Rome's balanced constitution which had been established on 'Revolution Principles'.[24] In other words the principles of the Roman Republic were the principles of 1688. Here the equation is as blunt as it gets. Edward Wortley Montagu, in the course of a discussion on Polybian balance in constitutions, compares 'The form of the Roman Republick', which was 'the production of necessity', of crises rather than reasoning, with England's achievement in 1688 when crisis dictated that a Polybian balance be established once and for all through the 'joint exercise' by Lords and Commons of the 'restraining power', 'conducted by Patriotism'.[25] There are many similar examples.

Central to the principles of the Revolution was opposition to a standing army. This key element was always referred to classical argument and precedent, as in Walter Moyle's 'An Argument against a Standing Army' (1697). Moyle turns the Whigs' Roman-republican perspective against them just as they have turned against their own Revolution principles on the issue: Marius, 'Head of the *Whig* Faction in Rome', first subverted Roman liberties by introducing standing armies.[26] Thus the Whigs of England are just like their models, the Whigs of ancient Rome, betraying the same principles.

Turning to the field of imaginative literature, Arthur Mainwaring's Jacobite *Tarquin and Tullia* (1689), a political allegory in which William III is Lucius Tarquinius, James II is Tullius, and Mary is Tullia, implicitly attacks supporters of the Revolution on their own classic ground for habitually identifying their cause, their rights, liberties and property with the Roman Republic: they blacken James's name with false charges and

dismal frights –
The loss of property, and sacred rights.
And freedom – words which all false patriots use,
The surest names the Romans to abuse,
Jealous of Kings, and always malcontent.[27]

The satire is effective in a double sense: the Whigs commonly 'abuse' the Romans by way of their false rhetoric of allusion; moreover, the Whigs, like the Romans to whom they appeal, really want to be rid of kings. In Charles Blount's 'A Dialogue between King William and the Late King James' (1690), William twice grounds his right in the social contract and the 'public safety' (*salus publica*, a justification of power often used on ancient Roman coins), but James despises him as

A marble Caesar pinioned to a throne,
The people regnant, and the monarch stone.[28]

Daniel Defoe's 'A New Satyr on the Parliament' (1701) supports the right of 'We the People' to 'punish and depose' their 'Senators' for not adequately supporting William's military needs.[29] William Shippen's 'Faction Display'd' (1704) castigates the Whigs for betraying the very principles they pretend to embody:

Blest Patriots these, who Liberty employ,
T'elude thy Laws, and Liberty destroy!
Where is the Noble *Roman* Spirit fled,
Which once inspir'd thy ancient Patriots dead?
Who were above all private Ends, and joy'd,
When bravely for the publick Weal they dy'd.[30]

The Whigs merely pretend to be Romans.

Other identifications aside from the Roman kind could always be employed according to inclination, of course. Polemical divines found a model for William III in the Old Testament. Analogies were useful but not essential: among various arguments that found print, William was justified by the simple law of conquest, and the Revolution defended in purely theoretical terms with reference to John Locke's second *Treatise of Government* (written during the Exclusion crisis of the late 1670s and early 1680s). Roman analogies were congenial to the beneficiaries of the Revolution, not *de rigueur*.

In some of the Whig political drama of the pre-Revolutionary years of crisis, for example in Nathaniel Lee's *Lucius Junius Brutus* (1681), early republican Romans are depicted as good Whigs living two millennia before their time, and the Glorious Revolution anticipated. In that play, banned after three nights, the Roman Republic is born in circumstances wrested to parallel contemporary events. When a character cries 'Guard and Defend the Liberty of Rome',[31] the real topic is English political liberty as understood and represented by the Whigs. The Roman-republican future is England's Whig future, as the emphases on religion, trade and manufacturing make clear: it will be a state of 'freeborn People'

> Where there's no innovation of Religion,
> No change of Laws, nor breach of Priviledge,
> No desperate Factions gaping for Rebellion,
> No hopes of Pardon for Assassinates,
> No rash advancements of the Base or stranger,
> For Luxury, for Wit, or glorious Voice;
> But on the contrary, a Balanc'd Trade,
> Patriots incourag'd, Manufactors cherish'd . . .
> O, Conscript Fathers, 'tis on these Foundations
> That *Rome* shall build her *Empire* to the Stars,[32]

and so on. Lee's play shows that the Whigs of the early 1680s were already identifying their cause with that of republican Rome. Roman analogies had been drawn for decades, but *Lucius Junius Brutus* is on a totally different plane of significance, and after 1688 and the establishment of Revolution principles it was natural that Lee's telling analogies should be made with greater frequency and point.[33] Addison's *Cato* was popular precisely because audiences were accustomed to paralleling the England of the Revolution settlement with republican Rome. The same analogising is strong in the opera, for example in Handel's *Lucio Cornelio Silla* (1713), where Sulla seems to represent liberty-threatening Marlborough as seen through Tory eyes.[34]

In 1712, a year before *Cato* was staged, Addison praised the English constitution as more perfectly mixed on Polybian and Ciceronian principles than even the Roman. This would become a common theme with Whig writers:

> I could never read a Passage in *Polybius*, and another in *Cicero*, to this purpose, without a secret Pleasure in applying it to the *English* Constitution, which it

> suits much better than the *Roman*. Both these great Authors give the Pre-eminence to a mixt Government, consisting of three Branches, the Regal, the Noble, and the Popular. They had doubtless in their Thoughts the Constitution of the *Roman* Common-wealth, in which the Consul represented the King, the Senate the Nobles, and the Tribunes the People. This Division of the three Powers in the *Roman* Constitution, was by no means so distinct and natural, as it is in the *English* form of Government. Among several Objections that might be made to it, I think the chief are those that affect the Consular Power, which had only the Ornaments without the Force of the Regal Authority. Their Number had not a casting Voice in it; for which reason, if one did not chance to be employed Abroad, while the other sat at Home, the Publick Business was sometimes at a stand, while the Consuls pulled two different ways in it. Besides, I do not find that the Consuls ever had a Negative Voice in the passing of a Law, or Decree of Senate, so that indeed they were rather the chief Body of the Nobility, or the first Ministers of State, than a distinct Branch of the Sovereignty, in which none can be looked upon as a part, who are not a part of the Legislature. Had the Consuls been invested with the Regal Authority to as great a Degree as our Monarchs, there would never have been any Occasions for a Dictatorship, which had in it the Power of all the three Orders, and ended in the Subversion of the whole Constitution.[35]

One notes the attention to detail with which the comparisons are thought out. They matter. Zera S. Fink has shown how 'ideas associated with classical republicanism lived on in English thought after republicanism itself was dead' and how 'the concept of mixed government became incorporated in what may be called the Whig theory of the English constitution'.[36] Despite its traditional association with republicanism, the concept of mixed government, current in England as early as the sixteenth century, had never been incompatible with monarchy (Sparta, a favourite model with classical republicans, was a dual monarchy). Even the Tories adopted it after 1688. It had been around for so long that many associated it with England's old 'Gothic' constitution, requiring Swift in 1701 'to protest against the prevalence of the notion that the idea of mixed government was of Gothic origin'.[37]

The Roman analogy was strengthened if one described England as a republic with a king. To this effect various writers, influenced by the classical-republican ideas of James Harrington, Algernon Sidney and others, cleared the word 'commonwealth', synonymous with the Latin *respublica*, of its Cromwellian associations and allowed it to include a monarchy of the English type.[38] The deist John Toland was one of these.[39] In *The State Anatomy of Great Britain* (1717) he contended that

> Such a Constitution as this of ours, is reckon'd the best of all others by the most judicious of the ancients, as *Aristotle*, *Polybius*, and *Cicero* ... As for the word *Commonwealth* (which is the common-weal or good) whenever we use it about our Government, we take it only in this sense: just as the word *Respublica* in *Latin*, is a general word for all free Governments, of which we believe ours to be the best. This is the sense in which King *James* I, call'd himself, *the great servant of the Commonwealth*; and in which Sir *Thomas Smith*, Secretary of State to more than one of our Princes, entitles his account of the *English* Government, *the Commonwealth of* England.[40]

Rousseau would later make the same point in the *Social Contract*: 'Any state which is ruled by law I call a "republic", whatever the form of its constitution; for then, and then alone, does the public interest govern and then alone is the "public thing" – the *res publica* – a reality. All legitimate government is "republican".' In a footnote he adds, 'So even a monarchy can be a republic.'[41] The commonwealthsman Thomas Gordon, author with John Trenchard of the anti-Walpolean *Cato's Letters* which appeared in the early 1720s, described England as 'the best republic in the world with a prince at the head of it'.[42] This use of the word 'republic' to mean 'commonwealth' was not new in England.[43]

In 1700 John Toland, dedicating his edition of James Harrington's classical-republican *Commonwealth of Oceana* (1656), a scheme for an oligarchic republic, to the Lord Mayor, aldermen, sheriffs and common council of London, identified key aspects of the constitution of the Bank of England and the government of the City with corresponding features in the Roman Republic. Referring to the Bank 'which, like the Temple of SATURN among the *Romans*, is esteem'd so sacred a Repository, that even Foreners think their Treasure more safely lodg'd there than with themselves at home', he praised its constitution for coming 'the nearest of any Government to HARRINGTON's Model'. Styling London 'a *New Rome in the West*' which deserved 'like the old one, to becom the Soverain

Mistress of the Universe', and stressing the importance of having men of 'good Qualitys' (solid independent means) as sheriffs so 'that as having the greatest Stakes to lose they will be the more concern'd for securing the Property of others', he compared the Lord Mayor to a Roman consul, the city's sheriffs to Roman praetors, the common council to Rome's popular assemblies and the Court of Aldermen to 'the Aristocratical Senat of the City', noting that 'the eldest Alderman', Sir Robert Clayton, 'is the same at *London* with what the Prince of the Senat was at *Rome*'. To honour Clayton for 'the courage with which he acted' in the late revolution, 'particularly in bringing in the Bill for excluding a Popish Successor from the Crown', the grateful people 'on this occasion first styl'd him *the Father of the City*, as CICERO for the like reason was the first of all *Romans* call'd *the Father of his Country*'. Clayton and his colleagues were models of civic virtue.

> To whom therfore shou'd I inscribe a Book containing the Rules of good Polity, but to a Society so admirably constituted, and producing such Great and Excellent Men? That elswhere there may be found who understand Government better, distribute Justice wiser, or love Liberty more, I could never persuade my self to imagin: nor can the Person wish for a nobler Address, or the Subject be made happy in a more sutable Patronage than THE SENAT AND PEOPLE OF *LONDON*.[44]

When Voltaire said he thought Addison's *Cato* 'faite pour un auditoire un peu philosophe et très-républicain',[45] and when he reported in the 1730s that 'The members of the English Parliament are fond of comparing themselves to the old Romans',[46] he was registering that tendency of the English to identify with the SENATVS POPVLVSQVE ROMANVS which Toland had shown in 1700. So was the Duke of Cumberland when he chose the inscription REPVBLICA SERVATA MDCCXLVI for the base of a bust of himself sculpted in 1746 following his victory over the tribal *barbari* at Culloden.[47] Republican Rome, its civic virtues and vices, its politics and class structure, the dangers it faced not just from Julius Caesar and autocracy but, it was implicitly understood, from the democratic element since the days of Marius and (for many) the Gracchi, all this became a compound metaphor for the state of England in the decades following 1688, exploitable by Whigs and Tories alike. Louis XIV might identify with Augustus but he thereby denied to the French state, insofar as it existed outside of himself, any connection with the free Roman Republic and its old institutions. It is the English ruling class's deep sense of affinity with this Rome and its oligarchic, not its popular, traditions, which gives English classicism an entire dimension of meaning absent from any of the contemporary continental classicisms until the French Revolution and the assimilation of Roman-republican iconography under the Republic.

It is unsurprising, then, that a proper understanding of Roman history and its relevance to contemporary England was, with a good knowledge of French, one of the first things the fourth Earl of Chesterfield tried to drive into the head of his son. Born in 1732, by 1738 the child was already learning that

> De toutes les histoires anciennes, la plus intéressante, et la plus instructive, c'est l'histoire Romaine. Elle est la plus fertile en grands hommes, et en grands événements. Elle nous anime, plus que toute autre, à la vertu; en nous montrant, comment une petite ville, comme Rome, fondée par une poignée de pâtres et d'aventuriers, s'est rendue dans l'espace de sept cents ans maîtresse du monde, par le moyen de sa vertu et de son courage.[48]

Liberty and civic virtue, Chesterfield stressed, were inseparable. Under Augustus Rome reached the high point of her grandeur, 'mais elle ne l'était plus d'elle-même; ayant perdu son ancienne liberté, et son ancienne vertu'.[49] There were lessons too in pre-republican Rome, points of close resemblance with modern England. Its monarchy was not absolute: 'Remarquez bien que le gouvernement de Rome sous Romulus était un gouvernement mixte et libre; et que le roi n'était rien moins qu'absolu;[50] au contraire il partageait l'autorité avec le sénat, et le peuple, à peu près comme le roi ici, avec la Chambre Haute, et la Chambre Basse.' For trying to violate the Senate's authority and the liberty of the people, Romulus was punished 'comme tout tyran mérite de l'être. Tout homme a un droit naturel à sa liberté, et quiconque veut la lui ravir, mérite la mort.'[51] The last king, Tarquin, 'avec toute sa famille fut banni de Rome, par un décret solennel . . . Telle est la fin que méritent tous les tyrans, et tous ceux qui ne se servent du pouvoir que le sort leur a donné, que pour faire du mal, et opprimer le genre humain.'[52] Tarquin is a type of James II. By the time the boy is ten, Chesterfield is concentrating on recent English history: had Charles I not been executed 'we had had no liberties left'; Charles II 'gave all he had to whores and favourites' and 'became a pensioner to France'; James II 'was of a sour, cruel, and tyrannical disposition' and 'the nation, very wisely and justly, turned him out'; William III 'would have been glad of more power than he ought to have; but his Parliaments kept him within due bounds, against his will', and so on.[53] Chesterfield was inculcating a thoroughly Whig reading of Roman and British history, and if he occasionally interprets Roman history anachronistically in the light of contemporary English experience, it was no more than what any Whig writer might do – this, for example: 'Had all the *Roman* Patriots been as much Whigs as *Cato*, *Julius Caesar* and his Tories would never have had an opportunity to subvert their Libertys.'[54]

As Britain's power increased abroad, analogies with the classical world became less and less deferential, developing a strongly expansionist aspect. For Pope the time was near when Britain would be acknowledged the equal of Greece and Rome for her attainments in peace and war, and for the skill with which her history was recorded on coins and medals:

> Oh when shall Britain, conscious of her claim,
> Stand emulous of Greek and Roman fame?
> In living medals see her wars enroll'd,
> And vanquish'd realms supply recording gold?
> Here, rising bold, the Patriot's honest face;
> There Warriors frowning in historic brass:
> Then future ages with delight shall see
> How Plato's, Bacon's, Newton's looks agree;
> Or in fair series laurelled Bards be shown,
> A Virgil there, and here an Addison.[55]

Britain's ability to surpass Rome was a common theme as Britain became an imperial power of the first rank. Horace Walpole's correspondence is illustrative if often sceptical. In 1759 he observed in regard to recent victories in the Seven Years' War that

> We have taken more places and ships in a week than would have set up such pendant nations as Greece and Rome to all futurity. If we did but call Sir William Johnson [commanding at the capture of Niagara], Gulielmus Johnsonus Niagaricus; and Amherst [Jeffrey Amherst, commander-in-chief in North America, commanding at the capture of Fort Ticonderoga], Galfridus Amhersta Ticonderogicus, we should be quoted a thousand years hence as the patterns of valour, virtue, and disinterestedness; for posterity always ascribes all manner of modesty and self-denial to those that take the most pains to perpetuate their own glory. Then Admiral Boscawen has, in very Roman style, made free with the coast of Portugal, and used it to make a bonfire of the French fleet. When Mr Pitt was told of this infraction of a neutral territory, he replied, 'It is very true, but they are burned.' – In short, we want but a little more insolence and a worse cause to make us a very classic nation.[56]

Walpole, who had flown in the face of English neo-classicism by re-animating the Gothic at Strawberry Hill to striking effect, had since the 1730s been dismissive of the self-congratulatory Roman analogising in which Opposition Whigs indulged at the expense of his father the Prime Minister.[57] His scepticism about the virtues of 'classic nations' was probably common enough. It reflects both a natural contrariness provoked by the general enthusiasm for things classical, and a refusal to mythologise history. William Hogarth, too, ridiculed classicist pretensions, including Burlington's, Kent's and Pope's.[58] Walpole was prescient on the matter of *agnomines*: Wolfe *of Quebec*, Clive *of India*, Montgomery *of Alamein*, Mountbatten *of Burma* are the English equivalents of Scipio *Africanus*. Some analogies were a little too just for Walpole. 'As this age is to be historic', he observed ironically in 1762, 'so of course it will be a standard of virtue too; and we, like our wicked predecessors the Romans, shall be quoted, till our very ghosts blush, as models of patriotism and magnanimity.'[59] Yet he could use Roman parallels with a straight face, lamenting the pillorying of the reprinter of the *North Briton* in 1765 as symptomatic of a period in which 'every man of virtue is proscribed', and this following on national triumphs over which he 'had felt all the Roman pride of being one of the first nation upon earth'.[60] 'There is nothing more like than two ages that are very alike',[61] he lamented in 1772 in reference to late-republican Rome and contemporary Britain. He could say seriously in 1780 that 'Like the Romans I would have Rome domineer over the world, and be free at home', even though 'The old man in me is sensible there is little equity in this, and that a good patriot is a bad citizen of the world.'[62] It was perhaps his attachment to a British *imperium*, something he had in common with Romanophiles since Toland (who had foreseen the 'New Rome in the West' becoming 'the Soverain Mistress of the Universe'), that led Walpole by 1785 to admire, above the usual Roman-republican heroes, the good emperors of the late first and second centuries, 'that marvellous period . . . when five excellent princes, though possessed of absolute power, succeeded to one another, Nerva, Trajan, Hadrian, and the two Antonines'. Fielding and Gibbon are among others who single out this group for particular praise.[63]

As the empire was expanded and consolidated through the middle decades of the century, a new identity of English, Scots, Welsh and Irish as a nation of 'Britons' engaged in a joint patriotic endeavour drew sustenance from appropriate classical analogies. Linda Colley has observed that 'classical literature was doubly congenial because the kind of patriotic achievement it celebrated was a highly specific one. The heroes of Homer, Cicero and Plutarch were emphatically men of rank and title. As such, they reminded Britain's ruling elite of its duty to serve and fight.'[64]

Edward Gibbon identified the British with the Roman pattern of colonisation, each colony becoming a little Rome, Romanising all about it. He had the idea from Hume. 'The American world . . . is already filled with [Europe's] colonies and institutions.'[65] On the loss of the United States Gibbon drew a contrast with Rome's loss of Britain – ancient Romans had behaved better: 'Britain was irrecoverably lost. But as the emperors wisely acquiesced in the independence of a remote province, the separation was not embittered by the reproach of tyranny or rebellion; and the claims of allegiance and protection were succeeded by the mutual and voluntary offices of national friendship.'[66]

There were profounder parallels accessible to those with a knowledge of late-republican Roman politics and society. Though he was not concerned with the Roman analogy, Sir Lewis Namier put his finger on a crucial affinity in the matter of elections. He described an eighteenth-century English politics principally determined and defined not by political parties and their supposedly distinct ideologies but by ambition and influence. The division that mattered was between 'ins' and 'outs', and patron–client networks (starting with the king as principal patron) based on family and social influence counted enormously. So did the ubiquitous bribery, which at least showed that the system was in healthy flux, clients up for grabs and the patrons less than totally secure.[67] Interestingly, this (aside from the fact of a king) was precisely the structure of politics in the late Roman Republic. The relationship between *patronus* and *cliens*, based on a mixture of familial and extra-familial influence, and bribery, was vital whether the political aspirant identified with the *optimates* or 'the people'. It was the system in which Caesar carved out his political career. In reading about a Roman politics of patronage and deference the eighteenth-century oligarchy were reading about their own.

Even the hustings at their most farcical smelt of Rome to Carl Philipp Moritz in 1782. After describing in grubby detail the scene of a no-contest victory speech by Sir Cecil Wray, 'publicly chosen' in Covent Garden, he added: 'All the enthusiasm of my earliest years, kindled by the patriotism of the illustrious heroes of Rome, Coriolanus, Julius Caesar, and Antony, were now revived in my mind: and though all I had just seen and heard, be, in fact, but the semblance of liberty, and that too tribunicial liberty, yet at that moment, I thought it charming, and it warmed my heart.'[68] A more thorough understanding of the electoral system as it operated across England would have deepened Moritz's appreciation of the affinities he sensed.

As Moritz knew, there was no 'tribunicial liberty' in England in the eighteenth century. Sir William Blackstone rightly distinguished British from Roman-republican politics in this important respect:

> This constitution of suffrages [based on a moderate property qualification] is framed upon a wiser principle, with us, than either of the methods of voting, by centuries or by tribes, among the Romans. In the method by centuries, instituted by Servius Tullius, it was principally property, and not numbers, that turned the scale: in the method by tribes, gradually introduced by the tribunes of the people, numbers only were regarded, and property entirely overlooked. Hence the laws passed by the former method had usually too great a tendency to aggrandize the patricians or rich nobles; and those by the

> latter had too much of a levelling principle. Our constitution steers between the two extremes.[69]

The concept of liberty as it was discussed and understood for most of the eighteenth century was inextricably bound up with property, far more so than in ancient Rome where the popular assemblies had given a voice to the urban poor. In Britain it was accepted that only the propertied men should vote and that the best defence of the nation's liberty lay in propertied hands. For Locke the relation of liberty to property was primary. Government was first created specifically to secure property – indeed 'Government has no other end but the preservation of Property.'[70] This was a feature of Locke's argument all could agree with even if his contract theory was too radical for many to accept. Naturally then, the concept of property was elevated along with liberty after 1688. The Revolution having secured the rights, including rights in property, of the citizen, logically those rights should be strengthened in law. J. G. A. Pocock, arguing against the seductively clear-cut Marxist idea that 'political man' was replaced by 'economic man' in the eighteenth century, has shown how the increased emphasis on property was sustained by and reinforced a classical-political frame of mind. The classical ideal, 'reborn with the great recovery of aristocracy which marks the later seventeenth and eighteenth centuries', ensured that 'property was always discussed in the political context of authority and liberty'.[71] In defining 'liberty', English classical republicans of the second half of the seventeenth century had followed Guicciardini for whom government existed to secure the propertied from tyrants and people, both enemies of 'liberty'.[72] This was one of the most important lessons taught by the expiring Roman Republic.

It is important to note that by 1720 men of all political persuasions, not just the Whigs, were regularly identifying their causes with the Roman Republic. The great majority in the articulate political nation until mid-century is pro-senatorial and anti-Caesarian, though far more anti-Julian than anti-Augustan.[73] Augustus had partly redeemed himself by giving the Empire a long peace after a century of recurring civil wars, by supporting the arts, by attempting to restore older standards of public and private morality and respect for the gods. Even Tacitus, so cynical in regard to Augustus, despaired of the old Roman spirit. Like the historian

Cremutius Cordus (early first century) he saw Brutus and Cassius as the last of the Romans. All civic virtue dead, the nation deserved the restraints and scourges the principate brought with it.

Nobody, however, Whig or Tory, not even the very few pro-Caesarean historians, proclaimed against the *virtuous* Republic of the days before luxury and vice. John Dennis and Aaron Hill admired Julius Caesar precisely for understanding that this once-admirable institution had become an empty shell. The tumultuous state of Roman affairs was to be put down to 'the whole Body of the Patricians' who, 'by their Ambition, their Avarice, and their Luxury . . . had brought the *Roman* Affairs into so much Confusion, that *Rome* was in Necessity of having a Master'. Had Caesar not crossed the Rubicon, another would have had to bury the dead Republic and institute a state of affairs productive of peace and political direction.[74]

The problem with this view was that it did nothing to justify the patriciate of England – quite the reverse. Not until Nathaniel Hooke's *Roman History* began to appear in 1738 did it gain wide currency. As a Tory populist in the tradition of Bolingbroke, Hooke's sympathies lay with the lower classes and he backed the popular side in Roman politics.[75] His *Roman History* provided classical analogies for those Tories who could see that an excellent form of attack on the Whigs who governed England was to show that they were as unrepresentative and greedy as the Roman senatorial oligarchy they so admired.[76] During the decades since 1688 many Tories in Parliament, though naturally unfriendly to Lockean notions of government as entrusted to its representatives by a sovereign people, had gradually accommodated themselves to the Revolution settlement and its rhetoric, presenting themselves as the friends of liberty, but, until works like Hooke's *Roman History* demonstrated more interesting approaches, in a generally copy-cat fashion – Country Tories, for instance, often following Bolingbroke in adopting classical-republican language of a neo-Harringtonian cast.[77] The Court Whigs under Walpole, assailed by Opposition Whigs fond of invoking Cato and ancient virtue, simply developed an alternative Roman-republican defence based on identification with another great republican hero, Cicero, who had the advantage of being more pragmatic than Cato.[78] Old classical republicans and commonwealthsmen like John Trenchard and Thomas Gordon, authors of the anti-Walpolean *Cato's Letters* (which ran in the *London Journal* in the early 1720s and were published as a collection in 1724), easily accommodated themselves to a now-limited monarchy and saw their rhetoric plagiarised by Tories and even Jacobites, who were not averse to invoking liberty in its radical forms.[79]

Within the generally pro-Roman-republican consensus, however, there were disagreements on historical particulars often reflective of a writer's visceral politics, which might be different from what his rhetoric of liberty leads one to expect. Swift, for example:

> Fair LIBERTY was all his Cry;
> For her he stood prepar'd to die;
> For her he boldly stood alone;
> For her he oft expos'd his own.[80]

Liberty of conscience was another matter. This votary of the goddess Liberty was at one with the high Tories in their support for the Test Act, and opposed to the policies of land reform fatally launched by the Gracchi in the second century BC. Swift's *Contests and Dissensions in Athens and Rome* (1701) is heavily biassed against the popular side of Roman politics. He neglects to mention that Tiberius Gracchus was acting in defence of poor farmers and of the old Licinian law, whose limits on the acreage one might own were being flagrantly disregarded by rich landowners in their development of the great slave-farmed *latifundia*. Swift's opposition is not to Gracchus' anti-constitutional methods which (unlike classical historians) he neglects to criticise, but to their levelling tendencies and the threat they offered to the nobility. The Gracchi 'fell violently upon advancing the Power of the People, by reducing into Practice all those Encroachments, which they had been so many Years gaining'. Following their example, Pompey and Caesar in their consulships 'used all Endeavours and Occasions for sinking the Authority of the *Patricians*, and giving Way to all Encroachments of the People'. By this time 'there was no Government left, but a *Dominatio Plebis*'. Dictatorship was the outcome.[81] In his use of Roman history Nathaniel Hooke was a more subtle and less visceral Tory than Swift. Implicitly identifying a selfish

Roman patriciate with England's Whig government, Hooke could praise Tiberius Gracchus to good tactical effect: 'He *fell off* from the Senate . . . [and] quitted the faction of the oppressors of their country, men determined to proceed in a course that was *contrary to all law and compassion, and directly tended to enslave* Rome.'[82] Some Whigs also thought well of the Gracchi.[83]

However, with the exception of genuinely radical Tories like Hooke, who through the mid-century gradually succeeded in undermining the once-spotless image of the Roman senatorial and oligarchic cause, most writers, whether Whigs, Tories or commonwealthsmen, who invoked Roman analogies in the first five or six decades after 1688 did so to support the privileges and power of the English patriciate, often quite explicitly. This is something which unites the Tory Swift and the commonwealthsmen John Trenchard and Thomas Gordon. Trenchard anticipated Bolingbroke's call for a populist king who would rule England in the interests of the people rather than party and dirty finance, but this clever rhetoric was aimed at Walpole and the new-money men, not at oligarchy. In *Cato's Letters* Trenchard opposed charity schools because they encouraged the plebs to get ideas above themselves, something which concerned Swift too. The Roman republicanism of Trenchard and Gordon, like that of Swift, worked against Walpole at the same time as it served the interests of the *optimates* generally.[84]

Later a tendency to deglamorise Roman-republican history would develop among some English historians, exemplified by Hooke's attacks on the Roman senatorial oligarchy and his revaluation of Julius Caesar, and by the dethronement of Cicero and even Cato as unalloyed models of civic virtue (in Cicero's case partly in reaction to Conyers Middleton's hagiographic *Life*).[85] Such revaluations would make the previously convenient, self-serving moral equation of English and Roman senatorial oligarchies self-defeating and encourage instead the kind of negative analogies made by Horace Walpole in the letters quoted above.

CIVIC VIRTUE AND THE ROMAN ANALOGY

It was Velleius Paterculus' highest praise of Cato of Utica that he was 'homo Virtuti simillimus' (a man most like to Virtue),[86] an apt description of one for whom a world without liberty dictated suicide, for *virtus* and *libertas* were understood as mutually sustaining, and by the mere fact of existing in Caesar's new unfree world, Cato would cease to be virtuous.

The inseparability of liberty and virtue is a constant theme in the classical sources from the time of Cato the Censor (great-grandfather of Cato of Utica) in the early second century BC and informs the political rhetoric of Cicero and most historians from Polybius through Sallust to Tacitus and beyond.[87] It was emphasised for the Renaissance by Machiavelli. His *Discourses on the First Ten Books of Livy* associated Roman civic virtue with a balanced constitution, the product of a long period of contention between nobles and plebeians. This constitution was subverted by luxury, greed and factionalism in the wake of military victories which civic virtue had made possible. Machiavelli's civic humanism was reinforced for Cromwellian England and anyone who cared to listen after 1660 by classical republicans including James Harrington in his *Commonwealth of Oceana* (1656), Henry Neville in *Plato redivivus* (1681) and Algernon Sidney in the *Discourses Concerning Government* (posthumous publication, 1698).[88] It would be the constant theme of Rousseau's *Social Contract* (1762). Everyone who wrote on the subject agreed that moral and civic virtue were two sides of the same coin. Cato of Utica was again exemplary in his personal as in his civic life.[89] As befitted a Stoic he was frugal, his passions were under control, and sex was appropriate only within marriage and for procreation.[90]

After 1688 England experienced a top-to-bottom moral reformation, a reaction against the low standards set by the court of Charles II, foremost of bad examples. This dramatic change, like that from Regency to Victorian, started at the top. William III wrote to the archbishops of Canterbury and York and to the Bishop of London to urge a reformation in manners directed by the clergy and focussed particularly on private vices. The statutes against blasphemy, perjury and drunkenness were read to congregations throughout the land.[91] From 1691 groups like the

Society for the Reformation of Manners used informers, instituted private prosecutions and published reports. The Society for the Promotion of Christian Knowledge was formed in 1699. Anne issued a 'Proclamation for the Encouragement of Piety and Virtue and the Preventing and Punishing of Vice, Profaneness and Immorality'. The new codes were reflected in the theatre, which Jeremy Collier had identified as a propagator of every kind of filth and vice.[92] All media co-operated in the venture.[93] This state-directed reformation had a famous precedent in Augustus' attempts to reform private and public morality,[94] but reflected the cultivation of Christian rather than classical sensibilities, and the enduring influence of seventeenth-century Puritan doctrine and practice.[95]

The concept of *civic* virtue, however, as it developed in England after 1688 was regularly associated with the classical past. Indeed it would have been difficult for a revolution anywhere in Europe proclaiming the defence of liberty as its purpose not to invoke classical lessons and precedents. Chesterfield's letters to his son justify the study of Roman history on the grounds of its richness in examples of civic virtue. The undraped busts of himself which he commissioned from Louis-François Roubiliac (*c.* 1745) and Joseph Wilton (1757), the latter (plate 1) supposedly representing the sitter 'as an elder Cato',[96] express the same ethic in their austere Roman-republican seriousness. The immediate question was how to secure England's liberty and prevent the degeneration of the new polity. The question of degeneration begged the issue of civic virtue.

The classical sources, above all Plato and Polybius, taught that all systems degenerated, monarchy into tyranny, aristocracy into oligarchy, democracy into ochlocracy or mob rule.[97] Polybius had claimed that the most stable systems – that devised by Lycurgus for Sparta, and that achieved through historical flux at Rome – combined monarchic, aristocratic and democratic elements in a mixed constitution.[98] Tacitus, however, whose authority stood high, had been sceptical, believing that mixed constitutions ultimately resolved themselves into one of their elements at the fatal expense of the others. Rome's mixed constitution had ended in a form of monarchy.[99] (Tacitus' view worried the American founding fathers.) Machiavelli claimed to show how liberty within a balanced constitution might be preserved, and how it might be lost; the chances of failure, he stressed, were high.

Well-read in Polybius and Tacitus, the English were acutely conscious of the dangers faced by their own experiment, not being able to foresee that a long period of relative stability lay ahead. John Sekora has shown how they constantly identified the causes of moral and political corruption in luxury, as the Old Testament and the classical historians taught them to do.[100] Striking parallels seemed to exist. Addison's *Cato* (1713) was the most discussed play of the age. Tories and Whigs vied with each other to praise it most fulsomely, each side wishing to be seen to identify with Cato's cause against Caesar. That Addison's sympathies were known to be Whig did not prevent Tories applauding his Cato for his 'Tory' principles. Bolingbroke ostentatiously presented the actor who played Cato with fifty guineas for his defence of liberty against the Whigs' great military hero, the Duke of Marlborough, identifying him with the Caesar of the play.[101] Alexander Pope, also a Tory, struck the appropriate chords in his prologue. He used the word 'virtue' four times in forty-six lines, identifying that quality with Cato in an echo of Velleius Paterculus' description of him as 'homo Virtuti simillimus':

> Virtue confess'd in human shape he draws,
> What *Plato* thought, and godlike *Cato* was . . .
> *Britons* attend: Be worth like this approv'd,
> And show, you have the virtue to be mov'd.[102]

The contemporary application of the play was taken for granted by everyone who saw it. Five years later came publication of Nicholas Rowe's translation of Lucan's *Pharsalia* (1718, just after Rowe's death), with a subscription list out of *Who's Who*. Lucan's Caesar is the incarnation of ruthless ambition operating to the destruction of the *res publica*, Cato is the most glorious of the republican heroes. Rowe's translation, dedicated by his widow to George I, had a preface by James Welwood pointing the significances of Rowe's having undertaken the project. Rowe's family, 'In all the Changes of Governments, . . . are said to have ever lean'd towards the side of Publick Liberty, and in that retir'd Situation of Life to have beheld with Grief and Concern the many

Incroachments that have been made upon it from time to time'.[103] Rowe

> had entertain'd an early Inclination for that Author, and I believe it was the darling Passion he had for the Liberty and Constitution of his Country, that first inclin'd him to think of Translating him ... As this is the happiest Nation in the World in its Constitution, and happy even in spite of our selves, he judg'd that all who are in Love with it, must needs be fond of an Author, who not only wrote for the Ancient Constitution of his own Country, but fell a Sacrifice for endeavouring to support it.[104]

Shaftesbury linked civic virtue with *virtù*, and hence with the arts generally, in two of his best-known sentences: 'I am persuaded that to be a *virtuoso* (so far as befits a gentleman) is a higher step towards the becoming a man of virtue and good sense than the being what in this age we call a scholar', and 'Thus are the Arts and Virtues mutually friends; and thus the science of virtuosi and that of virtue itself become, in a manner, one and the same.'[105] His distaste for the baroque and his advocacy of simpler, more classical forms, in which he anticipates English neo-Palladianism,[106] is also logical since virtue, which implies restraint, is properly unadorned, or not adorned to excess. The English taste for neo-Roman-republican sculpture, represented especially by Rysbrack and Scheemakers, reflects the same principle. Virtue hates luxury and excess. It sits best with simplicity and frugality. But how to reconcile frugality with the expenditure connoisseurship demands? The early models of virtue were frugal farmers: Cato the Censor and Lucius Quinctius Cincinnatus.[107] Cato's *De agri cultura* showed his preference for a healthy and independent farming life, identifying the virtues of the early Republic with the hearth and the soil: 'It is from the farming class that the bravest men and the sturdiest soldiers come, their calling is most highly respected, their livelihood is most assured and is looked on with the least hostility, and those who are engaged in that pursuit are least inclined to be disaffected.'[108] The patrician Cincinnatus, three centuries before, had been called from the plough to become dictator. The enemy defeated, the Republic served, he had returned to his farm, thereafter the epitome of Roman civic virtue.[109]

These models indicated that if one's means were derived from land, as distinct from commerce or usury, there need be no contradiction between virtue and wealth. Even connoisseurship and frugality might be reconciled. The purchase of a Poussin for £500 might be money frugally spent if it was a fine Poussin at the right price and contributed to the national stock of the virtue-improving arts. Predictably, the link between the defence of liberty and ownership of land (as distinct from mere wealth) was most loudly proclaimed by the Country Party – chiefly Tory[110] – and 'Patriot' Whig opposition to Walpole. It had been stressed by the classical republicans, much of whose rhetoric was assimilated in the 1720s and 1730s by Bolingbroke in his construction of an idealist political theory beyond party, though not beyond oligarchy.[111] The Country interest and the Patriots, including Richard Temple, George Lyttelton, and Thomas and William Pitt (the Elder), emphasised the corruptive effects of luxury and the power of the moneyed men who had made their fortunes with the financial revolution under William III and were now backing Walpole and sitting with him in Parliament. New City money was corrupting this institution, threatening the nation's liberty. The Bank of England and the National Debt were favoured targets too.

With the bursting of the South Sea Bubble in 1720 this line of attack had been re-invigorated. The directors of the South Sea Company, and others involved in the massive peculation, were stripped of their estates by Parliament.[112] Bolingbroke, above party now, spoke for a coalition of Tories and Opposition Whigs in his constant attacks on luxury, stressing the lessons of Sparta, Athens and Rome.[113] He ran the 'corruption' theme in the *Craftsman* and elsewhere,[114] while Trenchard and Gordon – and Lord Molesworth – used it in *Cato's Letters*. Venality and luxury (rather than any prerogative claims of the crown) would be the ruin of the constitution. Citing Aristotle, Cicero and Machiavelli, Bolingbroke pointed out that the people were only as virtuous as their leaders. As in Rome, the rot worked from the top down, party had replaced *patria*, luxury had displaced frugality and temperance. With civic virtue dead, liberty would soon expire.[115] Finally, in *The Idea of a Patriot King*, which cites the usual sources on luxury (Cato the Censor, Sallust, Machiavelli), Bolingbroke rejected the senate for the great *dictator* who would save the state from itself.[116]

When later in the century it became apparent that the commercial world was here to stay, the ethic of civic virtue had to shed its predisposition in favour of the land and instead became associated with a code of manners.[117] With accommodations of this kind the identification of liberty and virtue persisted into the new industrial age, thoroughly naturalised and increasingly free of classical associations, though these are still there in the 1780s, as we shall see, in Edmund Burke's prosecution of Warren Hastings over his conduct in Bengal, and, at the beginning of the nineteenth century, in the classical Temple of Liberty at Woburn Abbey, dedicated to the liberal Whig Charles James Fox, whose defence of the French Revolution had continued throughout the Terror. Within the cell of this temple (more extensively considered in the following chapter along with earlier temples at Stowe and elsewhere), Fox's bust rested on a pedestal inscribed with a poem by the Duchess of Devonshire:

> Here midst the friends he loved, the man behold,
> In truth unshaken and in virtue bold;
> Whose patriot zeal, and uncorrupted mind
> Dared to assert the freedom of mankind.[118]

In these lines the naturalised discourse of liberty and virtue shows its ability to assimilate the internationalist aspect of the French Revolution.[119] Just as it had frequently gestured back to republican Rome, so now it could invoke republican France, where a distinct variety of the discourse, incorporating the ideal of equality, had developed from 1789. The French variety reached its logical end in Robespierre's classical Republic of Virtue. This idea, popularised by Rousseau, is made visible and its Roman associations highlighted in the official revolutionary paintings of David (a member of the Committee of Public Safety), and articulated by Robespierre in his speeches to the National Convention, where a bust of the first Brutus presided, a terror to his erring children:

> Since the soul of the Republic is virtue, equality, and since your goal is to be found, to consolidate the Republic, it follows that the first rule of your political conduct ought to be to relate all your efforts to maintaining equality and developing virtue . . . If the mainspring of popular government in peacetime is virtue, amid revolution it is at the same time virtue and *terror*: virtue, without which terror is fatal; terror, without which virtue is impotent. Terror is nothing but prompt, severe, inflexible justice; it is therefore an emanation of virtue.[120]

Though praise of liberty or virtue need not imply reference to classical models, Robespierre, like Fox, was aware of them.

As commerce and empire brought ever-increasing prosperity and forced accommodations in the discourse, it became expedient to deny that growing national wealth necessarily threatened virtue and liberty (though in the late 1780s Burke was still arguing this vigorously in his prosecution of Hastings). Reassurance came from Adam Smith in *The Wealth of Nations* (1776). Prosperity brought dangers in its wake, but they could be successfully guarded against.[121] His friend David Hume countered the thesis of Longinus (and Shaftesbury) 'that the arts and sciences could never flourish, but in a free government' by reference to Renaissance Florence, Rome and the France of Louis XIV.[122] He nevertheless agreed with Smith and a long tradition of thinking 'that commerce can never flourish but in a free government',[123] and argued that the decline of virtue and public spirit at Rome had not been caused by prosperity but by 'an ill modelled government, and the unlimited extent of conquests'.[124]

Edward Gibbon pointed to Rome's 'loss of freedom, of virtue, and of honour' as central to her decline, the three virtues inseparable in his mind,[125] but blamed equally the rise of an anti-civic Christianity. For Adam Ferguson, peace and prosperity, not in themselves evil, could lead to complacency and remissness as citizenship became passive instead of active. This was pertinent after the Peace of Paris (March 1763) sealed immense imperial gains. The danger was that Britain, like Rome after the Second Punic War, would become complacent and soft.[126] In his *Essay on the History of Civil Society* (1767), he cites Sparta and contemporary Sweden as societies in which civic virtue gives vigour to the state.[127] His strictures on the causes of decline echo Cato the Censor, but Ferguson puts his observations into the present tense to give them contemporary point: decline sets in when men come 'to value their houses, their villas, their statues, and their pictures, at a higher rate than they do the republic. They may be found to grow tired in secret of a free constitution, of which they never cease to boast in their conversation, and which they always neglect in their conduct.'[128]

These remarks imply that the oligarchy's vocal civic-mindedness was mere rhetoric. When Samuel Johnson described patriotism as 'the last resort of a scoundrel'[129] he was showing his contempt for those who debased patriotism in the interests of party. High-political 'outs' had habitually called for the urgent defence of liberty when, as Johnson pointed out with the benefit of hindsight, liberty had never been seriously in danger.[130] Through the 1720s and 1730s the Opposition Whig 'Patriots' had adopted this vein of patriotic indignation in their paper war against Walpole. It has been well observed that in the first half of the eighteenth century 'the criticism of oligarchy is not to be studied as a description of oligarchy but rather as one of its products, one furthermore that oligarchy does not always succeed in absorbing and that may in the long run have something to do with how oligarchy is modified'.[131] A common error is to take the criticism seriously.[132] That it is embodied in literature of the quality of Swift's *Gulliver's Travels*, Pope's *Epistle to Burlington* and the *Dunciad*, or Thomson's *Liberty*, does not make it valid. One of the greatest criticisers, Thomas Gordon, who had collaborated in *Cato's Letters* for the Opposition *London Journal*, later wrote for the government, but of course he continued to defend liberty and civic virtue, and to translate Tacitus and Sallust. Why not? It was only a war of words, and the weapons were the same on both sides. Gibbon is interesting for the same reason. Following the publication of the first volume of his *Decline and Fall of the Roman Empire*, which evidenced his liberal Whig sentiments and hatred of political corruption, he accepted, as an MP, a place from Lord North worth £750 a year. This provoked Charles James Fox to write in his copy of the *Decline and Fall*:

> His book well describes
> How corruption and bribes
> O'erthrew the great empire of Rome;
> And his writings declare
> A degen'racy there
> Which his conduct exhibits at home.[133]

Then again Fox, human too, did similar deals with North.

Like all political discourses, that current in the century after 1688 was about power and self-promotion. The attractiveness of its central terms led to its being assimilated by all the major parties. This was its success and its limitation. Any opportunist could use it.

LITERARY *PERSONAE*: POPE, SWIFT, JOHNSON, THOMSON, FIELDING, BURKE

The adoption of an 'Augustan' tone and spirit in English neo-classical literature is a well-explored if nebulous subject,[134] and a broad historical study of the socio-political and aesthetic dimensions of the Roman temper in English eighteenth-century culture is not the place to explore it yet again. Of particular interest, however, is the (not always straightforward) assumption by poets and politicians of classical *personae* in treating topics where the invocation of Roman precedents or analogies is appropriate. Two of the more striking instances are James Thomson's character of Liberty in the poem of that name, and Edmund Burke in the role of Cicero as he conducts the prosecution of Warren Hastings, Governor of Bengal, who from Burke's point of view plays the role of Caius Verres. These will be examined in detail. They exemplify the limits of imitation and the constraints of a finally unbridgeable cultural distance. Other examples, in the works of Pope, Swift, Johnson and Fielding, also merit passing attention.

The popularity of Addison's *Cato* with all parties, already noticed, was such that he was often referred to as Cato, though his strong Christianity compromises the identification in an interesting way. A more important case in point is Alexander Pope, who assumed the *persona* of Horace in his *Satires and Epistles of Horace Imitated*, composed during the 1730s when, as a Tory and friend of Bolingbroke, he was writing in opposition to Walpole's Whig government. This identification, like Addison's with Cato, was uneasy, for Pope disapproved of Horace's subservience to Augustus.[135] When the Earl of Burlington left the Government in 1733, Pope's opposition to Walpole was reinforced and joined to that of the Whig 'Patriots' supporting Carteret. In the *Satires and Epistles* he adopts the tone and much of the character of Horace but turns the satire against targets in contemporary English society. The most powerful politically is the *Epistle to Augustus* (1737), which plays on the discrepancy between the Roman emperor and the addressee George II who, despite his second name being Augustus, was largely inaccessible to poets and showed little interest in them. The self-parodying panegyric sounds accordingly absurd:

> While You, great Patron of Mankind, sustain
> The balanc'd World, and open all the Main;
> Your Country, chief, in Arms abroad defend,
> At home, with Morals, Arts, and Laws amend;
> How shall the Muse, from such a Monarch, steal
> An hour, and not defraud the Public Weal?[136]

The satire probably works against Horace and Augustus to some extent too, for Pope was certainly critical of both. He writes from the side of the Opposition, Horace was a court favourite.[137] George II rules an England enjoying liberty, Augustus constrained liberty. In any case Pope is not wearing the mask of Horace seriously. English appropriations of Rome are inevitably more interesting when they are complex and ambiguous. Compare the dull predictability of the *Ode to the Earl of Chesterfield, Imploring his Majesty's Return. In Imitation of Horace, Ode II, Book IV* (1737):

> Applauding Senates shall record his Fame,
>   And hail the Arbiter of *Europe* home;
> Him haughty *Gallia*'s Dread they shall proclaim;
>   From him the *Turk* and *Tartar* wait their doom.[138]

There is invention in the idea of a British invasion of Turkey and Russia, but invention without tension or interest.

Pope's poetry, like much verse of his period and Dryden's before, embodies the Roman and specifically Horatian temper in its urbanity, formal regularity, public-centredness, and attitude of satiric detachment, though Pope breaks the Horatian bounds and incorporates Juvenalian elements within an original synthesis.[139] A neo-classical court poet like Dryden, poet laureate under kings (Charles II and James II) who imaged themselves imperially, had more in common with the Augustan court poets, pre-eminently Horace, than did Pope in an age of liberty, but after 1688 the great Augustans' literary supremacy ensured that they continued in favour despite their unrepublican obsequiousness towards the *princeps*. There were substantially more translations of Horace into English in the period 1660–1800 than of any other Latin or Greek author.[140] His appeal in a period when both satire and Roman models were in vogue is predictable. Formal verse satire was considered a Roman genre, the one form they boasted that they did not owe to the Greeks.[141] Even Swift, whom one generally thinks of as among the least formally classical writers of his period, was strongly attracted to Horatian forms and apparently prouder of his Latin poems *Ad amicum eruditum Thomam Sheridan* and *Carberiae rupes* than of most of his other verse. These neglected works show just how classical in sensibility a radical literary innovator like Swift could be when he chose to work within a Roman *persona*. The ode to Sheridan is suffused with a typically Swiftian humour (there are references to Sheridan's cicada-like voice and ridiculously frail body), but the tone is always convincingly antique, for instance in the concluding lines with their Virgilian tribute to Sheridan's inspirational teaching:

> Aureus at ramus venerandae dona Sibyllae,
> Aeneae sedes tantùm patefecit Avernas:
> Saepè puer, tua quem tetigit semel aurea virga,
> Coelumque terrasque videt, noctemque profundam.[142]

Although the Horatian imitations Swift wrote in English are generally less classical in tone and spirit than Pope's, his ode *To the Earl of Oxford, Late Lord Treasurer, sent to him when he was in the Tower, before his trial; out of Horace* is particularly faithful to the Horatian tone and phraseology, taking as its principal theme Horace's line, 'Dulce et decorum est pro patria mori', rendered by Swift in his first line as 'How blessed is he, who for his country dies'.

There is another important feature of Pope's Horatian Epistles which deserves notice in the present context. Pope had them printed with the original Latin text of Horace in italics on the left-hand page and his own text in roman on the right. This arrangement is iconographically important, quite aside from the vital literary interest it provides, in that it continually draws the reader's attention to the similarities and differences between the ancient Roman and modern English worlds. As Frank Stack has reminded us, especially relevant lines and phrases in the Latin text are highlighted by being printed in roman type, while index numbers and letters link points in one text to points in the other. The purpose of imitation was 'to endorse ideas of general nature and general truth, the conviction that human nature and human experience, despite changes of time and circumstance, had always been the same'.[143] Every personality, event and feature of society in Horace's milieu, many turns of phrase even, and so many of the mental habits and assumptions of Augustan Rome have their equivalents or contrasting variants in the English world of Pope's imitations. In this way Rome and England are fused, yet not confused, every turning of the page compelling us, in effect, to 'Compare *this* with *this*.' Contributing its small part to the tone of such poems was Pope's increasing preference for a purer, 'classical' typography in the printing of his works. David Foxon has persuasively argued that Pope led the way in the abandonment of capitals and italic in English printing, 'more influenced by the desire to appear as a classic author than by considerations of pure typography'.[144]

The *Epistle to Arbuthnot* offers an example of classical *personae* pushed to the absurd. Pope gives a satirical picture of his literary supporters, people whose praise consists in identifying him with his classical models all the way down to physiological and pathological details:

> There are, who to my Person pay their court,
> I cough like *Horace*, and tho' lean, am short,
> *Ammon*'s great Son one shoulder had too high,
> Such *Ovid*'s nose, and 'Sir! you have an *Eye* –
> Go on, obliging Creatures, make me see
> All that disgrac'd my Betters, met in me:
> Say for my comfort, languishing in bed,
> 'Just so immortal *Maro* held his head:'
> And when I die, be sure you let me know
> Great *Homer* dy'd three thousand years ago.[145]

The absurdity is somewhat self-cancelling, however, for while Pope satirises his supporters and their notions, it is really he who is making the connections here by virtue of creating the containing fiction.

Late in life he conceived the idea of an epic poem entitled *Brutus*, inspired by Geoffrey of Monmouth's *Historia regum britanniae*, a mythical account of the colonisation of Britain by the Trojan Brutus, great-grand-son of Aeneas, sixty-six years after the sack of Troy, thus making Italy and Britain Trojan sister-lands, inheritors of the same classical culture. As early as 1717, during the period when he was engaged in translating Homer's epics, Pope had translated Brutus' prayer to Diana from its source in Geoffrey, at the request of Aaron Thompson, who was preparing an English version of the *Historia*:

> Goddess of Woods, tremendous in the chace,
> To Mountain-wolves and all the Savage race,
> Wide o'er th'aerial Vault extends thy sway,
> And o'er th'infernal Regions void of day,
> *On thy third Reign look down*; disclose our Fate,
> In what new Nation shall we fix our Seat?
> When shall we next thy hallow'd Altars raise,
> And Quires of Virgins celebrate thy praise?[146]

The draft plans for the epic survive in two versions and indicate that it would have presented Brutus as a benevolent law-giver who laid out patterns of government, religion and morality. No doubt like Thomson's *Liberty* the poem was intended to contribute to the arsenal of the 'Patriot' Opposition.[147]

Samuel Johnson's poem *London: a Poem in Imitation of the Third Satire of Juvenal* was also a product of this period and reflects the same anti-court attitudes one finds in Pope's Horatian Epistles and in Thomson's work. For Johnson as for Pope, classical literary culture was part of his being, his love of the Latin culture causing him to translate his contemporaries' work, including Pope's, into Latin verse far more often than to imitate Latin verse in English. There are one or two sections in *London* where Johnson's Roman originals are inadequately anglicised in point of cultural and political realities. His Orgilio, for example, enjoys friends and a clientelage generous beyond anything a rich Londoner ever knew:

> Should heaven's just bolts Orgilio's wealth confound,
> And spread his flaming palace on the ground,
> Swift o'er the land the dismal rumour flies,

And publick mournings pacify the skies;
The laureat tribe in servile verse relate,
How virtue wars with persecuting fate;
With well-feign'd gratitude the pension'd band
Refund the plunder of the beggar'd land.
See! while he builds, the gaudy vassals come,
And crowd with sudden wealth the rising dome;
The price of boroughs and of souls restore,
And raise his treasures higher than before.
Now bless'd with all the baubles of the great,
The polish'd marble, and the shining plate,
Orgilio sees the golden pile aspire,
and hopes from angry heav'n another fire.

The problem with the passage was that Johnson had forgotten where it was that he was writing about. As he later noted, 'This was by Hitch a Bookseller justly remarked to be no picture of modern manners, though it might be true at Rome.'[148] In composing these anachronistic lines Johnson had slipped too unreflectingly into that antique frame of mind evident everywhere in his Latin poems.

Although satire is not his preferred genre, in some ways James Thomson embodies the Roman temper in an even more concentrated form than Pope or Johnson, not only identifying many of republican Rome's moral, political and aesthetic values with Britain's but assimilating the grammatical forms of the Latin language to his own. As in Pope, however, the process is never uncritical in its assessment of the earlier culture, and often deeply critical. *The Seasons* (1726–30) was already strongly neo-classical – in Mary Jane W. Scott's words, 'both a native georgic and an apology for the social values and virtues of Roman civilization, both Republican and Imperial'.[149] As the poem's Virgilian echoes and overtones suggest, Thomson had received a strongly classical education.[150] As a Scot he felt an affinity with antiquaries like Sir John Clerk of Penicuik (see chapters 3 and 4 below) who were working to enshrine the best of Roman values and civilisation in Scotland. Like Clerk, who had been a Commissioner for the Treaty of Union, Thomson was happy to see 'Caledonia', as Scotland is called in *The Seasons*, united with England in an imperial 'Britannia' whose capital was 'Augusta'.[151]

By the time he wrote *Liberty* (1735–6),[152] which he considered his greatest work, Thomson was identifying with Lyttelton's group of Patriots in opposition to Walpole, whom they castigated as a dictator at the head of a corrupt administration: thus the poem explicitly rejects imperial Rome as a worthy model, reserving its praise for the Republic. In its vocabulary and structures it is even more latinate than *The Seasons*. Rhyme was too Gothic for this work, the classical unrhymed pentameter of Milton (and *The Seasons*) being preferred. The latinate qualities are appropriate since the subject matter of *Liberty*, in large part, is the referral of the political and social ideals of contemporary Britain to their foreshadowing in republican Rome. The work, a five-part epic, is a detailed demonstration of what Rome meant for the Lyttelton group and for civic-minded defenders of liberty generally, the wider audience to whom the poem appeals. Analysis here will be concentrated upon the Roman republican connections.

The dominant voice is that of the goddess Liberty, but the poem opens with the poet's vision of the ruins of ancient Rome. While he contemplates the sad prospect, the goddess appears to him in her modern British aspect,

> her bright Temples bound with *British* Oak,
> And Naval Honours nodded on her Brow,
> Sublime of Port. Loose o'er her Shoulder flow'd
> Her sea-green Robe, with Constellations gay,
> An island-Goddess now. (1.29–33)[153]

Her crown combines the qualities of the Roman *corona civica*, oak-leaves and acorns (but British oak), with the *corona navalis*, which was ornamented with miniaturised beaks of captured ships, suitable to the protectress of a triumphing sea power, as are the sea-green robe and its ornamentation. Liberty's happiest reigns were in ancient Greece and Rome and in modern Britain where, as the imagery (sea associations, constellations) suggests, she has more scope than previously. Throughout, her affinity with Rome seems stronger than that with

Greece, to which part II is largely devoted. The first hundred lines of part I evoke Roman-republican glories, part III is devoted to Liberty's reign at Rome, and parts IV and V, on Britain, are rich in Roman associations. All this, together with the latinate syntax, suggests a Roman character, though as a moral and spiritual entity her origins predate any historical polity. She merely lends herself to particular cultures.

As the poet gazes on the ruins, the goddess conjures a vision of ancient Rome at its best (I.45ff.). This contrasts with the bleak Italian present. Oppression and superstition have laid the land desolate. There is a lesson in this:

> HENCE, BRITAIN, learn; my best-establish'd, last,
> And, more than GREECE, or ROME, my steady Reign;
> The Land where, *King* and *People* equal bound
> By guardian Laws, my fullest Blessings flow;
> And where my jealous unsubmitting Soul,
> The Dread of Tyrants! burns in every Breast:
> Learn hence, if such the miserable fate
> Of an heroic Race, the Masters once
> Of Human-kind; what, when depriv'd of ME,
> How grievous must be thine? (I.316–25)

It is clear that Thomson's identification with Rome is hedged with serious qualifications. He prefers Britain ('my best-establish'd ... Reign'), which is constitutionally superior to the old, more heroic, civilisation. Here a monarchy works best, and Liberty enjoys a 'more . . . steady Reign', in contrast to the political societies of Greece and Rome which were inherently unstable – a major criticism.

In part II Liberty traces her rise from the pastoral ages and pays the appropriate compliments to the 'public virtue' and 'smiling arts' of Greece, but as the goddess makes clear in part III, while Greece was a fairer product of Liberty's influence than Rome, which owed so much to the older civilisation, it was less great (III.78–9). Liberty's purpose at Rome was 'to diffuse / O'er Men an Empire' and 'set Nations free' (III.82–3, 87). This was her 'amplest Reign' (III.89). Beneath the '*Voted Laws*' of the 'parent State' the free citizens lived 'fraternal' (III.111–12), and from the '*Moral Nature*' of the *res publica*, strong with the 'Godlike Passion' of Liberty, Rome's virtues emanated (III.107, 113–17, 125–42) making her 'unconquerable' (III.120).

Victory over Carthage brought security, luxury, emulation, faction. Following the defeat of the Gracchi (heroes for Thomson), 'Aristocratic Pride', 'Usury', widening discrepancies in wealth, proscriptions and the mad mob turned Romans into slaves 'that lick'd the scourging Hand' (III.347–60). Henceforth Liberty lived only in the souls of exceptional individuals – Cicero, Cato, Thrasea Paetus (III.466–97). The evil effects of the worst emperors were soon compounded by 'Idiot SUPERSTITION' in its 'ten thousand Monkish Forms', poisoning reason and diffusing ignorance (IV.76–83). Rome became Romish, and Liberty, with the arts and sciences, sat out the dark ages in heaven.

Part IV traces a slow renaissance finally crowned in Britain. More extensively even than Rome, Britain will diffuse liberty through the world, from the Arctic to the Antarctic and out into 'The vast *Pacific*' (IV.414–17). The goddess marries herself to the British spirit, which includes a predisposition towards a religion 'rational, and free' (IV.479–581), but she adopts the vocabulary of republican Rome in discussing the struggles of the English Parliament, consistently termed the 'Senate', 'The *more than Roman Senate*' (IV.1020). She claims that under Charles II,

> The *Crown*, of its hereditary Wealth
> Despoil'd, on *Senates* more dependant grew,
> And they more frequent, more assur'd. (IV.1052–4)

This is an example of how Thomson takes Latin vocabulary and anglicises it to heighten the effect of the Roman analogy. 'Frequent', in addition to meaning regular, has the sense of the Latin *frequens*, 'full', in the stock phrase *senatus frequens* used in Roman senatorial procedure. Thomson indicates that the senates under Charles II were well attended, suggestive of their Members' strong commitment to the institution and the nation's liberties.

James II was a catalyst provoked by the goddess to precipitate the deliverance brought by William of Orange which ushered in her full reign in Britain (IV.1104ff.). At last Liberty's 'FABRICK stands compleat, / The PALACE OF THE LAWS' (IV.1179–80), equally sheltering all in freedom. Now the only danger is 'CORRUPTION' (IV.1190); Britain has nothing to fear but Walpole.

Part V describes the virtues required to sustain Liberty in Britain and the rapid progress of the arts and sciences under her rule. Within the essential 'PUBLIC VIRTUE' (V.94) reside a trinity of core virtues,

> INDEPENDENT LIFE;
> INTEGRITY IN OFFICE; and, o'er all
> Supreme, A PASSION FOR THE COMMON-WEAL'
> (V.120–2).

These were among the virtues of the early Romans, itemised in part III. Independence of life (i.e. property) is vital; without it there can be no integrity in office or passion for the commonwealth. This emphasis is founded on well-known classical *dicta* and exemplified in Cincinnatus and the Cato of the *De agri cultura*. As already noticed, it was a crucial part of the oligarchy's self-justifying rhetoric. Itself a sub-category of civic virtue, in Thomson's *Liberty* Independence is supported by a group of attendant virtues which ensure a happy life: '*Peace*', 'fearless *Truth*', 'Firm *Resolution*', '*Goodness*', '*Contentment*', '*Philosophy*' (V.137–43). But in Walpole's England these are undermined by indecent wealth and tasteless self-indulgence.

> See! how the Hall with brutal Riot flows;
> While in the foaming Flood, fermenting, steep'd,
> The Country maddens into Party-Rage.
> Mark! those disgraceful Piles of Wood and Stone;
> Those Parks and Gardens, where, his Haunts betrimm'd,
> And *Nature* by presumptuous *Art* oppress'd,
> The *woodland Genius* mourns. See! the full Board
> That steams Disgust, and Bowls that give no Joy! (V.160–7)

Readers were expected to recall Pope's Timon (*Epistle to Burlington*, 1731), Thomson no doubt believing that Pope intended him for Walpole.[154] Britain is on the verge of a moral decline like Rome's. It is a warning repeated by John Dyer in *The Ruins of Rome* (1740), inspired, like Gibbon's *Decline and Fall*, by the scene of the city's ruined splendour. In the same vein as Thomson decrying a nation 'damn'd to Wealth', Dyer identifies the principal threats as 'Ease and soft Delights', 'voluptuousness' and affluence.[155]

The rest of Thomson's poem is devoted to the rise of the sciences and arts in contemporary Britain. Classical good taste and urbanity are everywhere evidenced. In literature Liberty sees

the dread delightful *School*
Of *temper'd Passions*, and of *polish'd Life*,
Restor'd. (v.671–3).

In architecture the baroque and Gothic, associated with 'pompous Tyrants' and 'dreaming Monks' (v.688–9), lie buried for good, and simpler, classically inspired Palladian forms arise:

Lo! Numerous DOMES a BURLINGTON confess:
For *Kings* and *Senates fit*, the *Palace* see!
The *Temple* breathing a religious Awe;
Even fram'd with Elegance the *plain Retreat*,
The private Dwelling. Certain in his Aim,
Taste, never idly working, saves Expence. (v. 690–5)

Britain under Liberty is returning to the ideals and forms of ancient Rome in her senate houses[156] and temples, homes and landscape gardens, but one notices in these lines the distance of modern Britain from the ancient model, which was imperfect. In Britain 'Kings' share in a careful balance of power with 'Senates', and a 'religious Awe' contrasts with the spiritual vacuum of ancient Rome and her Popish inheritors.

The final sixteen lines are a conscious 'quotation' of the concluding lines of the *Epistle to Burlington*, full of the same imagery of future progress: 'PUBLIC WORKS' on every side, 'Connecting Sea to Sea, the Solid *Road*', 'the Proud *Arch*' bridging rivers, 'long *Canals*', expanding ports, '*Light-house* tow'rs', and 'the broad imperious *Mole*' repelling the force of storms (v.701–16). Engineering, the science in which the Romans excelled, is now, thanks to Liberty, an aspect of the British genius and bound to bring the same benefits once enjoyed by the parent civilisation.[157]

Liberty reveals the self-assurance with which classical analogies were being exploited at this time. Though Walpole is a danger, the tone is confident. On the other hand Rome, even at her best, is criticised for her constitutional instability. Thomson's admiration for the Republic has tension built in. Liberty prefers Christian, monarchical Britain to republican Rome. Her language and analogies suggest a Roman-like *persona* and repeatedly link the modern state to the ancient, but her intention is that the best features of the past are perfected in the present, not simply replicated.

Henry Fielding flattered Thomson by imitating him in *Liberty: to George Lyttleton, Esq.* (after 1735–6), in which the latinity of the language and the density of the antique iconography rival Thomson's. Among the divinities invoked, apart from God Himself and the Muses, there are 'Liberty, bright Goddess', Fortune, Venus, Pallas and Juno – this in a poem about *British* liberty. In honour of the dedicatee, Fielding urges that 'Altars' be raised and 'Incense' burned. In the present of the poem, Greece and Rome have long since lost their political liberty, but eighteenth-century 'Vandals' and 'Huns' enjoy it. In 'Iberia' the 'base Sword' has oppressed the bright goddess, and 'slavish *Gauls*' under Louis XV 'dare fight against thy Cause'.[158]

Fielding's *Liberty*, it has to be said, stands apart from much of his other work in that its classical analogies are meant to be taken at face value. Elsewhere in his poetry, and in his prose fiction too, he liked to burlesque the classical forms. Yet he embodied the classical spirit as authentically and thoroughly as any of his contemporaries, and in *Tom Jones* he argued the need for its re-animation in the present:

> I cannot conceive that *Homer* or *Virgil* would have writ with more Fire, if, instead of being Masters of all the Learning of their Times, they had been as ignorant as most of the Authors of the present Age. Nor do I believe that all the Imagination, Fire, and Judgment of *Pitt* could have produced those Orations that have made the Senate of *England* in these our Times a Rival in Eloquence to *Greece* and *Rome*, if he had not been so well read in the Writings of *Demosthenes* and *Cicero*, as to have transferred their whole Spirit into his Speeches, and with their Spirit, their Knowledge too.[159]

Thomson's warnings about the dangers to British liberty were party-political in purpose and out of all proportion to reality.[160] Through the mid-century the Patriot discourse to which they belong was rendered irrelevant by new political alliances.[161] It was not until the 1780s that Cassandras were again in full cry. The American colonies had become the United States, but a second British Empire quickly began to augment what was left of the first, and vast quantities of new money, dubiously obtained from the British East India Company's activities in the Orient, poured into England in such a way as to pose a far greater threat to British liberties than Walpole had ever done – or so it seemed to Edmund Burke and his Parliamentary friends as he undertook the impeachment of Warren Hastings for his alleged misgovernment of India. This view was reinforced by the apparently uncanny set of similarities between the cruelties and embezzlement supposed to have been carried out by Hastings and his clients in Bengal and the vicious misgovernment of Sicily by its propraetor Caius Verres (*c.* 120–43 BC), prosecuted in 70 BC by Cicero for the fiscal pillage of the province under his care, a prosecution which, in the form of Cicero's *Verrine Orations*, was known to countless Englishmen from their schooldays.

Burke had received a classical education at Trinity College Dublin, and modelled his oratory on Cicero's.[162] In this he followed most of the century's great orators. Joseph Spence observed that the Duke of Wharton, having decided to enter Parliament, was concerned over his rusty Latin. He went with Edward Young to Winchester 'where they did nothing but read Tully and talk Latin for six weeks – at the end of which the Duke talked Latin just like Tully's'.[163] The Duke's speeches to the Lords continually alluded to Roman history.[164] William Pitt the Elder, 1st Earl of Chatham, the greatest orator of his day, trained his son in the same classical models he himself followed, particularly Cicero, and taught by example as the boy watched his father perform in Parliamentary debates.[165] The younger Pitt's maiden speech to the Commons on 26 February 1781, in support of Burke's economic reform Bill, was praised for its form and delivery.[166] Yet compared to Burke's or Sheridan's, Pitt's oratory was less contrived and ornate, sparser in its generation of effect.[167] The Irish Burke by contrast showed little restraint, in print or speech, whenever he got into his high Ciceronian vein, which was often.

In concert with his friends in the Commons he devoted years to mounting a case for the impeachment of Hastings on the grounds of 'high crimes and misdemeanours', prosecuting it for another seven years before the Lords. Throughout both periods he repeatedly echoes and alludes to the *Verrine Orations*. Hastings, to his disadvantage, is cast in the role of Verres to Burke's Cicero.[168]

There is an important qualification: Burke's 'Gothic' side is never absent. As in his *Reflections on the Revolution in France* (1790), he is always ready to evoke the ancient 'Gothic' heritage of English liberty, just as his imagination evokes Gothic horrors, then very much in literary fashion. This complicates the Ciceronian role and guarantees that the distance between pupil and antique mentor will never be closed.

Long before 1788 and the commencement of proceedings Burke had already coloured Hastings's conduct in the darkest of classical tonings, replete with the imagery of omens, fate and catastrophe. On 29 April 1783, according to the Parliamentary record,

> He described the famine that at present raged at Madras, in the most pathetic manner, stating that two hundred persons perished daily with hunger in that city; that vultures appeared by hundreds, hovering over that ill-fated city, to share with the wolves and dogs in devouring the carcases of the dead; and to add to the misfortune of the miserable, they had also wolves and vultures in human shapes eager to devour them.[169]

The imagery foreshadows Burke's picture of Hastings at the impeachment when he described the plight of the Indians 'whose country he has laid waste and desolate'.[170] Hastings descended upon India like a malign fate: 'He came as a heavy calamity, like a famine or a pestilence on a country.'[171] His natural habitat is the Virgilian underworld: 'Mr Hastings feasts in the dark; Mr Hastings feasts alone; Mr Hastings feasts like a wild beast; he growls in the corner over the dying and the dead, like the tigers of that country, who drag their prey into the jungles . . . His is the entertainment of Tantalus, it is an entertainment from which the sun hid his light.'[172] Hastings 'gorged his own ravenous maw' 'from the collected morsels forced from the mouths' of the Indian nobility he despoiled and impoverished.[173] We have entered a world of myth and monstrosity. The imagery is from the sixth book of the *Aeneid*, the phrasing and rhythms from the Gothic novel.

In Burke's view, British (or Company) administration in India produces a *malaise* in the young men who go there, infecting them with attitudes destructive of English values and liberties. Speaking on Fox's India Bill on 1 December 1783, Burke explained how the 'intoxicating draught of authority and dominion', 'premature power' in the hands of the immature, resulted in 'excesses'. The corrupted youth return to England where

> They marry into your families; they enter into your senate; they ease your estates by loans; they raise their value by demand; they cherish and protect your relations which lie heavy on your patronage; and there is scarcely an house in the kingdom that does not feel some concern and interest that makes all the reform of our eastern government appear officious and disgusting.[174]

He quotes Cicero on Verres in the *Oration against Quintus Caecilius*: 'Nothing aggravates tyranny so much as contumely. *Quicquid superbia in contumeliis* was charged by a great man of antiquity, as a principal head of offence against the governor general of that day.'[175] Yet Verres never dispossessed the propertied of Sicily as Hastings did those of India. In Bengal, in 1772, 'They set up (Mr. Hastings set up) the whole nobility, gentry, and freeholders, to the highest bidder . . . Such an universal proscription, upon any pretence, has few examples.'[176] The India Bill will address such injustices effectively, though by introducing it Charles James Fox (then on the same side as Burke) has drawn on himself obloquy, 'a necessary ingredient of all true glory: he will remember, that it was not only in the Roman customs, but it is in the nature and constitution of things, that calumny and abuse are essential parts of triumph.'[177] Burke quotes Silius Italicus on Cicero, equating him with Fox.[178] The English-Roman hero will receive his Roman triumph. The proscription will be avenged, the Senate and people saved.

Along with the use of the Verrine analogy, Burke habitually echoed the language of the *Verrine Orations*. Compare Cicero, 'Today the eyes of the world are upon us . . . It is the present trial in which . . . the people of

Rome will pass its verdict upon yourselves',[179] with Burke at the impeachment, Speech in Opening, 15 February 1788: 'It is not only the interest of India . . . but the credit and honor of the British nation itself will be decided by this decision',[180] and, on 28 May 1794, 'It is not the culprit who is upon trial; it is the House of Commons that is upon its trial.'[181] Or compare Cicero, 'Where shall our allies seek refuge, whose help shall they entreat, nay, what hope will possess them that can make life seem worth living, if you, gentlemen, fail them?',[182] with Burke speaking anachronistically of colonies as 'the humble allies . . . who by their distance have a double demand upon your protection'.[183]

H. V. Canter cited other parallels: Cicero's strategy of voicing his anxiety regarding the power of money to secure an acquittal matched by Burke's identical tactic; Cicero's rejection, on the grounds that they were forced, of testimonials on the good character of Verres echoed in Burke's similar attack on Hastings's good references; Cicero's account of Verres' destruction of public records echoed in Burke's account of Hastings' similar actions; Cicero's demolition of Verres' claim that he did not himself receive the fruits of his extortion echoed in Burke's disposal of Hastings's identical defence; Cicero's denial of the idea that there is one standard for Rome and another for Sicily echoed in Burke's rejection of the idea in relation to England and India; Cicero's attack on Verres for betraying those who have bribed him echoed by Burke on Hastings.[184]

Burke's equation of Hastings with Verres was direct – 'He has got just the same character as Caius Verres got in another cause',[185] but Hastings was worse than Verres: 'We have all, in our early education, read the Verrine Orations. In these orations you will find almost every instance of rapacity and peculation which we charge upon Mr Hastings . . . But in the cause before your Lordships there is one species of disgrace . . . which I defy you to find in Verres'.[186] This was bond-breaking.

Other references are more subtle. In his Speech in Opening, Burke made the equation in a most learned way, but one that was surely lost on his audience and the accused alike. As Canter pointed out,[187] Quintilian relates how at one point in the trial of Verres the governor's counsel, Hortensius, who as Cicero knew had accepted a bronze model of the Sphinx from his client, became exasperated during Cicero's cross-examination of a witness, exclaiming 'I do not understand these riddles.' Cicero wittily replied, 'You ought to, then, as you have got the Sphinx at home.'[188] On 16 February 1788 Hastings was arguing that in India he was often working in the dark without any informed legal counsel. Burke interjected, '*At Sphingem habeas domi*'[189] (But you have a sphinx at home). Whether Hastings or their Lordships made anything of this arcane witticism can only be guessed. Even if Hastings managed to decipher the Latin he still had to interpret the riddle. The task was made more daunting by the fact that on this, the second day, he could hardly yet understand that he was two people, not one, sitting simultaneously in the House of Lords and the Forum of Rome.

Burke makes the Roman point that, the East conquered, Britain is herself conquered by oriental vices which come with the sudden influx of wealth and infect the ruling class. This was the theme of Polybius and the ancient historians who echoed him. It was used by Burke from the start of the prosecution,[190] its best expression coming in his speech on the Sixth Article, when he stressed that civic virtue and liberty, and the very character of the nation, were at stake.

> This prosecution . . . is a prosecution not only for the punishing a delinquent, . . . it is a great censorial prosecution, for the purpose of preserving the manners, characters, and virtues that characterize the people of England . . . Our liberty is as much in danger as our honor and our national character . . . *Opum metuenda potestas*. We dread the operation of money . . . Today the Commons of Great Britain prosecute the delinquents of India: to-morrow the delinquents of India may be the Commons of Great Britain.[191]

Burke's call for a verdict of 'guilty' would be rejected. For a start, Warren Hastings was not Caius Verres, nor like him, but personally frugal and without greed, though Burke was Cicero insofar as one can will oneself into the character of another. Secondly, history does not repeat itself. Eighteenth-century England was not the Rome of the second and first centuries BC, or like it in the senses Burke wished his audience to believe. India was not the Hellenistic East. The entire performance was a play, at the end of a century during which Roman roles were the vogue. Burke believed in the play. The Lords were sceptical.[192]

Yet the value of the classically framed discourse of virtue and liberty, for all its convenience to the ruling elite, and the self-serving it masked, should not be underrated. It reinforced the liberties won in 1688–9 and made it more difficult to contemplate a counter-revolution. It sanctified the Revolution by analogy with hallowed classical precedents and guarded it by ceaselessly warning of dangers which had destroyed liberty at Rome and might conceivably do so in England. It was a discourse which naturalised the classical frame of mind in a way impossible in any other European nation.

2

Virtue made visible

SENSIBILITY

The adoption by Thomson and Burke of classically figured language and appropriately classical *personae* in defence of political liberty and civic virtue – Roman-republican principles naturalised and qualified by recent English historical experience – was logical in a cultural milieu whose distinctive neo-classical character had developed with such vigour. That character had been largely authorised by a series of prominent arbiters of seemly self-presentation, from the 3rd Earl of Shaftesbury to the 4th Earl of Chesterfield. Much that was 'seemly' was French, as it had been since the Restoration brought a Frenchified court back to London, but much, especially after 1688, was classical Roman-republican. Before Shaftesbury's time, court art under Louis XIV, and the Italian Renaissance earlier again, had influenced culture throughout Europe in classical directions, though the models were normally imperial, not republican.[1] French literary neo-classicism had helped shape English Restoration literature.[2] It was immensely significant, too, that education was so heavily based on the classics.[3] All of these factors helped to prepare the ground for the distinctive emphasis Shaftesbury and Chesterfield put on the relation of classical culture to liberty and virtue, and hence to manners, in post-Revolutionary England.

Language, the allusive language of Thomson's *Liberty* or of Burke's Ciceronian speeches, was just one among several expressions of a new sensibility substantially established by 1714 when Thomas Tickell wrote his verse epistle prefixed to Addison's *Cato*:

France boasts no more, but, fearful to engage;
Now first pays homage to her rival's stage,
Hastes to learn thee, and learning shall submit
Alike to British arms and British wit:
No more she'll wonder, (forced to do us right,)
Who think like Romans could like Romans fight.[4]

That the English could be said to be thinking like Romans in 1714 indicates at this early date the vitality and comprehensive nature of the new classical spirit in England.

Voltaire's observation in the 1730s that 'The members of the English Parliament are fond of comparing themselves to the old Romans'[5] has been noted already and is supported by a wealth of other evidence. In the mid 1730s the identification of themselves with militant Roman republicans became the special mark of the 'Patriot' Whig (and, through Bolingbroke, partly Tory) opposition to Sir Robert Walpole, whose comment on their cast of mind is recorded by Chesterfield in his 'Character' of the Prime Minister: 'Well, are you to be an old Roman? a patriot? You will soon come off of that, and grow wiser.'[6] Yet as we shall see in the following section, even as he was facing up to his 'Roman' Opposition Walpole was imaging himself as a Roman in his busts and in the iconography of the interior of his own house, Houghton. Outside, at the apex of the central pediment, there is a statue of Walpole in the guise of Cicero.

In fact all parties in the Parliament identified themselves with the Roman Senate, including, as seen in the previous chapter, Tories. Bolingbroke himself repeatedly made the point that the Parliament was insufficiently Roman in the best senses and too Roman in the worst. According to him the problem with the British political system was that, from having been like the Roman-republican in form and spirit, it had similarly degenerated lately to a point where only form remained:

Q. *Can you give me an Instance where the Form of Government may be kept, and yet the Constitution destroy'd?*

A. Yes. The Forms of the Free Government of *Rome*, were preserv'd under the Arbitrary Government of the Emperors: There was a Senate, Consuls,

> and Tribunes of the People; as one might say King, Lords, and Commons, and yet the Government under the Emperors was always Despotick, and often Tyrannical; and indeed the Worst of all Governments is Tyranny sanctify'd by the Appearance of Law.
>
> Q. *By what Means fell that great People into this State of Slavery?*
>
> A. I have read the *Roman* History, and by what I can judge, it was by Faction, Corruption, and Standing Armies.[7]

Bolingbroke identified his own cause with that of Cato, Brutus and Cassius, proposing the latter two, whom the historian Cremutius Cordus termed 'the last of the Romans', as models for the 'ultimi Britannorum' who would fight to save England from Walpole/Caesar.[8] 'When I read the *Roman* History I am transported with Joy, and a profound Reverence for those Worthies who sacrificed their Lives, and what was perhaps dearer to them, to the Love of their Country', he wrote elsewhere, adding 'Nor is our own Country destitute of Examples of such Heroick Virtue', though they resided in the past.[9] Bolingbroke was too discreet to claim any such status himself, content instead to discern a vacuum of political heroism in contemporary England which was crying out to be filled:

> Q. *What is become of the Heroes, Philosophers, Orators, and free Citizens of* Greece*?*
>
> A. They are now Slaves to the *Great Turk*.
>
> Q. *What is become of the* Scipio's *and* Cato's *of* Rome?
>
> A. They sing now on the *English* Stage.[10]

Cicero and Cato provided him with ideal models of opposition to political parties and tyrants.[11]

Bolingbroke was by no means the only Tory politician to colour himself as a Roman republican, but he was the most prominent and consistent in the matter. Dozens of lesser Tories appear to have done the same, or to have wanted to give that impression to the world; the 'Hanover' Tory, Daniel Finch, 2nd Earl of Nottingham, for example, chose to be represented as a Roman Senator by Rysbrack (plate 2), and the Tory, Alexander Pope, was modelled as a latter-day Roman in a number of busts by Roubiliac.[12] Pope's Tory friend Allen Bathurst, 1st Earl Bathurst, is another example – his bust by Nollekens has him wearing the toga, though his house was in the old baroque manner rather than in the neo-Palladian style widely associated with Whig ideals of liberty and virtuous restraint.[13]

The 4th Earl of Chesterfield, a Whig, wrote from London to his son in Berlin on 12 February 1754 to inform him that

> your seat in the new Parliament is at last absolutely secured, and that without opposition, or the least necessity of your personal trouble or appearance . . . Thus, sure of being a Senator, I dare say you do not propose to be one of the *pedarii senatores et pedibus ire in sententiam* [place-fillers]; for, as the House of Commons is the theatre where you must make your fortune and figure in the world, you must resolve to be an actor, and not a *persona muta*.[14]

In the British Senate the great Parliamentary orators of the age were commonly identified with their Greek or Roman prototypes. Charles James Fox was the English Demosthenes, in whose works he was known to be steeped,[15] William Pitt the Elder was also compared to Demosthenes as well as to Cicero,[16] Richard Brinsley Sheridan was Hyperides (next in rank to Demosthenes) or an improved Tacitus for his 'correct periods'.[17] When Pitt the Elder set up a citizens' militia during the Seven Years' War he did so in emulation of Greek and Roman practice. Edward Gibbon describes in his *Memoirs of My Life* how the national mood, opposed to the institution of a standing army and the employment of mercenaries, favoured Pitt's design:

> The zeal of our patriots, both in, and out of, Parliament . . . complained that the sword had been stolen from the hands of the people. They appealed to the victorious example of the Greeks and Romans among whom every citizen was a soldier; and they applauded the happiness and independence of Switzerland which, in the midst of the great monarchies of Europe is sufficiently defended by a constitutional and effective militia . . .
>
> Two disgraceful events, the progress in the year forty five of some naked highlanders, the invitation of the Hessians and Hanoverians in fifty six had betrayed and insulted the weakness of an unarmed people. The country-Gentlemen of England unanimously demanded the establishment of a militia: a patriot was expected
>
> Otia qui rumpet patriae, residesque movebit
> . . . in arma viros.

> and the merit of the plan or at least of the execution was assumed by Mr Pitt who was then in the full splendour of his popularity and power...
>
> By the general ardour of the times, my father, a new Cincinnatus, was drawn from the plough: his authority and advice prevailed on me to relinquish my studies: a general meeting was held at Winchester; and before we knew the consequences of an irretrievable step, we accepted (June 12th 1759) our respective commissions of Major and Captain in the South battalion of the Hampshire.[18]

Both Chesterfield on the kind of Senator his son should be, and Gibbon here, demonstrate a playful Romanness undercut by only the mildest degree of irony. Even in the *Decline and Fall*, the values of the Roman world are generally secure from the ironies which occasionally undercut the nostalgia.[19] Chesterfield had always been explicit and generally unironical in advising his son to cultivate a manner part Roman, part French. The Roman elements would be primary, character-defining. A visit to Italy would reinforce and supplement the antique taste. France would provide the icing on the cake.

> I would wish you to be a Corinthian edifice, upon a Tuscan foundation; the latter having the utmost strength and solidity to support, and the former all possible ornaments to decorate. The Tuscan column is coarse, clumsy and unpleasant; nobody looks at it twice; the Corinthian fluted column is beautiful and attractive; but, without a solid foundation, can hardly be seen twice, because it must soon tumble down.[20]

That was the theory, but Chesterfield's years of patient advice in letter after letter bore little fruit. He urged the boy to adopt the precepts of Horace's *Art of Poetry*: 'the rules he there lays down are applicable to almost every part of life. To avoid extremes, to observe propriety, to consult one's own strength, and to be consistent from beginning to end, are precepts as useful for the man as for the poet.'[21] Graceful enunciation should be learned from the study of Cicero and Quintilian;[22] also 'correctness, purity and elegance of style, harmony of periods . . . Read over and over again the third book of the Cicero *de Oratore*, in which he particularly treats of the ornamental parts of oratory; they are indeed properly oratory, for all the rest depends only upon common sense, and some knowledge of the subjects you speak upon.'[23] Modern neo-classical writers might be useful too: Addison's *Spectators* are recommended as valuable guides to conduct.[24]

One could not learn everything at home, however. The cultivation of good taste meant examining at first hand the best models.

> The amphitheatre at Verona is worth your attention; as are also many buildings there and at Vicenza, of the famous Andrea Palladio, whose taste and style of building were truly *antique*. It would not be amiss, if you employed three or four days in learning the five Orders of Architecture, with their general proportions; and you may know all that you need to know of them in that time. Palladio's own book of Architecture is the best you can make use of for that purpose, skipping over the lowest mechanical parts of it, such as the materials, the cement, etc.[25]

Two and a half months later he made the same point: 'And for the minute and mechanical parts of [architecture], leave them to masons, bricklayers, and Lord Burlington; who has, to a certain degree, lessened himself, by knowing them too well.'[26]

Not only did travel to Italy reinforce the antique taste, it fleshed out much in one's classical reading:

> View the most curious remains of antiquity with a classical spirit, and they will clear up to you many passages of the classical authors; particularly the Trajan and the Antonine Columns; where you find the warlike instruments, the dresses, and the triumphal ornaments of the Romans. Buy also the prints and explanations of all those respectable remains of Roman grandeur, and compare them with the originals.[27]

'I must, from time to time,' he insisted in 1748, 'remind you of what I have often recommended to you, and of what you cannot attend to too much; *sacrifice to the Graces*.'[28] This was a piece of advice Chesterfield never tired of repeating. In his understanding of the correct elements of polite behaviour he represents the realisation of an important element in Shaftesbury's concept of virtuosity. Chesterfield's formula was simple: a familiarity with the ancient authors and the inculcation of grace, propriety and moderation learned there, made for a classical *gravitas* which would then be softened by an easy elegance, charm and gentility best learned on the Continent and especially from the French.

Nothing should be allowed to disturb one's equipoise. Above all one must never laugh, for to do so violated all restraint, moderation and decorum.

> Having mentioned laughing, I must particularly warn you against it: and I could heartily wish that you may often be seen to smile, but never heard to laugh while you live. Frequent and loud laughter is the characteristic of folly and ill manners: it is the manner in which the mob express their silly joy at silly things; and they call it being merry. In my mind there is nothing so illiberal, and so ill-bred, as audible laughter . . . A man's going to sit down, in the supposition that he has a chair behind him, and falling down upon his breech for want of one, sets a whole company a laughing, when all the wit in the world would not do it; a plain proof, in my mind, how low and unbecoming a thing laughter is. Not to mention the disagreeable noise that it makes, and the shocking distortion of the face that it occasions.[29]

Chesterfield is often ridiculed for this advice, but it was consistent with the views and behaviour of some of the best writers of the age. Congreve satirises the point of view by putting it into the mouth of Lord Froth, not a character to be taken seriously: 'There is nothing more unbecoming a man of quality than to laugh; Jesu, 'tis such a vulgar expression of the passion.'[30] Others, however, seem to have shared Chesterfield's view. According to Johnson, Swift 'stubbornly resisted any tendency to laughter', while 'by no merriment, either of others or his own, was [Pope] ever seen excited to laughter'.[31] Fontenelle boasted, like Chesterfield to his son, that never since reaching the age of reasoning had he '*fait ha! ha!*'[32] Addison and Shaftesbury should be added to this list, and were probably of seminal influence in the matter, though a century earlier Bacon had recommended a classical *via media* restraint: 'Entertain hopes; mirth rather than joy.'[33] Addison excluded from his ideal of humour everything unreasonable and conducive to laughter,[34] and Shaftesbury consistently took the same view, always emphasising the importance of decorous behaviour and the avoidance of vulgarity, of which laughter was of course an expression.

If laughter is 'Gothic' then it is *ipso facto* anathema to a classical frame of mind. Anything that excites it is to be shunned. To the mind of the judge, antiquary and quintessential Scoto-Roman, Sir John Clerk of

Penicuik, the wigs of judges were a ridiculous Gothic survival exciting mirth rather than respect, 'the imitation of the gravity and decency of a water spaniel'. The elimination of wigs and the cultivation of beards 'by our senators and executors of the law, like the gods and heroes of antiquity, will mean a return of a golden age and Roman gravity, vertue and frugality'.[35] *Gravitas, virtus, frugalitas*: these were core values of the Roman Republic in its glory, and of the newly Roman Britannia. Laughter seemed out of place there. In excluding it on the grounds that it was unseemly and unmannerly, Shaftesbury and Chesterfield probably found few demurrers, for their ideal of aristocratic conduct was a displacement of an earlier Stoic model popular in the seventeenth century, which was equally inimical to the vulgar and the unrestrained.

Stoicism is an important contributing element behind the Roman spirit of eighteenth-century England.[36] It is particularly significant that this philosophy, which had long been consciously promoted by Puritans, had always taught an active citizenship and engagement in the political life of the nation, with Seneca its leading martyr and finest example. As an honorary 'Christian' Stoic, Seneca had a particularly marked influence on seventeenth-century English codes of behaviour, while the Stoic emperor Marcus Aurelius' influence on Shaftesbury was pronounced.[37] Though as a code of conduct Stoicism gradually gave way to the new Shaftesburian emphasis on manners and taste, seen at its most marked in Chesterfield, in Shaftesbury himself it still exists alongside that emphasis, and its stress on civic engagement reinforced Shaftesbury's emphasis on the obligation of the oligarchy to promote civic consciousness and the arts under the panoply of political liberty.[38] More generally, it augmented the discourse of civic virtue flowing up through Machiavelli and the English classical republicans.

In his stress on the importance of classical reading and the right choice of models for seemly and civilised behaviour, Chesterfield follows Shaftesbury, though at a shallower level. In the *Characteristics* Shaftesbury compares the English of 1710, in the midst of war with France, with the Romans 'in those early days, when they wanted only repose from arms to apply themselves to the improvement of arts and studies'.[39] With the advent of peace, all that was necessary was the practice of 'virtue and emulation' of classical precedents (as the Romans had emulated the Greeks). High civilisation would result. An enlightened nobility might ideally form the vanguard of this cultural renaissance by way of moral support and patronage, 'would they freely help in this affair, and by a judicious application of their bounty facilitate this happy birth, of which I have ventured to speak in a prophetic style'.[40] Burlington was to take up this challenge in the 1720s.[41]

Although Shaftesbury was 'persuaded that to be a *virtuoso* (so far as befits a gentleman) is a higher step towards the becoming a man of virtue and good sense than the being what in this age we call a scholar',[42] he advocated wide classical reading, but reading assimilated into one's daily routine. When Shaftesbury first put it forward in 1710 this was a new idea, running clear counter to fashionable prejudice:

> Our youth . . . seem to have their only chance between two widely different roads: either that of pedantry and school-learning, which lies amidst the dregs and most corrupt part of ancient literature, or that of the fashionable illiterate world, which aims merely at the character of the fine gentleman, and takes up with the foppery of modern languages and foreign wit. The frightful aspect of the former of these roads makes the journey appear desperate and impracticable . . . As if . . . a Plutarch, a Tully, or a Horace, could not accompany a young man in his travels, at a court, or (if occasion were) even in a camp![43]

Shaftesbury's prescription would make a man's literary models intimate companions wherever he went. Inevitably they would be absorbed into his very being. By the same token he should avoid models of bad taste, such as the Gothic or the baroque, and take note only of the good:

> One who aspires to the character of a man of breeding and politeness is careful to form his judgment of arts and sciences upon right models of perfection. If he travels to Rome, he inquires which are the truest pieces of architecture, the best remains of statues, the best paintings of a Raphael or a Caraccio. However antiquated, rough, or dismal they may appear to him at first sight, he resolves to view them over and over, till he has brought himself to relish them, and finds their hidden graces and perfections. He takes particular care to turn his eye from everything which is gaudy, luscious, and of a false taste.[44]

Simplicity, austerity and severity were the hallmarks of good art, while the opposite qualities marked the cultural decadence both of imperial Rome and Bernini's Europe.[45] Symmetry and proportion were essential too, not only in good art but in the well-lived life:

> For harmony is harmony by nature, let men judge ever so ridiculously of music. So is symmetry and proportion founded still in nature, let men's fancy prove ever so barbarous, or their fashions ever so Gothic in their architecture, sculpture, or whatever other designing art. 'Tis the same case where life and manners are concerned. Virtue has the same fixed standard.[46]

Bad taste 'makes us prefer a Turkish history to a Grecian or a Roman, an Ariosto to a Virgil, and a romance or novel to an Iliad'.[47] Shaftesbury had modelled his own life and character on the best classical examples from an early age. He had spoken Greek and Latin fluently at eleven, conversing in those languages with his tutor, Mrs Birch. James Harris (an early biographer) wrote in the 1730s that throughout his life Shaftesbury's 'principal study was of the writings of antiquity, from which he formed to himself the plan of his philosophy'. Harris adds a footnote: 'Among these writings those which he most admired, and carried always with him, were the moral works of Xenophon, Horace, the Commentaries and Enchiridion of Epictetus as published by Arrian, and Marcus Antoninus. These authors are now extant in his library, filled throughout with marginal notes, references, and explanations, all written with his own hand.'[48] Addison, second only to Shaftesbury as an influence on the classical frame of mind of eighteenth-century England, was equally familiar from his earliest years with the best classical authors and his own style insensibly grew out of theirs, as Bishop Hurd pointed out:

> He employed his first years in the study of the old Greek and Roman writers; whose language and manner he caught at that time of life, as strongly as other young people gain a French accent or a genteel air. An early acquaintance with the classics is what may be called the good-breeding of poetry, as it gives a certain gracefulness which never forsakes a mind that contracted it in youth, but is seldom or never hit by those who would learn it too late. He first distinguished himself by his Latin compositions, published in the *Musae Anglicanae*, and was admired as one of the best authors since the Augustan age, in the two universities and the greatest part of Europe, before he was talked of as a poet in town.[49]

In Italy Addison visited Capri because both Augustus and Tiberius had lived there. Then, instead of travelling back to Rome by road, he took a boat in order to relive the voyage of Aeneas along this same coast and view the capes and headlands described by Virgil.[50] *Cato*, so redolent of the civic spirit of the Republic, was revised in Rome. By the time it was presented at Oxford, Addison's university, following its outstanding success in London, Addison was already known as Cato. Thomas Tickell wrote the prologue for the university production and, with a nice sense of appropriateness to the place, couched it in the language of Roman senatorial procedure:

> Great Cato's self, the glory of the stage!
> Who charms, corrects, exalts, and fires, the age,
> Begs here he may be try'd by Roman laws;
> To you, O Fathers! he submits his cause:
> He rests not in the people's gen'ral voice
> Till you the senate have confirm'd his choice.[51]

Addison earned the right to be 'Cato's self' not merely by writing *Cato* and producing superb Latin verse (which unlike most such compositions was also published in English translations), but, to the extent his Christianity would allow, by assimilating the spirit of Rome and its traditional civic values, and especially by living out those values as a Whig 'senator' whose ministerial career was crowned by his appointment in 1717 as Secretary of State.[52] Thus he functioned as a complete model of what civic virtue in England should look like, and his influence on the self-imaging of public figures must have been considerable.

What might otherwise have seemed eccentric was perhaps less so because of the example of 'Cato'. Sir John Clerk of Penicuik, Baron of the Scottish Exchequer, was much exercised over what might constitute an appropriate Roman title for himself. If a politician could be a senator, surely Clerk could find a suitable Roman title to substitute for his Gothic one. A friend, wanting to provide an inscription for Mavisbank, one of Clerk's residences, had proposed *Fisci Regii Baro*. To Clerk, within whose Roman habit of mind there was no corner for self-directed irony, this was ridiculous. There were no *reges* in the Roman Republic, and what ancient Roman had ever heard of the office of *baro*? The title had no authenticity let alone *gravitas*. True, there was in the Latin language the word *baro*, *baronis* (m.), and it meant a dunce. Clerk thought *Aerarii Tribunus* a lot better, and finally settled on *Aerarii Scotici Quaestor*.[53]

As noted in the previous chapter, Thomson's association with Virgil was almost as close as Addison's with Cato. The Scottish poet was strongly influenced by the Romanophile cultural milieu in which he grew up and in which Sir John Clerk played a central role, and by striking parallels between his own situation and Virgil's.[54]

Hume was another whose early reading in classical literature led to his cultivation of a Roman character. At fourteen he wrote a thesis defending classical *virtus* against what replaced it, 'monstrous' Gothic chivalry. He points out that our barbarian forefathers,

> struck with the Beauties of the antient Buildings, but ignorant how to preserve a just Mean; & giving an unbounded Liberty to their Fancy in heaping Ornament upon Ornament, they made the whole a heap of Confusion, & Irregularity. For the same Reason, when they wou'd rear up a new Scheme of Manners or Heroism, it must be strangely overcharged with Ornaments, & no part exempt from their unskillful refinements.[55]

When he should have been studying law he was devouring Cicero and Virgil.[56] He set about quite deliberately to form for himself a classical character:

> Having read many Books of Morality, such as Cicero, Seneca & Plutarch, & being smit with their beautiful Representations of Virtue & Philosophy, I undertook the Improvement of my Temper & Will, along with my Reason & Understanding. I was continually fortifying myself with Reflections against Death, & Poverty, & Shame, & Pain, & all the other Calamities of Life. These no doubt are exceeding useful, when join'd with an active Life; because the Occasion being presented along with the Reflection, works it into the Soul.[57]

He adds that at that age, however, his life was inactive and solitary, and his reading accordingly left him dispirited.

Such processes could be taken to extremes. After all, one lived in eighteenth-century Europe, not the ancient Rome in which Chesterfield had once dreamed of residing:

> At nineteen, I left the University of Cambridge, where I was an absolute pedant; when I talked my best, I quoted Horace; when I aimed at being facetious, I quoted Martial; and when I had a mind to be a fine gentleman, I talked Ovid. I was convinced that none but the ancients had common sense; that the classics contained everything that was either necessary, useful, or ornamental to men; and I was not without thoughts of wearing the *toga virilis* of the Romans, instead of the vulgar and illiberal dress of the moderns.[58]

Study of Roman literature and history naturally made one want to be there. His memory playing nostalgically around the Eton days they shared as children, Walpole tells his friend George Montagu that 'The beginning of my Roman history was spent in the Asylum, or conversing in Egeria's hallowed grove, not in thumping and pummelling King Amulius's herdsmen . . . One of the most agreeable circumstances I can recollect is the Triumvirate, composed of yourself, Charles [Lyttelton, later Bishop of Carlisle], and / Your sincere friend, / HOR. WALPOLE.'[59] The interest of the playful Roman self-imaging here, which could be matched at other points in Walpole's correspondence, is not diminished by the fact that the places at and around Eton to which he refers cannot now be identified.

Like Hume and Chesterfield, Gibbon developed early a self-consciously classical style whose full flowering is seen, of course, in the *Decline and Fall*. The balanced sentences of his prose (like Samuel Johnson's) can be traced to Isocrates, and much of the ornamentation to Cicero,[60] but at school his first models, he tells us himself, were Phaedrus and Cornelius Nepos.

> The *lives* of Cornelius Nepos, the friend of Atticus and Cicero, are composed in the style of the purest age: his simplicity is elegant, his brevity copious: he exhibits a series of men and manners; and with such illustrations, as every pedant is not indeed qualified to give, this Classic biographer may initiate a young Student in the history of Greece and Rome.[61]

Later, under the spell of Conyers Middleton's biography, he read Cicero, '*all* the Epistles, *all* the Orations, and the most important treatises of Rhetoric and Philosophy', with intense satisfaction.[62] 'Cicero in Latin and Xenophon in Greek are indeed the two ancients whom I would first propose to a liberal scholar, not only for the merit of their style and sentiments but for the admirable lessons which may be applied almost to every situation of public and private life.'[63] This suggests how closely Gibbon's everyday consciousness was formed by his classical reading. He looked back with envy on the Renaissance, when any learned man in Europe could converse with any other in the common Latin idiom.[64] Gibbon would have been at home there: at the age of nineteen he was already corresponding in Latin with the Zurich librarian Johann Jacob Breitinger on Roman history.

Like Addison, Gibbon not only wrote about Rome but cultivated certain Roman attitudes and sensibilities, and in this respect he was representative of the age. The affinity with Rome, particularly the republic, is found equally in the historian Adam Ferguson, whose *Essay on the History of Civil Society* (1765), which pioneered the field of social science in England, gives the Roman Republic a central place in its analysis and apotheosises its last heroes, Brutus and Cato.[65] Ferguson's *History of the Progress and Termination of the Roman Republic* (1782) adopts a more restricted field of view than the *Decline and Fall*, focussing on a period of Roman history whose proper understanding continued to be regarded during the rest of the century and throughout much of the next as crucial for anyone seriously interested in the political present.

In 1765 Gibbon formed the Roman Club in order to surround himself with people who shared his spiritual affinity with Rome.[66] They were no doubt less actively engaged in promoting British Romanness than the Society of Roman Knights, examined in the following chapter, and perhaps more than were the Society of Dilettanti, who quickly transferred their aesthetic allegiance to Greece. Founded around December 1732, the Dilettanti were initially a dining club of self-appointed arbiters of taste. Early members included Richard Temple, Viscount Cobham, the leading figure in the Opposition 'Patriot' circle at Stowe, whose Roman self-imaging is examined below. On 1 February 1741 it was resolved 'That a Roman dress is thought necessary for the President of the Society'.[67] Exactly a month later they voted that it be scarlet, not crimson, and 'That the President puts on the Roman dress when the

Books are open'd' and 'Quits the Roman dress when he leaves the Chair and not before'. The President sat in the 'sella Curulis' which was covered in crimson velvet. As their self-indulgences included large quantities of wine, it was appropriate that the Society's books be kept in a box called Bacchus' Tomb, the ornamented lid of which had as its principal ornament a reclining Bacchus. There was some disagreement over the choice of a device for the Society's Great Seal. The proposal that it be 'a Consular Figure in the chair with the Fasces and the inscription Auctoritate Reipublicae . . . passed in the negative'. Instead, 'the figures of Minerva and Apollo' were chosen. *Seria Ludo* was fixed upon as the motto, and the device changed to 'Medusa's head in silver gilt'. Horace Walpole, who was never a member, told Sir Horace Mann that 'The nominal qualification is having been in Italy, and the real one, being drunk.'[68] The toast was originally 'Viva la Virtu', later changed to 'Grecian Taste and Roman Spirit' (it was not accepted until 1789 that a toast to the king should precede any other). The Society was intensely fashionable, not only reflecting shifts in antique taste faster than any other group but dictating them through its support of James Stuart and Nicholas Revett who, as newly elected members, travelled to Athens to do the field-work for their *magnum opus*, *The Antiquities of Athens* (first volume, 1762). In fact a fragment of the Parthenon frieze was already in the Society's possession by 1744. In helping to pioneer the taste for a more strictly faithful neo-classical architecture modelled on Greek rather than Roman originals, the Dilettanti must have coaxed many men of influence away from that fascination with things Roman one sees in the Society's own early iconography.[69]

Yet while an increasingly exact understanding of 'Grecian taste' would finally elevate it above Roman in England, 'Roman spirit' would continue to be a *desideratum* even for the Dilettanti themselves. Through the second half of the century it would be endorsed by Edward Gibbon and Adam Ferguson in history and social science, Hume in philosophy, Burke, Pitt and Fox in Parliament, among many others. Beyond the scope of this book, it would determine much of the political character and iconography of the young United States and, carrying over into the next century, influence the idea of the British Empire.[70]

SCULPTURE

Until well into the seventeenth century, the privilege of having oneself visually imaged as a Roman was largely restricted to princes. The models chosen were not generally the heroes of the Republic. It was the Empire these princes wished to evoke or restore, with themselves as *principes*. Charlemagne is the outstanding example. The Western Empire, dead after 476, left a legacy of Caesarism to its successor states, and, through the centuries which followed, kings across Europe were inspired to emulation by Roman examples, above all by the Empire's founder and his adopted son: Julius and Augustus. The titles Czar and Kaiser testify to this habit of mind, as do the images and inscriptions on a mass of European coinage from the early Middle Ages.

Aside from the laurel wreath, the appropriate costume was slow to be adopted into the iconography of these latter-day Caesars. It has been pointed out that while Roman military costume continued to be used by commanders in Byzantium into the Middle Ages and may have influenced the Carolingian court to some extent, it had little impact on princely self-imaging until the Renaissance, when the new interest in antiquity, particularly as expressed in the prestigious genre of history painting, made this form of costume well known. Even then, its depiction was long restricted to subjects out of the past and was generally marked by anachronisms.[71] Cosimo I was probably the first modern prince to have himself depicted in Roman military costume, in a painting by Vasari and a bust by Cellini, and his example was followed in France by Charles IX and Henri IV, and later in England by Charles I. Meanwhile Roman costume was being popularised in the masques of Inigo Jones and in seventeenth-century French heroic drama[72] and Italian *opera seria*. In the second half of the seventeenth century Louis XIV of France took self-glorification to new heights, directly identifying himself with Apollo, the Sun god.[73] He habitually imaged himself as a latter-day Roman emperor and was emulated all over Europe, including in England, where Charles II and James II filled their imperial roles with less security, threatened as they were by strong senatorial oppositions unbecoming a Caesar. The 'classical' portraits of these monarchs generally preserve seventeenth-century features, most obviously the long wig, and various anachronisms in the habits.[74] The same is true of many of the busts and statues. The equestrian statue of Louis XIV in the Place Vendôme, for example, crowns a Roman figure with a contemporary periwig. Some of the royal statues Louis inspired in England show greater fidelity to classical style, in particular Grinling Gibbons's bronze statues of Charles II (*c.* 1676) at the Royal Hospital, Chelsea, and James II as Augustus (*c.* 1686), now in Trafalgar Square. Each of these is in the military dress of a Roman *imperator* and holding a baton as symbol of authority, and each wears a laurel wreath over short hair. In this feature, however, Gibbons was ahead of his time. Other 'Roman' statues of Charles II and James II have periwigs, including the equestrian Charles II on the Royal Mile at Edinburgh.

The depiction of English non-regal personages as Romans begins in earnest after the Revolution, though there are early anticipations, like Nicholas Stone's monuments to Francis Holles (d. 1622) and George Holles (d. 1626) in Westminster Abbey.[75] It was to be expected that after 1688 the nobility and gentry, and particularly Members of Parliament and of the Government, their newly enhanced political status securely based in the Bill of Rights, should image themselves as representatives and defenders of the classical principles of political liberty and civic virtue. The 'Roman' busts, statues and monuments of themselves which they commissioned were intended to suggest their qualifications for the authority and privileges they enjoyed, in particular their adherence to high moral and civic standards. As we shall see from examples below, it is misleading to say of Roman military costume that as it 'descended the social scale, from royalty, to nobility, and thence to gentry, some of whom had no heroic qualifications whatsoever', it 'soon became little more than a masquerade costume, and as such it survived in the eighteenth century'.[76] It is even more untrue of Roman costume generally. The primary qualifications for the Roman self-imaging in which the oligarchy indulged after the Revolution were moral and spiritual, and of course political. This is the case also in a number of those monuments in which the subject is depicted in military costume. Roman self-imaging, including the military sort, did not merely 'survive' in eighteenth-century England, it flourished and perfected itself. Like the Roman-republican military 'heroes', their eighteenth-century English emulators act within the *res publica* and their exploits are to be understood not as individualistic Herculean feats (in fact the very human Pompey, Brutus and Cato were all defeated) but as functioning civically within a community of shared moral, spiritual and political values, something which has not previously received the attention it deserves.[77]

A good illustration is Roubiliac's monument to John Campbell, 2nd Duke of Argyll and Greenwich in Westminster Abbey (completed 1749), and more particularly the terracotta model of 1745 (plate 3) on which it is based. This work draws on seventeenth-century precedents in monuments designed by Le Brun and Fischer von Erlach,[78] but the political messages are distinctly British and more to the point here. A knowledge of pertinent biographical details makes Argyll's monument easier to read. The first significant historical fact about Argyll is that on 30 June 1685, the day his grandfather was executed on the orders of James II for fighting unsuccessfully in support of Monmouth under the banner 'For God and Religion, against Poperie, Tyrrannie, Arbitrary Government, and Erastianism',[79] the four-year-old John Campbell fell unharmed from an upper-storey window. The memory of this fact was obviously preserved because it was considered an auspicious omen, rich in political meaning. His education, under private tutors, was heavily biased towards philosophy and classics, and he quickly demonstrated a military bent. As a young Brigadier-General in Marlborough's campaigns his valour was remarked at Ramilies, Ostend, Oudenarde, Lille and Ghent. As Lieutenant-General at Malplaquet on 11 September 1709 'he accomplished the critical enterprise of dislodging the enemy from the woods of Sart, displaying in the attack extraordinary valour and resolution. In the struggle he had various narrow escapes, several musket-balls having passed through his coat, hat, and periwig.'[80] Marlborough's vast ambitions, however, turned Argyll against him. According to Swift,

> When he was consulted [by Queen Anne] what course should be taken upon the Duke of Marlborough's request to be general for life; and whether any danger might be apprehended from the refusal; I was told, he suddenly answered, That her Majesty need not be in pain; for, he would undertake,

> whenever she commanded, to seize the Duke at the head of his troops, and bring him away either dead or alive.[81]

What is most remarkable here is Argyll's undertaking to seize Marlborough at the head of his troops. He proposes a civic-minded action, classically heroic, against a military strongman who is already seen by his political enemies as a would-be Caesar and in the face of whose ambitions the government of the free commonwealth trembles. One is reminded, and probably meant to be reminded, of the resolution of the military defenders of the Republic, Brutus, Cato, and above all Pompey, with whom Argyll particularly identified himself, as we shall see. His opposition to Marlborough so endeared him to the Tories that late in 1710 he was created a Knight of the Garter. Subsequently, under a Whig government, he played a leading role in crushing the 1715 Jacobite rebellion in Scotland, and in 1737 he defended Edinburgh in the face of the Porteous riots. Though his contribution to the political life of the nation was less significant than his military exploits, his oratory in Parliament was legendary. Pope referred to him as born to wield 'the State's whole Thunder . . . / And shake alike the Senate and the Field',[82] and Thomson commented,

> For, powerful as thy Sword, from thy rich Tongue
> Persuasion flows, and wins the high Debate.[83]

He was swayed by passion more than by reason and his political career was inconsistent in direction. In the late 1730s he alienated Walpole and played a significant role in his fall, but spurned attempts by the Jacobites to enlist him in their cause. He died in 1743.

Roubiliac's design for the Argyll monument gives classical expression to a life that was undoubtedly largely classical in its inspiration. Argyll, in Roman armour, sits on his sarcophagus (its base ornamented with sword, baton, coronet and garter), leaning against the winged figure of Fame who bends forward as she inscribes his name on the pyramid (signifying eternity) behind him. In her left hand she holds a book (the historical record of Argyll's life) which rests appropriately on a cannon-ball and bears the inscription 'NATVS DIE 10 mensis 8. MDCLXXX OBIIT

DIE 3 mensis 8. MDCCXLIII'. Below, a bas-relief shows Liberty between two columns, being presented with a sword and shield by putti (liberty, once won, must be defended against her enemies by force of arms). There is a scroll at Liberty's feet which in Roubiliac's 1748 drawing of the monument is inscribed 'Magna Charta'.[84] To the left the dramatic figure of Eloquence, arm outstretched to the spectator, signifies Argyll's oratorical powers and his political services to the state. By her side leans a shield inscribed 'DEMOSTHENES in Greek capitals. On the right sits Pallas, looking up towards the Duke. She holds a shield inscribed 'CN POMPEIVS' and bearing the portrait of Argyll's model general, defender of the free state against the ambitions of Caesar, just as Argyll defended it against the ambitions of Marlborough-as-Caesar and later those of Walpole-as-Caesar. The monument as a whole defines the intimate relations of the political and the military in a state presided over by liberty. Argyll's exploits are contained and explained within a civic context, outside of which they would make no sense.[85]

The same is true, in a less impressive way, of the monument (*c.* 1721) by Denis Plumier, Laurent Delvaux and Peter Scheemakers commemorating John Sheffield, Duke of Buckingham ('Buckinghamshire' until 1703), in Westminster Abbey (plate 4).[86] Buckingham had carved out a distinguished naval and military career before holding high political offices under James II (Privy Councillor, Lord Chamberlain), William and Mary (Privy Councillor, member of the Cabinet Council, temporarily Speaker of the House of Lords), and Anne (Privy Councillor, Lord Privy Seal, Lord President of the Council). His politics were Tory. He was also a poet, author of an 'Essay on Poetry' and an 'Essay on Satire' (a scurrilous lampoon), and reviser of Shakespeare's *Julius Caesar*, out of which he produced two plays titled *Julius Caesar* and *Marcus Brutus*, interesting here because he classicised his Shakespearean material by adding choruses. He was the dedicatee of Dryden's translation of the *Aeneid*. His monument combines his attachment to the classical past with his military and political achievements. There is not much gesturing to liberty and any role he may have played in its defence, though an inscription, 'Pro Rege saepe, pro Republica semper', insists that for him the Republic always came before the king. The Duke, in Roman armour and with his hair in

Roman style, mourned by an adoring wife to his left, reclines with the symbols of military and civic authority about him – a standard on which the letter 'R' of 'SPQR' is not visible, since he served the *senatus populusque* of England, not of Rome; banners and weapons; the *fasces*, perhaps representing his position of 'consul' as Lord President of the Council; and so on. Above, the winged figure of Time carries medallions bearing bas-relief portraits of the Duke's children.[87]

Roman military garb, and civil garb too for that matter, is not a 'masquerade costume'[88] in eighteenth-century sculpture. It expresses the idea that the subject maintains the values of the classical past in the English present. Frequently a deliberate juxtaposing of the past and present emphasises just this point. Henry Cheere's statue of Christopher Codrington (1734), in the Codrington Library of All Souls College, Oxford, is a good example (plate 5). While a student at Oxford, Codrington established himself as a wit and a scholar, thereafter fought in Flanders and was made captain of the first regiment of foot by William III, whom he accompanied to Oxford in 1695, delivering the university oration in the king's presence. Addison's disciple Thomas Tickell in his poem *Oxford* (1707) links Codrington with Richard Steele as a soldier–poet, classicising both:

> When *Codrington*, and *Steele* their Verse unrein,
> And form an easie, unaffected Strain,
> A double Wreath of Laurel binds their Brow,
> As they are Poets and are Warriors too.[89]

Codrington, who came originally from a planter family, became Governor-General of the Leeward Islands. When he died in 1710 he left his library, valued at £6,000, to All Souls, and £10,000 for the erection and furnishing of the College's Library. Cheere's statue has him in Roman military costume and carrying a baton, appropriately, as he had commanded against the French in the West Indies; but he stands, anachronistically, beside a pile of leather-bound and obviously modern large folios partly draped by his long mantle. He is at once soldier, scholar and benefactor, Roman in both *virtus* (civic and military) and *munificentia*, yet a devoted son of contemporary Oxford. The juxtaposing of roles and

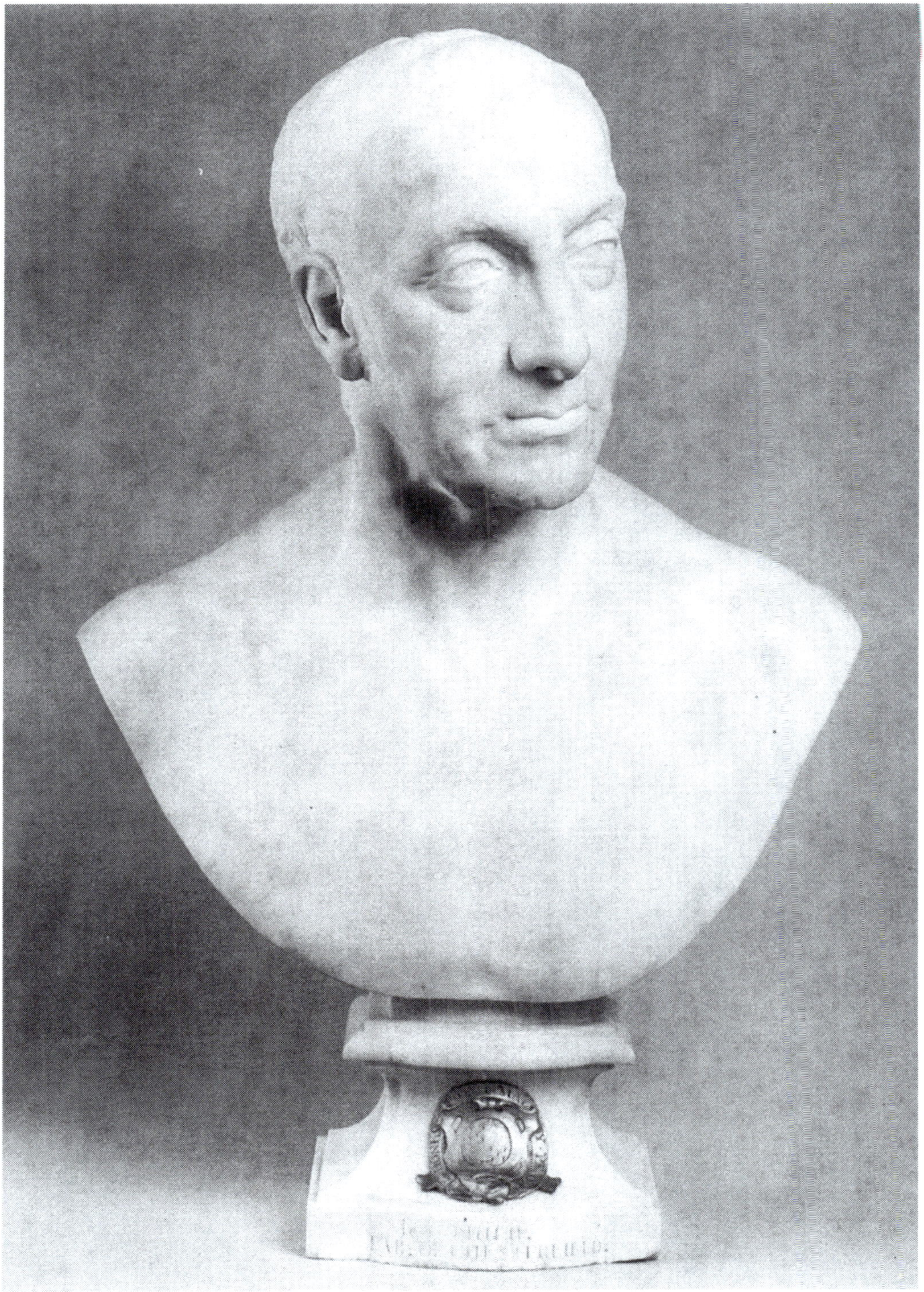

[1]
Philip Dormer Stanhope, 4th Earl of Chesterfield, by Joseph Wilton.

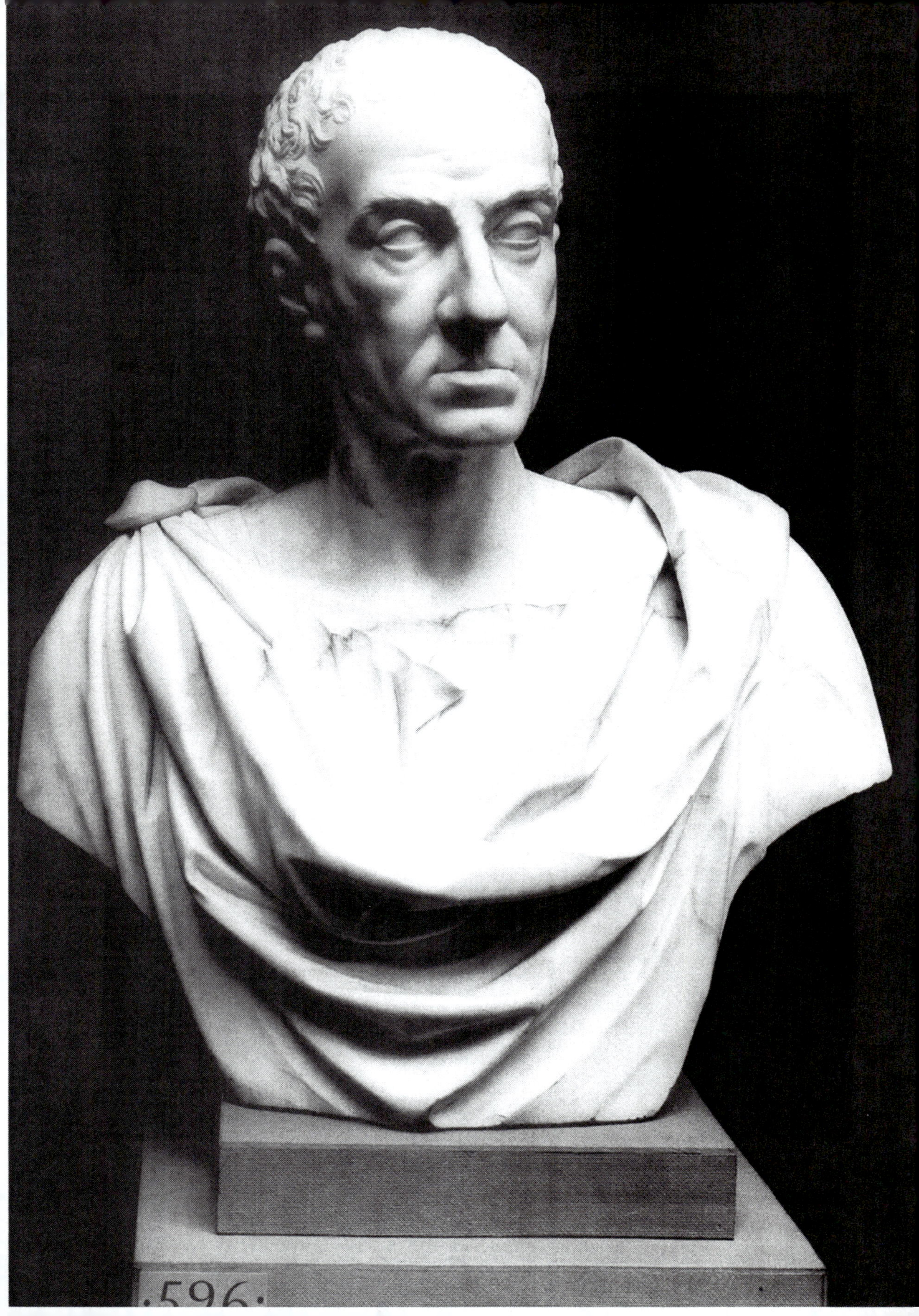
.596.

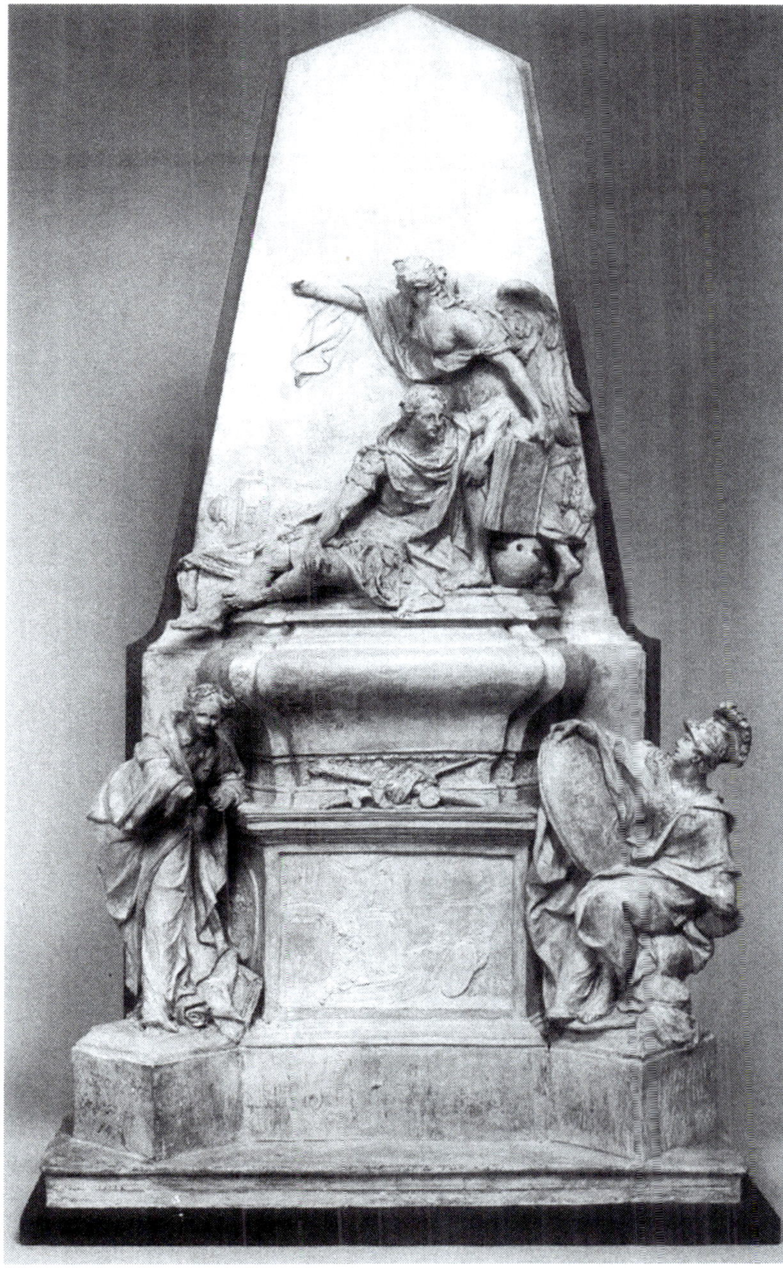

[2] (opposite)
Daniel Finch, 2nd Earl of Nottingham, by Michael Rysbrack.

[3]
Model for monument to John Campbell, 2nd Duke of Argyll, in Westminster Abbey, by Louis-François Roubiliac.

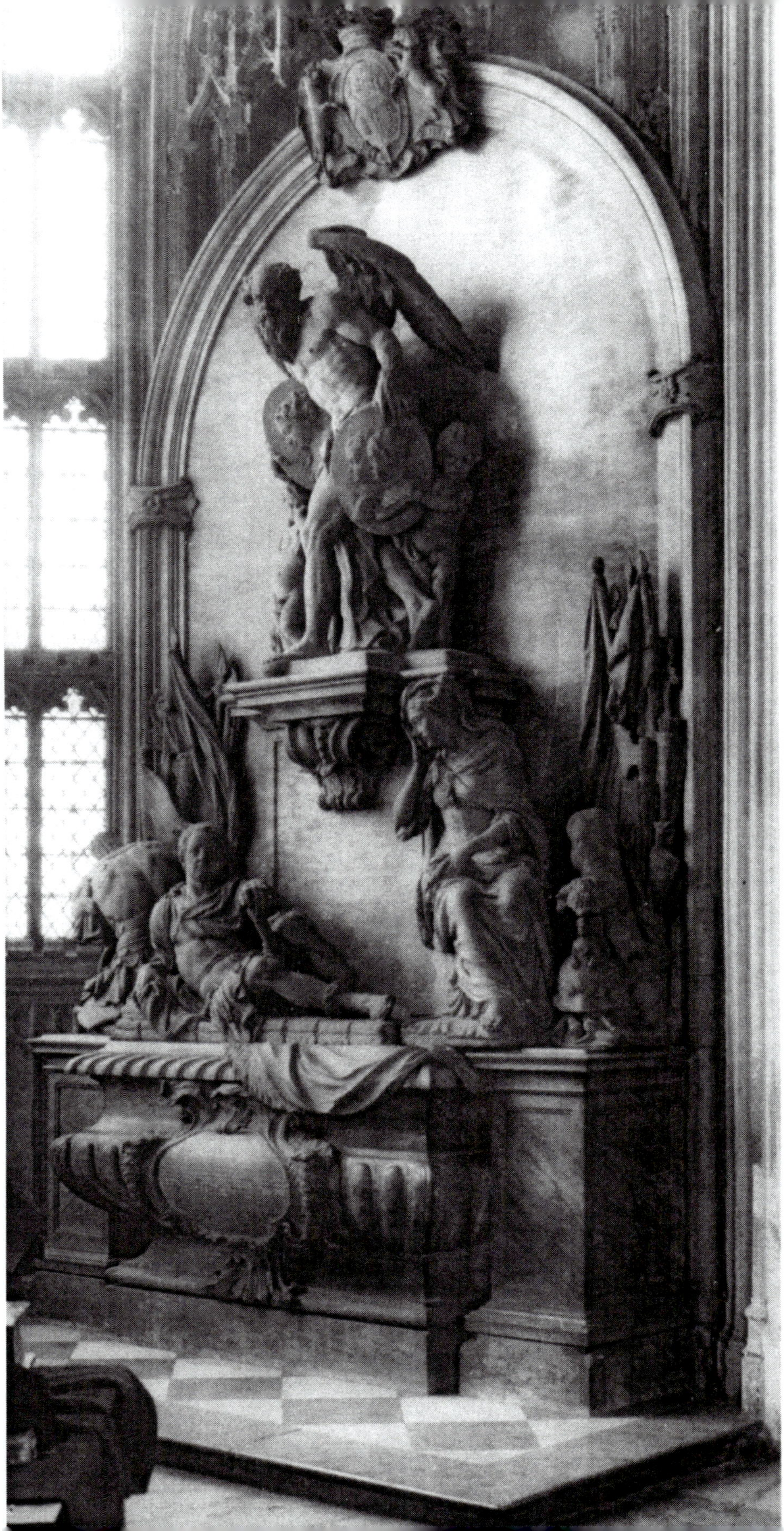

[4]
Monument to John Sheffield, Duke of Buckingham, by Denis Plumier, Laurent Delvaux and Peter Scheemakers.

[5]
Christopher Codrington,
by Henry Cheere.

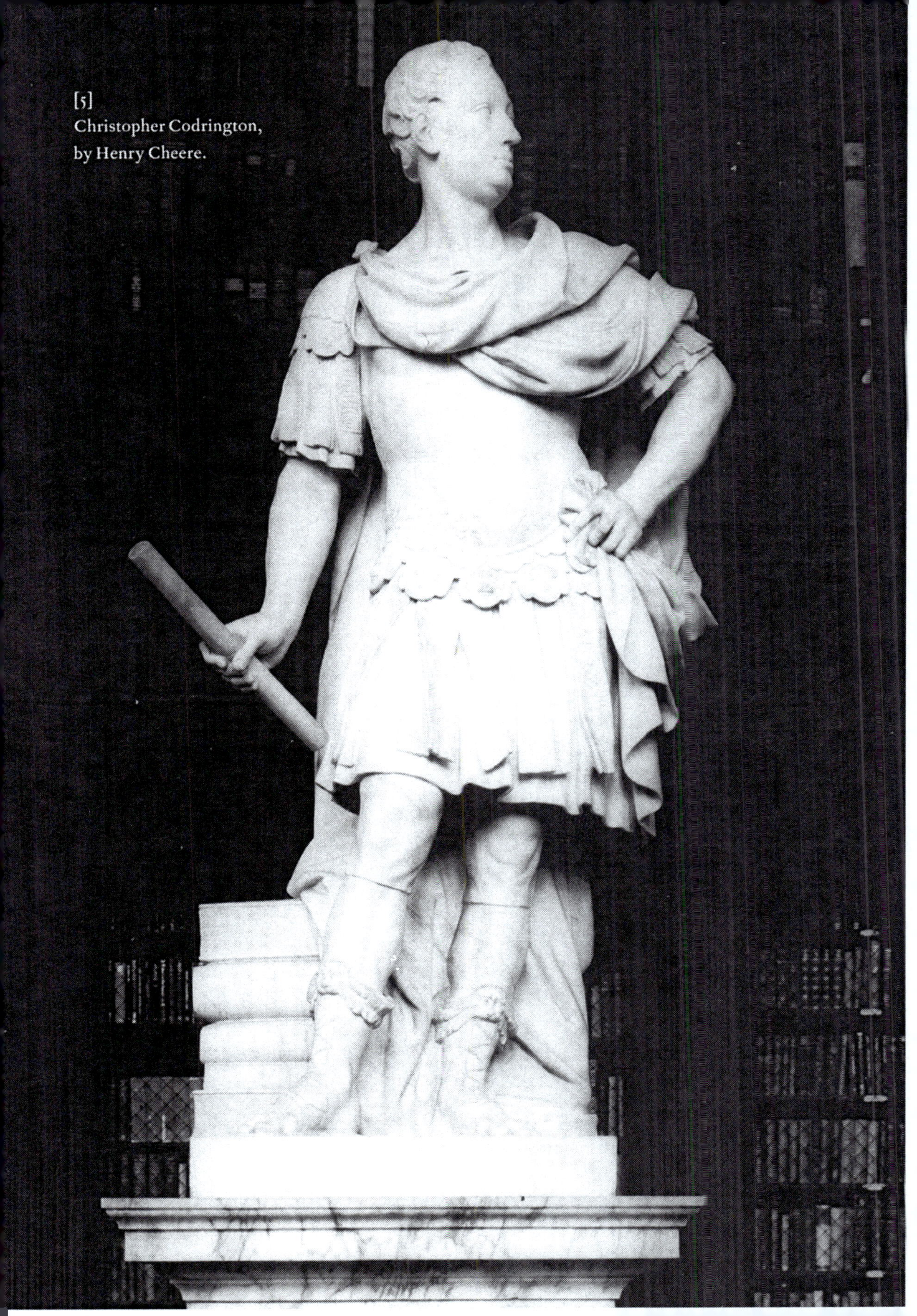

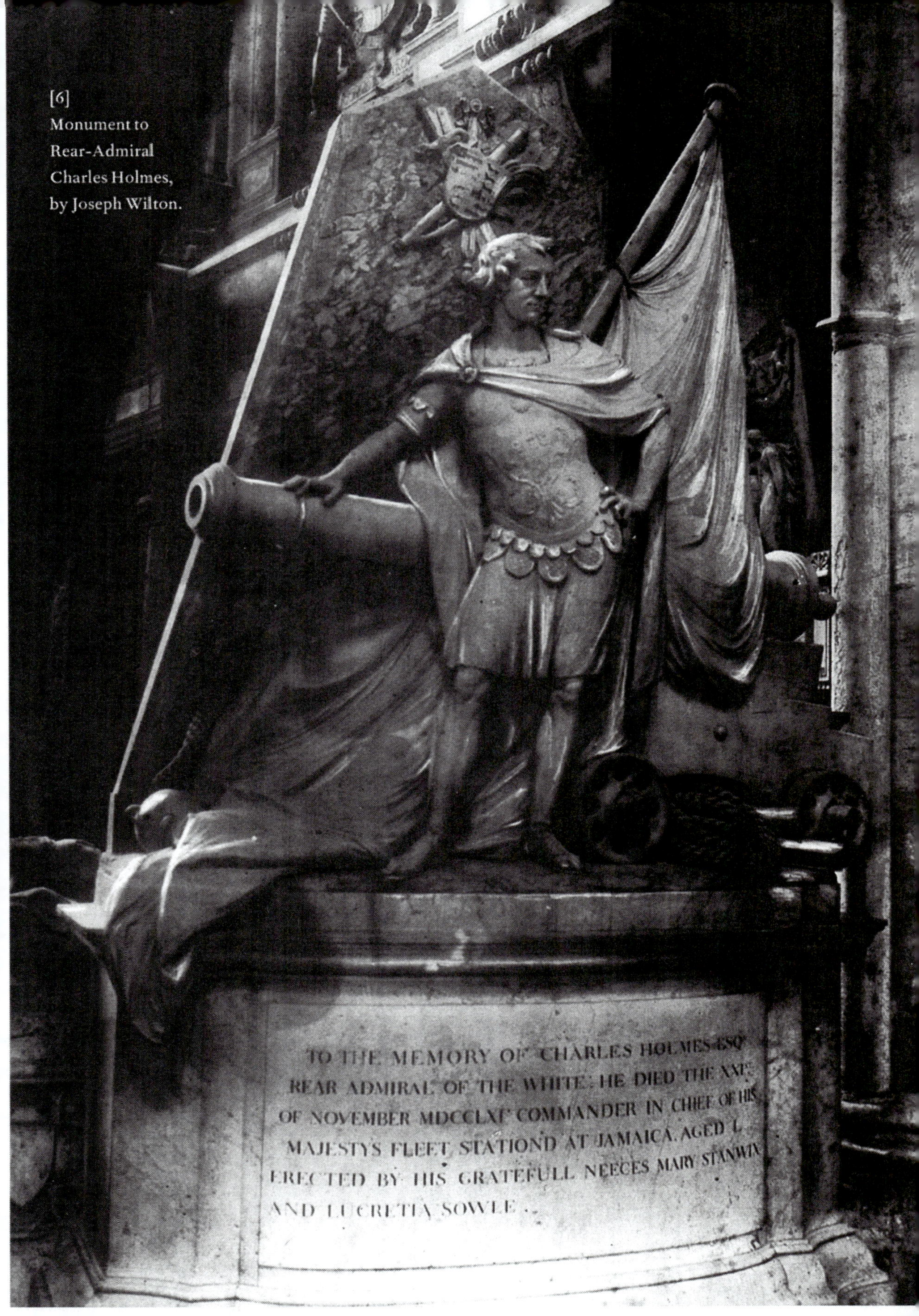

[6]
Monument to Rear-Admiral Charles Holmes, by Joseph Wilton.

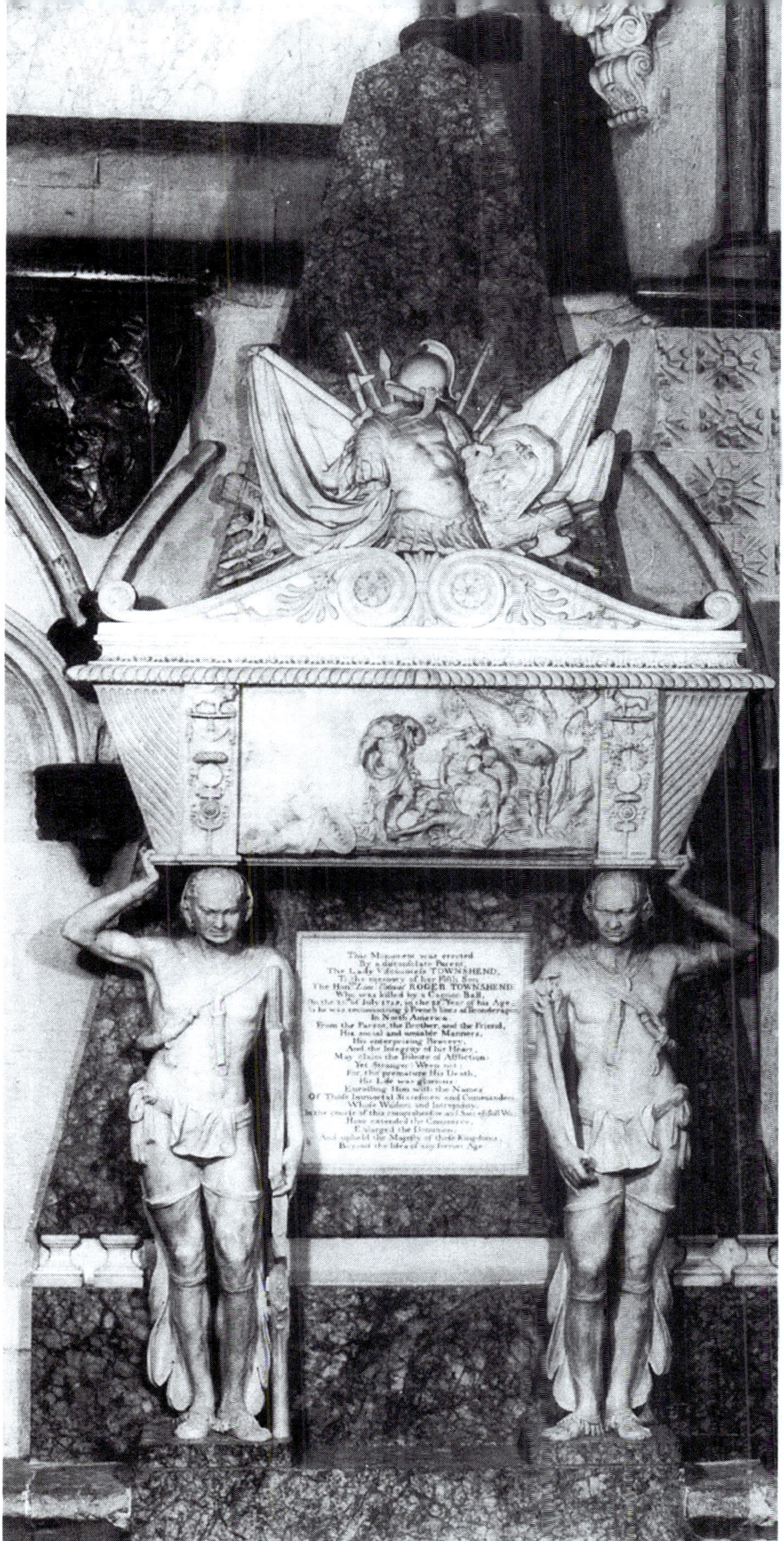

[7]
Monument to Lt. Col. Roger Townshend, by Benjamin and Thomas Carter and John Eckstein.

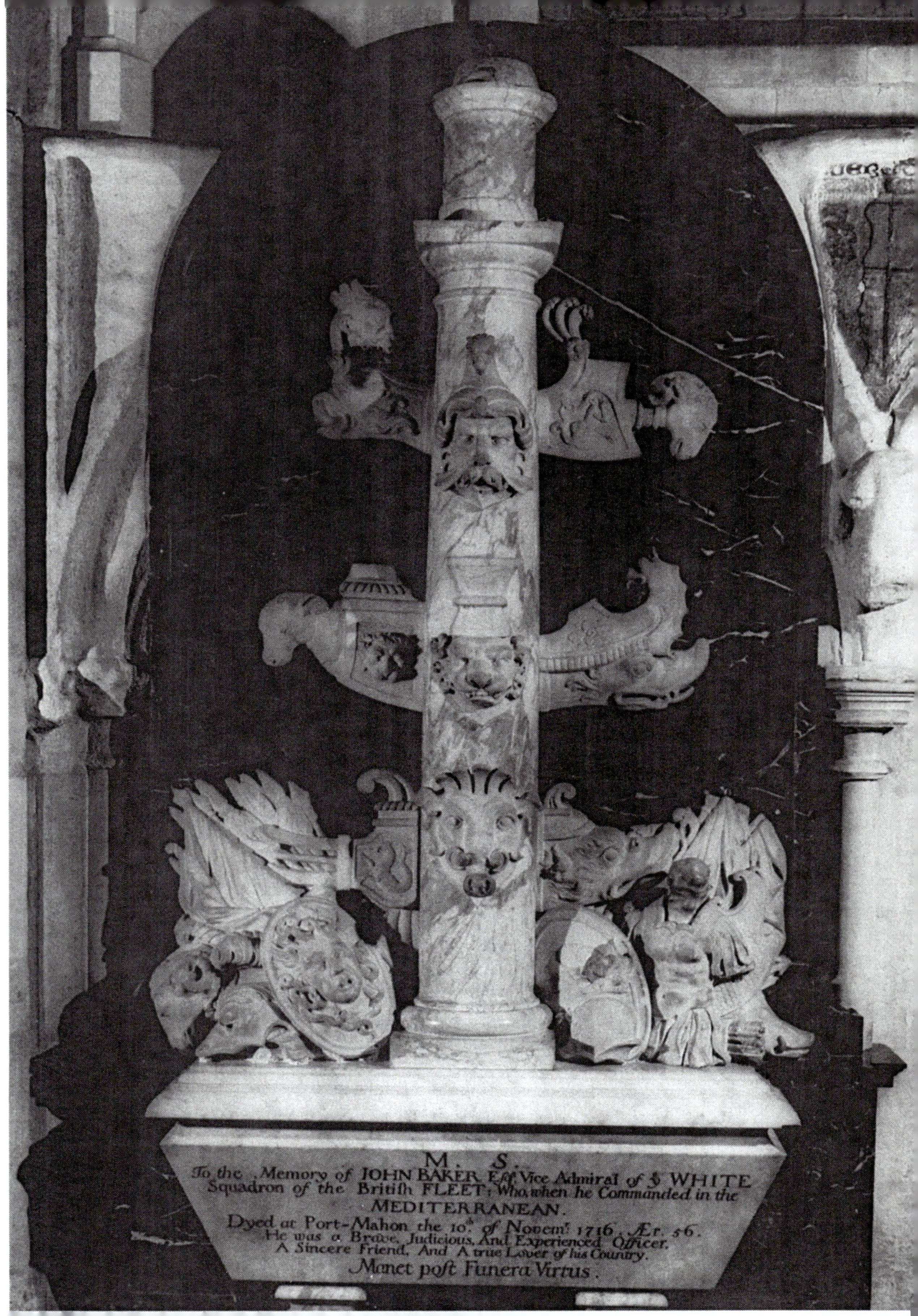
M. S.
To the Memory of JOHN BAKER Esq. Vice Admiral of ye WHITE
Squadron of the British FLEET; Who, when he Commanded in the
MEDITERRANEAN.
Dyed at Port-Mahon the 10th of Novemr. 1716. Ær. 56.
He was a Brave, Judicious, And Experienced Officer,
A Sincere Friend, And A true Lover of his Country.
Manet post Funera Virtus.

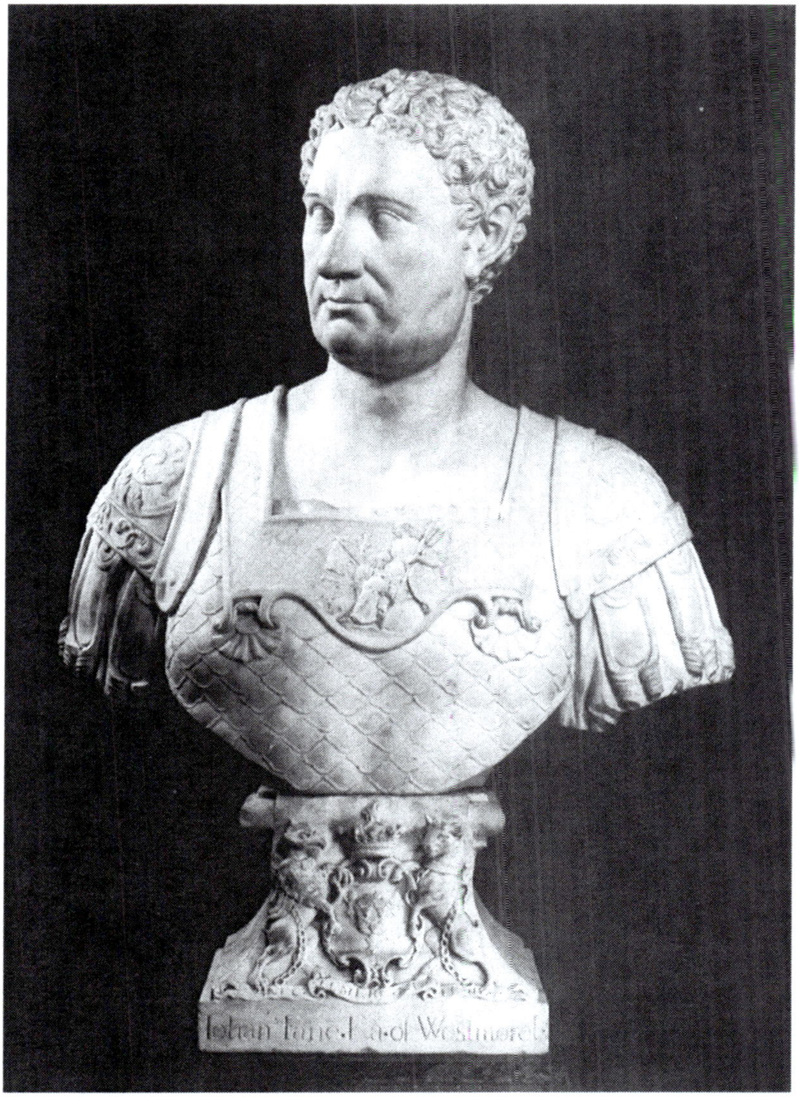

[8] *(opposite)*
Monument to Vice-Admiral
John Baker, by Francis Bird.

[9]
John Fane, 7th Earl of Westmorland,
by Thomas Ady.

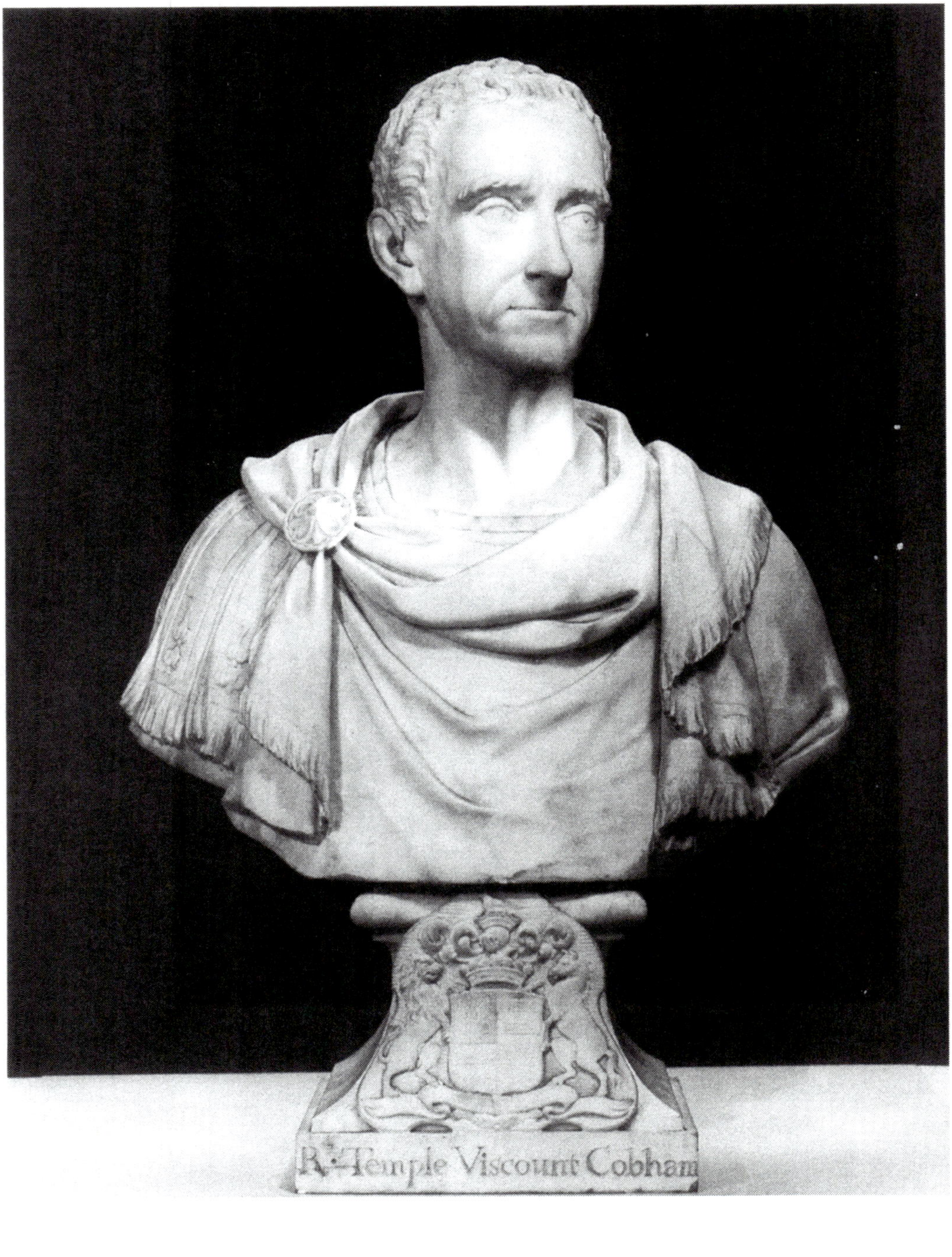

[10]
Richard Temple, Viscount Cobham,
by Peter Scheemakers.

[11] *(opposite)*
Robert Clive, 1st Baron Clive,
by Peter Scheemakers.

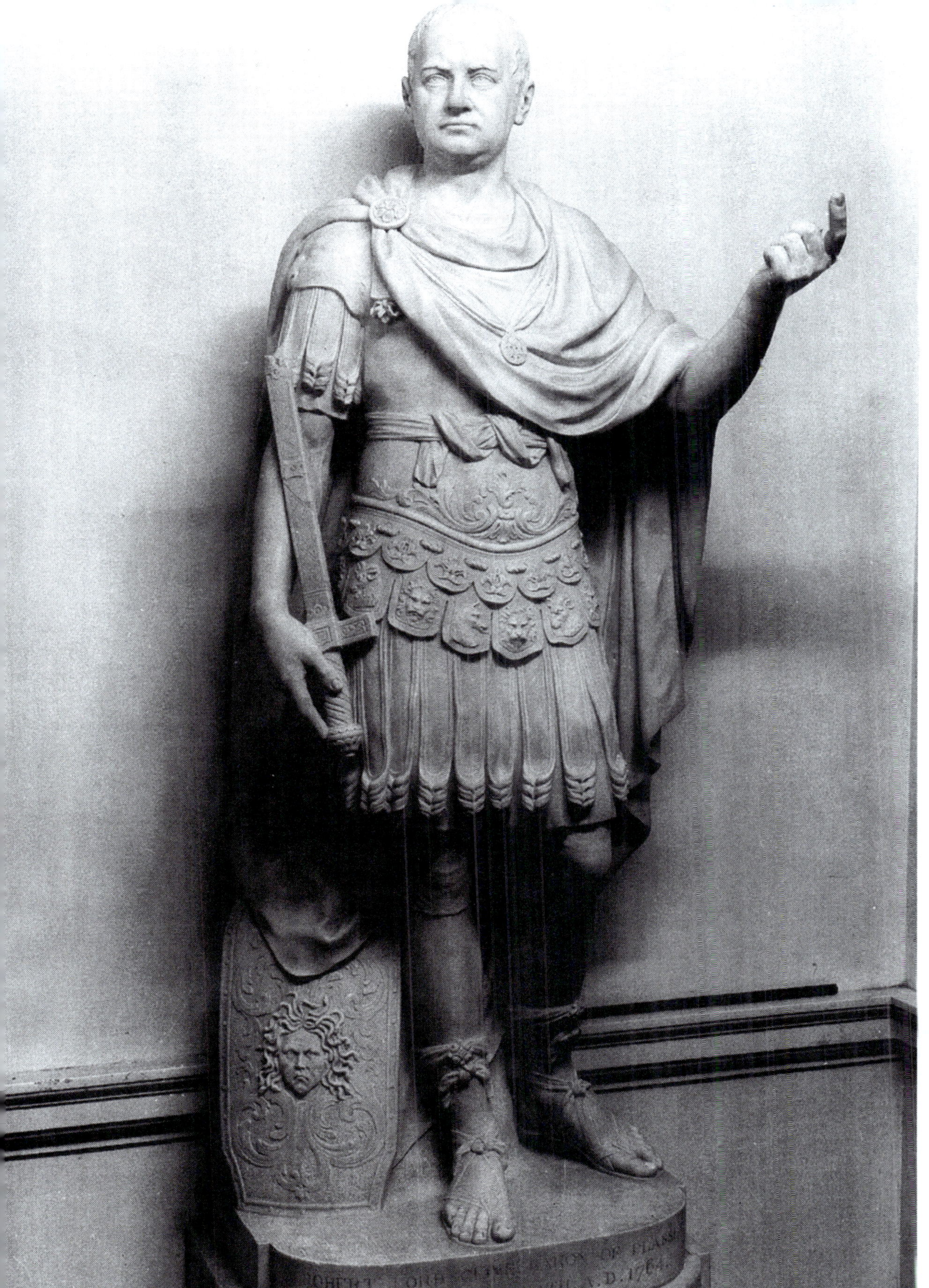
KNIGHT OF

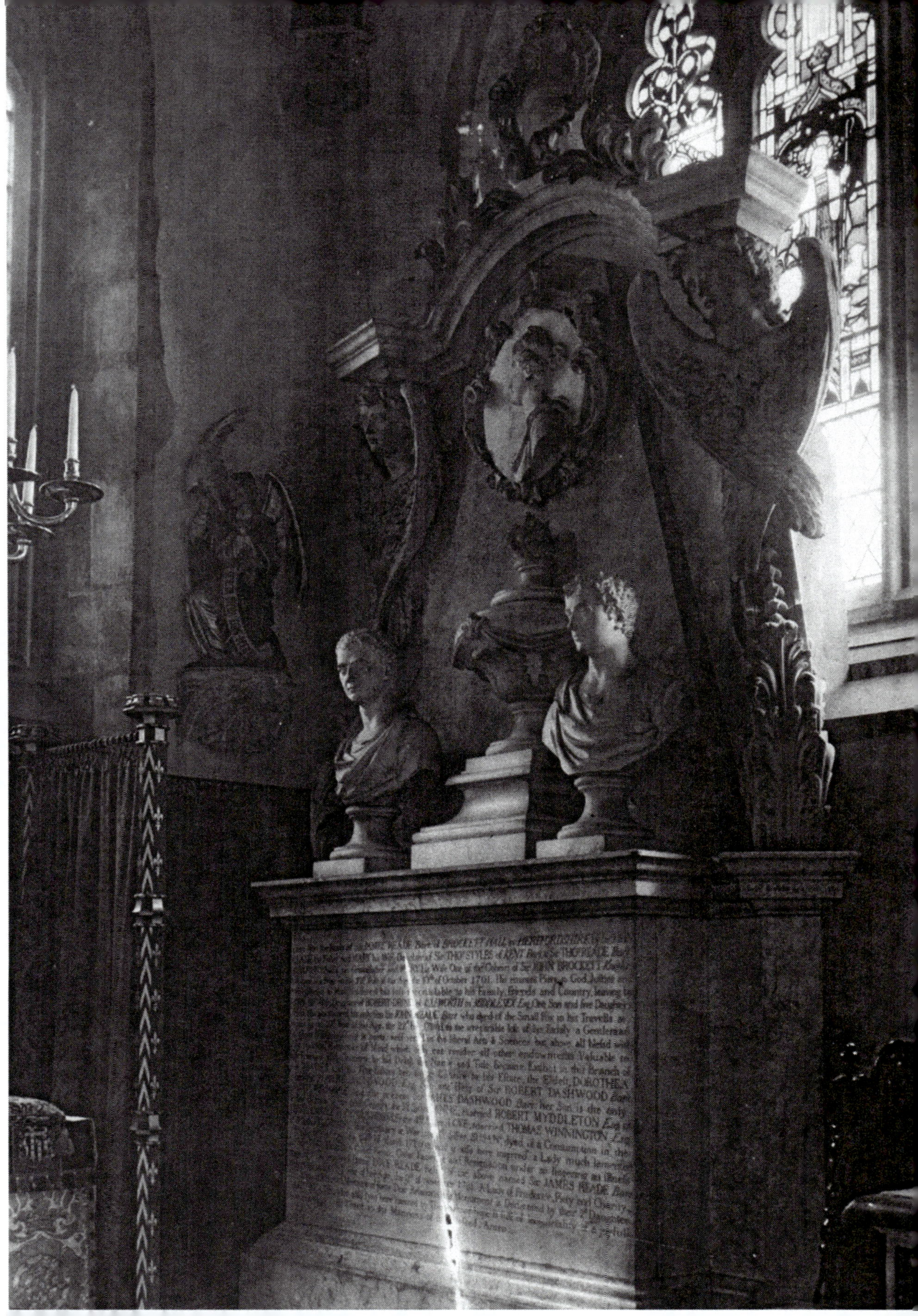

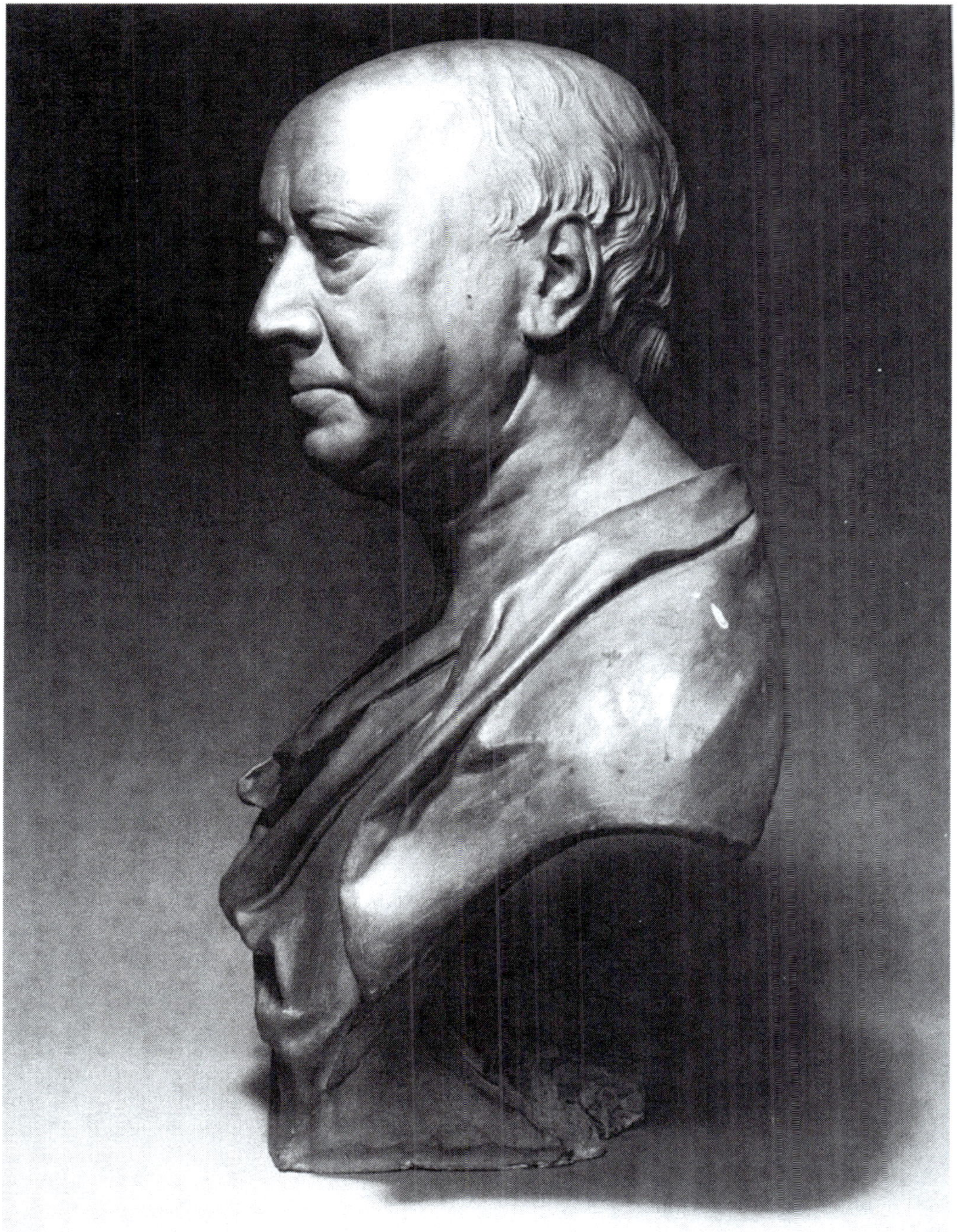

[12] *(opposite)*
Reade Family Monument at Hatfield,
by Michael Rysbrack.

[13]
Sir Andrew Fountaine,
by Louis-François Roubiliac.

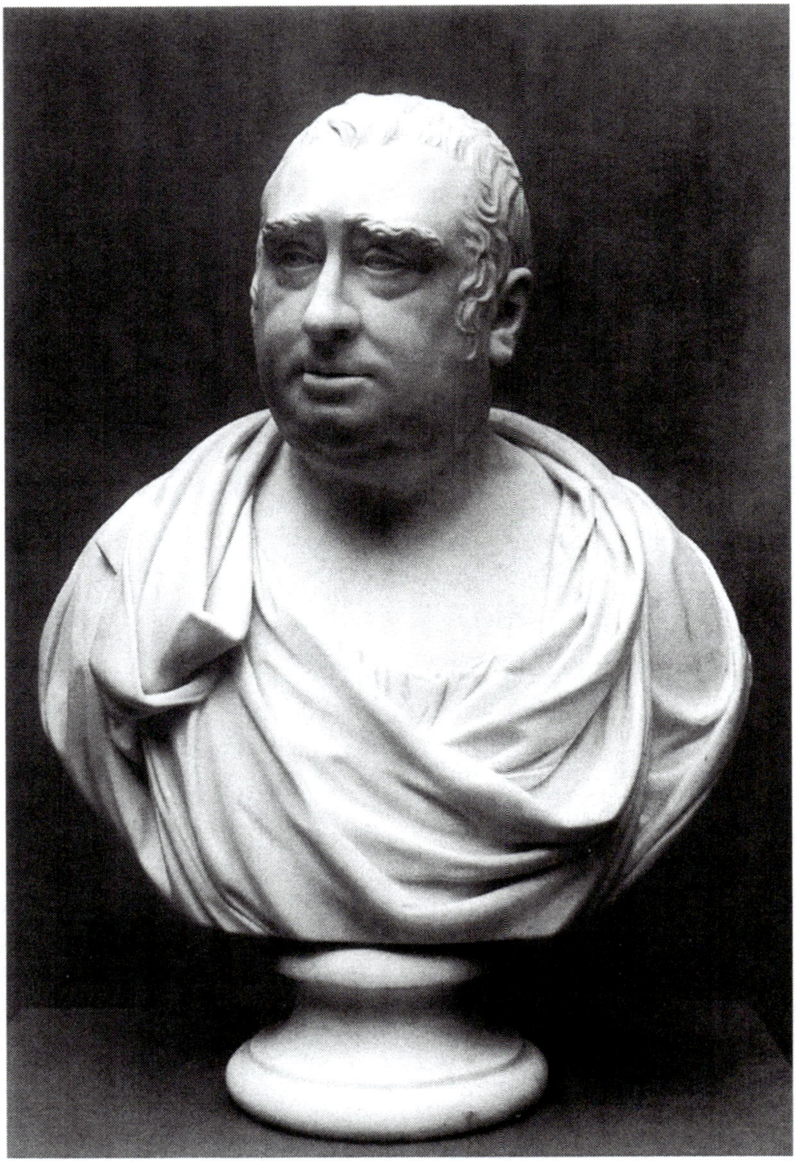

[14]
Charles James Fox, 1801,
by Joseph Nollekens.

[15]
Temple of Ancient Virtue, Stowe. William Kent.

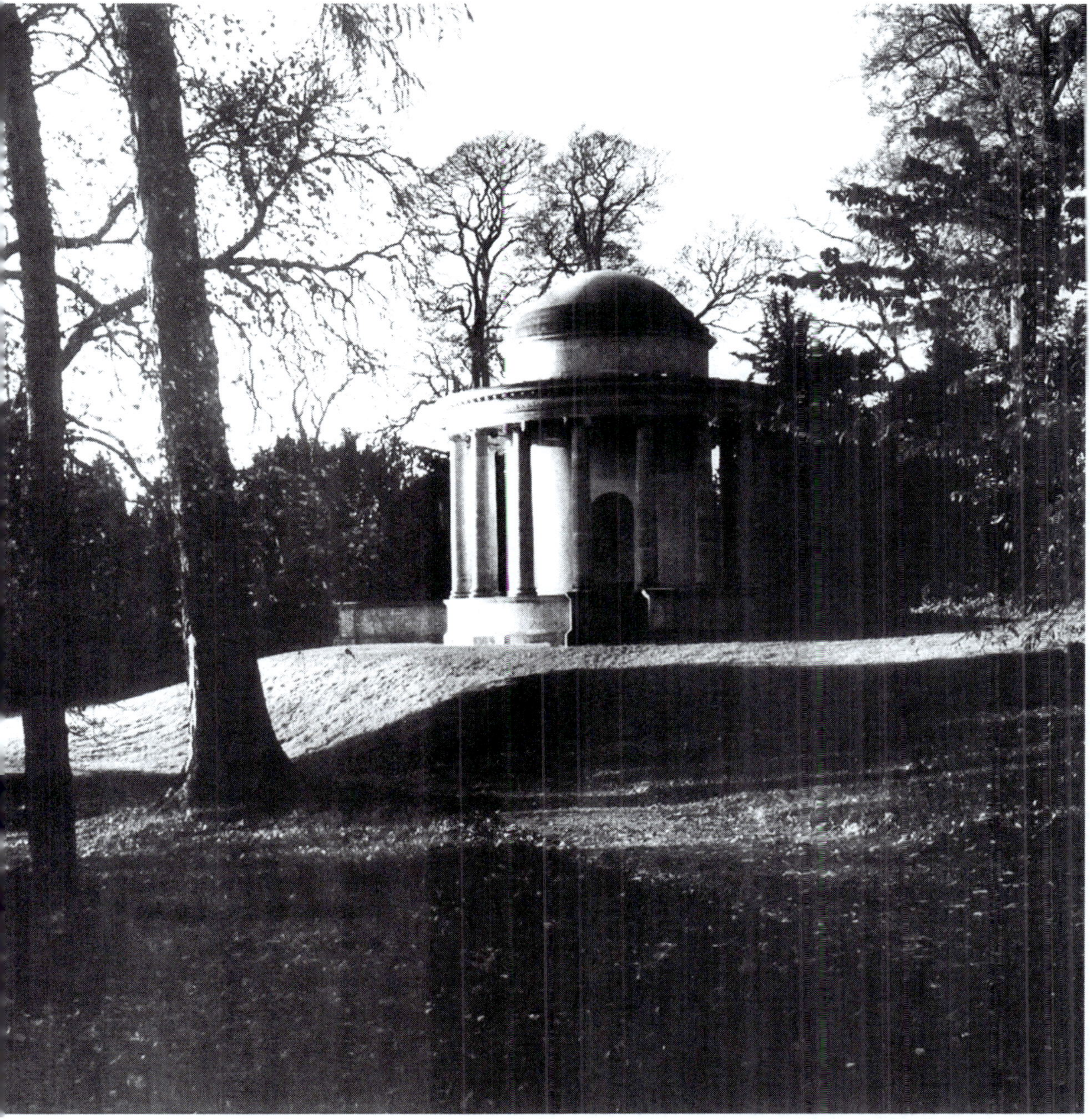

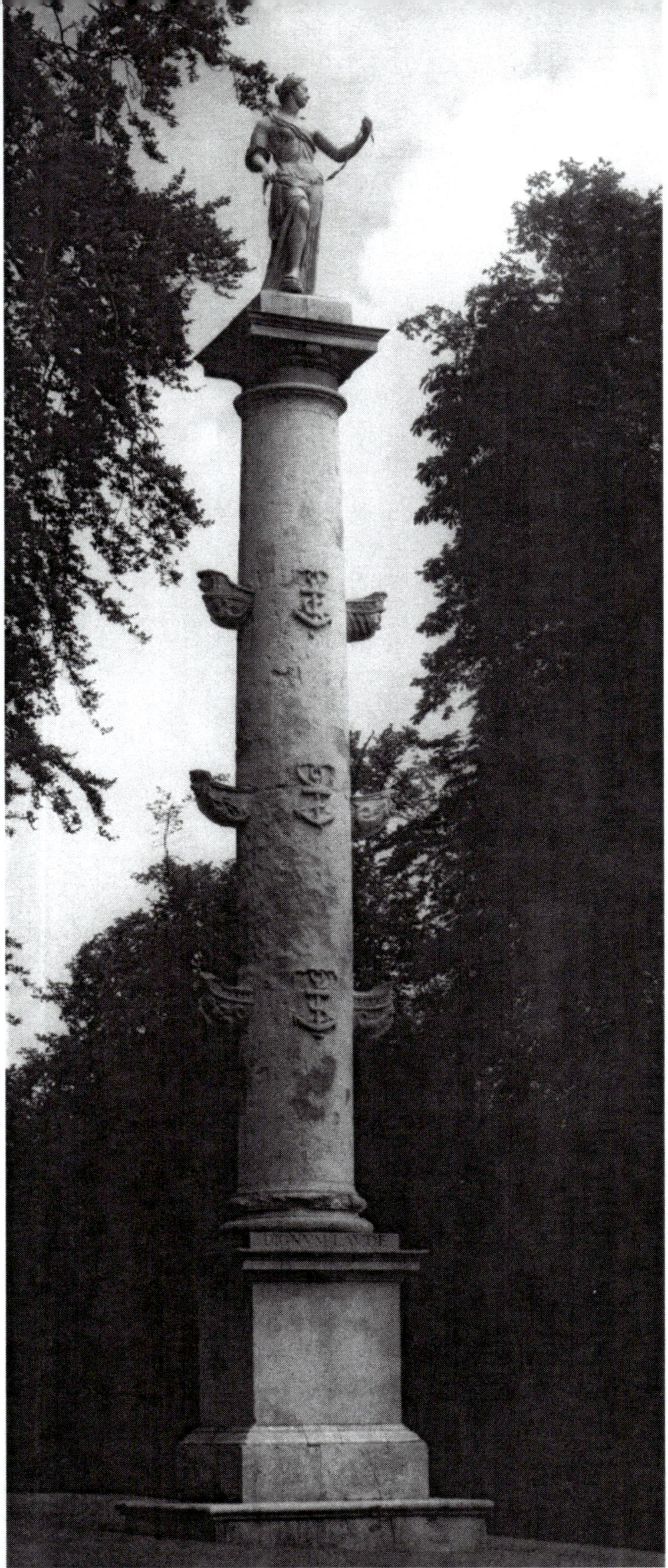

[16]
Grenville Monument, Stowe.
Designer unknown.

[17]
Temple of Concord and Victory, Stowe. Richard Grenville (with William Kent and G. B. Borra).

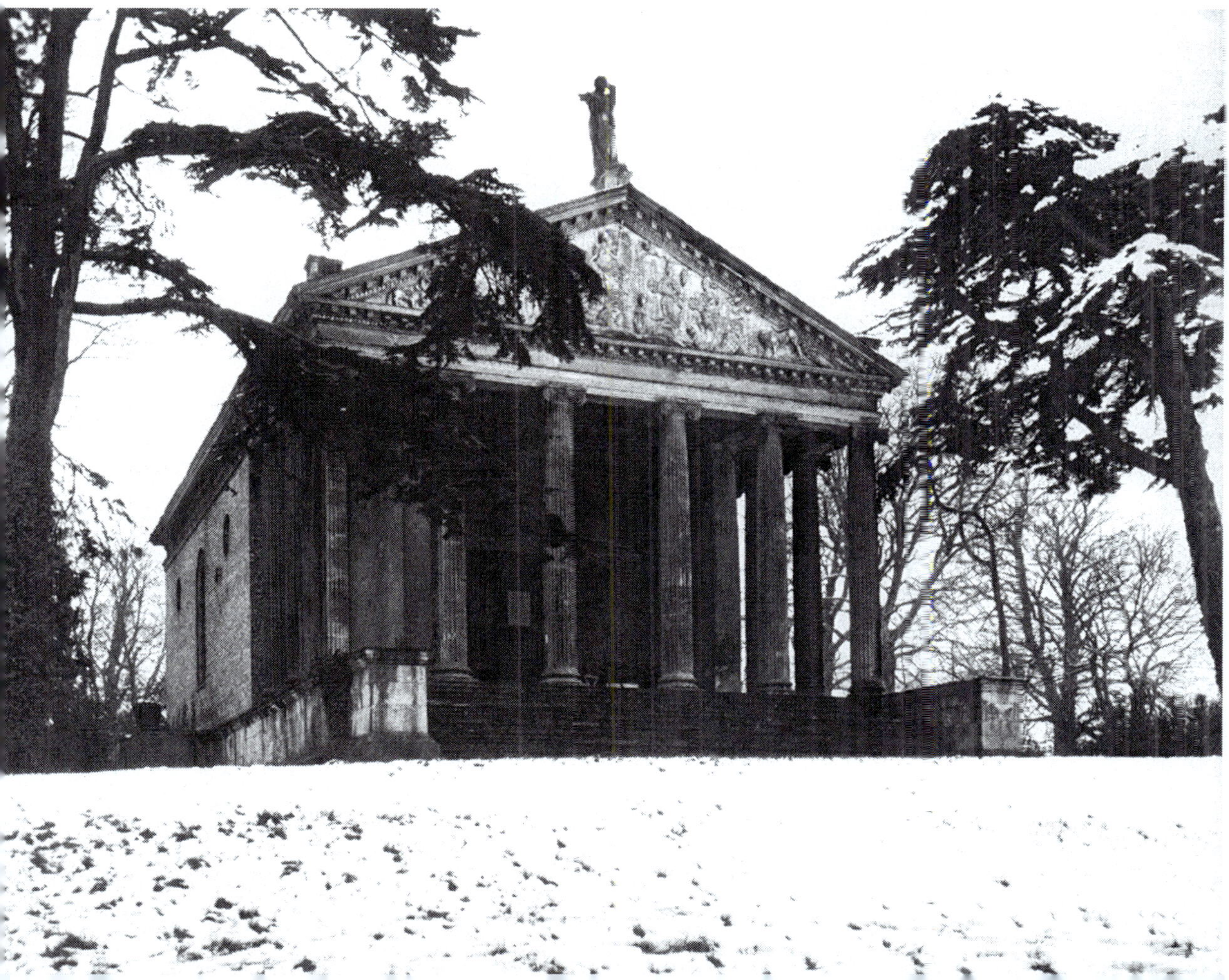

[18]
Temple of Liberty, Woburn
Abbey. Henry Holland.

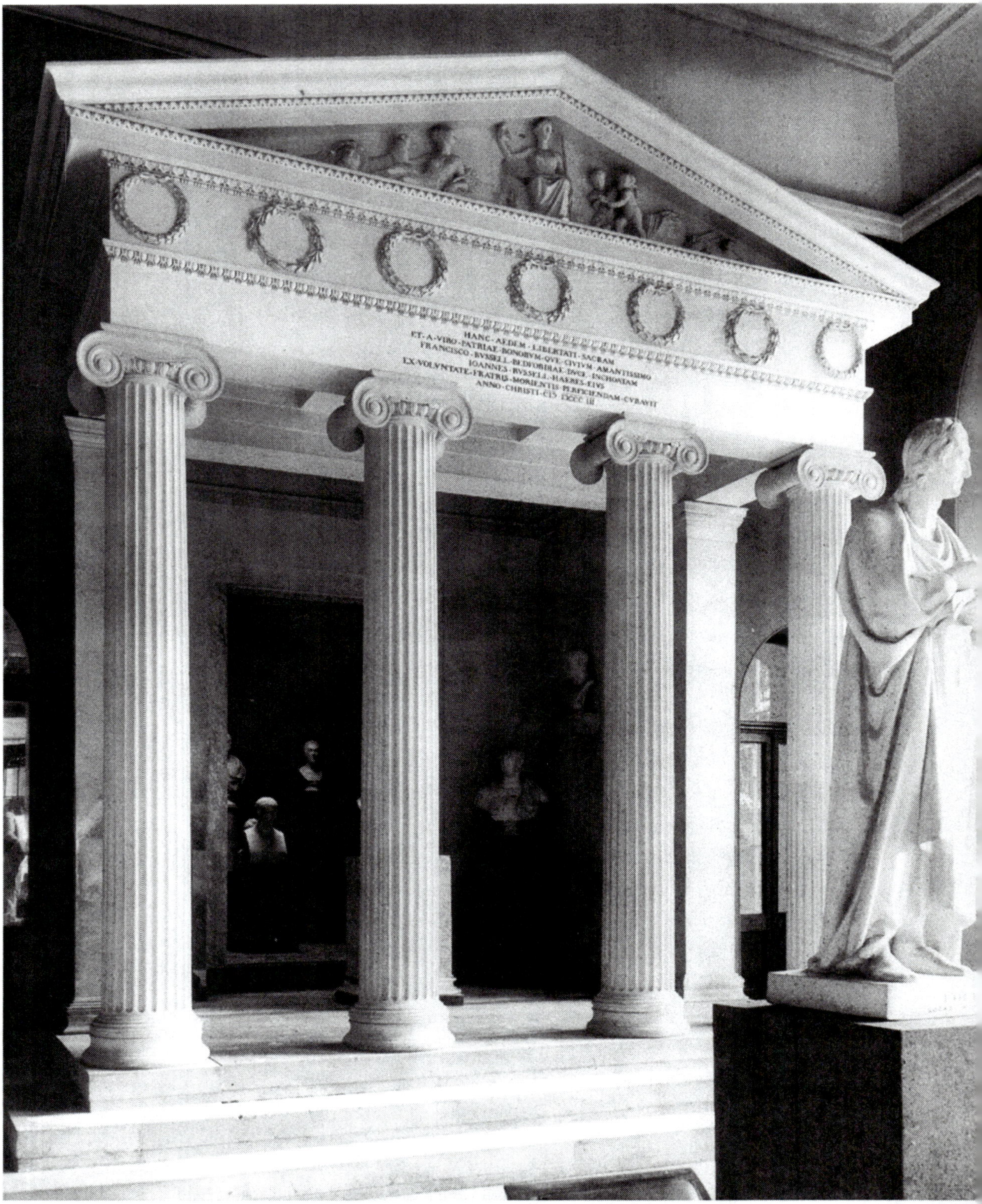

periods underlines the fact that the best values of the past are alive in the present, which may be like, but can never be, the past.

A similar effect is created in Joseph Wilton's monument to Rear-Admiral Charles Holmes (*c.* 1761) in Westminster Abbey (plate 6). Holmes, in Roman armour, rests his right hand on a very up-to-date cannon with a coil of equally up-to-date rope beneath it.[90] As Rear-Admiral of the Blue, he played an important role in the capture of Quebec and the destruction of French shipping in the Caribbean. The deliberate anachronisms in Wilton's monument are more flattering to Britain than to Rome, making the point that Rome's naval prowess, so significant in the establishment of her *imperium* around the Mediterranean, has been reborn far more potently in the navy of Britannia as she establishes her empire, at French expense, in America and the Caribbean. The same point is made by the monument to Lt. Col. Roger Townshend by Benjamin and Thomas Carter and John Eckstein, also in the Abbey (plate 7). Two American Indians support a sarcophagus topped by an arrangement of classical armour, weapons and *fasces*. Lt. Col. Townshend died in July 1759 'As he was reconnoitring the French lines at Ticonderagoe' (Fort Ticonderoga, New York), 'Enrolling Him with the Names of Those Immortal Statesmen and Commanders, Whose Wisdom and Intrepidity, In the course of this comprehensive and Successful War, Have extended the Commerce, Enlarged the Dominion, And upheld the Majesty of these Kingdoms, Beyond the Idea of any former Age'. A more purely Roman effect of a naval kind is produced by Francis Bird's rostral monument to John Baker, Vice-Admiral of the White, 'a true Lover of his Country. Manet post Funera Virtus.' It too is in the Abbey. Significantly, this monument, which is content to reflect, rather than to diminish, Rome, is earlier – *c.* 1717 (plate 8).

In many instances the style of the portrait is an authentic expression of the interests and aesthetic inclinations of the sitter, as in the case of Thomas Ady's bust of John Fane, 7th Earl of Westmorland (1742) in the Victoria and Albert Museum (plate 9). The work was sculpted in the year Westmorland was made major-general and lieutenant-general and he had himself depicted as a Roman general, but an English Roman, for on the breast his uniform bears the figure of Britannia. Westmorland commissioned Colen Campbell to design Mereworth Castle for him, the first and most faithful translation of Palladio's Villa Rotunda to English soil (*c.* 1722–5) and a landmark in the development of a purer classicism in domestic architecture. He had also been an MP and was a member of the 'Patriot' circle centred on Viscount Cobham, whose Temple of Friendship at Stowe once housed this bust.[91] Westmorland had earned the right to image himself as an English Roman.[92] The same is true of Cobham himself, and his bust (plate 10), by Scheemakers, like the others that were once in the Temple of Friendship, is naturally in the Roman style.[93] The eyes are incised (cut to represent the pupils), as they never were in Rome until after the republican period, but otherwise the work is severely classical.[94] Scheemakers was still working in the same style at the age of seventy-three when he completed the marble statue of the 1st Baron Clive as a Roman general in 1764 (plate 11).

The popularity of this style is owing above all to the influence of Michael Rysbrack, the most classical of the sculptors working in England and indeed anywhere from the 1720s to the 1760s.[95] He was clearly regarded by Horace Walpole as the most important sculptor at work in England. In the *Anecdotes of Painting* Walpole devotes three times as much space to Rysbrack as to Roubiliac, dismisses Guelfi and Delvaux with a paragraph each, and totally neglects Scheemakers.[96] That this estimate is not idiosyncratic is shown by the fact that in the *Gentleman's Magazine* through the 1730s and 1740s there are many references to Rysbrack but hardly any to other sculptors.[97] Although he had never been to Italy, Rysbrack had been trained in the classical tradition in Antwerp by Michael Van der Voort (or Vervoort), whose classicism was in the line of Fiammingo and the Quellins, though influenced too by Le Brun and the classical period of sculpture at Versailles in the 1660s and 1670s before it succumbed to baroque influences.[98] After arriving in London in 1720, Rysbrack's first important contacts were with the Marlborough circle, but he must also have met Burlington at an early stage, perhaps gaining access to the court through him. Burlington had recently returned from his second Italian tour, which was devoted to studying the work of Andrea Palladio in and around Vicenza. Palladio already had an English propagandist in Colen Campbell, the first volume of whose *Vitruvius britanni-*

cus had appeared in 1715, but Campbell's work was not sufficient to cause a thoroughgoing revolution in taste. By 1720 it is likely that Burlington saw himself as providing that leadership for the project of a purer classicism in England which Shaftesbury had defined as reserved for those who had the fortune, influence and public spirit to carry it through. Rysbrack was exactly the kind of sculptor Burlington was looking for, and Rysbrack soon won his favour to the cost of the formerly patronised Guelfi, a sculptor whom the Earl had brought to England and lodged (with Kent) at Burlington House.[99]

Commissions quickly came Rysbrack's way. One of the earliest, in 1722, was from Daniel Finch, 2nd Earl of Nottingham (plate 2). Margaret Whinney, while detecting certain baroque elements in this bust, has described it as

> a landmark in English sculpture (and indeed probably unique in the Europe of its day) . . . There can be no doubt that it is a novel and deliberate attempt at portraiture in the Roman manner . . . The noble but individual features, the close-cropped hair arranged in small waves which do not break the outline of the skull, the loose undergarment, and the cloak broached on the right shoulder are all derived from Roman models. The head, which is almost frontal and in which the eyes are not incised, must be inspired by a Late Republican bust (possibly a Julius Caesar), while the general pattern of the drapery is closer to that more normally used in Late Imperial busts.[100]

It should be noted that Nottingham was a Tory. As we have seen in the previous chapter, the cult of civic virtue and the fondness for Roman-republican models were not peculiar to the Whigs. Rysbrack avoided identifying himself with a political party and his work was in demand from both sides. In the same year he completed the Nottingham he also sculpted the Whig Charles Spencer, 3rd Earl of Sunderland, wigless and in Roman drapery. Important commissions like these so quickly established his reputation that he soon found himself working at court. The *Roman Marriage*, a large and important marble bas-relief in the cupola room at Kensington Palace, was completed in 1723. It was based on an antique original in the Palazzo Sacchetti in Rome, which Rysbrack copied from Pietro Santi Bartoli's engraving of it in Bellori's *Admiranda romanorum antiquitatum* (1693), and it established his reputation in this form also.

It was soon being copied for country houses throughout England. Rysbrack evidently had a profound insight into the ethos of the oligarchy among whom he moved for he perfectly represented their view of themselves as inheritors of classical standards of civic virtue and political liberty. He more than anyone set off the vogue for the classicising bust, depicting the English ruling class as they now saw themselves – spiritual Romans of the republican period. The new style in monuments achieves the same effect.[101] Roman dress was also appropriate for the poets who had established in English literature those standards they so admired in Roman Augustan poetry. It was fitting that Rysbrack should choose to present Edmund Waller as a Roman crowned with bay leaves and suitably garbed,[102] since following the Restoration Waller had pioneered a highly polished style, much admired by Pope, in rhyming iambic pentameters. Pope noted that through Waller and the French influence behind his writings and translations (he helped turn Corneille's *Pompey* into English), 'Wit grew polite, and Numbers learn'd to flow.'[103] Rysbrack's bust of Pope is not in the classical mode,[104] but Roubiliac's busts of him are.[105]

Rysbrack's commissions in the Roman style included a statue of George I in armour, at Cambridge, and a George II at Greenwich, both as Roman emperors, the second celebrating its subject as (among other distinctions set out around the pedestal) 'Princeps' and 'Pater [Patriae]'. However, the most politically important of his patrons was Sir Robert Walpole. Rysbrack's marble bust of the Prime Minister (1738) sits over the fireplace in the Stone Hall at Walpole's Houghton in Norfolk. The work is less severely classical than the Nottingham, less so too than his very Roman bust of the Tory Bolingbroke,[106] though clearly from the same hand and in the same tradition. The Prime Minister is a very English Roman, wearing the Star of the Garter on his cloak, and his eyes are incised. As if to confirm the pretended fears of his opponents, in the Stone Hall Walpole presides over a company of Roman emperors in the form of portrait busts on pedestals, none as highly placed as himself. Bas-reliefs by Rysbrack decorate the room with Roman images – a *Sacrifice of a Bull* (taken from Montfauçon's *L'Antiquité Expliquée* (1719), an important source for Rysbrack's classicism), a *Sacrifice to Diana* (being performed immediately behind the Prime Minister, in whose interests it was that the goddess of agriculture be propitiated at Houghton), and others. A bas-relief outside the room shows Neptune locking admiringly towards Britannia, ruler of the oceans. These bas-reliefs were heavily influential and copied across the country.[107] With Britannia Romana a living reality in the Stone Hall at Houghton, the Prime Ministerial residence itself reflecting the influence of Colen Campbell and Burlington as well as advertising William Kent's handiwork, the Shaftesbury–Campbell–Burlington project for a revival of classical artistic values in England could be seen to have triumphed at the apex of power and influence within three decades of its conception. Not that the Prime Minister's influence was all-powerful, even within his own family. It was his son Horace, after all, who re-introduced the Gothic at Strawberry Hill, and while Horace was particularly proud of his Roman eagle (discovered in the area of the Baths of Caracalla and prominent, as an emblem of connoisseurship, in the Reynolds portrait of 1755–6), his attitude to the Romans was just as ambivalent as his feelings for Houghton.[108]

Rysbrack's evocation of the ancient Roman world could be subtle and learnedly allusive, as in the Reade monument at Hatfield in Hertfordshire, a late work (1760) commemorating three members of the family (plate 12). On either side of a funerary urn are placed the classicised busts of two of the dead, and it has been pointed out that the design intentionally recalls the Roman custom of carrying the busts of one's patrician ancestors to the funeral. Behind and above them, towards the apex of the pyramid, in a rococo cartouche, is a portrait medallion of Susan Reade, the most recently deceased. Rysbrack organised these and other elements of the design to create a work both rich and simple, subtle and noble in its Roman allusiveness.[109]

Roubiliac, far more baroque than Rysbrack, frequently found himself working in a severely classical mode not out of momentary inclination but because particular sitters were obviously insistent on the matter. Sir Andrew Fountaine is a good example. This important collector and connoisseur of classical antiquities had had himself imaged in Roman style several times before commissioning Roubiliac, for instance in a portrait medal (copy in the British Museum) done in 1715 by Antonio

Selvi during Fountaine's stay in Florence, the reverse showing Pallas amidst classical ruins and works of art. This was the world with which Fountaine identified, and Roubiliac's 1747 bust (plate 13), at Wilton House in Wiltshire, makes the connection again. There is an uncompromising austerity to it, with no concessions whatsoever to vanity. The same sculptor's bust of the 9th Earl of Pembroke, owner of the largest collection of classical and pseudo-classical sculpture in England, is more dynamic and probably inspired by the Caracalla in Pembroke's possession, but like the Fountaine is far more Roman than the sculptor's usual style.[110]

Joseph Wilton was in some ways even more classical than Rysbrack. His bust of Chesterfield (plate 1), in the British Museum, is particularly austere, not simply by virtue of being undraped. There is no questioning the world with which the sitter desires to associate himself. Spiritually he belongs to antiquity, and to that uncompromising Roman-republican ethos epitomised by the elder Cato. The French side of Chesterfield, so evident in his letters, is totally absent here.

After Wilton, Joseph Nollekens carried the fashion for the classicising bust well into the nineteenth century, though in his late work the new fashion of side-whiskers severely undercuts the effect.[111] Nollekens had a vast amount of work, and his most famous busts were reproduced in great numbers for a market eager to decorate their fireplaces patriotically with copies of his 1791 or 1801 versions of Charles James Fox (1801, plate 14, at Woburn Abbey), or the William Pitt of 1807 (Windsor Castle).[112] John Kenworthy-Browne has described the 1801 Fox as having 'the dignity of a Roman republican'[113] (a remarkable achievement given the very un-Roman demeanour and habits of the sitter). In this, appropriately, it is exactly like all the other busts in the Temple of Liberty at Woburn Abbey, examined below. Like Sir Robert Walpole two generations earlier, Fox and Pitt, political enemies, each believed that in his work for the nation he was acting according to classical political and civic codes whose validity had been established for all time.

Not only the politicians of Georgian England but its most significant military officers, its connoisseurs and many of its literary figures chose to be depicted as belonging spiritually to an ethos that was both 1800 years in the past and eternally valid. By placing themselves within it they claimed a more than transitory recognition.

POLITICAL GARDENS AND TEMPLES

The idea of the part-cultivated, part-natural *jardin anglais* as developed by William Kent, Charles Bridgeman and their contemporaries involves abolition of geometric pruning and the garden wall in favour of unbounded prospects, and a degree of irregularity and wildness even in the more artfully cultivated surrounds of the house. As Martin Battestin has stressed, however, 'the aesthetics of regularity were not discarded at a stroke', and indeed the new movement reflects and confirms the idea of a divinely ordered natural world.[114] Its inspiration comes from Shaftesbury, Addison and Pope. Less immediate but equally important influences include the Italian landcape and its idealised depiction in the paintings of Poussin and Claude, Pliny's accounts of the gardens and lansdcapes of his own country seats, and other classical sources.[115] The subject has been thoroughly chronicled.[116] It constitutes an important movement in the history of English taste and was in important ways bound up with the political consciousness of the English oligarchy, though it distorts a more complex reality to identify the *jardin anglais* with Whig politics.[117] The connection of the English landscape garden with ideals of political liberty and civic virtue, and the political and cultural significances of the architecture constructed to decorate the new gardens and give them contemporary meaning, have been demonstrated by others with reference to particular gardens.[118] I shall examine here two striking examples of how the Whig oligarchy employed garden architecture and garden sculpture to reinforce its self-image as the guarantor of the nation's newly won liberties, giving greater attention than has previously been paid to the Roman elements.

As a Whig poet interested in the development of the arts of Hanoverian England, James Thomson believed that the landscape garden, like good art generally, could flourish only under liberty, defined for his times by the political party to which he gave his allegiance. The foundation of much eighteenth-century gardening theory and practice was Pliny's detailed description of his own gardens, which were tentatively 'reconstructed' in Robert Castell's *Villas of the Ancients* (1728). Pliny's gardens had been developed well within the period of the emperors, an unhappy historical fact which Thomson simply ignores, though he might have circumvented it to some extent by pointing out that Trajan, Pliny's friend and correspondent, was a good emperor who restored a measure of liberty and civic pride to his country. For Thomson, Liberty is not merely the *sine qua non* of the flourishing arts but their begetter:

> BEHOLD! all *thine again* the SISTER-ARTS . . .
> SEE! SYLVAN SCENES, where *Art*, alone, pretends
> To dress her *Mistress*, and disclose her Charms:
> Such as a POPE in Miniature[119] has shown;
> A BATHURST o'er the widening Forest spreads;
> And such as form a RICHMOND, CHISWICK, STOWE.[120]

The gardens at Richmond Lodge, Chiswick and Stowe were commissioned by Whigs. Pope and Bathurst, on the other hand, were Tories, but Thomson is not so partisan as to exclude them on that account from the blessings of Liberty, who smiles on all of England, not just a faction. Tories, however, were less inclined to claim credit for the benefits of English liberty, and it is to the Whig landscape gardens and their carefully developed classical and political associations that one goes to find the iconography of self-congratulation.

Stowe epitomises it. In its gardens everything is made to point a simple message: the best moral and political values of classical antiquity, together with the native Anglo-Saxon 'Gothic' heritage of mixed government and liberty, are being kept alive by a group of patriotic Whigs led by Stowe's owner, Richard Temple, Lord Viscount Cobham. These men have opposed themselves to the Caesarian encroachments of the Whig Prime Minister, Robert Walpole, and Stowe is their base and spiritual home. That, at least, was the message constructed there through the 1730s. By the 1750s it had been supplemented by an imperial theme.[121]

In the words of Pope, a regular visitor, Stowe was 'a Work to wonder at'[122] and he addressed the first Epistle of his *Moral Essays* (1734) to Cobham, whose ruling passion Pope identified as patriotism.[123] Cobham employed Sir John Vanbrugh, William Kent, Charles Bridgeman, James Gibbs and others on the house and gardens, and Capability Brown's career began as head gardener there. The Stowe circle commemorated itself in the Temple of Friendship, which housed busts of Frederick, Prince of Wales (patron of the 'Patriot' Opposition), the Earls of Westmorland, Chesterfield and Marchmont, Lords Cobham, Gower and Bathurst, Richard Grenville, William Pitt and George Lyttelton. Like any political grouping, this one was not particularly stable across the years, a point Horace Walpole made with telling effect,[124] but its collective impact on the country was considerable and reached beyond its own time. William Pitt the Younger, for example, whose father, the 1st Earl of Chatham, was Cobham's brother-in-law and stayed for extended periods at Stowe, received his earliest political lessons under its influence.

Before mid-century Stowe had become the best-known of all English gardens, and its thousands of visitors were well supplied with detailed guide books. Two of these, William Gilpin's *A Dialogue upon the Gardens of the Right Honourable the Lord Viscount Cobham at Stow in Buckinghamshire* (1748), which Gilpin compiled following his visit of 1747, and George Bickham's illustrated and more detailed *The Beauties of Stow* (1750), provide lively contemporary views and interpretations of what they survey, Gilpin's in the form of a dialogue between a couple of visitors, Polypthon and Callophilus. Gilpin is particularly sensitive to the philosophy behind the gardening programme at Stowe and had obviously read Shaftesbury with care: 'there appears a very visible Connection between an *improved* Taste for Pleasure, and a Taste for Virtue . . . I cannot help imagining a Taste for these exalted Pleasures contributes towards making me a better Man',[125] he observes, echoing Shaftesbury's conflation of virtue and virtuosity. Shaftesbury would have appreciated being quoted here in the context of Stowe and its radical Whig agenda. One can follow Bickham around the gardens as they were in 1750. The focus in the following paragraphs will be on the Romanness of the iconography and inscriptions, which has not previously been analysed in any detail.[126]

Not every structure at Stowe taught a moral or political lesson. Some objects were there for amusement, others merely to provide a sense of association with the ancient world.[127] An example of a more serious message was provided at Vanbrugh's Nelson's Seat (now demolished), where an illustrated Latin inscription taken from the Arch of Constantine proclaimed Rome's wide dominion, inviting contemplation of the even more widely flung empire Britain already ruled.[128] An equestrian statue of George I, by the house, made a more direct equation:

IN MEDIO MIHI CAESAR ERIT –
ET VIRIDI IN CAMPO SIGNVM DE MARMORE PONAM
PROPTER AQVAM. COBHAM.

Bickham's translation is elegant: 'Imperial *Caesar* shall the Centre grace; / A Marble Statue to my Prince I'll place, / Near the clear Water, on the verdant Grass'.[129] More wittily, the Latin inscription on Rysbrack's statue of Queen Caroline, a patron of the arts, not only Romanised her but, going the whole Roman way, deified her into the bargain: 'HONORI, LAVDI, VIRTVTI DIVAE CAROLINAE' (to the honour, praise and virtue of the divine Caroline).[130] Her deep interest in ecclesiastical patronage and theological matters adds to the wit and appropriateness, and the incongruously pagan impact, of the inscription, disarmingly daring in its flattery: why should not the divinely human, in the eighteenth century, become a goddess?

Bickham comes closer to the heart of Cobham's scheme when he approaches Kent's Temple of Ancient Virtue (plate 15), modelled on the Temple of Vesta at Tivoli,[131] with a reference also to the Roman Temple of the Sibyl, as Ronald Paulson emphasises.[132] The Temple of Ancient Virtue housed statues of Lycurgus, Socrates, Homer and Epaminondas, chosen because in Bickham's words they first sought respectively 'To establish a well-regulated Constitution, to dictate the soundest Morality, to place Virtue in the most amiable Light, and bravely to defend a People's Liberty'[133] – the concerns closest to the heart of the Cobham circle. Over the two doors Latin inscriptions pointed the Stowe ideals: to deserve the love rather than the detestation of the state (a tendentious glance in Walpole's direction); and to cultivate the social affections in such a way that they embraced all citizens. The steps were narrow, suggesting the difficulty of practising ancient virtue. Nearby, a despicable pile of ruins called the Temple of Modern Virtue, with a headless statue alongside meant to be Walpole, showed how insubstantial and decrepit modern virtue was compared with the eternally valid ancient variety.

Appropriately looking up towards the Temple of Ancient Virtue were (and still are) the busts of the British Worthies in their open 'Temple', a semi-circular affair by Kent, perhaps modelled on a grouping of Roman emperors at the Villa Brenzone.[134] In a central niche sat Mercury, the god who conducts the souls of the blessed to Elysium. The British Worthies, at least eight of them and perhaps all sixteen by Rysbrack,[135] were housed eight on either side of Mercury, each in his/her own niche and all except one with an inscription indicating the reason for inclusion.[136]

The Temple of Liberty[137] was a Gothic structure dedicated 'LIBERTATI MAIORVM' (to the liberty of our ancestors). It contained Saxon deities, and over its door was the inscription, taken from Corneille, 'Je rends graces aux Dieux de nestre pas Romain' (I thank the gods I'm not a Roman). This inscription, together with the pride in the Anglo-Saxon past manifested here and in the Temple of British Worthies, and the strong tributes to Greece already noticed, serve as important checks on the Romanising aspects of Stowe. Cobham's programme for England involved reanimating the best in all these worlds.

Where it glances at Britain's military power and imperial destiny, however, Stowe's iconography is generally Roman in tone and spirit, imperial as well as republican, as in the Imperial Closet housing Titus, Trajan and Aurelius, the 'good emperors'. The Grenville Monument (plate 16) is a rostral column crowned first by a statue of Hercules, later by one of Heroic Poetry, who held out a scroll to the British Worthies.[138] With its projecting beaks of captured enemy ships it is thoroughly Roman. Erected by Cobham in 1749, it commemorates his nephew, Capt. Thomas Grenville, who as captain of a ship in the Royal Navy when it was commanded by George Anson was mortally wounded 'DVM CONTRA GALLOS FORTISSIME PVGNARET' (while fighting most valiantly against the Gauls) and who declared in his dying moments that it was far better to die than to be judged a coward. In Gilpin's guidebook Callophilus tells Polypthon that the monument 'joins with the Nation in applauding a Man, who pushed forwards by Honour, and a Love for his Country, met

Danger and Death with the Spirit of a *Roman*'.[139] Roman too are Scheemakers's alto-relievos, initially on the Palladian Bridge, later removed to the Temple of Concord and Victory, showing the four quarters of the world bringing their various produce to Britannia.

The Temple of Concord and Victory (plate 17) is always said to have been modelled on the Maison Carrée at Nîmes,[140] but another debt, to which its name gives the clue, is never noticed. Particularly in its Ionic capitals, and the proportion of its width to its height, it is in fact much closer to the Temple of Concord in Rome as reconstructed by Palladio in the fourth of his four books of architecture.[141] It was completed around 1764 and commemorated on its medallions the triumphs of Britain and her allies in the Seven Years' War, which added Canada and much of India to the First British Empire. The Peace which ended this war is classicised and personified as a 'CONCORDIA CIVIVM ET FOEDERATORVM', as if England were Rome and her allies the Italian states aligned with Rome. Concordia, to whom many ancient temples were raised, was the Roman goddess of harmony and peace. Now, with the defeat of the Gauls, against whom Capt. Grenville had bravely fought, she had become the Concordia of England too.

Stowe's temples were used as well as admired. Cobham and his friends regularly met in the Temple of Friendship, for example.[142] Horace Walpole told a correspondent in 1770 that during his recent stay at Stowe, 'Twice a day we made a pilgrimage to almost every heathen temple in that province that they call a garden . . . We supped in a grotto in the Elysian fields [laid out by Kent], and were refreshed with rivers of dew and gentle showers that dripped from all the trees.'[143] The whole point of the gardens and temples at Stowe was that one should entertain one's political friends in them, for their chief value lay in the political and classical associations they evoked.

No other gardens rivalled Stowe's in political importance, though a number no doubt reflected their owners' Whig politics in more subtle ways. The Earl of Carlisle's development of the landscape at Castle Howard was an attempt to create a classical Elysium and its associations are literary and mythological,[144] but in its scale and uncircumscribed vistas it could also be said to express the Whig aesthetic of freedom that

Carlisle's friend Addison had applied to the laying out of gardens when he extended the meaning of the word to embrace entire estates.[145]

We should be wary, however, of identifying the landscape movement too exclusively with Whig politics. As noted already, Pope, a Tory, was one of its earliest articulators and propagandists. At Stourhead, as James Turner has shown, Henry Hoare developed a landscape through the late 1750s and 1760s which, by way of its classical allusions (particularly to the first book of the *Aeneid*) and its idealisation of Alfred the Great, reflected his Tory fears for the state and belief 'in a world order based on peace, patriotism, virtue, social hierarchy, naval supremacy, and a powerful monarch'.[146] The Tory agrarian ideal is an important influence on the English landscape garden,[147] while Pliny, the chief classical authority, was a friend of Trajan's and no republican. An analogous movement was afoot in Bourbon France. The Earl of Oxford, a Tory, employed the landscapist Charles Bridgeman, who also worked at Stowe. In regard to Oxford's patronage of Bridgeman it has been claimed that the latter's work was somehow 'baroque' (and thus presumably fancied by an anti-Palladian Tory like Oxford),[148] but then why should a 'baroque' landscapist also be employed at Whig Stowe? The landscape garden was in fashion, and fashion is a far more potent stimulator than politics.

Through the mid-century, as the Hanoverians succeeded one another with dull predictability, as the last Jacobite rebellion was routed in a manner sufficiently thorough to show that the Stuart cause was finished, and as the Revolution settlement matured into unchallengeable history, liberty lost its novelty and, no longer so obviously endangered, ceased to be celebrated by self-proclaimed, self-congratulating defenders. The message of Stowe was only marginally relevant even in the 1730s, when its political enemies spoke the identical language of liberty, if less stridently; it was a joke in the 1760s and 1770s, as Horace Walpole's reflections on his visits there make clear. In retrospect we can see that Stowe's political message was relatively unimportant historically. The number of recently published books and articles on the liberty-loving opposition to Sir Robert Walpole is sustained largely by the fact that its propagandists included Pope and Swift.[149] The message of Stowe is only important because it epitomises the tendency, so strong from 1689 to Walpole's demise in the early 1740s, of the triumphant Whig oligarchy to blazon themselves in the symbols and paraphernalia of the classical world at its liberty-loving best. For almost half a century no cause was sufficient to inspire a similar iconographical extravagance.

Only in 1789 did such a cause arise in the form of the French Revolution, and when that quickly turned radical and then imperial, the only political group who were at once daring enough to espouse its principles openly and wealthy enough to indulge in Stowe's kind of self-congratulatory self-imaging were the minority Foxite Whigs. In what amounted to a combination of the purposes of Stowe's Temple of Friendship and (Gothic) Temple of Liberty, these men were celebrated by one of their number, the 5th Duke of Bedford, in the Temple of Liberty at Woburn Abbey. This is an expression of the classical frame of mind in its most radical English form, when its ideals included a widening of the franchise, the abolition of slavery and Catholic emancipation.[150] The Woburn Temple (plate 18 shows the front) may also have been inspired by the construction in revolutionary France of Temples of Liberty like that dedicated at Nantes in 1790. Built inside the new Conservatory and scaled down from its Greek Ionic original as illustrated in Stuart and Revett's *Antiquities of Athens* (1762), its purity and plainness are part of its political message,[151] which is confirmed by busts of the Elder and Younger Brutus: the Foxites who in their stony conclave celebrate Liberty here are, like the virtuous Marcus Junius Brutus, selfless and natural heirs of their forefathers who first securely established it. The Elder Brutus, as already noted, was an important figure in revolutionary France, where his bust presided over the deliberations of the National Convention, and where the man who would later turn that Republic into an Empire was declared 'first consul' in 1799. The Woburn Temple housed Romanised busts of all the leading Foxites, without wigs and with their hair in the 'radical' short fashion of the late Roman republic (though with the very English side-whiskers then in vogue).[152] The inscription on Fox's bust proclaims his 'virtue', 'patriot zeal', 'uncorrupted mind' and boldness in asserting 'the freedom of mankind'. Centrally featured in the Temple's pediment is of course the figure of Liberty herself. She wears the Roman *pileus* or cap of liberty so popular in revolutionary France. On her right reclines the figure of Peace bearing an olive branch in one arm, the other resting on a lamb. A lion reposes at the feet of Peace, its docility and proximity to the lamb signs that the classical golden age has been restored. To Liberty's left sits a cat, suggesting love of freedom. Two genii, representing Agriculture and Commerce, empty a horn of plenty at Liberty's feet. Behind are symbols of agricultural and industrial activity – plough, rabbit, sheaf of corn, textiles. The whole is a compressed allegory of what Britain is missing for want of entrusting herself to a Foxite programme: liberty for all, not just Protestants; peace in place of the long war with revolutionary France; abundance and prosperity instead of the war economy.

Woburn's Temple of Liberty is an important reminder that in the early nineteenth century, despite things Grecian being strongly in fashion, the icons of liberty and civic virtue – or imperial authority as in Napoleonic France – were still Roman. The imagery of ancient Rome was above fashion and ready to hand wherever anyone in authority or seeking it desired to evoke associations with the longest-lasting and most powerful of ancient free republics or its imperial successor. From the prominently displayed *fasces* in the United States House of Representatives to the eagles and wreaths on the legionary standards of the National Socialists in Germany to the glorification of 'tribune' power in the old Marxist republics of eastern Europe, this association has been insistently proclaimed by dictators, patricians and plebeians alike. It is a game almost anyone can play. The oligarchy of Georgian England, however, understood what they were appropriating. Struck by the affinities with their senatorial counterparts in antiquity, they were bearers of civic and spiritual values learned out of Cicero, Sallust and Tacitus, and their sensibilities reflected what they admired.

3

Britannia Romana

ROMANO-BRITISH ARCHAEOLOGY: PIONEERS

It is hardly surprising that Romano-British archaeology enjoyed a golden age during the late seventeenth and early eighteenth centuries.[1] At the same time that classical civic ideals were being adapted to current political purposes, the classical temperament was naturalised in a still profounder dimension by an intense focussing on Britain's own Roman past.

This activity might at first sight seem to represent a reflection of the 'ancient' disposition as it defined itself in the contemporary 'battle of the books' over the respective virtues of ancient and modern learning. Paradoxically, however, the archaeologists to be considered here were engaged in a profoundly 'modern' endeavour, using the latest philological and scientific techniques to uncover and 'read' their country's ancient history. Like other admirers of classical values and virtues considered in the preceding chapters, they were 'ancients' in their cultural sympathies and affinities. In the important matter of their procedures, however, they were decidedly progressive and wholly on the side of 'modern' learning.[2] Dr Richard Bentley's career reflects the identical paradox. He was the greatest classical scholar and teacher of the period precisely because his techniques were so analytical, exacting and 'scientific', in other words modern.[3] Significantly, in his Boyle Lectures[4] he invoked the Newtonian system against atheism, thus locating himself at the cutting edge of modern science. It was because of his advanced methodology that Bentley was cast in the role of a leader of the 'moderns' by Swift in *The Battle of the Books* (1704). Bentley no doubt wore the label with pride.

The Roman influence in Britain could be represented as having stretched over the best part of five centuries.[5] Following Caesar's landings of 55 and 54 BC, however, there had been a century-long hiatus, though there may have been small colonies of Roman traders resident in Britain during this period. The Roman colonisation of Britain effectively commenced in AD 43 under Claudius and ended with the departure of the last legionaries in 410 when Honorius told the British that from now on they would have to govern themselves and defend the Saxon Shore, and the north, alone. There may have been some form of military reoccupation or support subsequently, but if so it lasted only a few years.[6] The final British appeal for Roman military assistance was made to the consul Aetius in 446 and turned down.[7] There were thus at least 367 years and perhaps a few more of Roman Britannia, an extensive period replete with impressive traces through which diligent antiquaries and nostalgic romantics might wander, recording and annotating the objects and inscriptions they came across, building their collections, publishing their findings and theories, contemplating the classical civilisation Britain had enjoyed and lost, and the chances of its restoration in a neo-classical present.

The first general survey of the subject, the field's *magnum opus* until John Horsley's *Britannia romana* came out in 1732, and the foundation on which all subsequent Romano-British archaeology is built, was William Camden's *Britannia*, which first appeared, in Latin, in 1586.[8] Before Camden, only John Leland in his *Itineraries* – the records of his journeys through England during the 1530s and 1540s – had transcribed Roman inscriptions and described remains with anything approaching a system.[9] Camden's work, which like Leland's covered medieval as well as Roman antiquities, was more systematic. It was continually corrected and updated in the light of the author's latest researches, and several Latin editions had already appeared by the time Philemon Holland published his English translation of it in 1610. Camden felt obliged to defend antiquarianism against the sceptical who saw it as a waste of time, but the outstanding success of his *Britannia* established at once the respectability of its field.[10]

As far as I am aware Camden was the first to contemplate the genetic and spiritual continuity of Roman and modern Britons. As we shall see, the endeavour to establish such a continuity would be a vital ingredient in early Georgian attempts to explain and 'authenticate' the Roman spirit shown by such patrons of Romano-British archaeology as the 8th Earl of Pembroke and the 3rd Earl of Burlington. These men would be represented as descendants of the British and Romano-British patriciate of ancient Britain. In his general remarks on 'The Romans in Britain' Camden makes the following important point:

> Whilst I thus treat of the Roman Empire in Britain (which lasted, as I said, about 476 years) I cannot but consider with my self, how many Colonies of Romans must be transplanted hither in so long time; how many souldiers were continually sent from Rome for Garisons; how many were dispatch'd hither, to negotiate either publick or their own private affairs, who intermarrying with the Britains, seated themselves here, and multiplied their Families. For *whatsoever* (says Seneca) *the Romans conquer'd, they inhabited.* So that I have oftentimes concluded it much more probable, that the Britains should derive themselves from the Trojans by these Romans (who doubtless descended from them) than either the *Arverni*, who *from Trojan Blood* stile themselves brethren to the Romans; or the *Mamertini*, the *Hedui*, and others, who claim kindred with the *Trojans* upon fabulous grounds. For Rome that common Mother, (as one calls her) challenges all such for her citizens,
>
> *Quos domuit, nexuque pio longinqua revinxit.*
> Whom conquer'd she in sacred bonds hath tied.
>
> And 'tis easy to believe that the Britains and Romans, by a mutual *engrafting* for so many years together, have grown up into one Nation; since the *Ubii* in Germany, twenty eight years after their Colony was planted, made this answer with respect to the Romans in it: *This is the natural country of those that were transplanted hither; as well those that have issue by us. Nor can we think you so unjust, that you would have us murder our Parents, Brethren, and Children.* If the *Ubii* and the Romans, in so short a space of time came to the natural relation of *Parents, Brethren*, and *Children*; what shall we think of the Britains, and the Romans, who were so many years associate? What likewise may we say of the Burgundians, who, from a tincture of their blood (during a short abode in the Roman Provinces) call'd themselves the offspring of the Romans? Not to repeat what I have already said, that this island was call'd *Romania*, and the *Roman Island*.[11]

In short, the British had become genetically Roman.

Perhaps because it represented such a novel activity, Camden's great work did not generate any immediate surge of archaeological publications in the Romano-British area (though the papers of Camden's Society of Antiquaries circulated widely in manuscript[12]). The next really significant event was Inigo Jones's survey of Stonehenge in 1620 at the request of James I, considered below in the discussion on Burlington. Jones's argument that Stonehenge was a Roman temple waited until 1655 for its posthumous publication – *The Most Notable Antiquity of Great Britain called Stone-Heng, Restored*, edited by Jones's disciple John Webb. Three years later came the next major contribution, William Burton's landmark work on the Antonine Itinerary, again published posthumously.[13]

The *Antonini itinerarium* is a detailed account of the principal roads and sea-roads of the Roman Empire, compiled perhaps in the early third century.[14] Every town of significance on each of the many roads throughout Roman Asia, Africa and Europe is named, along with its distance from Rome. The section of the Itinerary devoted to Britannia is the most important source for any reconstruction of its geography, which involves among other tasks identifying the hundreds of itemised Roman towns and military places with their modern equivalents and locating and digging up those which have disappeared beneath the fields. William Burton's *A Commentary on Antoninus his Itinerary* was immensely learned and went far beyond a synthesis of previous research on the subject. It represented the labour of Burton's last years, and later workers in the field acknowledge their great debt to him. Like Camden, Burton emphasises the thoroughness of Romanisation in Britain and quotes Tacitus' *Agricola*, another important source for the geography of Roman Britain, on the rapidity with which the British elite took to Roman ways: 'Moreover the Noble-mens sons he [Agricola] took and instructed in the liberall Sciences, preferring the Wits of the Britains before the Students of *Gaul*, as being now curious to attain the eloquence of the Roman Language, whereas they lately rejected the speech. After that our attire grew to be in account, and the Gown much used among them.'[15] The fact that Camden and Burton, and those who followed, go to such pains to insist on a thorough Romanisation of Britain is problematic and interesting because they obviously knew that the colony was primarily military in purpose. Most of the tangible evidence available to earlier archaeologists, until the important discoveries of considerable numbers of villas in the nineteenth century revealed the extent of this feature of Romano-British life, was related to the camp. There was certainly a vast quantity of it, but it was not such as to allow one to conclude that life for the majority of Britons had been as extensively and deeply Romanised as it had been, say, for the majority in Gallia Narbonensis.[16] Hence the tone of special pleading in Camden's observations on this subject and those of William Stukeley and others examined below. Burton cites Tacitus on the rapid Romanisation of the British elite and the reader is encouraged to imagine that the process must soon have reached down to the entire population. The certainty, backed by a wealth of evidence, of widespread intermarrying in the towns is made to justify Camden's enthusiastic but dubious vision of two peoples become one across the whole nation, rural as well as urban, through a profound and extensive 'association'. It is a nice thought because it allows modern Britons to see themselves as Romans in a very essential way, but it is based, insofar as it overstates the case, on wishful thinking.

Burton's work on the British section of the Antonine Itinerary was followed by that of Thomas Gale, Professor of Greek at Cambridge and later High Master of Paul's School and Dean of York, and his son Roger. Thomas Gale, whom David C. Douglas has described as 'in many ways almost a Renaissance figure, a successor to Isaac Casaubon and Scaliger',[17] edited and annotated the section as the *Antonini iter britanniarum*, which Roger published in 1709 with notes of his own. Another of Thomas's sons, Samuel, also devoted himself to antiquarian studies. He, Roger, and Humphrey Wanley were among the revivers of the Society of Antiquaries, which had come into a brief existence towards the end of the sixteenth century.[18] Roger Gale was the first vice-president of the revived Society, Samuel its first treasurer, elected at the beginning of 1718. William Stukeley, a disciple and close friend of Roger Gale (his brother-in-law from 1739), was the first secretary.[19] Roger Gale and William Stukeley probably did more than anyone else to put Romano-British studies under the patronage of the oligarchy and involve these people directly in field-work, not a difficult task given the number of rich English virtuosi who could be expected to show an interest in the Roman impact on Britain. Gale, a man of considerable means, Member of the Parliaments of 1705, 1707, 1708 and 1710, and a commissioner of excise from 1715 to 1735, was well placed to enlist powerful connections in the cause of archaeology, cultivating the friendship of Sir John Clerk of Penicuik, among others. Clerk's interests, aside from his first field, the law (he was Baron of the Scottish Exchequer), included music (which he had studied in Italy under Corelli), philosophy, mathematics and poetry, but his first passion was Roman antiquities. He became the patron and principal stimulator of Romano-Scottish studies and was one of Gale's most important students in the field. Stukeley, a medical man who later entered the church, became friends with the lawyer Maurice Johnson, one of the founders in 1709–10 of the Gentlemen's Society of Spalding, a group with both archaeological and literary interests which attracted such notable members as Isaac Newton, Richard Bentley, Alexander Pope, John Gay and Michael Rysbrack. Stukeley and Gale were early members, as was Sir John Clerk. For Stukeley these connections opened up others. He was soon enjoying the friendship of members of the aristocracy such as the 8th Earl of Pembroke, the 7th Earl of Hertford and the 5th Earl of Winchilsea and engaging them in his own enthusiasm for Romano-British field-work, measuring Caesar's Camp on Hounslow Heath in the company of Lords Winchilsea and Hertford on 18 April 1723, for instance.[20] He sat to Kneller for his portrait.[21] The best library in the land, that of Robert Harley, Earl of Oxford, was open to him.[22] On Christmas Eve 1725, with his best Romano-British work already behind him, he made a note to himself:

> Whilst I lived in London for 9 years together, in the flourishing time of my life, I had the greatest intimacy with Thomas Ld Pembroke, Heneage Earl of Winchelsea, Sr Isaac Newton, Dr Halley, Mead, Sr Hans Sloan, Ld Oxford, James West, John Bridges, D. of Argyle, Tom Rawlinson, Dr Friend, Dr Arbuthnot, Dr Morton, Dr Waltr. Harris, Sr Godfrey Kneller, & in short with the whole sett of learned men & vertuoso's, wh. at that time abounded, & by having recourse to their librarys I arriv'd to a considerable degree of knowledg & equal reputation.[23]

As we shall see, the enlistment of the oligarchy in the cause of Romano-British archaeology added immensely to the movement's self-confidence and prestige and should be recognised as one of the most important factors behind the field's great flowering through the 1720s and 1730s.

Meanwhile in 1695 Edmund Gibson had brought out his newly translated, corrected and considerably enlarged edition of Camden's *Britannia*.[24] This, as Stuart Piggott has pointed out, was undoubtedly a major stimulus.

> By producing this edition of Camden, so augmented as to constitute something approaching an original work, Gibson placed in the hands of the country gentry, doctors, and clergymen, a basic summary against which they could see the results of their own local inquiries in history and archaeology. An annotated copy of the 1695 or subsequent editions of Camden formed the almost inevitable nucleus around which comment and additions would grow as local investigations were carried out by these amateurs who were beginning to build up the tradition which crystallized into the great nineteenth-century county histories and the foundation of regional archaeological societies.[25]

Other significant work through the 1690s and into the early years of the new century included William Somner's *A Treatise of the Roman Ports and Forts in Kent*, published posthumously by James Brome in 1693, with notes by Edmund Gibson; Sir Robert Sibbald's pioneering *Historical Inquiries, Concerning the Roman Monuments and Antiquities in the North-Part of Britain called Scotland* (1707), covering the Roman Walls, colonies, forts, ports, temples and military ways, and including engravings; the same author's similarly focussed *Miscellanea quaedam eruditiae antiquitatis quae ad borealem britanniae majoris partem pertinent* (1710); John Battely's *Antiquitates Rutupinae* (1711);[26] and Sir James Dalrymple's supplementation of Camden's material on Scotland – learned, detailed, and much admired by later workers in the Romano-Scottish field including Alexander Gordon. In addition we should note that in the wake of the Great Fire of London (1666) and the rebuilding it occasioned, much work had been done on Roman London, a subject which interested Sir Christopher Wren, Dr John Woodward and others.[27]

THE ROMAN KNIGHTS AND THE RECRUITMENT OF THE ARISTOCRACY

By the early 1720s, then, the field had been thoroughly surveyed and a great deal of investigative work carried out. What had been unearthed excited speculation on how much remained unexcavated. Field itineraries were expensive in time and money, and there was a ready opportunity here for members of the ruling class to demonstrate their patriotic credentials and classical spirit by supporting such activities and even engaging directly in them. Any pretender to connoisseurship, given the necessary money and advice, might import antique marbles from Italy, any politician could pretend to Catonic virtue in defence of the *res publica*, but to assist in uncovering Britannia was to engage directly with one's own Roman roots, rescue the nation's antique past from the accumulated detritus of the dark ages and a thousand years of Gothic neglect, and unite it at last with the sympathetic present. It is not surprising that men like William Stukeley and Roger Gale had little trouble enlisting notables in the cause.

Stukeley had the acumen to see that in 1722 the time was ripe for a specialised antiquarian society devoted exclusively to Britain's Roman past.[28] The Society of Antiquaries, as its members Alexander Gordon and Sir John Clerk pointed out in the strongest terms, were largely ignoring this field in favour of what these Scotsmen contemptuously termed 'Gothicism',[29] yet it must have been obvious that Romano-British studies were potentially the most prestigious side of British antiquarian and archaeological inquiry. In 1722 the classical spirit was particularly strong in politics – this was the period of *Cato's Letters*, for instance – and in the arts, with English Palladianism, which looked back beyond the baroque to Inigo Jones's early neo-classicism and its sixteenth-century source in Andrea Palladio, just seven years old in its current vogue, which dated from the appearance of the first volume of Colen Campbell's *Vitruvius britannicus* in 1715. The new architectural movement had just enlisted Lord Burlington, recently returned from making a close study of Palladio's work in and around Vicenza during his second tour of Italy in 1720–1. Rysbrack's severe 'Roman-republican' classicism was enjoying its first major commissions. 1722 also saw the publication of a newly revised version of Gibson's edition of Camden's *Britannia*. In this atmosphere Stukeley had the wit to offer Roman citizenship, at the high level of *equites* or knights, to those who considered themselves Roman in spirit and dreamed of a restoration of Roman Britannia. For some, like Lord Pembroke, membership of Stukeley's 'Equites Romani' or Society of Roman Knights (whose first *praetorium* was convened on 23 July 1722) was a recognition of support provided to the cause of Romano-British archaeology, for others it was an encouragement to make similar contributions. Most importantly, the Roman Knights provided a forum in which findings might be compared and future projects planned and co-ordinated. Partly as a result of the stimulus supplied by this society, Romano-British studies were elevated through the 1720s and 1730s to the highest prestige of any antiquarian inquiry, making the investigation of Saxon England and 'monkish manuscripts' by antiquaries like Thomas Hearne look decidedly dull by comparison.[30]

The Roman Knights existed formally for little more than four years but during that time they represented the discipline of Romano-British studies and evangelised on its behalf at a crucial cultural moment. After 1726 they lost cohesion mainly because they lost Stukeley, whose energies had helped to bring and keep them together, though as a field of inquiry Romano-British studies continued to gain in strength. In addition to his interest in Roman Britain, Stukeley had always been fascinated by the Druids, and after 1726 he devoted more of his time to this enthusiasm, which represents the less scientific and reliable side of his work.[31] He also quarrelled with a number of the Knights, including Alexander Gordon and Roger Gale, and in 1726 ceased attending the Society's meetings.[32] From 1722 to 1726, however, the Society oversaw important field-work, enlisted influential members of the aristocracy in its activities, and provided a new rationale for the classical spirit in Britain by urging the recovery of its Roman past.

The Knights, drawn from a wide range of backgrounds, were given Celtic or Roman names, many of them from the period of Julius Caesar's invasion and the first half-century of colonisation up to the governorship of Agricola, though some are later. Celtic names, including those of warriors who had opposed the Romans, were perhaps considered appropriate because of the belief (expressed, as we shall see later, by leading members) that the British ultimately welcomed their conquerors. Each name was in some way appropriate to the member, typically reflecting his county of origin or profession. Extraordinarily for the period, women were admitted.

The Society boasted the aristocrats Thomas Herbert, 8th Earl of Pembroke ('Carvilius', who attacked Caesar's naval base and whose burial-place was thought by Stukeley to lie in Pembroke's Wilton estates – see below); Heneage Finch, 5th Earl of Winchilsea ('Cingetorix', who attacked Caesar's camp and who like the Earl lived in Kent); Algernon Seymour, 7th Earl of Hertford, also president of the Society of Antiquaries ('Segonax', another of Caesar's British opponents, presumed to have come from the vicinity of Lord Hertford's county seat at Marlborough near Avebury); and the Countess of Hertford, to whom James Thomson would later dedicate *The Seasons* ('Boudicca' or 'Boadicea').

The 'professional' archaeologists (among whom one should probably include Lord Hertford) were Stukeley ('Chyndonax', an arch-Druid); Roger Gale ('Venutius', husband of the Brigantine queen Cartismandua whose territories included Gale's Yorkshire); Samuel Gale ('Cunobelinus' or 'Cymbeline', 'Rex Britanniae' as he is styled by Suetonius); Sir John Clerk of Penicuik, Baron of the Scottish Exchequer, FSA ('Agricola', appropriate for the foremost Romanophile of Scotland, which Agricola had brought under Roman arms by defeating Galgacus at Mons Graupius); Alexander Gordon, FSA, another Scot ('Galgacus'); Maurice Johnson, instrumental in refounding the Society of Antiquaries ('Prasutagus', King of the Iceni, whose widow was Boadicea); James Hill, FSA, FRS ('Caradocus' or 'Caratacus', son of Cunobelinus); and John Warburton, FRS, FSA[33] ('Asclepiodotus', prefect of Constantius who retook Britain from the usurper Allectus – a key moment in the history of Britannia, commemorated on a well-known medal proclaiming the restoration of the light of Roman civilisation).[34] In 1723 the membership more than doubled.[35]

The typical *praetorium* began with a speech by the secretary and proceeded to the election of consuls and an orator, the proposal of new members for the following year and other business.[36] Stukeley's speech to the *praetorium* of 27 May 1723, apparently the first 'official' meeting of the full Society, survives and affords a unique entrée into the most Romanophile society of Georgian England. Towards the end he spelt out its purposes:

> My Lds. & Gent. the business of this Society whereof You are the founders, is to search for & illustrate the Roman Monuments in the Britannic Isles. The name of Knights (Equites) dictates to us that travelling is part of our Province. & we are so far to answer our title of Roman, as never to return home without conquest, without large spoils and trophys that merit the civic Crown. We are to encounter time, & Goths & barbarians those destructive enemys of our territorys. We are to fight pro aris & focis. To save citys & citysens, Camps, temples, walls, Amphitheaters, monuments, roads, inscriptions, coyns, buildings & whatever has a Roman stamp on them, we are to redeem & illustrate whole nations & people, recover past ages, to cancel the obscuritys of the envious corrupter of valorous actions, & snatch from his rapacious jaws, the memorable transactions, the laws, religion & polity of our glorious predecessors, whatever concerns Romano-British Antiquitys. We must consider our selves as in a Praetorium, where Roman Chiefs & Emperors would not be ashamd to take their places & consult on the fate & fortune of Kings and states. Such was the tent of the great Pompey in Syria where tributary crowns of the eastern & western world awaited with submissive silence for irreversible decrees. & such was the Praetorium of the greater Caesar on Hounslow heath where the Princes of the Trinovantes, the Cenimagni, the Segontiaci, the Ancalites, the Bibroci, & the Casci sent their Legates to offer subjection & receive his commands. The Eternal Empire in you revives with fresh lustre & the Roman Eagle after long inactivity shakes its torpid wings, from the happy dawn & warm influence of British nobility feels new vigor again affects her lofty flight, & Phoenix like emerges out of the ashes the dust & rubbish of Antiquity to a better life.

He then proceeded to explain the significance of the ring, with the Society's device impressed upon it, which was presented to each member upon admission:

> Sirs, the ring the emblem of love & friendship & unanimity which by its circle denotes its perpetuity . . . is the mutual band & signature of true cordial amity & of Roman vertue, whereto all the endeavors of this Society are tending as

> radii to the central point. . . 'Tis the metal of eternity . . . This ring was the peculiar ornament of Roman Knights as now of Roman Antiquarys.
>
> The impress thereof is an eagle displayd holding a book upon his breast, the colors argent & sable dictates to us that we are to commit our works to writing. His double head was supposd to be first born by our Country man Constantin the Great regarding the East & western Empire. But as the Eagle is a proper emblem of the sharpsightedness & sagacity necessary for our studys, his double regard with more happy auspice points out the end & purport thereof. Time is but of two denominations, for the present is but a moment & scarce an entity or quantity, time past is the object of the enquirys of this Society & time future is the terminus. The Motto is Temporis utriusque vindex which intimates to us that we are to be the Secretarys the interpreters & preservers of the memorials of our Ancestors & to commit them to the eternal cognisance of posterity. Whence the mystical circle of time that infolds all things shall center in us, here place its beginning here find its medium & its termination.[37]

Poetic and flamboyant, but more rambling than these extracts suggest, Stukeley's speech demonstrates that the classical impulse does not always promote order and reason. He was supposedly trying to achieve a Ciceronian eloquence. There is no doubt, though, that he successfully conveyed and reflected the immense enthusiasm of his audience for the enterprise on which they were jointly embarked.

As he emphasises, publication of the fruits of members' researches was central to the Society's *raison d'être*. The most significant publications to come out of the Society of Roman Knights were Stukeley's own *Itinerarium curiosum* (1725) and Alexander Gordon's *Itinerarium septentrionale* (1726). Stukeley's book illustrates how Romano-British studies engaged the aristocracy in field-work and promoted seriously intended 'historical' connections between the Georgian oligarchy and the aristocracy of Romano-Celtic Britain, a procedure repeated in the 1730s on Lord Burlington's behalf by Francis Drake in his important work on York, *Eboracum* (1736), examined below. Gordon's book reveals in its list of subscribers the extensive network of political and cultural connections Romano-British studies could enlist in its service by 1726 and the field's intimate association with the burgeoning classical spirit.

Stukeley's primary purpose in the *Itinerarium curiosum* was to redirect homewards some of the intense interest the British were showing in the antiquities of Italy, arguing, for example, that 'it is not impossible to make a classic journey on this side the streights of Dover'.[38] This idea must have seemed even more startling at the time than it still seems now. Stukeley evokes a Britannia once replete with 'the glorious show of towns, cities, castles, temples, and the like', now represented by 'the prodigious quantities of their ruins and memorials beyond that of any other part of Europe, scarce excepting imperial Rome',[39] a claim which takes note of quantity rather than quality, since in the state of their preservation the Roman remains in Britain could not begin to compete with those in Provence, Spain, Africa and Asia, let alone Italy. His message is directed at the taste-setting grand tourists: 'Hither let the young noblemen and gentry travel, to admire the wonders of their native country, thick sown by that great, wise and industrious people, and learn with them how to value it.'[40]

The message was urgent at a time when the most significant Roman remains, like the pharos at Dover which, with that at Boulogne, was probably the earliest lighthouse in western Europe and which Stukeley illustrated in its then-still-impressive dimensions, could be allowed to decay and fall without qualm or protest. In 1725 at Housesteads, by Hadrian's Wall, one could witness

> the august scene of Romano-British antiquities, in the most neglected condition: a dozen most beautiful and large altars; as many fine *basso relievo's*, some with their heads down the hill; particularly an admirable image of Victory, both arms knocked off... Many soldiers with heads broken off... three ladies sitting close together, with globes in their hands; their heads all gone.[41]

Stukeley's Britannia is compounded of facts, conjectures, special pleading and a vast amount of nostalgia, all serving to represent it as the most favoured province of the Empire. He notes 'How fond the Romans were of this island; whence the cities, castles, roads, temples, altars, sculptures, and in general the whole face of the country here, vastly exceeded that of the continent.'[42] It is an absurd claim, particularly in regard to sculpture, but Stukeley was a propagandist trumpeting a glorious classical past to an

England ready to buy the idea that the buried paradise lost might yet be regained, given enough archaeologists and right-spirited modern architects. He even calls it paradise: in Roman Britain, 'either naturally or by their industry, all things smiled like the garden of Eden'. Where the land is now bad 'it was much better in their days, in the hands of those who could almost conquer Nature herself'.[43]

No wonder so much of their civilisation yet remains, for 'As well as use, they studied eternity in all their works, just opposite to our present narrow souls, who say, it will serve our time well enough.'[44] The conclusion to his 1725 'Iter boreale', undertaken with Roger Gale, strikes all the appropriate chords, not only an anthem to the nation's classic past but a clarion-call to the classic future:

> The amazing scene of Roman grandeur in Britain which I beheld this journey, the more it occurred with pleasure to my own imagination, the more I despaired of conveying it to the reader in a proper light by a rehearsal. It is easy for some nations to magnify trifles, and in words gild over inconsiderable transactions till they swell to the appearance of an history . . . but if in any people action has outdone the capacity of rhetoric, or in any place they have left historians far behind in their valour and military performances, it was in our country; and we are as much surprised in finding such infinite reliques of theirs here, as that we have no history of them that speaks with any particularity of the last 300 years that the Romans dwelt in Britain, and rendered it perfectly provincial. The learned memoirs are very short; and it is well they were guided with such a spirit, as left monuments sufficient to supply that defect, when handled as they deserve . . . I hold myself obliged to preserve, as well as I can, the memory of such things as I saw; which, added to what future times will discover, will *revive the Roman glory among us, and may serve to invite noble minds to endeavour at that merit and public-spiritedness which shine through all their actions*. This tribute at least we owe them, and they deserve it at our hands, to preserve their remains.[45]

Stukeley here fuses, in effect, Britain's antique past and its neo-classical present and future, united once and for all, it is implied, by Roman-spirited men of noble virtue – virtuous nobles like Pembroke and Burlington whose bank accounts and drawing-boards were helping to make the revival possible.

By way of return, the archaeologists might do something for them: prove their antique character, insofar as archaeological research could, by showing that their country seats came down to them from Roman Britons or (even more impressively) a British king whose name was recorded by Julius Caesar in section v of his *Gallic War*. This is what Stukeley did for Pembroke at Wilton. Later, as I shall show, it would be done for Burlington. It was a procedure remarkable for its boldness and deserves notice.

Pembroke had directed Stukeley's attention to the well-known King-barrow, situated on an eminence overlooking Wilton and the valley formed by the concourse of the Nadder and the Wylye. This tumulus, round, flat-topped and without a surrounding ditch, among the highest barrows in Britain, had interested Pembroke for years. He had determined its height above sea-level by accurate calculations but his speculations on its origins had not got beyond the assumption that it was the burial-place of a Celtic king. Stukeley recounts how as they walked over it 'and paid our respects to the illustrious *manes* of the royal defunct', he pointed out to Pembroke that the barrow enjoyed a prospect not only of Stonehenge but of Long-barrow beyond and the extensive ridge of Martinsall Hill, St Ann's Hill and, further away, Runway Hill, 'upon which goes the great Wansdike', which Stukeley took to be the northern boundary of the Belgic kingdom at the time Julius Caesar mounted his invasions. He successfully persuaded Pembroke that the barrow must be the grave of the Belgic king Carvilius, immortalised in Caesar's *Gallic War* as one of several kings who attacked his naval camp on the Rutupian shore. Stukeley's reasoning was stunning in its simplicity: Carvilius obviously lived among the *Carvilii*, near the River Wylye and almost certainly at a town named Carvilium, which in the course of centuries had become Pembroke's Wilton.[46] Not surprisingly, Pembroke was persuaded. Consequently he took the name Carvilius in the Roman Knights, and in his correspondence Stukeley began referring to Pembroke as Carvilius Magnus and Wilton as the Villa Carviliana.[47]

The *Itinerarium curiosum* reveals how close was Stukeley's professional relationship with Pembroke. They regularly worked together in Wiltshire and met for discussions in London. Pembroke was no mere

Watson to Stukeley's Holmes. For instance it was Pembroke who pointed out to Stukeley the logic of the proposition that Clarendon (near Wilton) ought to be called Clorendum after the well-known Roman camp of that name close by a Roman road evidently made or repaired by the emperor Constantius Chlorus (who fathered Constantine the Great and died at Eboracum).[48] It is precisely the kind of working relationship Francis Drake later enjoyed with Lord Burlington, examined below. The already classically minded aristocratic patron is enlisted by the archaeologist as fellow-field-worker, then flatteringly 'connected' via scholarly evidence with classical antiquity – proved Roman.

The Earl of Hertford ('Segonax') and the Earl of Winchilsea ('Cingetorix') also earned their membership of the Roman Knights. Stukeley refers to some of their recent field-work in a letter of October 1724.

> Mr Lord President Hartford was with us at the Antiquarians, being just arrived. He has discoverd lately a whole Roman palace & city coverd over with wood, which he has bought, & in December we goe to cut it down & make observations about it: this is in Wiltshire. Ld Winchelsea has done much this summer, fought valiantly against that all devouring enemy of antiquitys, Time. He has visited many Roman stations in his country & has emissarys abroad or spys to pick up all the urns, lares, pateras, fibulas, &c., that can possibly be met with. He has really amassd together a huge sight of crocks & pans enough to furnish the kitchen of an Apicius. He intends when he comes home to make a collation to some vertuoso ladys, where the whole entertainment is to be servd up a la romain, instead of china ware.[49]

Unfortunately no record survives of the ensuing feast.

The activities of Stukeley, Roger Gale and the aristocratic Knights in England were complemented in Scotland by the work of Alexander Gordon ('Galgacus') and Sir John Clerk ('Agricola'), in whose household Gordon was employed for a while as a tutor. Certain aspects of Clerk's philoromanism have been noticed in chapter 2 and others will be examined in the following chapter.[50] Gordon's *Itinerarium septentrionale* (1726), like Stukeley's *Itinerarium curiosum*, stresses the classical achievement in Britain and sees all modern arts as, at their best, a rediscovery of classical models. Gordon's principal patron was Charles Douglas, 3rd

Duke of Queensberry and 2nd Duke of Dover, first cousin to Lord Burlington and, like Burlington, a patron of John Gay. Gordon's work on Roman Scotland and the north of England naturally gives much of its attention to the Walls, the most outstanding of enduring Roman military monuments anywhere, though John Horsley would soon produce far more impressive work on this topic. Gordon's achievements include his discovery of the Roman signal stations on the coast of Cumberland. He would later migrate to South Carolina as secretary to the Governor.[51]

His philoromanism is noticeably more tempered than Clerk's: in Scotland, he says, the Romans struggled for conquest, the Scots for liberty, and he specifically identifies his patron with the defence of Scottish 'Honour and Liberty'. Gordon's name in the Knights, 'Galgacus', identified him with the Caledonian leader who unsuccessfully opposed Julius Agricola at Mons Graupius in 84. Sir John Clerk, in a letter to Roger Gale from Penicuik dated 2 June 1726 following publication of the *Itinerarium septentrionale*, ridicules Gordon for believing that on the eve of the battle of Mons Graupius Galgacus actually delivered the speech containing the memorable statement 'They make a desert and call it peace' which Tacitus 'reports' as his in the *Agricola* – 'I once endeavored', he wrote, 'to persuade him that it was onely a fiction of Tacitus.'[52] Gordon was too pro-Caledonian for Clerk, who thought 'The best that could have been said for the Caledonians was that though they had been conquered, yet the Romans could not retain their conquests. I am, I confesse, of the opinion of some learned men that it is a reproach to a nation to have resisted the humanity which the Romans laboured to introduce.'[53] Roger Gale agreed: it was

> a great misfortune not to have submitted to their arms, since their conquests were so far from enslaving those they vanquisht, that they tended onely to the civilizing and improving their manners, reducing them under the Roman laws and government from their wild and savage way of life, instructing them in arts and sciences, and looking upon them as fellow-citizens and freemen of Rome, the common mother of all that had the happynesse to fall under her subjection, and every nation that was subdued by her might truly say she was *Felix adversis, et sorte oppressa secunda*.[54]

Despite Gordon's pro-Caledonian bias, however, in his preface the praise of the Roman accomplishment in Britain is almost as strong as Stukeley's:

(*China* excepted) the whole World cannot show a greater Sight of amazing Grandeur, than what the *Romans* have left behind them in *Cumberland*, *Northumberland*, and *Scotland*. Which, by the bye, shews the Value they had for our Island; and, indeed, I must, with equal Justice and Pleasure, confess, That no Nation in *Europe*, since *Cambden*'s Time, has been at more Pains to collect and preserve their Monuments of Antiquity, than the *English*.[55]

This sentiment becomes forward-looking and programmatic by virtue of Gordon's militant anti-Gothicism. Thus he wishes the Society of Antiquaries, who had recently elected him to their number, 'Prosperity, that by them Antiquity and Learning may flourish in the Island, to the total Extirpation of *Gothicism*, Ignorance, and a bad Taste'.[56] Their president the Earl of Hertford and their vice-president the Earl of Winchilsea, Roman Knights and significant connoisseurs and collectors, are specifically appealed to in that context. In this sentence Romano-British archaeology converges with and reinforces the independent but complementary influence on contemporary aesthetics of Shaftesbury, Addison and Pope, by linking the Romano-British past to the English quest for a proper Rule of Taste based on classical models. Gordon goes on to cite the important private art collections of his day, specifically those of the Earl of Pembroke, the Duke of Devonshire, the Earl of Burlington and others, to whose credit it is 'that *England* seems now to be the true Seat of the Muses, and *London* is become *Apollo*'s favourite Residence'.[57] For Stukeley, London is 'the *Augusta* of Britain', and 'destined to be the *altera Roma*'[58]. The direction of modern architecture is especially important to Gordon. He singles out James Gibbs, one of his subscribers – Lord Burlington was another, though his most important work was still in the future – in his praise for 'the noble Taste that now reigns . . . in the Island'.[59]

A glance through Gordon's subscription list reveals the extent to which Romano-British archaeology had attracted the cultural elite. There are 231 names. Naturally the Roman Knights are well represented.[60] Beyond this charmed circle, important members of the aristocracy included Pope's friends the Earl of Burlington and Lord Bathurst, the dukes of Devonshire, Queensberry (six copies) and Rutland (four), and the intellectual Countess of Eglinton (four), among a host of dukes, duchesses, earls and countesses. Dr John Arbuthnot subscribed, Sir Hans Sloan, Dr Richard Mead (four) and General Wade, the landscape gardener Charles Bridgeman, the architect James Gibbs, and Christopher Wren, son of Sir Christopher. Among other antiquaries who supported the project[61] was Dr John Woodward, owner of the most famous 'Roman' shield in Britain, which happened to be a fake. Woodward, one should observe in passing, is a notorious example of the tendency, so often displayed by men at that time, to find in Roman antecedents whatever they wanted to find, and unconsciously to manufacture the evidence. He desperately wanted his iron shield to be an example of the highest stage of Roman art, stubbornly refusing to accept repeated advice that iron could never weather so many centuries in such pristine condition. He went through all the ancient literature on the subject of Roman shields, extracting just those bits which he could twist to his purposes, and even managed to charm or cajole continental experts into lending him some support. Like many other antiquarians of his day, he allowed his zeal to outrun discretion and fact.[62]

Gordon sought additional support for the expense of the many engraved plates his book included, each being inscribed to its 'donor' (not all donors were subscribers – Sir Andrew Fountaine, for instance). The fact that Burlington, Bathurst, Bridgeman and Gibbs subscribed strongly suggests that contemporary architecture and landscape gardening were drawing sustenance from the enthusiasm for Britain's Roman past, that the new classicism was in search of native roots. This previously unexplored factor in the development of English Palladianism is further considered below in relation to Burlington's work.

Although John Horsley was never a member of the Society of Roman Knights, his *Britannia romana* (1732) was the culmination of what the Society stood for, and he was in touch with such *Equites* as Lord Hertford, Stukeley, Roger Gale, Sir John Clerk and Alexander Gordon, with all of whom he discussed his work or corresponded, for the most part after the Society's formal existence had ceased.[63] As late as 1907 the eminent archaeologist and historian Francis Haverfield could describe the *Britannia romana* as 'till quite lately the best and most scholarly account of any Roman province that had been written anywhere in

Europe'.[64] In 1933 Sir George Macdonald called it 'an astonishing achievement', 'an indispensable instrument of research', praising 'the accuracy of the details', 'the soundness of the general principles', the 'admirable clarity'.[65] In 1936 R. G. Collingwood pronounced it 'in many ways still the best book on Roman Britain as a whole'.[66] Horsley's thorough and exhaustive study, which was published just a few weeks after his premature death on 12 January 1732 at the age of forty-six, was the product of four years' writing-up and, behind that, many years of research and thousands of miles of travel. One stimulus for publication was probably dissatisfaction with Gordon's *Itinerarium septentrionale*. This book had appeared shortly before Horsley began to put his own materials together into what became the *Britannia romana*. Gordon had done far less field-work than Horsley and had disguised his indebtedness to him.[67]

The first of Horsley's three volumes (bound together in most copies) surveyed the history of Roman Britain, gave full details of the military aspects of the occupation and provided a description of the Walls complete with many detailed maps. Stukeley in his 'Iter boreale' (in the *Itinerarium curiosum*) and Gordon in the *Itinerarium septentrionale* had recently published their analyses of the Walls, but Horsley's is vastly superior in the quality of its reasoning, even if he does ascribe Hadrian's Wall to Severus. The second volume was a catalogue of all Roman inscriptions and sculptures found in Britain, exhaustively illustrated and impeccably transcribed – most of *Britannia romana*'s more than 100 copper plates were in this volume. Of its roughly 340 inscriptions, over 140 were new and others correctly transcribed or contextualised for the first time.[68] The third volume gave a thorough consideration to every aspect of the Roman geography of Britain and reprinted the most important primary sources. Its map of Roman Britain according to the Antonine Itinerary is reproduced on plate 19. At the end Horsley provided a handy 'chronological table of occurrences relating to the Roman affairs in Britain', a chapter-by-chapter index to all the inscriptions and sculptures, 'an index of the Roman names of people and places in Britain', 'an index of the modern names of Roman places in Britain' and a 'general index'. With its indexes and prefatory material this extremely attractive and usable book ran to just under 600 folio pages. Georgian England had everything there was then to know about its Roman past in one set of covers – everything except any information on the life of the Celts under Roman occupation, for Horsley's interests were almost exclusively focussed on the Romans themselves.[69] Though the book was obviously expensive to produce, Horsley met the costs from his own small resources as a Presbyterian minister and schoolmaster. Because there was no subscription list it is not possible to analyse its readership in the way one can with Gordon's *Itinerarium septentrionale*, but Lord Oxford paid for three copies in advance, Horsley ensuring that one of these was on superfine paper.[70] Burlington bought a copy and had it bound in his best russia.[71] Dr Richard Mead, FRS, possessor of a considerable collection of antiquities, owned a copy on large paper.[72] In other words, like Gordon's book, it was selling to the cultural elite and not just to specialists.

As Stukeley does with Pembroke, so Horsley confers Romanness on his patron, Sir Richard Ellys, Calvinist theological writer, MP, a Greek scholar admired on the Continent, and intimate friend of Maittaire. Much of Ellys's time was given to antiquarian research. Horsley praises him for his 'Eminence in religion and learning' but is more interested in his virtues, which are the Roman-republican ones, *pietas*, *virtus* – 'piety and true virtue' – and support of *libertas*.[73] He is also praised for his 'elegance of life', which Horsley makes Roman too: 'In the following account of the remains of the *Roman* grandeur in our island, you will find some traces of that elegance of life, which you, SIR, so happily enjoy.' In a 'degenerate and corrupt age' his role is to 'protect the cause and interests of piety, liberty and virtue',[74] like everyone else in England's oligarchy of virtue and its virtuous Opposition.

Though Horsley confers spiritual Romanness on Ellys, this patron lacked the means to recreate the classical past physically, and it is the ability of their patrons to do just this that is most celebrated and encouraged by William Stukeley and later by Francis Drake, whose *Eboracum: or, the History and Antiquities of the City of York* (1736) was supervised by Lord Burlington. As we shall see in chapter 4, it was an ability the 8th Earl of Pembroke had shown at Wilton in a great variety of ways, including populating his house and gardens with scores of the most eminent Greeks and especially Romans. With Burlington, the interest in Roman Britain went hand in hand with the will to rebuild it.

ARCHITECT AS ARCHAEOLOGIST: BURLINGTON

The first modern European attempts to replicate, more or less exactly, surviving ancient Roman buildings, or their putative forms as drawn by Palladio, were made in England. Inigo Jones's St Paul's Covent Garden (1631–3), the earliest of these, was based on Palladio's paper reconstruction of Vitruvius' Tuscan temple in Daniele Barbaro's edition of Vitruvius (1556).[75] Jones's classicism was complemented and reinforced by his interest in Roman Britain and his desire to see in modern England the inheritor of the best in Roman civilisation. It was this thinking that led him to prove, to his own satisfaction, that Stonehenge was an open Tuscan temple to Caelus, the Roman god of the heavens (the Greek Uranus), the greatest work of its kind ever constructed by the Romans, not a Druidic temple as traditionally believed.[76] Vitruvius was enlisted in support of the argument. Jones's findings, published posthumously by his disciple John Webb, created a controversy and Webb produced a strong defence.[77] Jones's realisation of Vitruvius' Tuscan temple at Covent Garden is historically important as the first exercise in a literalist reconstruction of Roman Britain, or a Roman West for that matter. It is not surprising that this important seventeenth-century example should have been followed in the 1720s and 1730s by others designed by Lord Burlington, Burlington's disciple Kent, and other architects of the Burlington school, given Burlington's intense admiration for Inigo Jones. Vitruvius, Palladio and Jones formed the trinity inspiring all of Burlington's work. Particularly noteworthy is the extent to which Burlington shared Jones's deep interest in Roman Britain. In October 1724, shortly before a new edition of Jones's and Webb's essays on Stonehenge was to appear, Stukeley told Alexander Gordon that 'My Lord Burlington is very angry with me because he hears I shall demolish Inigo Jones's notion of Stonehenge being a Roman work, & vindicate it to the Britons to whom it of right belongs.'[78] Burlington took any criticism of Inigo Jones as a slight to himself.

Some time before 1727 Burlington erected a circular temple in his gardens at Chiswick. This temple was illustrated by William Kent on plate 73 of the first volume of his *Designs of Inigo Jones* (plate 20).[79] Fiske Kimball long ago recognised its historical importance: 'Nothing like it [had] been attempted in modern Europe. It has, in small, the scheme of the Roman Pantheon. Against a circular cell crowned by a Roman saucer-dome with steps, stands a pedimented portico of four Ionic capitals.' As Kimball pointed out, Burlington took his simplified version from Palladio's *I quattro libri dell'architettura* (1570) which contains, in addition to the Pantheon, a simpler form of it near San Sebastian.[80] He would no doubt have been encouraged in his replicating interests by Colen Campbell's second volume of *Vitruvius britannicus* (1717), which contained Campbell's plans for a church based on the Maison Carrée at Nîmes (plate 21).[81] Later, following his original far more faithfully, Burlington reproduced in the Great Hall of his York Assembly Rooms the basilican 'Egyptian Hall' described by Vitruvius and illustrated by Palladio (see plate 22). Despite the name Vitruvius gives to it, his 'Egyptian Hall' was a thoroughly Roman building, intended for entertainment (a good analogy for the name is the Victorian *palais de danse*).[82] Burlington's only significant departure from the design as given by Palladio was to specify pilasters above instead of engaged columns.[83] The adaptation by Hawksmoor of the Temple of Vesta at Tivoli and the Tomb of Sulla's widow Caecilia Metella, on the Via Appia, for the Mausoleum at Castle Howard (1728–41) involved Burlington again, this time as overseer.[84]

The lead he gave in this field of replica and recollection architecture was followed at Stowe by William Kent, whose Temple of Ancient Virtue (*c.* 1735; plate 15), taken from the Temple of Vesta at Tivoli, was recognised by Christopher Hussey as 'Kent's most impressive building at Stowe, perhaps indeed anywhere'.[85] The Temple of Concord and Victory, originally called the Grecian Temple, also at Stowe and noticed in the previous chapter (plate 17), was begun in the 1740s and influenced by the Maison Carrée and, as I suggested in the previous chapter, by Palladio's paper reconstruction of the Temple of Concord in Rome.

Ambrose Phillipps's triumphal arch at Garendon (plate 23) is noticed below, together with the other 'Roman' structures he built there. Many more, of varying fidelity to their originals and most of them predating the arrival of 'neo-classicism' proper, are noticed in chapter 4, including the Pantheon (1753–6, to designs by the Burlingtonian Flitcroft – plate 24) at Henry Hoare's Stourhead, where the classical spirit was made to infuse the landscape more impressively than anywhere else in England apart, perhaps, from Stowe.[86]

Burlington's establishment of the vogue for replica and recollection architecture in England should be seen in the context of his archaeological interests. As in the case of the Adams and other British neo-classical architects of the mid and later eighteenth century, there was a symbiotic relationship between Burlington's architectural practices and his interest in archaeology.[87] The depth of this interest has not been recognised, though it is evident to some extent in his publication in 1730 of examples from his private collection of Palladio's drawings of Roman *thermae* (which inspired Pope's *Epistle to Burlington*),[88] and in his patronage, if that is what it was, of Robert Castell's *Villas of the Ancients*.[89] As we shall see, the depth of Burlington's enthusiasm for archaeology was reflected in his library at Chiswick[90] and, even more significantly, in his encouragement of and active involvement in the field-work and publications of Romano-British archaeologists. These factors, together with an appreciation of the nostalgic and patriotic aspects of Romano-British archaeology, and of course the fact that Inigo Jones had done it, make Burlington's decision to recreate ancient Roman architecture in England intelligible.[91]

The extent to which Burlington carried out examinations of classical Roman buildings during his first tour of Italy in 1714–15 is not known. Three of the four months he spent in Rome seem to have been passed in recovering from fever.[92] The accounts are the only records to have survived from this tour and they reveal purchases of paintings and other art objects but no interest at all in architecture. His second Italian tour in 1719 was devoted particularly to the north of Italy, where he examined the Palladian villas at and near Vicenza. It was at this time that he purchased Palladio's drawings of Roman baths. Given Burlington's enthusiasm for

Palladio, nothing could have stimulated his interest in the archaeology of Roman architecture more than these.[93]

The Catalogue for his library at Chiswick was drawn up much later, in January 1742,[94] but it is probable that a number of Burlington's books on archaeology were purchased around the time of his second Italian tour and in the years immediately following. An annotated shelf-list for the relevant titles is given in the appendix. As a collection they constitute a neglected and crucial example, from one of the most culturally significant early eighteenth-century private libraries, of the contemporary enthusiasm for the antique.[95] The collection merits attention for this reason and because for Burlington and his followers their replica and recollection architecture was consciously linked to their enthusiasm for Roman archaeology and the search for Britain's Roman self.

As I have shown elsewhere, Burlington's Chiswick library, unlike the purely ostentatious library of Burlington's antithesis, Timon, satirised in Alexander Pope's *Epistle to Burlington*, was a working collection, its volumes contributing directly to his own designs, his particular interests and activities.[96] Together with his drawings, the library's catalogue provides the starting point for any serious enquiries into his work. In the present context it represents the foundation of knowledge on which his support of and collaboration with British archaeologists rested.

This support and collaboration took a variety of forms, from his interest (if not participation) in Castell's work, which provided a scholarly background for later investigations of Roman villas in Britain, to his support for Alexander Gordon's *Itinerarium septentrionale* (subscription and underwriting of the cost of the plate which is dedicated to him[97]), his purchase of a copy of Horsley's *Britannia romana* and, most significantly of all, his patronising of Francis Drake's monumental archaeological study of York and collaboration with Drake in his field-work in and about the city. In working with Drake, Burlington was developing a practical side to the academic archaeological interests reflected in his library. He was doing this, moreover, at the same time that he was engaged in realising for York, the second most important city of Roman Britain, a Roman building that had been described by Vitruvius and putatively reconstructed by Palladio, the 'Egyptian Hall'. Drake had been collecting material for *Eboracum* from the late 1720s and developed a practice of consulting Burlington on matters of mutual interest. Finally the entire work was submitted to his scrutiny before publication.

A good example of their collaborative archaeological activity was their attempt to fix the site of the Romano-British town of Delgovitia. This was a significant problem in scholarly efforts to define the geography of Roman Britain. Their most important source of information on the subject was the Antonine Itinerary. Roger Gale, who also helped Drake on the *Eboracum*, had published his father's edition of the Antonine Itinerary in 1709, to which he had added his own scholarly notes.[98] According to the Antonine Itinerary it was seven Roman miles from the camp of the Sixth Legion (Legio VI Victrix) at Eboracum to Derventio, and another thirteen miles from Derventio to Delgovitia. This provided the framework within which hypothesis and archaeology had to operate on the problem. Some had speculated that Delgovitia should be identified with Market Weighton or Wighton, from the common -vic- element in the names if one pronounced Delgovitia as Del*govic*ia, and Weighton as *Wic*ton or *Vic*ton. Market Weighton was the correct distance from York, but no evidence of its having once been a Roman station had ever come to light, and the etymological argument struck Drake as spurious. Others thought Goodmanham a likelier candidate, from Bede's reference to it as a 'locus idolorum', but Drake thought this was likelier to refer to Saxon than to Roman idols. Burlington, as lord of the manor of Goodmanham, took a personal interest in a problem whose classical–archaeological nature interested him in any case. It was Burlington who drew Drake's attention to a large area of ground on the eastern side of the village. By the uneven and pocked aspect of the turf here, it seemed this might cover long-buried ruins. Burlington authorised Drake to bring in a team of labourers and make several digs across the area, each to a considerable depth. Nothing was discovered apart from chalk- and lime-pits.[99]

As a result, Drake became convinced that Delgovitia must be sought elsewhere. He knew that the terminations -burgh and -chester led in many cases to Roman stations, and he began to consider Burlington's Yorkshire seat of Londesborough as a possibility. It was the correct distance, and Drake believed he could prove, from detailed evidence he had been given by Burlington's head gardener at Londesborough, that a Roman road ran directly through Burlington's park. What clinched the issue in his mind was a pair of supportive facts: Roman coins of the middle and later periods had been unearthed there, and Roman funerary repositories had come to light in the course of digging in the park, gardens and under the hall of the house. Burlington was literally living above the graves of his Roman predecessors. He owned Delgovitia. Drake had achieved for him precisely what Stukeley had for Pembroke – given him a tangible hereditary connection with Roman history in the very soil he sat on.

Drake was anxious lest this discovery be seen as flattery disguised as archaeology, and as if to confirm his *bona fides* he changed his mind in 1747 when more convincing information came to light. In that year John Burton published an article for the Royal Society regarding the location of Delgovitia and Drake backed him up in a supplementary article.[100] In a letter to Stukeley of 27 July 1747, Drake, writing from York, refers to the discovery of the site of Delgovitia and goes on to mention Burlington's recent contributions to this and other aspects of local Romano-British archaeology:

> I have sent up an accurate survey of the Roman roads leading to and from this place [Delgovitia], with the stupendous remains of the fortifications by earthen ramparts, for some thousands of acres, to the Lord Burlington. His lordship has put this map into the hands of Mr Vertue to contract and make a plate of, at his own expense. When it is finished I will send you a print of it, as also of the platform of a Roman hypocaust lately discovered in this neighbourhood, which is engraving also, at the charge of the same worthy nobleman.[101]

The 'plate' mentioned here is reproduced on plate 25. Two years later Drake told Stukeley of 'a Roman bagnio and pavement found lately at Hovingham, near us, and published [from an engraved plate] at the expence of Lord Burlington'.[102] In another letter, undated but written after the publication of *Eboracum* (1736), Drake described for Stukeley his recent excavation of a major Roman military road in Burlington's park:

> Being at Londesborough last week, I prevailed with Lord Burlington to dig for the Roman causeway in his park, menticned p. 32 of my York. At about 19 inches deep, through a very fine soil, by the side of the canal, the workmen came to the stratum, and bared the whole breadth of it, which measures 24 foot. This is the broadest Roman road I ever mett with, and on it is plainly to be seen the impressions of wheel carriages. Most certainly this was the great military way, mentioned in the first Iter, from York to Praetorium, one way, and crosse the Humber to Lincoln the other; but more of this when we meet. My lord proposes to lay bare as much of this road as is in his territorys, and then it may tempt so curious a person as yourself to go from hence to see it; I will do myself the pleasure to accompany you.[103]

Drake naturally regarded Burlington as the last word on Roman architectural remains and in the course of his research for *Eboracum* consulted his patron on whether or not an arch in Micklegate-bar, a principal gate of York, was Roman. Drake had long thought it so but did not have the intimate knowledge of Roman architecture his patron possessed. As the two were walking about the city examining Roman remains, Drake drew Burlington's attention to the arch: 'His lordship having considered it a little, said pleasantly this must be a *Roman* arch or else built since *Inigo Jones*'s time. The improbability of the latter is apparent enough. In short his lordship assured me that it was a *Roman* arch and of the *Tuscan* order. The arch is a *triplit*'.[104] In every way, Burlington shared Drake's reverence for Roman Eboracum. It is indicative, for example, that in his direction of Kent's design of a new pavement for York Minster he preferred classical patterns.[105]

In the York Assembly Rooms, of course, Burlington brought the Roman city back to life (plate 22). Appropriately, Burlington's drawings for this, based on Palladio's, were displayed in *Eboracum*. Drake understood the significance of the fact that it was in his city that ancient Rome was being physically recreated, insofar as Palladio's drawings of a Roman 'Egyptian Hall' can be considered an accurate paper reconstruction of this type of building as described by Vitruvius, as Burlington certainly would have taken them to be. Vitruvius wrote, and of course practised as leading architect, under Augustus, so any building based on Vitruvius was not just Roman but golden-age Roman. Burlington's beautifully engraved plans were featured fully and handsomely. Drake also made all the right connections between his patron and the Roman world – the same sort of connections Stukeley had made for Pembroke ('Carvilius') and Horsley for Sir Richard Ellys (fount of *pietas*, *libertas* and *virtus*). Drake's identification of Burlington with the Roman world and Roman Britain in particular epitomises this form of analogising: 'Where should the history of an ancient *Roman* city, in *Britain*', he asks in the dedication, 'find greater favour, or meet with a better reception, than from a nobleman, whose particular genius, almost, speaks him of *Roman* extraction?' Burlington's Roman inheritance, represented for Drake in 1736 by his understanding that Londesborough was Delgovitia, has now gone the final step and become genetic. Drake goes on to point out that Burlington's '*English* titles make no small figure in this very history; having been, indubitably, one of them a *Roman port*; and, the other, your paternal and favourite seat, a *Roman station* in our neighbourhood' – references to Burlington Bay (Gabrantuicorum Sinus Portuosus) and of course Londesborough (Delgovitia). Burlington also happened to be governor of modern Eboracum, as we are reminded. In Drake's eyes and no doubt his patron's, Burlington was Romanised to his bones. Accordingly it was perfectly appropriate and logical that, in the words of Drake's dedication,

> *York*, by your means, is now possessed of a structure, in a truer and nobler taste of architecture, than, in all probability, the *Roman* EBORACUM could ever boast of. Your Lordship's great knowledge in this art, soars up to the *Augustan* age and style; and, that *Praetorian* palace, once in old EBORACUM, made ever memorable for the residence and deaths of two *Roman* emperors, and, in all likelihood, for the birth of a third, must, if now standing, have given place to your *Egyptian* hall in our present *York*.[106]

Elsewhere Drake gives Burlington his appropriate Roman name: 'that truly *English* VITRUVIUS',[107] the same name Alexander Pope gives him in the concluding lines of the *Epistle to Burlington*.[108]

Other architects drew much of their inspiration from archaeological interests and activities, of course, particularly after the mid-century, when first-hand archaeological experience in the eastern Mediterranean basin became almost a *sine qua non* for the serious neo-classical architect. Burlington, however, is an important example of how archaeology, including the Romano-British variety, inspired early attempts to recreate antique structures in a once-Roman province well before the arrival of neo-classicism proper. Moreover, he was not alone in this. Another clear case in point is the amateur architect Ambrose Phillipps of Garendon, an early member of the Society of Dilettanti. He travelled through France and Italy in the early 1730s, making drawings of important Roman structures. On his return he proceeded to reproduce a number of these on his Garendon estate in Leicestershire, including a triumphal arch (plate 23), based on the Arch of Titus and partly on the Roman arch at Orange in France; a Temple of Venus, obviously inspired by the Temple of Vesta at Tivoli; and an obelisk. His epitaph overstates his contribution to British architecture but accurately reflects his ideals and ambition:

EX ITALIA REVERSVS
INSPECTIS ANTIQVORVM AEDIFICIORVM RELIQVIIS
ARTES ROMANAS IN PATRIAM TRANSTVLIT
ET INTER PRINCIPES VIROS QVI IAM ARCHITECTVRAM
IN ANGLIA RESTITVERE ET PERPOLIRE COEPERANT
ENITVIT PENE PRIMVS.[109]

Romano-British archaeology in the 1720s and 1730s had an important revivalist message – the uncovering of Britain's Roman self should proceed side by side with its revivification by modern Britons imbued with a true classical taste. This message is very clear in Drake's *Eboracum* and in the work of William Stukeley, Alexander Gordon and John Horsley. All reflect the psychology of nostalgic patriotism that marked Romano-British archaeology at the time Burlington and others were making modern Britain look increasingly like its lost self. Together, the Romano-British archaeologists played a crucial role, too long neglected by art historians, in giving an authentically British and hence patriotic aspect to the prevailing classical temper. In their work the national classic past took on an idealistic quality, and their patrons were praised for helping to preserve its remains. Because the archaeologists appealed directly to a tangible and local classical antiquity (in distinction to neo-Palladianism, which looked back to a classicism mediated and transformed by sixteenth-century Italian architects), arguing for its restoration and the revival of its values, they effectively encouraged, inspired and validated attempts to replicate and 'recollect' Roman architecture as a project both nostalgic and natural. All that was required was a classically minded architect with sufficient knowledge of Roman architecture who shared the Romano-British archaeological enthusiasm and was keen to put such a project into effect.

As Francis Drake recognised when he identified his patron and fellow field-worker with Vitruvius and praised him for his reincarnation of Roman Britain in its old northern capital, it was this important role that Burlington first filled, tentatively at Chiswick and later, more seriously, at York. In this he was encouraged, no doubt, by Inigo Jones's brief essay into the same field. Burlington would soon be followed by his disciple William Kent, and a variety of like-minded architects and patrons, in their designs for the temples and other professedly 'Roman' structures that would soon be decorating the landscape gardens of mid eighteenth-century England.

[19]
Map of Roman Britain from John Horsley, *Britannia romana*, 1732.

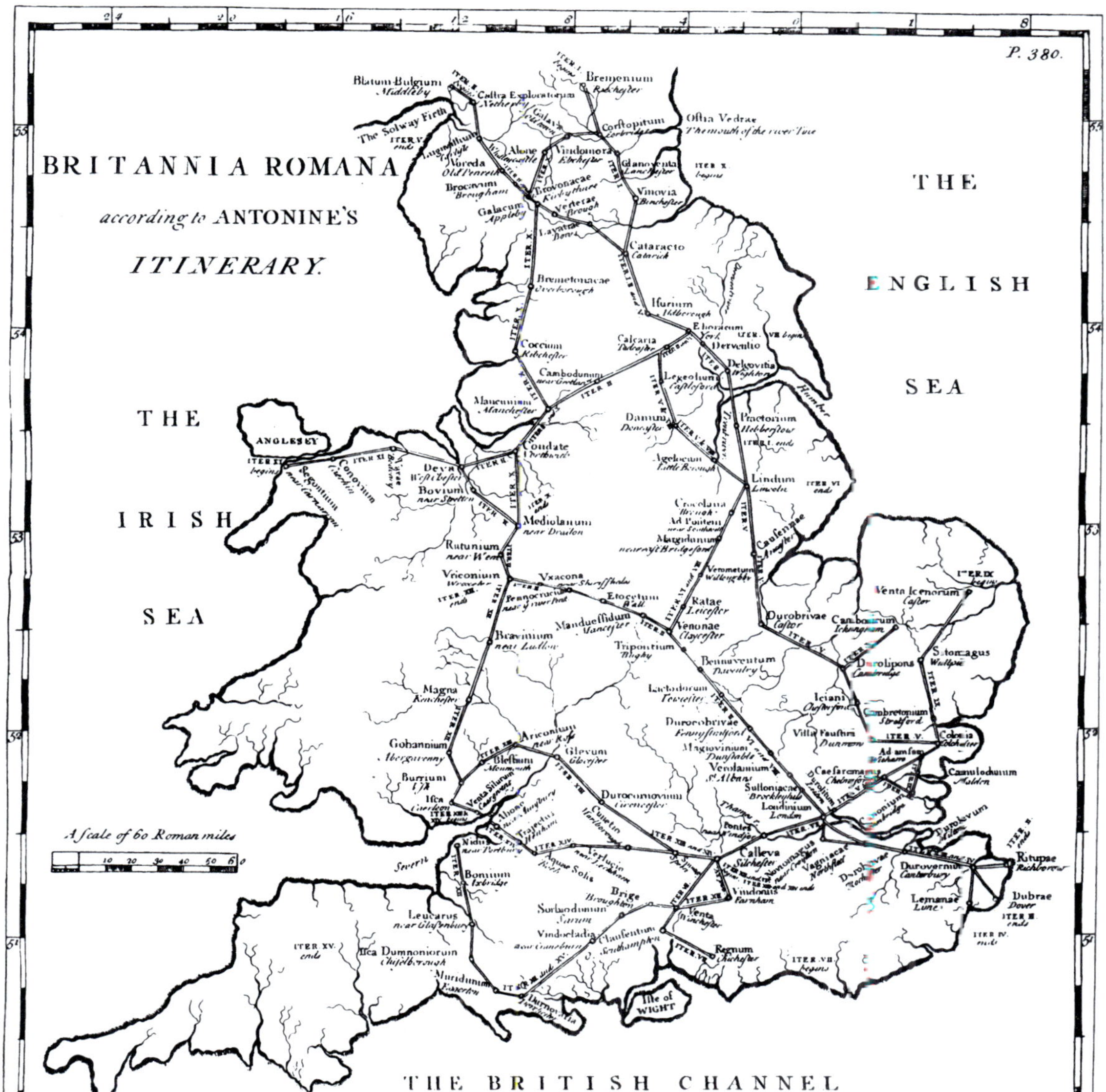

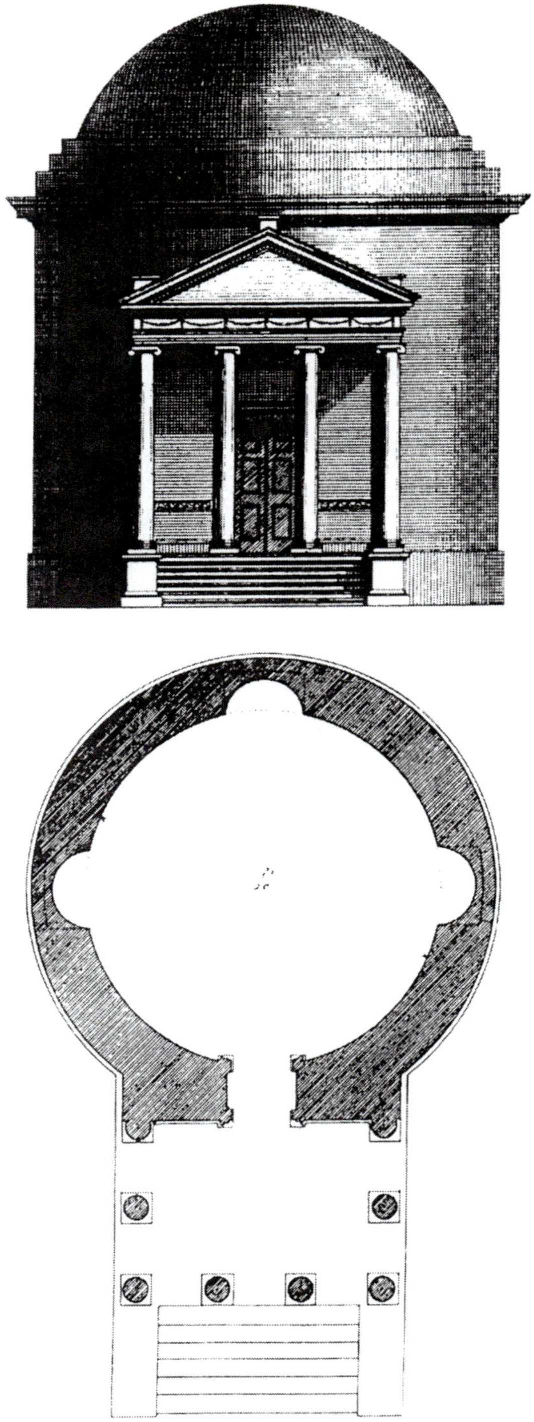

[20]
Garden temple by the 3rd Earl of Burlington, Chiswick, from *Designs of Inigo Jones*, ed. William Kent, vol. 1, 1727.

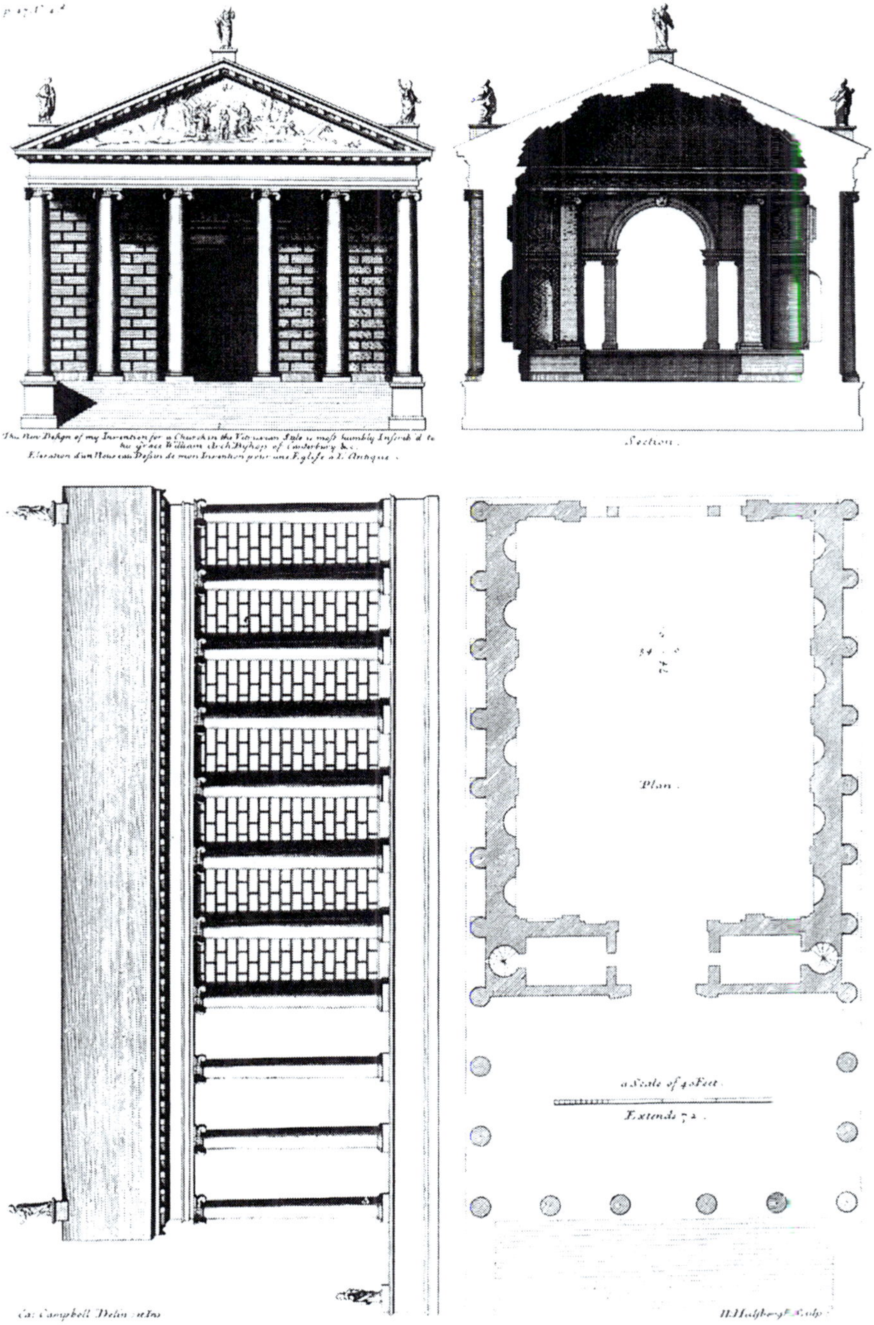

[21]
Design for a church in the Vitruvian style by Colen Campbell, *Vitruvius britannicus*, vol. II, 1717.

[22]
Assembly Rooms, York, by the 3rd Earl of Burlington.

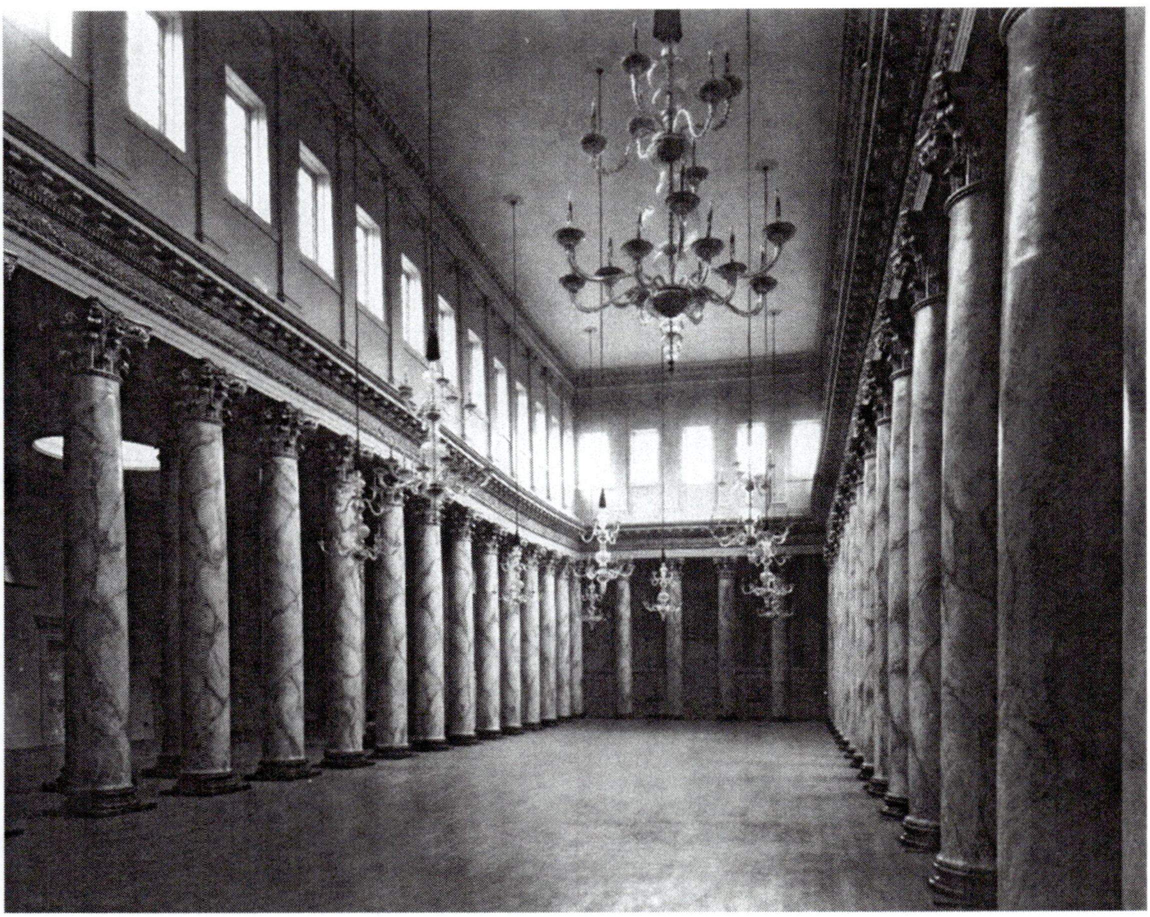

[23]
Triumphal Arch, Garendon.
Ambrose Phillipps.

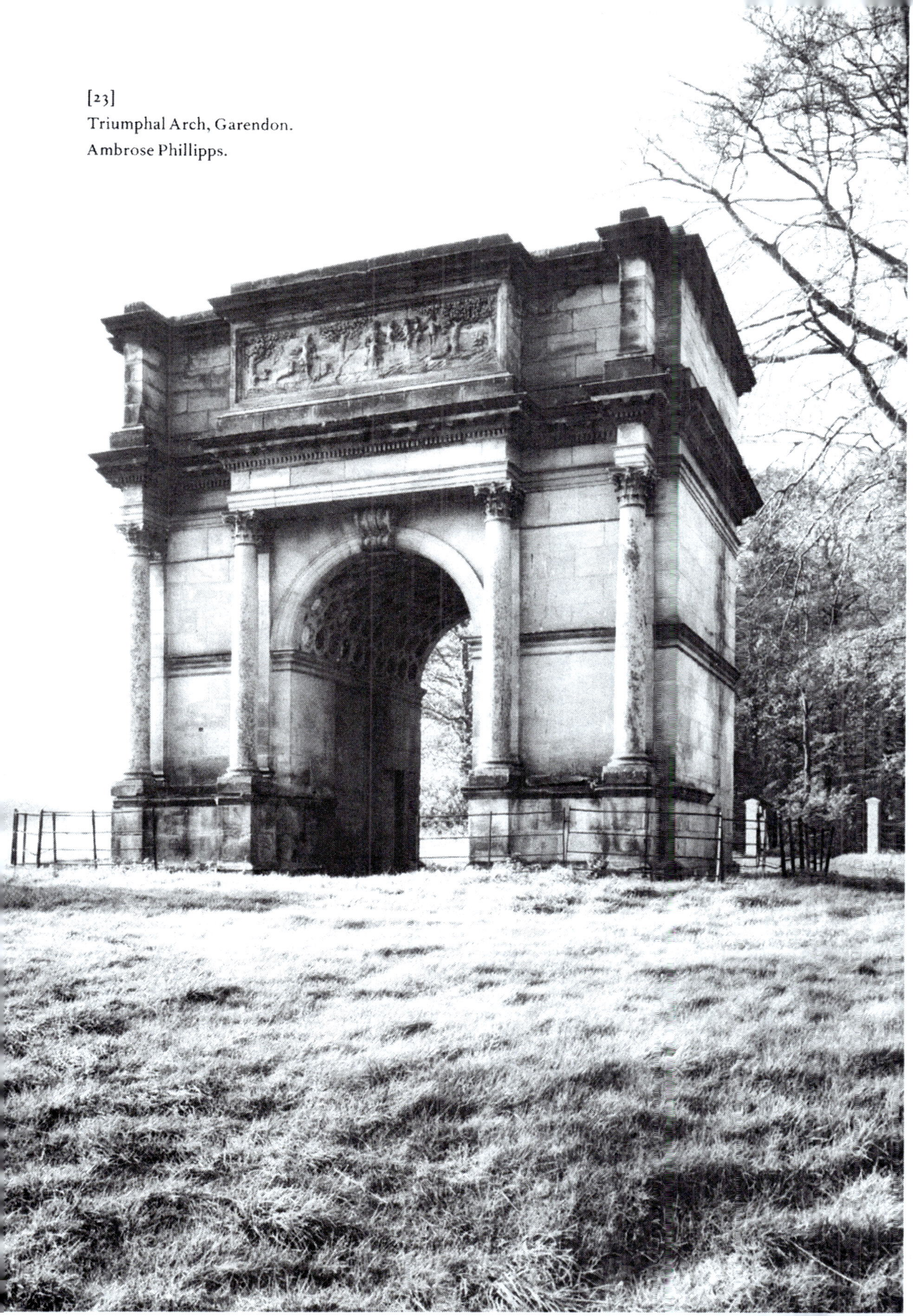

[24]
The Pantheon, Stourhead.
Henry Flitcroft.

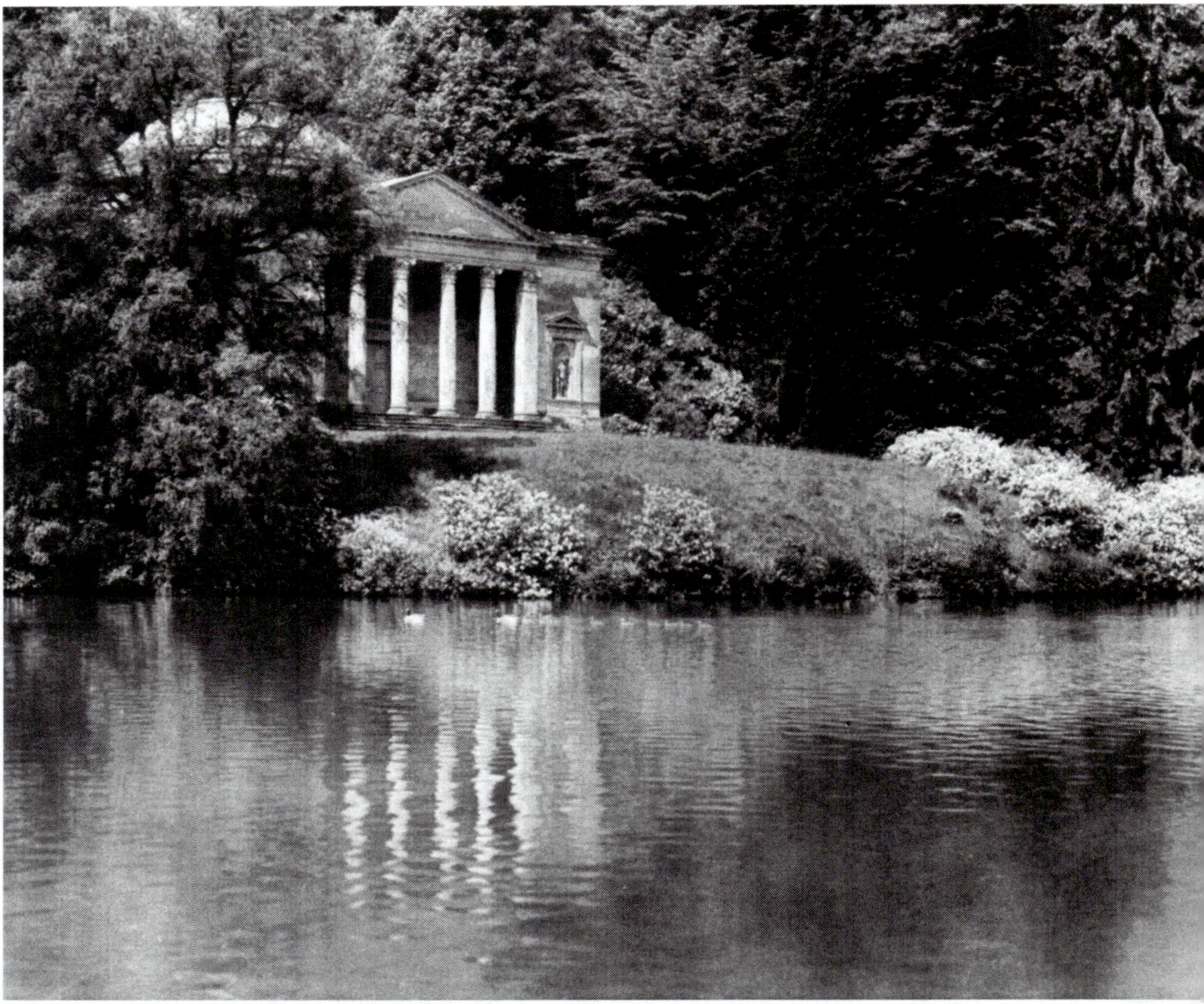

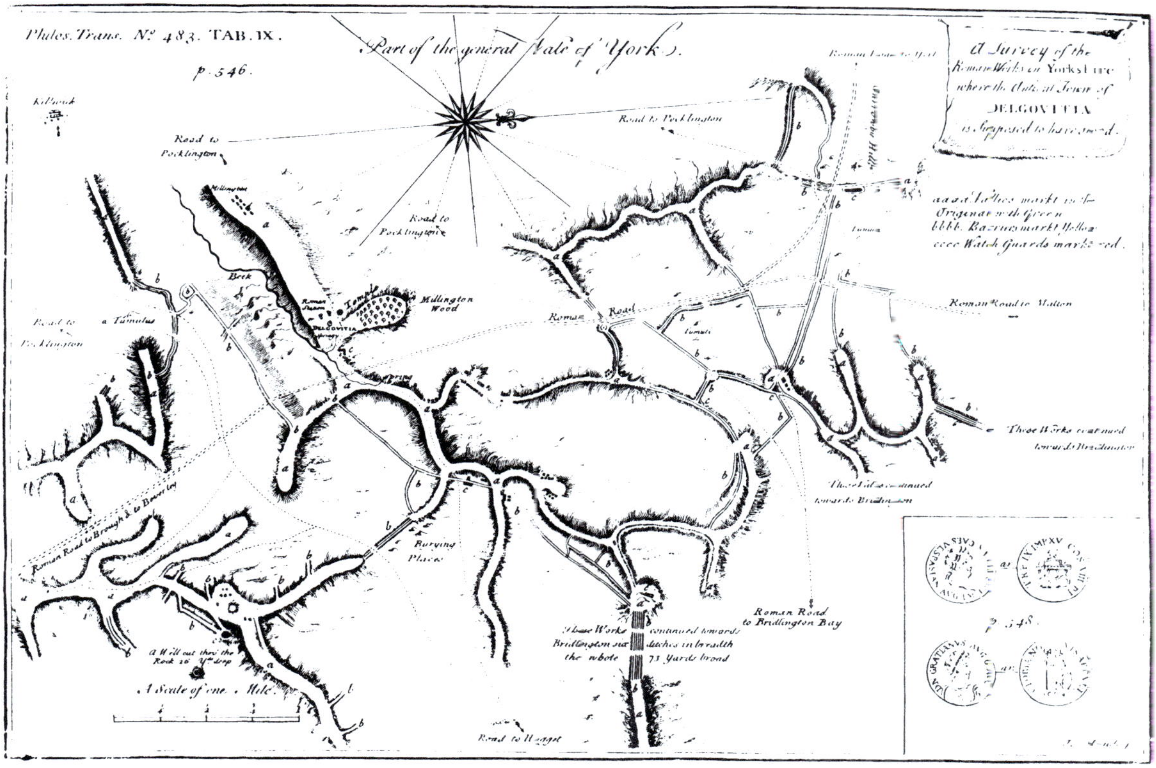

[25]

Archaeological plate commissioned by the 3rd Earl of Burlington through George Vertue, *Royal Society: Philosophical Transactions*, 44 (1747), 546.

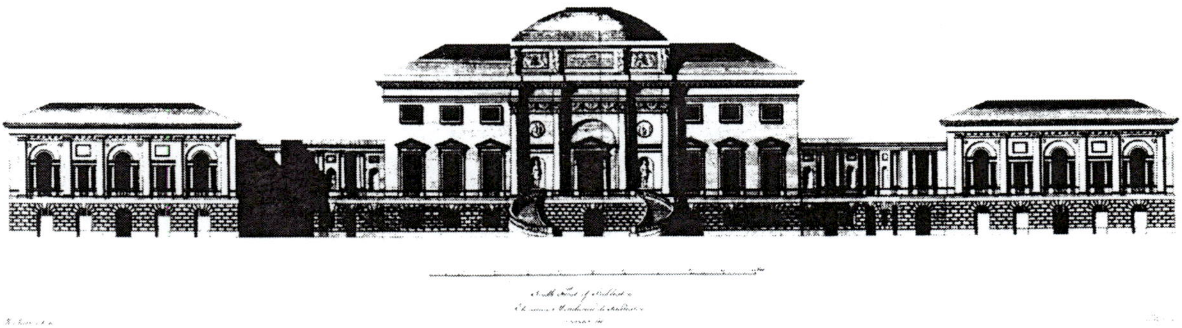

[26]
South front, Kedleston Hall, designed by Robert Adam, from John Woolfe and James Gandon, *Vitruvius britannicus*, 1767.

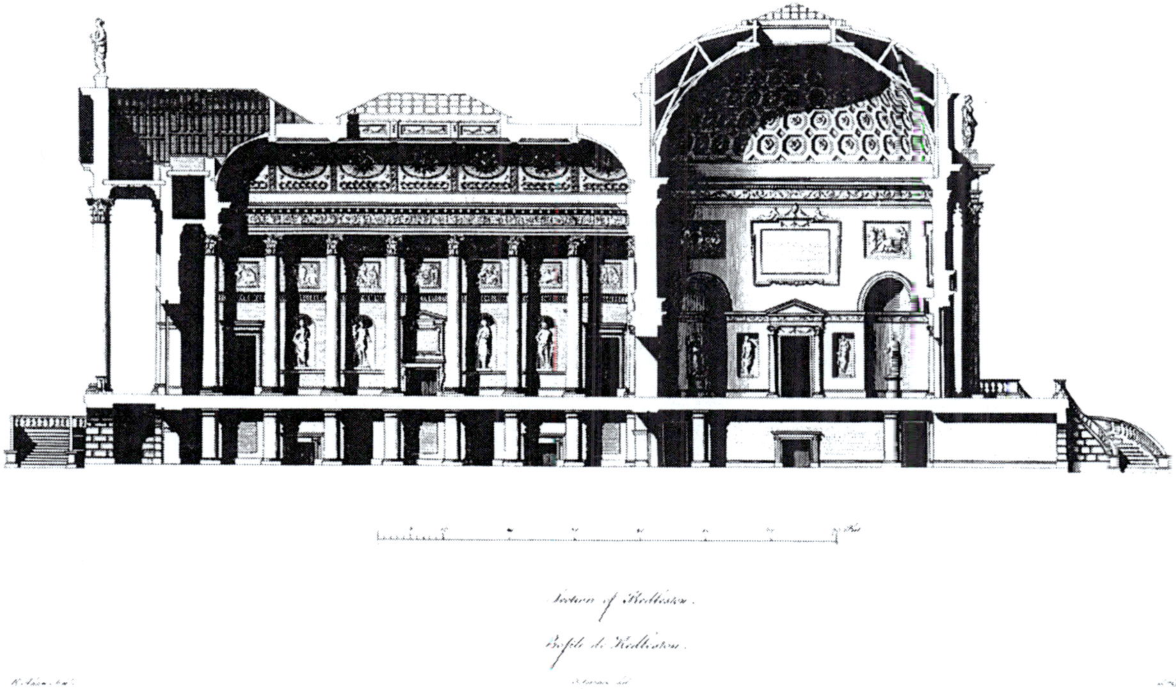

[27]
Section of Kedleston Hall, from John Woolfe and James Gandon, *Vitruvius britannicus*, 1767.

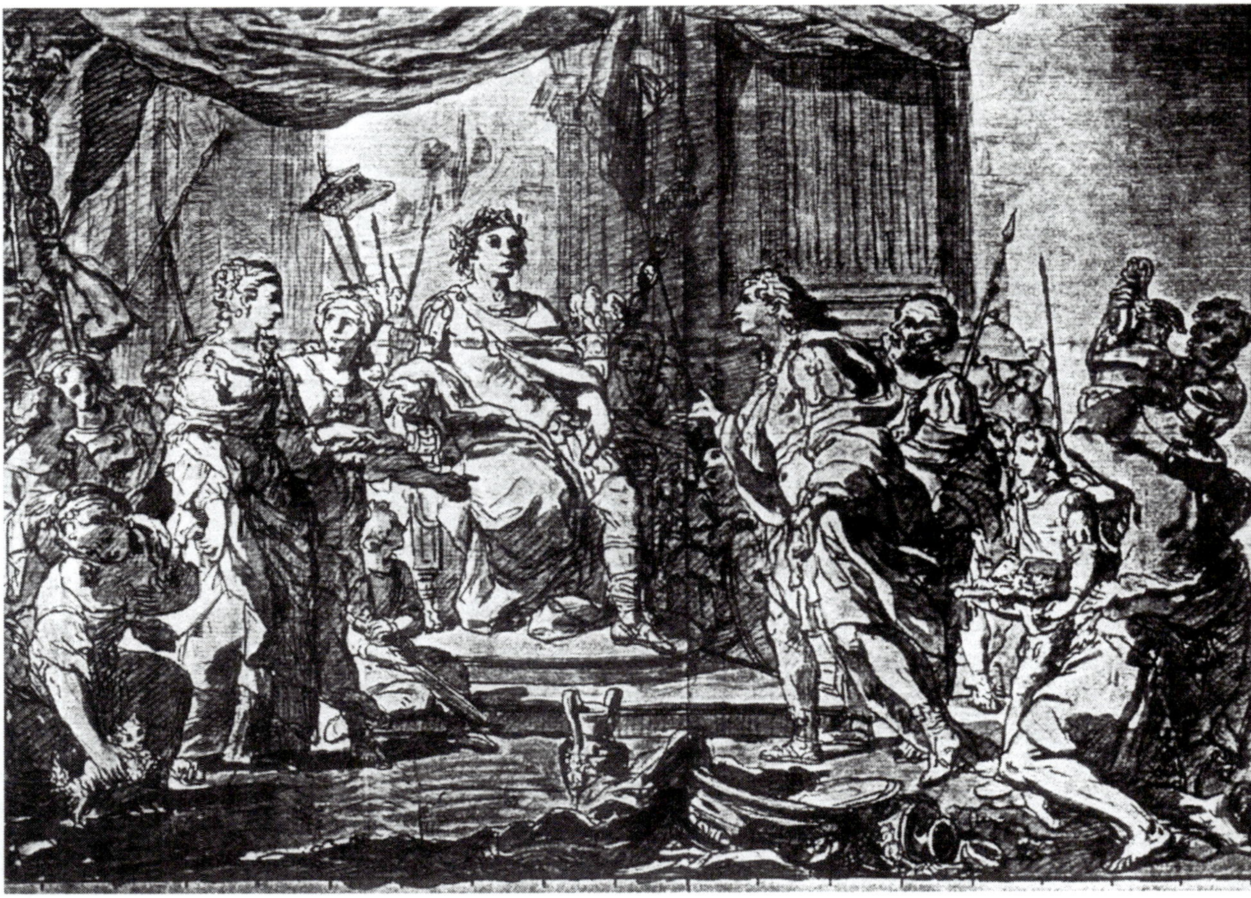

[28]
Drawing, attributed to William Kent, of
The Continence of Scipio by Giuseppe Chiari.

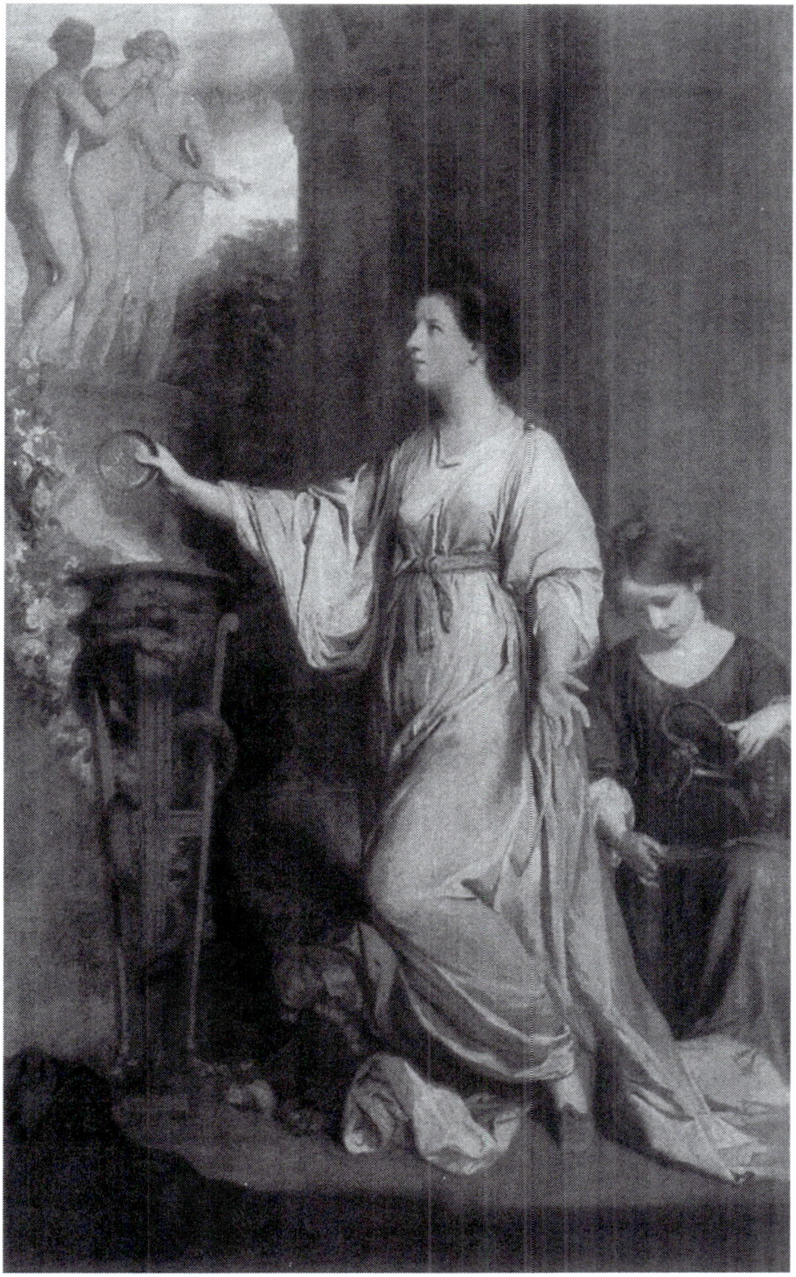

[29]
Lady Sarah Bunbury Sacrificing to the Graces, by Sir Joshua Reynolds.

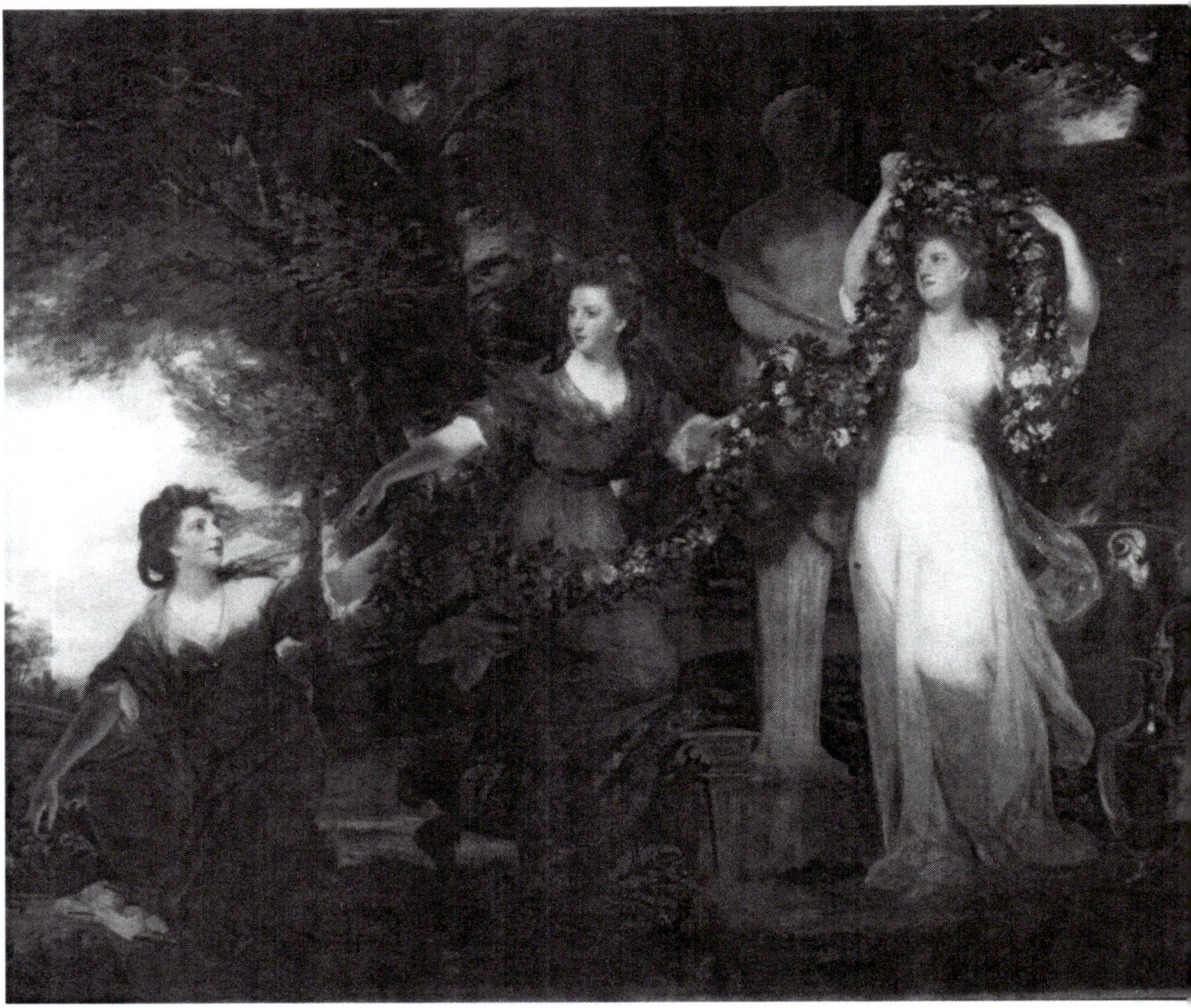

[30]
The Daughters of Sir William Montgomery as 'The Graces adorning a Term of Hymen', by Sir Joshua Reynolds.

4

Britannia Romana revived

ARCHITECTURE

It has been claimed that 'at least until the nineteenth century, there was no thoroughgoing attempt to re-create classical antiquity'.[1] This begs a question in regard both to 'thoroughgoing' and 're-creation'. Certainly the production of strictly neo-classical civic architecture in the nineteenth century vastly outdoes that of the preceding period. However, during the first half of the eighteenth century there were numerous projects which aimed consciously to recreate in early Georgian buildings the spirit of classical antiquity, and while neo-Palladianism is not on the whole a pure-classicist movement, it represents a nostalgic attempt to 'recollect' antiquity generally and specifically. In some instances it becomes pure classicism in its attempts to duplicate ancient buildings or parts of them.[2] The English neo-Palladians saw themselves working within the tradition of Vitruvius, and hence within the classical tradition. This chapter surveys a variety of attempts to re-create, mainly before the arrival of that stricter Roman- and (increasingly) Greek-based neo-classicism in the later eighteenth century,[3] what was perceived in England as 'the Roman world', especially in architecture and the display of sculpture. These attempts should be seen as realisations of the Shaftesburian project and as a conscious revival of that *Britannia romana* recorded and celebrated in the work of John Horsley and other practitioners of Romano-British archaeology, in which, as we have seen, the arbiters of taste were themselves heavily involved.

While Shaftesbury concerned himself with the inculcation of

'correctness' in all aspects of English cultural life, architecture was of particular importance. In a free nation, he argued, the state of architecture was of direct concern to 'People' (those with property and thus a tangible stake in the commonwealth), and above all to the architect as a citizen with 'a passionate Concern, and Interest' in liberty, the laws, government and property. When liberty prevails, 'Judgments are form'd; Criticks arise; the publick Eye and Ear improve; a right Taste prevails . . . Nothing is so improving, nothing so natural, so con-genial to the liberal Arts, as that reigning Liberty and high Spirit of a People.'[4] He hoped the nation would reject the baroque excesses represented by Christopher Wren's St Paul's, the crowning shame of the 'one single Court-Architect', which he thought full of 'Gothick' excrescences, and begin an age of simpler, purer forms based on a 'right Taste' by undertaking 'two of the noblest Subjects for Architecture', a new royal palace and a worthy building for Parliament.[5] These were to remain the frustrated ambitions of neo-Palladian architects, nothing coming of them until much later – and then the Parliament would be neo-Gothic. Nevertheless Shaftesbury's broad aesthetic ideal was to be quickly realised, the key moment being the appearance of the first volume of Colen Campbell's *Vitruvius britannicus* in 1715.[6]

This is generally and, on the whole, persuasively regarded as a Whig architectural manifesto. It is an interesting and complicating fact that Campbell's subscription list boasts, in addition to its numerous Whigs, the foremost Jacobites who within months would be leading, assisting in or apologising for the first rising – the Duke of Ormonde, the Earl of Mar, the Duke of Shrewsbury, the Earl of Nottingham and Sir William Wyndham among them.[7] It has been argued recently, though without very persuasive evidence, that Burlington himself was a Jacobite.[8] The buildings represented in the book, however, are overwhelmingly for Whig clients. Sir Christopher Wren is handsomely admitted into Campbell's pantheon at the front, where his St Paul's is followed by what it was thought to rival, St Peter's at Rome. Then come designs for a somewhat more restrainedly baroque church by Campbell himself, suggestive of how the vogue might be purified of excessive ornament. Vanbrugh at his most baroque is predictably included, Blenheim and Castle Howard being comprehensively illustrated.

With all its deference to Wren and Vanbrugh, however, Campbell's first volume is clearly the manifesto of a new movement which promptly set itself apart from them and all their works, and the main thrust of the campaign was undeniably Whig in inspiration. Campbell's chief deities are the very un-baroque Andrea Palladio and his seventeenth-century English disciple Inigo Jones.[9] Within a decade and a half of the appearance of this volume the neo-Palladians under the direction of Lord Burlington and his protégé William Kent had captured almost all the important positions in the King's Works and the patronage of the most influential elements in the oligarchy. Though the influence of Wren continued to be felt in the work of the later Vanbrugh, Nicholas Hawksmoor, James Gibbs and others, the dominant aesthetic from the 1720s to the mid-century was the Vitruvian–Palladian one. The Palladians' first victory in the state sphere was the appointment (short-term as it turned out) of William Benson to the office of Surveyor-General of the King's Works in 1718.[10] Benson and his friend Campbell (appointed Deputy-Surveyor and Chief Clerk) shared the credit of having 're-discovered' Palladio. Other important early Palladians were Giacomo Leoni and Nicholas Dubois. After 1725 a second wave entered the Works, led by William Kent, who came in as Master Carpenter in that year, quickly followed by another close disciple of Burlington's, Henry Flitcroft, by Roger Morris, Isaac Ware and later John Vardy. Blessing the professional circle from above were Burlington and the 9th Earl of Pembroke, very much practitioners though 'amateur' in the old sense, often working in close association with their protégés; the Palladian Bridge at Wilton, for instance, was the combined work of Pembroke and Morris. Others, like John Wood the Elder at Bath, concentrated on the provinces. In the work of James Paine and Sir Robert Taylor, English Palladianism remained a force right through the 1760s and 1770s alongside the work of Robert Adam and the neo-classicists, so that when these were just beginning their work, John Woolfe and James Gandon could say in their 1767 continuation of *Vitruvius britannicus* that an antique correctness had already been extensively achieved in England and elevated that nation above the rest of Europe:

> The many elegant and sumptuous buildings already recently erected, and still erecting throughout Great Britain, have furnished us with an opportunity of convincing the world and posterity, that architecture was brought to as great a point of perfection in this kingdom in the eighteenth century, as ever it was known to be among the Greeks and Romans; and that if we were not inferior to the ancients in this respect, we far surpassed our contemporaries of every other country.[11]

Though by 1730 Palladianism had effectively captured the King's Works, most of the school's important projects were private, for by the 1730s the King's Works were a shadow of their former self. It was still logical for Shaftesbury in 1711 to imagine that a 'correct' architectural taste based on classical models would be set first and foremost by the monarch and his government in the form of Houses of Parliament and royal palaces, and overseen by the King's Works. Under the Hanoverians, however, the Works suffered a dramatic, in some ways scandalous, decline from the status they had enjoyed under the Surveyorships of Inigo Jones and Christopher Wren.[12]

In 1702 Vanbrugh had succeeded to the Comptrollership of the Works. This was a political appointment which modern authorities see as the beginning of a *malaise* which within a few years reduced the Works to insignificance in comparison with what they had been.[13] Thus, although by 1730 most of the relevant positions in the Works were held by Palladians, not all of them to Burlington's and Kent's liking, the chances of a Burlington or a Kent being commissioned to design flagship projects like those Shaftesbury envisaged were increasingly slim.[14] This fact is crucial in understanding the tone of the conclusion of Pope's *Epistle to Burlington* (1731), which is far more complex than generally recognised.[15] Pope advances a set of state programmes for which the existing Works are absurdly inadequate, a programme of 'Imperial Works' requiring nothing less than Burlington's direction of a resurrected King's Works akin to what they had been under Inigo Jones and Christopher Wren, or (even better) like the Augustan Works under Marcus Pollio Vitruvius:

> You too proceed! make falling Arts your care,
> Erect new wonders, and the old repair,

Jones and Palladio to themselves restore,
And be whate'er Vitruvius was before:
Till Kings call forth th'Idea's of your mind,
Proud to accomplish what such hands design'd,
Bid Harbors open, public Ways extend,
Bid Temples, worthier of the God, ascend;
Bid the broad Arch the dang'rous Flood contain,
The Mole projected break the roaring Main;
Back to his bounds their subject Sea command,
And roll obedient Rivers thro' the Land;
These Honours, Peace to happy Britain brings,
These are Imperial Works, and worthy Kings.[16]

This passage, its opening and closing lines echoing Horace and Virgil,[17] subtly but deliberately identifies the future Britain with Augustan Rome. All of these works Pope sees as appropriate to a truly Vitruvian surveyorship, which should be filled by Burlington himself (or perhaps by Kent, with Burlington pulling the strings).[18] The phrase 'be whate'er Vitruvius was before' is terminated in all the authoritative editions by a colon, indicating that in the remainder of the verse-paragraph Pope will define exactly what Vitruvius 'was' as well as what Burlington should 'be'. The extent of the parallels here has gone unrecognised. In embracing a wider range of activities than architecture, Burlington's office would be just like the surveyorship of Vitruvius, who also controlled the plumbing of Augustan Rome, for example, and devoted his attention to harbour construction, storm protection and flood control,[19] all three mentioned by Pope as appropriate concerns for his patron. A programme of this kind for Britain, properly supervised by Burlington, must have seemed especially appropriate in the 1730s. Not only was the general cultural atmosphere obviously ready for it, but Burlington had proved his Vitruvian credentials in his own work as architect; according to Francis Drake, as we have seen in the last chapter, Burlington was 'that truly *English* VITRUVIUS'.[20]

This architect's Vitruvian associations, the way in which they are mediated by the *Epistle*, and the associated question of the domestication of Vitruvius in England at this time, are matters which have been largely ignored and deserve to be noticed in the present context. Burlington's close association with Palladio (who had gone to Vitruvius for his first principles) is reiterated in all discussions of the poem, but there has been insufficient attention given to Burlington's and Pope's direct knowledge of Vitruvius, and none at all to the way in which a familiarity with the opening section of Vitruvius' *De architectura*, taken for granted by Pope, elucidates the concluding passage of the *Epistle to Burlington*.[21] The passage Pope had principally in mind, Vitruvius' preface to book I, was addressed to Octavian some time after the Battle of Actium (31 BC) but before his assumption of the title 'Augustus' (27 BC). Vitruvius held an office under Octavian/Augustus in the latter's rebuilding of Rome (it was among Augustus' proudest boasts that he had found Rome built of brick and left it built of marble). This office is rendered in translation by the Loeb editor as the 'surveyorship'. The specific analogies informing the close of Pope's *Epistle* are Augustus/George II (ironic at the expense of the latter, who was christened Augustus, a fact of which Pope makes ironic play in his 1737 imitation of Horace's *Epistle to Augustus*), the Augustan Works/the Royal Works (ironic at the expense of the latter), and Vitruvius/Burlington (non-ironic). All three paragraphs of Vitruvius' preface are relevant to the *Epistle*. They tell us, in Pope's words, 'what Vitruvius was before', what Burlington should 'be', and inform us regarding the public 'works' of Augustus, 'Imperial Works', of a kind which a right-minded English king may, in future, choose to 'call forth' through Burlington. In glaring contrast to the great programme of state-directed public works undertaken by Augustus during the surveyorship of Vitruvius stood the programme of the Royal Works of Britain when Pope was writing – anything but 'Imperial Works, and worthy Kings'.

That Burlington was as thoroughly familiar with the *De architectura* as he was with Palladio's *Quattro libri dell'architettura* (1570), of which he possessed multiple copies, is not open to doubt. During his 1719 journey to Italy, at the Villa Maser near Asolo, he had purchased a large number of Palladio's drawings (which he published in 1730[22]) from the direct descendant of Palladio's friend and patron Daniele Barbaro. Barbaro's translation of Vitruvius into Italian had first appeared in 1556, complete with his own outstanding commentary, and illustrations by Palladio – Burlington had multiple copies at Chiswick.[23] Through his friendship with Barbaro's family, Burlington's link with Vitruvius was almost personal.

When Pope wrote the *Epistle*, however, it was to England, not to Italy, that one went for the closest of all links to the Augustan master, thanks to an event seven years previous to the poem. On 6 August 1724 Humphrey Wanley, librarian to Edward Harley, 2nd Earl of Oxford, had noted in his diary that

> This morning I recd a Letter from Mr Mattaire, dated yesterday: concerning Sigr Zamboni's MSS. and his last Price for the whole Parcel he being unwilling to separate them. Which Letter being produced to my Lord, he gave me the sum demanded: with which I went immediatly to Mr Mattaire, who brought to me (tarrying at a place appointed) the said Parcel, which I have now brought into this Library; to which, some of them will be always Ornaments. They are . . .
>
> 12. Vitruvius. fol. min. Exemplar fere 800 annorum.[24]

Lord Oxford had purchased what the British Museum would catalogue several decades later as Harleian MS. 2767, not only the earliest but the best manuscript of the *De architectura*, almost certainly dating from the eighth century, before the establishment of the Carolingian miniscule.[25] As Wanley appreciated from the beginning, it was one of the great ornaments of the Harleian Library. It would be remarkable had Pope not been familiar with it – if he had not examined it under the supervision of Wanley, who was fond of showing the treasures in his care – for as their voluminous correspondence attests, Pope was an intimate friend of Oxford's (perhaps, in the 1720s, the closest of all),[26] and a frequent visitor to Wimpole and its Library, of which he made the freest use. He turned up whenever he liked, announced or unannounced, knowing he was welcome to stay as long as he pleased.

Burlington was also a (less intimate) friend of Oxford's. The latter, however, whose collection of books on architecture was at least as immense as Burlington's and even more significant, was critical of Burlington's style of architecture, preferring Wren. The interests he shared with Burlington, rather than bringing them closer, created a form of rivalry. They were political opposites, and the Tory Oxford identified Burlington's Palladian programme with Whig politics. Perhaps a non-political factor that 'qualified' Oxford to be critical was his proud possession not only of the earliest and best but of two other manuscripts of Vitruvius' *De architectura* – Harleian MSS. 3859 (eleventh century) and 2760 (fifteenth century), both deriving ultimately from 2767. Oxford could identify himself (far more directly than could Burlington) with the fountainhead via these, and particularly MS. 2767. Burlington had to rest content with just one (relatively late) manuscript of the *De architectura*, early printed editions of Vitruvius including the Ioconda edition of 1511, and three copies of the first edition (as well as numerous other editions) of Vitruvius' disciple Palladio. Through the efforts of Burlington and his circle Britain may have become the inheritor of the Palladian–Vitruvian tradition, but thanks to Oxford's wealth, Britain (in the shape of the Library at Wimpole) had become the home of the 'word' in its earliest and purest form – if one likes, of Vitruvius himself.

It was the York Assembly Rooms, building as Pope wrote the *Epistle*, which most clearly established Burlington's claim to be a Vitruvian architect in the *public*, not merely the private, domain. The Vitruvian venture at York prepared him for what his supporters saw as his rightful work in the other great Romano-British city, London – the Houses of Parliament. A century earlier Inigo Jones had drawn up magnificent plans for this project, but civil war had intervened. James Ralph's *A Critical Review of the Publick Buildings . . . in, and about London and Westminster* (1734), dedicated to Burlington, is a faintly disguised in-camp promotion of Burlington as the man to lead a renaissance of public architectural works in London, beginning with the Parliament. In his dedication Ralph tells Burlington that the critical analysis the book contains is merely an application of those 'rules in theory, which you reduce into practice'. Ralph is particularly interested in public buildings and compares contemporary England unfavourably in this respect with Italy and France: ''Tis high time therefore for us to look about us too, and endeavour to vie with our neighbours in politeness, as well as power and empire.' He looks back nostalgically to the surveyorship of Jones, when

'There was not any excellency that we might not have hoped to attain.'[27] Civil war, however, led to 'all darkness and obscurity', which endured until the time of Wren. Ralph has high praise for aspects of his St Paul's, but voices major criticisms too (for instance, 'the form of a cross is more favourable to superstition than beauty', the dome is out of proportion to the whole, etc.).[28] He would have had an ally in Shaftesbury in thinking it fortunate that Wren had not been allowed to make of a new Parliament the 'gothick' disaster he had made of the cathedral. Ralph nominates a new building for Parliament as the first priority of a concerted programme of public works, identifying Burlington as the obvious architect:

> if it falls into the noble hands to execute, we have long been flatter'd to believe it would, there is no room to doubt but the grandeur of this appearance will answer the majestick purposes 'tis to be employ'd in. The *British* taste in architecture, is, to be sure, more obliged to that *Nobleman*, than any other person now living, and if *Inigo Jones* has any advantage, 'tis only in having lived before him.[29]

It was not to be, however, and Pope's concluding lines to the *Epistle* suggest that both Pope and Burlington knew it. As Battestin has observed,[30] the passage is implicitly critical of George II. One might add that Pope's criticism is informed by his awareness of the derelict state of the King's Works, the implied contrast in public-spiritedness between Augustus and George II (thus the generalised 'Kings' in the line 'Till Kings call forth th'Idea's of your mind'), and the likelihood, things being as they are, that the 'truly *English* VITRUVIUS' will have to wait a long time to reach his fulfilment in the public domain ('Till Kings' suggests a reign or two at least). Accordingly, any triumphalism in the poem's conclusion is wry and wistful, shot through with ironies and the knowledge that the new *Britannia romana* is not coming into being by the grace of George II. The poem's critical and satirical edge runs to the very end.

It would be the oligarchy who would make the new Roman Britain, with private money. This was also appropriate politically, for they constituted the real power in the land. Networks of patronage and influence sped the process. To take one instance, in regard to the important classical-nostalgic project at Stourhead it is not happenstance that the owner,

Henry Hoare, nephew of the neo-Palladian pioneer William Benson, used another more famous neo-Palladian pioneer, Colen Campbell, as his architect, that he was Burlington's banker, that he consistently patronised Rysbrack (Burlington's favourite sculptor) and the Burlingtonian Flitcroft, and that he quoted Burlington's close friend Pope in stone in his Grotto. The result, inside and out, was that Stourhead was 'correct' in every detail. A good measure of correctness could be attained without all these connections-within-connections, however, simply by following the precisely conceived Palladian theories and prescriptions of Robert Morris as set out in his *Essay in Defence of Ancient Architecture* (1728), his *Lectures on Architecture, Consisting of Rules Founded upon Harmonick and Arithmetical Proportion in Building* (1734–6) and his book of drawings for villas, *Rural Architecture, Consisting of Regular Designs of Plans and Elevations for Buildings in the Country* (1750). Morris based his designs on precise harmonic and mathematical proportions which he believed affected the mind via the eye in the same way that music did through the ear. In this, as Battestin has shown, he was at the end of a Pythagorean tradition of architectural theory running back through René Ouvrard and François Blondel to Palladio and Alberti and finally to Vitruvius himself.[31] The literal-minded emphasis on harmony, together with his adherence to the three virtues of convenience, proportion and regularity,[32] had the result that Morris's drawings, while exquisite to look at, never surprise. His books lent a certain theoretical respectability to cut-rate Palladianism based on pattern-books which William Halfpenny and others had been producing since the early 1720s, by means of which the merely rich and the nearly rich could aspire to live as 'correctly' as the noble and the great. Pope noted the consequences of this tendency in 1731, when it was already ten years old, in the *Epistle to Burlington*: the emulation of Palladio and, behind him, of ancient Rome becomes piecemeal and absurd:

> You show us, Rome was glorious, not profuse,
> And pompous buildings once were things of Use.
> Yet shall (my Lord) your just, your noble rules
> Fill half the land with Imitating Fools;

Who random drawings from your sheets shall take,
And of one beauty many blunders make;
Load some vain Church with old Theatric state,
Turn Arcs of triumph to a Garden-gate;
Reverse your Ornaments, and hang them all
On some patch'd dog-hole ek'd with ends of wall,
Then clap four slices of Pilaster on't,
That, lac'd with bits of rustic, makes a Front;
Or call the winds thro' long Arcades to roar,
Proud to catch cold at a Venetian door;
Conscious they act a true Palladian part,
And, if they starve, they starve by rules of art.[33]

As Pope indicates here, Palladianism and the re-creation of the ancient Roman world were understood to go together in Burlington's practice. The same point is made implicitly by Campbell in the second volume of his *Vitruvius britannicus* (1717). Campbell included in this collection four views of a 'New Design of my Invention for a Church in the Vitruvian Stile' (plate 21).[34] This was a proposal for the reconstruction in Britain of a modified form of the best-preserved of all ancient Roman temples, the Maison Carrée at Nîmes, which had been constructed during the reign of Augustus and dedicated to the *principes iuventutis*, Gaius and Lucius Caesar, some time between 12 BC and AD 2. Campbell's church would have been Ionic rather than Corinthian, larger in all of its dimensions than the Maison Carrée, its width proportionally greater in relation to its height, and with a Venetian window in the east end, but at first glance the similarity between the two is striking. On the pediment, in relief, angels observe St John baptising Christ in the Jordan as the Holy Spirit descends. This proposal probably represents Campbell's ideal for British church architecture, Vitruvian temples lightly Christianised.[35] Dissenters would later favour neo-classical styles, but nothing so uncompromising as this would be attempted. Its historic importance is that it represents an ideal classicism waiting to be attempted and points the way for Burlington and Kent, who would soon be designing 'Vitruvian' edifices and supervising their construction at Chiswick, at York (where Burlington's Assembly

Rooms, it has been justly claimed, 'constitute the central shrine of classicism in Europe'[36]), at Stowe and elsewhere.

Such edifices, in their convincing concreteness, must have immensely enhanced their owners' and visitors' affinities with the virtuous Romans they claimed to emulate in the civic world. The type of domestic building best guaranteed to do this was the neo-Palladian villa. During the period 1720–40 the compact villa gradually supersedes the large country house, and its development is closely associated with the development of English Palladianism.[37] The word 'villa', however, was not in common use before around 1730.[38] In the appropriate country house, surrounded by gardens in which art complemented nature in the ways recommended by Shaftesbury, Addison and Pope, one might almost be Pliny away from the cares of Rome at Laurentinum or in Tuscany.[39] Although the typical English country house through to the mid-century would come via Campbell or Burlington from Palladio, it frequently contained features which were thought to come directly from Roman houses. Giles Worsley has identified at least five attempts by neo-Palladians from the 1720s to the 1760s 'to recreate a Roman house'. They were 'inspired by their love of the Antique to design buildings that were not merely influenced by Classical architecture but could have been mistaken (or so they believed) for buildings erected by the Romans', such houses clearly illustrating 'the importance of pure neo-Classicism in neo-Palladianism'.[40] These projects were based on descriptions in Pliny and Vitruvius reinforced by the authority of Palladio, Scamozzi, and Robert Castell's *Villas of the Ancients* (1728).[41]

Of these houses the most important, Holkham Hall in Norfolk, dates from 1734, probably the joint product of Burlington and its owner Thomas Coke, Earl of Leicester, assisted by Kent and Matthew Brettingham.[42] The chief source for its hall, properly to be understood as a Roman atrium, is not (as Wittkower claimed) Burlington's Vitruvian 'Egyptian' Hall in the Assembly Rooms at York but Barbaro's interpretation of Vitruvius' description of a Roman house.[43] The hall's heating was not by fireplaces but underfloor, inspired by the Roman hypocaust, like the central heating at West Wycombe Park in Buckinghamshire, which was modelled on an actual Roman hypocaust discovered near Lincoln.[44]

Holkham's Roman features were its most celebrated aspect in the eighteenth century and these were proudly detailed in Matthew Brettingham's *Plans, Elevations, and Sections of Holkham in Norfolk* (1761). Leicester specified brick for the construction because Vitruvius had recommended this for villas – the dimensions of the bricks used were determined by those of a real Roman brick – and his adoption of the split pediment at Holkham was based on Palladio's claim that this had been a feature of Roman domestic architecture.[45] The gardens are probably based on Pliny's descriptions by way of Castell's interpretation of these. Other 'Roman' houses include Rokeby Park in Yorkshire, built in the late 1720s and early 1730s,[46] the work of its owner, the amateur Palladian Sir Thomas Robinson, and Hovingham Hall in Yorkshire, rebuilt from 1751 to his own designs by its owner Thomas Worsley, and perhaps inspired by the discovery of the remains of a Roman villa on the site.[47]

Even if the modern British villa were not deliberately Roman in form, objects within or around it could provide the requisite associations with the Roman world. Sir John Clerk of Penicuik was so confidently and spiritually Roman that the physical properties of his country houses were probably less important.[48] Penicuik, eight miles from Edinburgh, was the old family seat while Mavisbank, which Clerk built four miles closer to town, was 'in a true palladio tast' as Roger Gale observed, calling it (as Clerk did) a villa and observing of it that 'You would there think yourself rather in a valley near Tivoli than Edenborough'.[49] Clerk explored the literary sources for the Roman villa and and gave application to the idea before Castell ever turned his thoughts to it. Clerk was using the word in reference to one of his houses as early as 1710. He modelled Mavisbank on the Plinian villa, inscribed the word in stone on the east front of the house in 1724, used it as a Roman would have used his, and always referred to it as his villa, pioneering the contemporary use of the term. His views on architecture and gardening were set out in his long, unpublished poem, 'The Country Seat' (*c.* 1727). Influenced by the concept of the *ferme ornée* as developed in Stephen Switzer's three-volume *Ichnographia rustica* (1718),[50] as well as by Bridgeman and Castell, a copy of whose *Villas of the Ancients* he owned, his gardens reinforced the other antique associations of his life at Penicuik and Mavisbank. At Penicuik he developed a grotto and tunnel with strong and precise Virgilian associations.[51]

James Thomson is already using 'villa' for 'country house' in 'Summer' (1727), l. 1454, suggesting that the word had quickly caught on in Scotch philoroman circles. As we have seen, Thomson's philoromanism turned about the ideas of liberty and civic virtue and thus had a programmatic aspect to it. In the 'Britannia' sequence in 'Summer', classic Italy is reborn in modern Britain. Burlington's villa at Chiswick, not yet finished when the poem appeared, is joined by a myriad like itself:

> On every hand,
> Thy Villas shine. Thy Country teems with Wealth;
> And Property assures it to the Swain,
> Pleas'd, and unweary'd, in his guarded Toil.[52]

It is Liberty who is addressed here, and it is important to note that the 'villas' are hers. The connections which this poem makes between Roman and British liberty, property and architecture have not been appreciated. Thomson emphasises here that the guarantors of the people's wealth, as of the people's liberty, are the propertied who are building the new Britannia. This reinforces what he has spelled out a few lines earlier – that the nation's riches, cultural as well as material, are the product of the liberty which this class has won:

> Happy BRITANNIA! where the QUEEN OF ARTS,
> Inspiring Vigor, LIBERTY abroad
> Walks, unconfin'd, even to thy farthest Cotts,
> And scatters Plenty with unsparing Hand.[53]

Thus the villas which 'shine' 'on every hand' are the logical expression of the class which constructs and occupies them, the properly Roman retreats (hence 'villas') of men imbued with Roman civic consciousness. We should note that the subscribers to the *Seasons* included Burlington (five books), Sir John Clerk (three books), Charles Bridgeman and Alexander Pope (three books), among a host of significant taste-formers, and the work accurately reflects their aesthetic and civic values.

If Clerk in Scotland pioneered the idea of the 'Roman' villa for Britain, the English, as Thomson foresaw, were not far behind. When

Burlington, following on a smaller scale the example of Colen Campbell, who had just designed Mereworth (*c.* 1722–5) for John Fane, adapted the design of Palladio's Villa Rotunda for his villa at Chiswick from around 1725, he enhanced the building's classical affinities by replicating in his portico the capitals of the Temple of Castor and Pollux as illustrated by Palladio, while in the gardens he kept close to the spirit of antiquity as graphically illustrated in Robert Castell's conjectural recreation of Pliny's gardens,[54] though there were debts to modern Italy too.[55] We have already noticed in the previous chapter Burlington's pioneering replication of a Roman temple in the small circular temple he had erected at Chiswick some time before 1727. The incorporation of carefully considered and archaeologically correct Roman elements in English houses and gardens is commonplace from the 1720s. Marble Hill, another villa in Twickenham, by Pembroke and Roger Morris, and largely completed when Burlington was beginning work on Chiswick, contained a hall based on Vitruvius' description of a Roman atrium as interpreted by Palladio.[56] In the hall (or more properly the atrium) at Holkham, Leicester and Burlington took the fluted Ionic columns for the screen, the entablature moulds and the important elements of the frieze from the Temple of Fortuna Virilis as illustrated in Desgodetz's *Les edifices antiques de Rome* (1682), and the recessed coffered panels from the dome of the Pantheon, again via Desgodetz. The same authority supplied the octagonal panels of rosettes in the saloon's ceiling coves (from the Temple of Peace) and the griffins on the frieze of the drawing-room (from the Temple of Antoninus and Faustina).[57]

Piecemeal though these borrowings often were, they lent a convincing *auctoritas* to the structures to which they were attached. Undoubtedly the grandest example of a Roman element borrowed for incorporation into an English country house in the eighteenth century is the Arch of Constantine as grafted by Robert Adam onto the south front of Lord Scarsdale's Kedleston Hall in Derbyshire around 1761 (plate 26). Wittily, this leads directly into a miniature of the Pantheon (plate 27). A similar idea on an absurdly smaller scale was the reduction of the Arch of Severus to a sideboard screen at Raynham Hall. There is an even grander example than Kedleston's in civic architecture, John Wood I's Circus at Bath, begun in 1754, 'a miniature Colosseum turned inside out'.[58] Wood's original plans for Bath, drawn up in 1725–6, would have gone much further in restoring the city to the ancient Roman character it once possessed as Aquae Sulis. He intended to provide an extensive 'Royal Forum' and an 'Imperial Gymnasium', for example.[59]

If such examples are exceptional in their boldness of conception, they typify the prevailing tendency to recollect Roman antiquity in early Georgian buildings, their contents and their gardens. This tendency is both a reflection of the rule of taste and a quest to make tangible that political and class affinity with the Roman oligarchy explored in previous chapters. Above all it expresses the self-validating identification of this class with antique civic values, something reflected repeatedly in Pope's Shaftesburian view of the function of a national architecture, already evident in *Windsor Forest* (1713) and still strong in 1731 when, in the *Epistle to Burlington*, he evoked what he hoped would be Burlington's national destiny.[60] He introduced into his own gardens at Twickenham the classical principles of landscape design he had lauded as early as 1713,[61] and which he found laid out not only in Virgil and Pliny but in Homer, particularly in the Garden of Alcinous, with which the garden at Twickenham had much in common, including diminutiveness.[62] Just as he assimilated Homer by making him speak correct English verse, Pope assimilated the antique world into Twickenham itself, classicising his garden and his house.[63] Busts of Inigo Jones and Palladio presided over the library. Even trees could be turned to antique effect. He takes the common association of groves of poplars with Gothic cathedrals and classicises it: 'I have sometimes had an idea of planting an old Gothic cathedral, or rather some old Roman temple, in trees. Good large poplars, with their white stems, cleared of boughs to a proper height, would serve very well for the columns, and might form the different aisles, or peristiliums, by their different distances and heights. These would look very well near, and the dome, rising all in proper tuft in the middle, would look as well at a distance.'[64]

Garden temples provided the most ready way to replicate or recollect Roman antiquity. Stowe's temples of Ancient Virtue and of Concord and Victory have already been noticed. Like these, many other examples at least approximated to classical Roman originals, and were themselves, in several cases, copied all over England.[65] At Stourhead, Flitcroft's Pantheon (1752–6) was a scaled-down version of the original and his Temple of the Sun (*c.* 1765) was taken from the Roman Round Temple of Venus at Baalbek, which also provided the model for Sir William Chambers's Temple of the Sun at Kew (1761).[66] These exemplify the demand for new Roman models resulting from the extension of archaeological inquiry ever further to the east. As noted earlier, the main body of Hawksmoor's Mausoleum (begun 1728) at Castle Howard was inspired by the Tomb of Caecilia Metella on the Via Appia.[67] Though not properly a temple, the Mausoleum inspired garden temples of similar if reduced form. At Studley Royal the Temple of Piety, central to the moon ponds which John Aislabie developed in the 1720s, was indebted to Labacco's paper reconstruction of the Temple of Jupiter.[68] At Chiswick, as we have seen, there was Burlington's small Pantheon-like temple (before 1727), which he modelled on the Roman temple near San Sebastian on the Via Appia as this had been represented by Palladio. At Bramham Park the round temple or Rotunda (*c.* 1750) was perhaps derived from one of the two temples of Vesta illustrated by Palladio, or from Kent's Temple of Ancient Virtue at Stowe. Duncombe Park's Tuscan and Doric temples (*c.* 1730) were probably adaptations of the two Corinthian temples of Vesta just mentioned, one with a raised and one with an unraised pavement as at Duncombe,[69] while Duncombe's Ionic temple (1758) is reminiscent of the Ionic Temple of Fortuna Virilis in the Forum Boarium at Rome, but called the 'Maison Carrée' despite the latter's being Corinthian and all the other obvious differences.

In addition to their Roman temples, English gardens through this period became home to triumphal arches based, loosely in most cases, on Roman originals. Ambrose Phillipps's arch at Garendon in Leicestershire has been noticed in the previous chapter. Others include Thomas Pitt's Corinthian arch for Stowe (1765–6)[70] and Sir William Chambers's arch at Wilton (*c.* 1759), reminiscent of the Arch of the Sergii at Pula and topped by a replica of the Marcus Aurelius statue.[71]

These structures, and hundreds of others less specifically indebted to their classical originals, lent impressive substance to that nostalgic association with Roman antiquity evident in so much English art and literature of the period and so important in the gardening programmes at Chiswick, Wilton, Stowe, Stourhead, Castle Howard, Claremont, Bramham Park, Rousham and many others. Though after the mid-century new archaeological excursions prompted a developing vogue in the replication of Greek originals, they also expanded the known canon of Roman architecture, and in England the cultural associations with ancient Rome were strong enough to ensure a continuing Roman element in civic, domestic and garden architecture in the work of Sir William Chambers, Robert Adam, Sir John Soane and others.[72] Indeed, it was not until the 1790s that Greek forms became a really strong force in the architecture of Britain.

COLLECTIONS

In their concerted attempt to make the ancient world reappear in their midst in the form of antique objects, the English had been anticipated to some extent at Fontainebleau by Francis I, and far more comprehensively by Louis XIV at Versailles. The former commissioned the copying in bronze of famous antique statues, causing Vasari to remark that Fontainebleau had become 'almost a new Rome' in consequence. Louis was more interested in the creation of his own distinct baroque classicism than in collecting and copying the past, but Francis's example was later followed by Napoleon, who preferred originals to copies, however, and had the means to steal them.[73] On the other hand in England, as we have seen, the reduplication of the classical past developed as a complement to the nation's newly won political liberties under which, it was believed, a 'correct' taste based on antique values of proportion and harmony should naturally flourish precisely as it had in Greece and Rome for as long as those states remained free.[74] All the arts were involved, from architecture and sculpture to the 'correct' poetry that Pope, following the advice of the critic William Walsh, saw himself pioneering in English.[75] The reduplication of antiquity by way of collecting antiques, though it was underway for decades before the Revolution, naturally came to be associated after 1688 with the cultural programme of the oligarchy.

For the virtuoso and the young gentleman seriously interested in what his tutor had to show him on the grand tour, the greatest attraction Italy had to offer was the sensation of living in the capital of the antique Roman world, face to face with the classical architecture and private collections of famous works of sculpture one had only read about or seen in illustrations, and with the great works of the Italian Renaissance one had been taught to revere too. Ancient Roman busts were particularly dramatic because they brought the persons of the past into the present. John Northall, who toured Italy in 1752, observed that when one is physically confronted by 'emperors, consuls, generals, orators, philosophers, poets, and other great men, whose fame in history engaged our earliest notice, standing as it were in their own persons before us', one is given 'a cast of almost 2000 years backwards' and the past becomes present.[76]

Yet in respect at least to this category of sculpture one might save the cost of the Italian tour and go instead to Wilton. There 'Carvilius Magnus', 8th Earl of Pembroke, had brought the ancient world to him, peopling his house and gardens with eminent Greeks and especially Romans in the form of the busts and statues that were regarded as the largest if not the best collection of ancient marbles in Europe.[77] In fact many were mediocre and a number later turned out to be modern fakes.[78] The core consisted of 133 busts, but there were also 36 statues, 15 bas-reliefs, and nine 'miscellaneous' in the collection Stukeley set about cataloguing in the early 1720s.[79] Much of it derived from the great collection of Thomas Howard, 2nd Earl of Arundel, who began to import large numbers of antiquities in the second and third decades of the seventeenth century, and who, with Sir Kenelm Digby and Charles I, was one of the first English virtuosi.[80] Their collections encouraged Sir Francis Kynaston to establish his Musaeum Minervae in the 1630s as an academy for the nobility and gentry with a curriculum that included antiquities and numismatics, and though this never became properly established, by the late 1630s it was possible for connoisseurs to enjoy, without going to Italy, the thrill of direct contact with classical civilisation that good collections of antique marbles, coins and medals provide.[81]

The busts at Wilton had all been 'identified' and naturally included the greatest philosophers, poets and dramatists of Greece. The majority, however, were declared to be famous Romans and most of these purported to be political figures.[82] Here there was no prejudice in favour of the Roman Republic – not because authentic republican busts and statues are notoriously rarer than their imperial counterparts (after all, one might declare a bust to be anyone it conceivably resembled), but because powerful emperors, even bad ones, have a cachet all their own, their presence undeniably flattering to owners like Pembroke and Walpole. To take just the first two-and-a-half centuries of Caesars, all were domiciled at Wilton.[83] Their wives and mistresses were in attendance too (the licentious Poppaea's bust 'naked', naturally), as were the second-rank leaders like Drusus and Germanicus. Republican heroes, mostly of eminent civic virtue, included the two Bruti, Scipio Africanus, Cato the Elder, Scipio Nasica, Marius, Sulpicius Rufus, Dolabella, Cicero, Pompeius Magnus and Sextus Pompeius. Augustan literature was represented by a Livy and a bust claiming to be Horace, though Stukeley was not so sure – 'I am inclined to believe it Ovid', he demurred.[84] The effect of this vast collection was that 'Wilton is become tramontane Italy.'[85] As Stukeley pointed out, one was in 'tramontane Italy' even before arriving at Wilton. Along the roads running to it Pembroke had 'revived the Roman method of placing a numbered stone at every mile, and the living index of a tree to make it more observable; which ought to be recommended as a laudable pattern to others: thus C. Gracchus planted a stone at every mile, with the distance inscribed, says Plutarch'.[86] Stukeley's *Itinerarium curiosum* is archaeological in focus but logically devotes considerable space to Wilton and other seats whose interiors and gardens were rich in classical objects which revived the past through association because, like his fellow archaeologists, it was not just excavation and preservation that Stukeley was preaching but revival.

Smaller collections, some of them open to the public, created the same ambience all over England – for instance at Easton Neston in Northamptonshire with its new house designed by Hawksmoor for Thomas Fermor, 2nd Baron Leominster or Lempster, and from 1721 Earl of Pomfret, illustrated by Colen Campbell shortly after its completion.[87]

Pomfret's collection had been badly restored, a fact which did not escape perceptive visitors like George Vertue[88] and Horace Walpole.[89] Like Pembroke's, much of the collection at Easton Neston had derived from the dispersal of the Arundel Collection in the previous century.[90] Stukeley's detailed account of the contents of the house and garden provides not only an idea of the disposition of the sculptures but of the ingenuous and trusting way the eighteenth century looked at what purported to be classical portrait busts and statues. For instance, after describing how, on descending into the garden 'along the middle walk', one found in the parterres around the fountain four immaculately carved Greek statues 'of most admirable art' in the draperies, Stukeley notices, 'between them and the house on the south side',

> that celebrated statue of Cicero intire, with his *sudarium* in his right, and a scroll in his left hand: the sight of the eyes is cut hollow. I could not possibly excuse my self half a quarter of an hour's serious view of this master-piece, frequently going round it: where so much seeming simplicity of the carver, has called forth all the fire of that divine genius that could make statues hear, as this artist has made them speak, and left an eternal monument of contention between him and the great orator: it grieved me to think it should stand a day longer in the open air. Answering to this on the left, is another statue of more robust shape and workmanship: his left hand holds a scroll, his right is laid in a passionate manner upon his breast: if sinewy muscles denote one that worked on the anvil, it may possibly be Demosthenes. The two next that correspond beyond the fountain, are Scipio Africanus and Asiaticus, in an heroic dress. Beyond, on each side the steps going down to the lower garden, are two *colossi*, Fabius Maximus the cunctator, and Archimedes with a square in his hand. At each end of this cross-walk, or terrace, which terminates the middle or principal one, is built a handsome stone-work with niches and pediment supported with pilasters, contrived on purpose to receive other pieces: in that on the left hand, or north side, is the tomb of the famous Germanicus, adorned with carving of bas-relief: upon it two admirable busts of him and Agrippina his wife.[91]

Stukeley's eagerness to believe that the statues were sculpted from the life involves him in overlooking the vast numbers of multiple copies made in classical times, to say nothing of the error of ascribing a Cicero with incised eyes to the first century BC. Among the collection of antiques in the house itself he notices 'Caius Marius in a senatorial habit' and 'M. Antony, a naked figure', both life-size.[92] It is clear that such works were valued more for their historical associations than their aesthetic qualities. They had carried their subjects down into the present, that was the miracle. Rarely is any doubt expressed regarding the identifications.

In purchasing (frequently through agents abroad) the best available examples or, when these could not be had, the finest copies of the mythological and historical characters of antiquity, British collectors were doing no more than following the procedures of Roman antiquity itself, though their immediate preceptors were the great patrons of Renaissance Italy and France. Statues in marble and bronze from the golden age of Greek art, the fifth and fourth centuries BC in which Pheidias, Polycletus, Alcamenes, Myron, Praxiteles, Scopas and Lysippus worked, were reproduced in large numbers for the Roman market from the second century BC when, following the incorporation of the Greek states into the Roman Empire, Hellenistic ideas and taste quickly permeated Roman society. The Greek manufactories were vastly expanded in the imperial period, especially during the prosperous second century.[93] Cicero's letters to Atticus evidence the extent of this one man's imports as early as 67–66 BC. Of all classic authors Cicero was the most read in eighteenth-century England, and his passion for collecting must have encouraged men like Pembroke and Pomfret:

> I am delighted at your news about the Hermathena. It is a most suitable ornament for my Academy, since no class-room is complete without a Hermes, and Minerva has a special appropriateness in mine. So please do as you suggest and send as many ornaments as possible for the place. The statues you sent before I have not seen yet. They are in my house at Formiae, where I am just thinking of going. I'll have them all brought to my place at Tusculum, and if that ever gets too full I'll begin decorating Caieta.[94]
>
> I have raised [20,400 sesterces] for L. Cincius for the statues of Megaric marble, as you advised me. Those figures of Hermes in Pentelic marble with bronze heads, about which you wrote, I have already fallen in love with: so please send them and anything else that you think suits the place, and my enthusiasm for such things, and your own taste – the more the merrier, and the sooner the better – especially those you intend for the Gymnasium and the colonnade. For my appreciation for art treasures is so great that I am afraid

most people will laugh at me, though I expect encouragement from you.[95]

Please do as you say about the statues and the Hermeraclae: and have them shipped as soon as you can conveniently, and any other things you come across that are suitable for the place – you know what it is like – especially for the Palaestra and Gymnasium. That's where I am sitting and writing now, so my thoughts naturally run on it. I give you a commission, too, for bas-reliefs for insertion in the stucco walls of the hall, and for two well-covers in carved relief.[96]

In addition to the demands of the numerous private villas like Cicero's and up to the scale of Hadrian's, the imperial mansions on the Palatine, the multitude of temples and basilicas, theatres and baths all required their copies of the most famous statues of what was already 'Greek antiquity', often reduced, enlarged or turned out in mirror reversals and ordered by the shipload – what has been called 'the tradition of art by the mass consignment that would survive until the British country houses of the eighteenth and early nineteenth centuries, or Lord Astor's country home at Cliveden as late as 1900'.[97] As well as copies there were scores of important originals in imperial Rome – among those the elder Pliny reports are a Cupid of Praxiteles in Octavia's Rooms, a Flora, a Triptolemus and a Ceres by the same artist in the Gardens of Servilius, and others on the Capitol, in the collection of Asinius Pollio and elsewhere; Scopas' *Apollo* on the Palatine, his *Seated Vesta* in the Gardens of Servilius, his composition centring on Neptune in the Flaminian Circus, and several more; and many other works whose authorship was in controversy.[98] Pliny's account of how, some time after 39 BC, 'Asinius Pollio, being an ardent enthusiast, was accordingly anxious for his collection to attract sightseers',[99] provided a classical precedent for those great eighteenth-century English collectors who, following in the footsteps of famous Italian patrons, opened their doors to the admiring public.

It is also notable that in private Roman collections, just as in those of eighteenth-century England, the value of portrait statues was largely determined by the sense of association they provided. Pliny records

a novelty that has also been invented, in that likenesses made, if not of gold or silver, yet at all events of bronze are set up in the libraries in honour of those whose immortal spirits speak to us in the same places, nay more, even

> imaginary likenesses are modelled and sense of loss gives birth to countenances that have not been handed down to us, as occurs in the case of Homer. At any rate in my view at all events there is no greater kind of happiness than that all people for all time should desire to know what kind of a man a person was.[100]

This was precisely the spirit in which Chesterfield set up an antique bust of his admired Cicero[101] in the library of Chesterfield House, South Audley Street, Mayfair, a house designed by the Burlingtonian Isaac Ware in an appropriately Palladian style.[102] The walls of Chesterfield's library were adorned with portraits of all the great writers. Naturally the busts Chesterfield commissioned of himself were in the same antique style as the Cicero, and just as Cicero had used his friend Atticus as an agent in his purchases of antique sculpture, so Chesterfield used his godson the diplomatist Solomon Dayrolles. The needs of the recently completed Chesterfield House were uppermost in his letter of 25 May 1750 to Dayrolles at the Hague, asking his friend to bid at the forthcoming sale of Count Obdam's collection of *virtù* in the middle of 1750. As he wrote, Chesterfield referred to his copy of the catalogue:

> Comte Obdam's *virtù* will, I think, for the reason you give, go very cheap; few people in Holland understanding those things, or even thinking that they do. I would not give sixpence for his bronzes, nor a shilling for his books; but for some of his antique marbles, I would give reasonably. Those which, upon the face of the catalogue, I should choose, are the following ones:
> 297. *Hermes* (Buste) *juvenis Romani cum lorica et sago, in marmore. Ant.*
> 298. *Bacchus, cum corona hederacea. Ant.*
> 302. *Caput juvenis Romani, supra basin. Ant.*
> 305. *Statua cum anaglyphis, sacrificium in honorem Priapi efformantibus. Ant.*
>
> There are also in the appendix two bustos, one of Homer, the other of Apollo, by Girardon; which, if they go extremely cheap, as possibly they may, I should be glad of them; by extremely cheap, I mean about ten pounds a-piece. For the four antiques above-marked, *l'un portant l'autre*; if they are fine, I would go as far as five and twenty pounds a-piece. But should these which I have mentioned have great faults, and others which I have not mentioned have great beauties, I refer to your decision.[103]

In using a diplomat as his agent Chesterfield was working within an already old British tradition. Ambassadors had long been instrumental in securing important purchases, including the Arundel Marbles in the previous century. Through the middle and later decades of the eighteenth century several British diplomats, among them Consul Joseph Smith at Venice, provided advice or acted as agents for British collectors. The ideal, of course, was to buy your antique marbles on the spot, as Thomas Coke, 1st Earl of Leicester, did while travelling through Italy as a young man in 1717 in the company of the young William Kent, purchasing first of all a gigantic bust of Lucius Verus that had recently been unearthed and would later dominate the dining room at Holkham from above the fireplace. Thereafter he acquired a large statue of Jupiter, an important Diana and an equally significant 'Lucius Antonius',[104] later a Venus and Meleager, a Faun crowned with vine leaves, and a valuable and putatively contemporary bust of Thucydides, among others. Thus began what would grow into one of the most important collections in England. Later, when he could not be in Italy, he had Matthew Brettingham the Younger purchase additional works for him.[105] They filled their niches in the long Sculpture Gallery at Holkham in an impressive fashion. The collection of antique marbles at Sir Robert Walpole's Houghton was, as we have seen, appropriately more political: Roman emperors survey the Stone Hall from their pedestals. Quality for quality, political portrait statues were more impressive than political portrait busts. In his gardens at Chiswick Burlington had placed antique statues of Caesar, Pompey and Cicero in the exedra, perhaps following a similar arrangement at the Villa Mattei.[106] These statues had the best possible provenance. They came from Hadrian's Villa, thus providing a highly potent physical link between Chiswick (a deliberate attempt to recreate the Roman villa in England) and the most impressive villa of Roman antiquity.

Amidst the wealth of imported antiques no statues or busts considered at the time to be of the very first rank ever came to England, none of the recognised gems of the canon. By the eighteenth century this canon had become very well defined. Each item within it had been endowed with its own mystique. A detailed catalogue of its 'register', together with its development from the Renaissance, has been provided by Haskell and Penny.[107] Of the ninety-five works they catalogue, not one came to England, perhaps because, like Chesterfield, the English were never sufficiently inclined to go beyond the 'reasonable' bid. They note, moreover, that 'it is in fact impossible to trace to an English collection any piece of antique sculpture which had previously been illustrated in an Italian anthology of the most famous and beautiful statues with the exception of Mr Coke's *Diana* and *Lucius Antonius*'.[108] Many went to France, others to Spain and Germany.

The canon was so well known in England, however, that large numbers of copies and casts were purchased and displayed in baroque, Palladian and neo-classical settings. Even copies of copies were proudly set up, as in the case of Le Sueur's duplicate of Charles I's much-admired bronze copy of the *Borghese Gladiator*, among the most famous of them all; though only great at third hand, Le Sueur's replica of a replica was given pride of place at Wilton by the 4th Earl of Pembroke where it remained until presented by the 8th Earl to Sir Robert Walpole for display at Houghton. Most of the canon was supposed to be either golden-age Greek or golden-age Roman – in fact the majority of its items are today catalogued as first- or second-century copies of lost originals.[109] The important casts and copies of canonical works in the houses and gardens of eighteenth-century England were not intended by their copiers as fakes. The originals were too famous, and the connoisseurs knew where they all were. Not all of the copies in England were full-scale.[110]

In addition there were casts and copies of less famous statues in collections such as those at Syon House and Holkham Hall and many cheaper copies in lead decorating the skylines of country houses like Kedleston. For gardens, cheap lead copies of the most famous antiques, and for libraries and other rooms, plaster casts were produced in very large series by Sir Henry and John Cheere, and by the brothers Benjamin and Thomas Carter in their yards at Hyde Park Corner, where anyone could purchase a *Farnese Hercules* and equally inexpensive copies of other famous works.[111] From here they streamed out in their thousands into gardens like those at Timon's Villa, satirised in Pope's *Epistle to Burlington*:

> Here Amphitrite sails through myrtle bowers;
> There Gladiators fight, or die in flowers.[112]

It is worth noting that these lines depend on the reader's recognition that copies of the *Borghese Gladiator* and the *Dying Gladiator* had already become garden clichés by as early as 1731. Whereas the English preferred to have copies of antique sculptures in their gardens, the French in the eighteenth century generally adorned their gardens with modern sculptures. Modern statues, unless they were copies of the antique or done after an antique style, would have been quite inappropriate in English gardens modelled to such an extent on classical sources. The difference here between French and English practice also reflects again the unique vigour and authenticity which England's recent political history had given to its classical temper.

Not only sculpture but any object that brought the classical and particularly the Roman world into the English present was set up for reverence, like the bronze eagle, supposedly from the top of a legionary standard, displayed at Castle Howard along with Roman urns, columns and what Horace Walpole acknowledged as 'the finest collection in the world of antique tables of the most valuable marble'. In addition there were the more usual antique bronzes and marbles including ones claimed to be Antoninus Pius and Marcus Aurelius, and an important collection of antique gems kept in London.[113] Such objects were in keeping with the idyllic and epic Virgilian spirit Lord Carlisle had been at such pains to evoke in the Yorkshire landscape.[114] The Earl of Leicester had his Roman table-tops too, from Hadrian's Villa moreover. It was only right that so much of Hadrian's should find itself in England, for that emperor had confirmed his attachment to Britain by his personal supervision of the most impressive work of defensive military engineering undertaken anywhere in the Empire.

The examples given here of the oligarchy's use of sculpture and other collectable items for purposes of tangible association with the Roman past could be multiplied many times over, though the standards of authenticity and quality would decline in the examples cited. An example with a difference might be noted in conclusion. As a young man the Earl of Leicester had himself included as Allucius in a historical painting, the *Continence of Scipio*, which he commissioned from Giuseppe Chiari. The painting is no longer at Holkham, but a drawing of it, attributed to

William Kent, architect of Holkham, exists (plate 28).[115] The scene is set in Spain, where the strikingly beautiful maiden betrothed to the leading young Celtiberian Allucius is returned to him untouched by a virtuous Scipio, to whom she had been brought by the Romans. In response, Allucius will bring into the service of the Roman state a contingent of 1,400 cavalry. Leicester here reverses his usual procedure of bringing the Roman world to England, pre-incarnating himself into the antique past. Yet in so startlingly marrying the modern to the ancient, the painting invites us to view it as a learned joke, a paradoxical essay in the unreachable otherness of the classical world.

THE NUMINOUS IN LANDSCAPE AND HOUSE

On 12 September 1776 John Wesley visited Stourhead and recorded in his journal his reaction to the works of art in Flitcroft's Pantheon, among them Rysbrack's *Hercules,* his *Flora,* John Cheere's *Meleager* and *Diana,* and an antique statue of Livia Augusta as Ceres: 'I cannot admire the images of devils', he confessed, adding, 'I defy all mankind to reconcile statues with nudities, either to common sense or common decency.'[116]

Wesley's sensibilities may have been rather narrow but he was no simpleton. His instincts told him that these statues were more than ornaments to further the association with classical antiquity which the banker and antiquarian Henry Hoare, nephew of the pioneer Palladian William Benson, sought to create in his lake-landscape at Stourhead. They represented his quest for the numinous in that association, as Kenneth Woodbridge, Ronald Paulson and others have shown.[117] In this quest he was following not only the example of continental painters – Claude Lorrain, Nicholas Poussin and Salvator Rosa – who adorned their idealised landscapes with antique temples, but, like them, classical precedent which encouraged the placement of temples and statues appropriate to their setting in the landscape. More particularly, Hoare seems to have been following Pliny the Younger, who describes, in his *Letters*, the source of the Clitumnus:

> At the foot of a little hill, covered with venerable and shady cypress trees, a spring issues, which . . . forms itself, after several windings, into a spacious basin, so extremely clear, that you may see the pebbles . . . The banks on each side are shaded with great numbers of verdant ash and poplar trees, as distinctly reflected in the stream, as if they were actually existing in it . . . Nearby it stands an ancient and venerable temple, wherein is placed a statue representing the river-god Clitumnus in his proper vestment; and indeed the prophetic oracles here delivered, sufficiently testify the immediate presence of that divinity. Several little chapels are scattered round, dedicated to particular gods distinguished by different names, and some of them too presiding over different fountains . . . Several villas, attracted by the beauty of this river, are situated upon its borders.[118]

Hoare may have visited the scene during his tour of Italy in the 1730s. Above the springs of the River Stour he erected a temple, originally intended to house the Hercules but subsequently dedicated to Flora (Hoare's choice of goddess – Flitcroft had intended it for Ceres). Both Hercules and Flora were associated with gardens in classical antiquity. Over the entrance to the Temple of Flora was the injunction spoken by the Cumaean Sybil in the sixth book of Virgil's *Aeneid* and commonly used in Roman religious ceremonies, 'Procul, o procul este profani' (Be far off, begone, ye unhallowed!).[119] Below the Temple of Flora lies the Grotto. Like the temple by the source of the Clitumnus in Pliny, the Grotto houses the statue of a River God, and also that of a 'nymph', both by John Cheere. The second of these is a copy of the Belvedere *Cleopatra*.[120] Under it is Pope's verse:

> Nymph of the grot, these sacred springs I keep,
> And to the murmur of these waters sleep;
> Ah, spare my slumbers, gently tread the cave!
> And drink in silence, or in silence lave.

Kenneth Woodbridge has observed how, 'As the springs flow about the statue of the nymph, something of the awe surrounding pagan sanctuaries survives, which makes her more than a garden ornament.'[121] Nearby, Cheere's River God holds an urn, turned on its side, from which the Stour flows as from its source. Around 1765 Flitcroft's Temple of Apollo, also called the Temple of the Sun, adapted from the Temple of Venus at

Baalbek, logically completed Stourhead's tribute to the natural sources of life.

Henry Hoare's patronage of Rysbrack and Flitcroft and the influence of Kent's ideas on the Stourhead landscape, as well as other factors noticed in the previous chapter, associate him with the Burlingtonian tradition, though his politics, like Pope's, were Tory. That tradition, like philoromanism generally, required of its acolytes money, not attachment to party. Like Shaftesbury and Chesterfield, Henry Hoare epitomised the connection between classical sensibility and a heightened social exclusivity. The family's wealth derived from banking and from the South Sea Company, and some had been invested by Henry Hoare's father (the so-called 'Good' Henry) in the purchase of the manor of Stourton in Wiltshire. A new house, Stourhead, designed by the Palladian Colen Campbell, author of *Vitruvius britannicus*, was built in place of the old. After the father's death his son, Henry Hoare 'the Magnificent', developed Stourhead with the inherited wealth which he supplemented through his banking business in Fleet Street. He later told his nephew Richard that his reading was motivated by 'the pursuit of that knowledge which distinguishes only the Gentleman from the Vulgar and teaches him to adorn the fortune he acquires or possesses'. The contemplation of the distance between 'the Gentleman' and 'the Vulgar' was one of his principal pleasures. He admitted that as a younger man he had been disposed, when in Fleet Street, to 'murder my sweet precious time in looking at the insensible Vulgar who passed under the window'.[122] His thematic fusion of landscape, neo-classical architecture and statuary is reminiscent of Cobham's Stowe, but his emphasis on the sacred gave Stourhead a sublimity beyond anything achieved by Cobham, whose political theme makes the real world ever-present. At Stourhead Henry Hoare constructed a landscape directly out of antiquity, in which it was possible to contemplate one's distance from the vulgar aesthetically and even spiritually, as well as intellectually and geographically, though he deferred to Christianity outside his garden.[123] As time went by his gardens acquired a strong political significance,[124] and non-classical elements such as Alfred's Tower (a tribute to the native tradition of political liberty), a Druidic cell, Chinese bridge, Turkish tent and so on, to provide associations with the developing tastes of the age, but the classical spirit with which the garden had been laid out and first developed remained dominant.

The programme of temple-building and appropriate choice and placement of classical divinities at Stourhead was underway when Joseph Spence published the first of several editions of his heavily subscribed *Polymetis* (1747), which, in addition to its other information on classical art and literature, sets forth the principles for placement of temples and classical statuary within landscape gardens.[125] Spence's section on this matter in *Polymetis* is the only systematic treatment of the topic in English. There had been other books, of course, which had informed their readers on the general subject of the ancient deities, such as William King's *An Historical Account of the Heathen Gods and Heroes; Necessary for the Understanding of the Ancient Poets* (1710), essentially a school textbook for an age in which classical education was universal; this saw many editions until 1788, when it was replaced as the authoritative book on the classics by Lemprière's *Classical Dictionary*. Spence's book takes the form of a dialogue. Polymetis is an Englishman with a villa on the Thames not far from town. In his library, which overlooks the gardens, he explains to his friends that

> I have followed the taste in fashion . . . of making my gardens rather wild than regular . . . The lower part, in particular, joins in with the view of the country, as if it made a part of it . . . The statues I got formerly from Italy, and which used to croud up all my house, are placed in [garden temples]: and what I a little value myself upon, is the order in which I have placed them . . .
>
> You see that Rotonda, with a Collonade running round it, on the brow of the hill? Within that, are the great celestial deities; as the milder ones relating to the human mind and civil life, (Fidelity, Clemency; Peace, Concord; Plenty, Health; all the Mental or Moral Deities, of the better sort;) are placed in the Collonade about it; one in each opening between the pillars. That temple, lower down the hill to the right, contains the beings which preside over the element of fire: which, according to the antients, had its place next to the supream mansion of the gods. You may call this, if you please, the temple of the Sun and Stars. There I have lodged all my antiques that relate to the Sun, to the Planets, to the Constellations; and to the Times and Seasons, as measured by the former. That Octogon, opposite to it on the left, is the temple

> of the Winds, and of the imaginary beings of the air. Those two temples on either hand below them contain, one the deities of the Waters, and the other the deities of the earth.[126]

The passage suggests the care and attention to detail which might inform the placement of neo-classical garden architecture and associated statuary, but there has been no very detailed analysis of the relation of Spence's theory to other people's practice. Among the important parallels between Stourhead and Spence's model is the treatment of the water deities. Spence devotes an entire dialogue to these. Polymetis houses them in a structure that 'looked more like a great grotto rather than a temple'. They naturally belong 'somewhere near the place whence each river took its rise: where, if there was any grotto, they usually had some figure of the presiding deity of the stream in it; with his urn, and the waters gushing out of it; to denote the source of the river'. They were normally represented more or less reclined (at Stourhead the River God is seated). 'Every River-god was supposed to be attended by several goddesses of an inferior nature, called Naiads . . . They were supposed to live in the places of the presiding deities of fountains, lakes, and rivers.'[127] The grotto at Stourhead shows great fidelity to such details. On the other hand, by Spence's logic Stourhead's Pantheon, on the edge of the lake, would seem too low, though the Temple of Apollo, which is near to, but not upon, the top of its hill, is correctly placed.

Elsewhere in England neo-classical landscapes combined the associative with the numinous in similar manner, as at Castle Howard in Yorkshire. The rationale behind the conception here was described in the poem *Castle Howard*, published around 1733 and presumed to have been written by Lady Irwin, daughter of Charles Howard, Earl of Carlisle, Whig and former First Lord of the Treasury, to whom it is addressed. Christopher Hussey has shown how the poem reveals an intimate appreciation of Howard's purpose: 'to recreate the ideal world envisaged in classical poetry'[128] – the Golden Age. The poem identifies Howard's first aim in this connection: 'to make those happy who on you depend', 'those' being Lord Carlisle's immediate family, for, as Hussey emphasises, 'the happiness of dependants did not prevent the removal of the village of Henderskelf without rebuilding elsewhere. It was for the elite of birth and taste that this felicity was designed through escape from false, worldly values into an elysium where the ideal truths of morality and art were made visually real.'[129] The poem's frequent allusions to Virgilian idyllic and epic poetry suggest that classical literature provided a primary and direct inspirational source at Castle Howard (as at Stourhead) of more significance than the mediated visions of paintings. There was a consistency in Lord Carlisle's directing vision that gives the Castle Howard landscape a sublime coherency in spite of its huge scale and changes in architects. The ornaments were functional and the divinities, who included Diana (as presider over woods, in this case Wray Wood) and Venus (like Flora, goddess of gardens), suitable to the spirit of the place.[130] Carlisle's vision culminated in two sublime masterpieces, Vanbrugh's Temple of the Four Winds and Hawksmoor's Mausoleum. The temple symbolically celebrates the unconfined idyllic spaces it opens upon. As one Vanbrugh scholar has observed, 'In the clear North Yorkshire air it has an unexpectedly Mediterranean aspect, entirely and marvellously in harmony with the Virgilian feeling of its landscape setting.'[131] It received its title only after it was built, but the name is highly appropriate given the setting, and one might also note that the Ionic order, as Spence's Polymetis points out, is correct for temples of the Winds.[132]

Within a smaller compass General Dormer at Rousham created a similarly idyllic landscape in which his collection of copies of famous antique sculptures – the Capitoline *Horse and Lion*, the *Dying Gaul*, the Barberini *Faun*, the *Venus de' Medici* among them – could be displayed to advantage. The most striking feature is Kent's Praeneste Terrace, at once an amusingly diminutive reminder of the largest ancient temple in Italy, that of Fortuna at Praeneste, and an invocation of Praeneste's religious associations as the seat of a celebrated oracle. In its elevated position Kent's structure gives architectural substance to the classical effect of the whole enterprise, which seemed to Horace Walpole 'as elegant and antique as if the Emperor Julian had selected the most pleasing solitude about Daphne to enjoy a philosophic retirement'.[133] Kent also reshaped the Vale of Venus at Rousham, taking the idea for his rustic cascades from the Villa Aldobrandini at Frascati.[134]

Stowe, already considered in regard to the political uses of landscape and antiquity, repeatedly used classical religious references to enhance its contemporary social messages. As Nikolaus Pevsner has remarked, Mercury was originally central to the Temple of British Worthies, 'as the god who leads souls to Elysium – apparently British as well as Grecian'.[135] Previously neglected Roman analogical elements in the inscriptions, some with strong religious overtones, have already been noticed in chapter 2, among them the 'Concordia' of the Temple of Concord and Victory and the 'deification' of the late Queen Caroline in the inscription to Rysbrack's statue.

Examples could be multiplied. Like so much western art and literature from the Renaissance onwards, the eighteenth-century English landscape garden employed classical ornaments and mythology for the tangible association they provided with the spirit of antiquity, but beyond that because they gave specific and appropriate spiritual dimensions to the sense of sublimity the landscape was intended to evoke. There is ample evidence that their owners used garden temples as contemplative *loci* in which to pass idle hours profitably. Tobias Smollett, condemning the overly formal Italian gardens of his day, praises by way of contrast the English 'garden or park' whose 'arbours, grottos, hermitages, temples, and alcoves' not only shelter their owner from the sun but 'afford him means of contemplation and repose'.[136] Sir John Clerk of Penicuik, member of the Roman Knights, writing in Latin to Hermann Boerhaave at Leiden, provided Roman precedents for almost every aspect of his Scottish 'villa' and the manner of his life there.[137] His Roman Centurion's Bridge and Roman Outlook Tower lent heavy substance to the classical atmosphere. As an old man he would make a daily contemplative walk to his grotto, knowing that, in his own words,

> Your stately house and pleasant fields at last,
> With other Charms of Life you must forego,
> And this way travel to the shades below.[138]

Such landscapes provided exercises in classical sensibility. Robert Lloyd facetiously referred to the extensive statuary yards at Hyde Park Corner which turned out *en masse*

The Gods of Athens, and of Rome.
Here squabby Cupids take their places,
With Venus, and the clumsy Graces:
Apollo there, with aim so clever,
Stretches his leaden bow for ever;
And there, without the pow'r to fly,
Stands fix'd a tip-toe Mercury.[139]

As Wesley intuited, however, their uses and implications might sometimes run a little deeper than the casual observer cared to think. Horace Walpole wrote of his stay at Stowe in the middle of 1770,

> Twice a day we made a pilgrimage to almost every heathen temple in that province that they call a garden . . . We supped in a grotto in the Elysian fields, and were refreshed with waters of dew and gentle showers that dripped from all the trees; and put us in mind of the heroic ages, when kings and queens were shepherds and shepherdesses, and lived in caves, and were wet to the skin two or three times a day. Well! thank heaven, I am emerged from that Elysium, and once more in a Christian country! – Not but, to say the truth, our pagan landlord and landlady were very obliging, and the party went off much better than I expected.[140]

Walpole's ironising of his experiences depends for its effect on our recognition that while games were being played in the grounds of Stowe they were at least half-serious. The associative quality of their gardens mattered to the host and hostess, which is the object of the satire.

If landscape was to provide exercises in classical sensibility it was essential to eliminate the ruder reminders of eighteenth-century reality and particularly 'the insensible Vulgar' as Henry Hoare disarmingly termed them. If there was a village in sight there was little option but to do as Lord Carlisle of Castle Howard had done with Henderskelf and level it, moving the inhabitants elsewhere if one was so disposed or (like Lord Carlisle) allowing them to shift for themselves.[141] Similar things happened at Sir Robert Walpole's Houghton and all over England through the middle decades of the century and informed Goldsmith's *The Deserted Village* (1770), which focuses particularly on the fate of the village at Nuneham Courtenay, demolished by the 1st Earl Harcourt, founding member of the Society of Dilettanti. There was seldom any resistance.[142] When the tenants at Milton Abbas in Dorset did resist on the grounds that their leases had not expired, Lord Milton released the dam holding Capability Brown's lake and flooded them out.[143]

In the sixteenth and seventeenth centuries it had been a point of honour for a landlord to provide in himself and his house a centre of sustenance and hospitality for his tenants and villagers, as part of a relationship that acknowledged mutual dependency and respect for tradition, if we are to credit the country house poems of Jonson and Marvell.[144] In the eighteenth century the defenceless tenants of landlords who imaged themselves in the iconography of civic virtue found themselves banished out of sight and mind by the ideal of pastoral sublimity and for the contemplative good of their masters.

Inside the eighteenth-century house, as in the park, the sacred was an important part of the neo-classical frame of reference. A significant proportion of Rysbrack's commissions were for classical reliefs on religious themes, in more or less close fidelity to their originals as these were illustrated in Montfauçon's *L'antiquité expliquée* and similar works of the period. Those at Houghton have been noticed in chapter 2. He did a *Sacrifice to Apollo* for Woburn, which was copied, probably by Rysbrack himself, for Godsmersham Park in Kent. He did two reliefs of classical sacrifices for Clandon Park in Surrey, and a *Roman Marriage* in marble for the Cupola Room in Kensington Palace.[145] Statues of classical divinities within the interiors of houses were of course commonplace. To outdo them all the Earl of Leicester contemplated a *coup de théâtre* for his Marble Hall at Holkham. He intended to raise an enormous statue of Jupiter on a pedestal at the base of the steps, the logical place for an altar. Changes were made in the plans and nothing came of the idea.[146]

There are well-known portraits of the sitter sacrificing to a suitable classical deity. For example Sir Joshua Reynolds's *Lady Sarah Bunbury Sacrificing to the Graces* (1765 – plate 29) depicts its subject in classical drapery and a pose adapted from a classical relief, offering incense to the goddesses of grace and beauty, daughters of Jupiter.[147] *The Daughters of Sir William Montgomery as 'The Graces adorning a Term of Hymen'* (1774 – plate 30) is a more complex exercise in iconography. E. H. Gombrich has pointed out that at the time the Rt Hon. Luke Gardner, MP, commissioned Reynolds to do the portrait, the central figure engaged in the decoration of the term of the god of wedlock was Gardner's fiancée. They married before the work was completed. Her two sisters are shown assisting at the sacrifice. The first of these, the already married youngest daughter, has passed the image of Hymen. The eldest daughter, who did not marry for another year, is still gathering flowers for the rite. Reynolds, influenced by Poussin's depiction of a bacchanal, a painting by Rubens of the three Graces attiring Nature, and possibly earlier Italian sources, has employed classical mythology to elevate a portrait (low on the hierarchy of kinds) into the higher genre of the 'historical', suitable to the sitters, who were all amateur actors. Thirteen years earlier Reynolds had painted Lady Elizabeth Keppel performing the same rite.[148]

Medallion portraits, which in most cases strongly classicised their subjects, should also be mentioned in the present context, for when the subjects were women an analogy with Minerva was frequently implied. Samuel Johnson's poem 'On Seeing a Portrait of Mrs Montagu' (Elizabeth Montagu, a friend) illustrates the point:

> Had this fair figure which this frame displays,
> Adorn'd in Roman times the brightest days,
> In every dome, in every sacred place,
> Her statue would have breath'd an added grace,
> And on its basis would have been enroll'd,
> 'This is Minerva, cast in Virtue's mould.'[49]

For their owners there was no doubt an amusing aspect to these pictures, but they were intended to do more than amuse. By granting their subjects an eternal participation in the cultural life of classical antiquity they signify their absolute cultural exclusivity in the present.

5

Beyond the mainstream: classical nostalgia and freethinking

Eighteenth-century England was a deeply Christian society, even a 'confessional State'.[1] Its most representative authors, among them Addison, Steele, Pope, Swift, Defoe, Richardson, Fielding, Sterne, Cowper, Johnson and Burke, were Christians. During the eighteenth century over 20,000 separate titles of sermons were published, many of them titles to *collections* of sermons.[2] Prominent churchmen from the time of Archbishop Tillotson in the late seventeenth century might espouse rationalist attitudes, but the paper debates in which they engaged hardly affected the spiritual lives of ordinary Englishmen.[3] Isaac Newton could be a conforming Anglican while quietly denying the doctrine of the Trinity. So could the Boyle Lecturer and critic of deism (but 'Arianiser'), Samuel Clarke, and other senior churchmen. Such tendencies, however, never constituted more than a fraction of the broad church, or of the social elite. Deists and freethinkers, mostly Whigs, were even thinner on the ground.[4] This section examines the neglected classicist core of their thought.

Deists were properly located outside Christianity, though some espoused a 'rational' Christianity.[5] The most effective reply to their arguments was Bishop Butler's *Analogy of Religion* (1736).[6] Through the mid century, scepticism tended to displace deism as the enemy in Christian eyes,[7] though deism continued to have its adherents. According to Elisha Smith, Shaftesbury and Matthew Tindal were 'the two Oracles of Deism'.[8] Together with Leibniz, Shaftesbury influenced Bolingbroke and Pope (who remained a Catholic) among others, and, through Diderot and Voltaire, the Continental Enlightenment.[9]

From the outset a principal prop of English freethinking was a nostalgic classicism which facilitated a doctrinally indifferentist but God-acknowledging philosophical cast of mind as represented, for instance, by Cicero.[10] For freethinkers from Shaftesbury to Gibbon, ancient Rome, in contradistinction to Roman Catholicism and even credal Christianity as a whole, becomes a model of toleration and doctrinal indifferentism, of a rational and natural religion whose enlightened *pietas* underpinned civic-minded *virtus*.[11] In many ways philoromanism was propagated in England as an intentional contrast to Roman Catholicism. Thus, throughout Shaftesbury's *Characteristicks*, 'superstition' and 'bigotry' are code-words for Roman Catholicism.[12] Often, however, Shaftesbury and his freethinking followers use these terms in a more general attack on what they see as an overly dogmatic Christianity.

The connection between admiration for the classical past and free-thinking is suggested by a range of evidence from one end of the century to the other. Richard Steele's defensive *The Christian Hero* (1701) attacks Stoicism (which by way of the neo-Stoicism of Montaigne, Charron, Du Vair and others was still a strong influence when he wrote) and 'the Fashionable Vice of Exploding Religion',[13] and particularly the idealisation of Brutus, Cassius and the younger Cato. Steele asks why it is 'that the Heathen struts, and the Christian sneaks in our Imagination',[14] how it has come about 'that when we say a thing was done like an old *Roman*, we have a generous and sublime Idea, that warms and kindles in us, together with a certain Self-disdain, a desire of Imitation; when on the other side, to say, 'twas like a Primitive Christian, chills Ambition, and seldom rises to more than the cold approbation of a Duty that perhaps a Man wishes he were not oblig'd to'.[15] This was five years after the publication of John Toland's notorious *Christianity not Mysterious* (1696), which purported to explode both revelation and the supernatural.[16]

In 1718 Maittaire commented on the dispute arising out of Bishop Hoadly's sermon before the king in March of the previous year, in which Hoadly had denied doctrinal authority to the church. To Maittaire the sermon was 'worse-than-heathenish' since 'even Heathens have a greater regard for religion than he', and the dispute

> a vile reproach upon our Church in particular, as well as Christianity in general. Hoadly puts me in mind of another free-thinker, Toland (the much abler and better writer of the two, tho' of as vile principles)... We see the dire effects of the so much commended and fashionable spirit of moderation, we feel the wane of ecclesiastical Power... God's will be done; and if he in his unsearchable wisdom thinks fit to suffer this inundation of Heathenism, we ought to resign patiently the event to his Providence. Yet I can't forbear being zealously concerned, that the church of England is thus trodden under foot.[17]

Like Steele, Maittaire wildly exaggerates, but the connection he makes with 'Heathenism' is interesting. This word, when applied in Christian parlance to writings and speeches, frequently signalled a pre-Christian classical-philosophical bent. It has nothing to do with Roman religion or polytheism, which everyone regarded as absurd. In the quotation from Steele, the Stoical Brutus, Cassius and younger Cato are 'Heathens'.

Freethinkers exaggerated their own numbers and distorted reality. David Hume claimed that 'Our ancestors, a few centuries ago, were sunk into the most abject superstition, last century they were inflamed with the most furious enthusiasm, and are now settled into the most cool indifference with regard to religious matters, that is to be found in any nation of the world.'[18] Elsewhere he identified the principal causes of this alteration as 'the progress of learning and of liberty'.[19] The party-political implication of this is spelled out in another essay: 'Since the origin of *whig* and *tory*, the leaders of the *whigs* have either been *deists* or profest *latitudinarians* in their principles; that is, friends to toleration, and indifferent to any particular sect of *christians*.'[20]

The word 'sect' is important. Christians here are being seen from outside, as the 'sect' they were in the eyes of the classical world in their first three centuries. Conventionally used by self-consciously orthodox Christians to categorise those they consider heretical, within Hume's neo-classical outlook it is a pejorative code-word applicable to every subset of Christians, and deists as well, whose arguments were for Hume equally without convincing proof.[21] Hume, 'the Great Infidel', anticipates the way Gibbon, like the philosophical pagans he flatteringly presents in *The Decline and Fall of the Roman Empire*, looks upon the early Christians.[22] Some of the deists had used the same technique.

'Enthusiasm', 'bigotry' and 'superstition' were among their code-words for revelation-based Christianity. Matthew Tindal and Anthony Collins, examined below, provide plenty of examples of such usage.

Those who defended orthodox Christianity tended to categorise Christians with a bias towards natural religion as little better than deists. John Witherspoon's *Ecclesiastical Characteristics: or, the Arcana of Church Polity* (1753), a satirical attack on the Moderate party within the Church of Scotland, associates freethinking with the 'heathen writers' who provide the authority, with a classical sensibility and a cultivated demeanour.[23]

Edward Gibbon expected his critical survey of early Christianity in the *Decline and Fall* to outrage few English readers. The strength of its hostile reception surprised him. England, he had thought, was by the 1770s not dissimilar to ancient Rome at her best in its tolerant indifference towards religion;[24] but eighteenth-century England, below the cultural surface, was no New Rome. In his memoirs for June of 1775 he admitted having 'flattered myself that an age of light and liberty would receive without scandal, an enquiry into the *human* causes of the progress and establishment of Christianity', and on 3 February 1779 he pointedly noted, 'Had I believed that the majority of English readers were so fondly attached even to the name and shadow of Christianity . . . I might, perhaps, have softened the two invidious Chapters, which would create many enemies, and conciliate few friends.'[25] It was as though Gibbon, who as Joseph Ward Swain has observed was 'thoroughly at home in the polished and sceptical society of the eighteenth century',[26] had suddenly found himself seeming not to belong there.

One reason why Gibbon was so wrong on the extent of freethinking is that categories had been blurred. Thanks to an extensive body of writing from the late seventeenth century, a synthesis of the ideal classical philosopher and the 'true Christian' had been developed with the convenient result that one could be both. James Burnett, Lord Monboddo, was building on a long tradition when towards the end of the period he illustrated in the sixth volume of his *Ancient Metaphysics* (1779–99) the uniformity in many particulars of Christian and non-Christian concepts of the deity. Monboddo showed the congruity not only of classical and Christian but of Greek, Egyptian, Buddhist and other beliefs as well. He was interested in the pervasiveness of the ideas of the Trinity and the Fall, suggestive of a universal natural religion underlying specific religions and philosophies. Like Pope in the *Essay on Man*, but in his own distinct way, he used the concept of a Great Chain of Being to illustrate the nature of God. In Monboddo's universal scheme everything is, in Pope's words, as perfect as it ought to be, partial evil being reconciled within universal good.[27]

Pope's 'Universal Prayer' is the most succinct literary expression of the idea of a natural religion underpinning the world's multifarious forms of worship.[28] Its first stanza announces the theme with confident directness:

DEO OPT. MAX.
Father of All! in every Age,
In every Clime ador'd,
By Saint, by Savage, and by Sage,
Jehovah, Jove, or Lord![29]

The Latin dedication 'to God the greatest and best', looking in its abbreviated form like an inscription in marble from the Capitoline Temple dedicated to 'Jupiter Optimus Maximus', was an early Christian adaptation of the title given by the pagan Romans to the omniscient and prescient lord of heaven. No doubt the early Christians understood themselves to be demoting the pagan Jove, but Pope, a Roman Catholic with a catholic imagination, insists that Jehovah, Jove and Lord are alternative names for the one supreme God. Jehovah and Jove even sound alike, and Pope may have known of an early attempt to impute revealed knowledge to learned pagans – the tradition of a separate revelation given by Moses ('Musaeus') to the Greeks, encoded by sages as mythological stories embodying philosophical allegories.[30] As Pope's friend Joseph Spence pointed out in *Polymetis*, which includes a comprehensive iconology of Roman religion, intelligent Romans and Greeks were monotheists. 'The thinking part of them believed that there was but one great Being, that made, and preserved, and actuated all things; which is just as much as to say that they believed there was but one God, in our sense of the word. Their best authors say this expressly.'[31]

To Pope's mind, Jehovah, Jove and Lord are likewise distinctions without insuperable difference. He combines elements of the Lord's Prayer (as in the tenth stanza's 'That mercy I to others show, / That Mercy show to me') with classical imagery –

> Let not this weak, unknowing hand
> Presume Thy Bolts to throw,
> And deal Damnation round the land,
> On each I judge thy Foe.

Classical too is this spirit of religious tolerance, and the piety Pope recommends towards a generous God to whom all sincere forms of worship are pleasing, and of whom all mankind and Nature sing in praise:

> To thee, whose Temple is all Space,
> Whose Altar, Earth, Sea, Skies,
> One Chorus let all Being raise!
> All Nature's Incense rise!

The poem's spirit is in conformity with the sermons of Henry Wharton, whose broadmindedness appealed to deists like Tindal who loved to enlist contemporary Christian authorities on their side:

> GOD's Goodness and Mercy were, from all Ages, equal and uniform; his Justice always impartial and universal, in excluding none from his Favour, but for reasons common to them with all Mankind . . . It is so pleasing a Delusion, to fancy themselves dear to God in an extraordinary Manner, and for unaccountable Reasons . . . This seduc'd the *Jews*. – This Prejudice has corrupted great Numbers of Christians.[32]

The early Fathers, not always disposed to see God in Jove, had recognised that certain pagan philosophers including Plato, Cicero, Virgil and Seneca had been graced with a partial apprehension of the divine moral law. Within minority quarters in the early eighteenth century the terms of this comparison, so flattering to those who made it and insulting to the only half-blind philosophers, began to turn in the pagans' favour.

Shaftesbury, who defined himself as 'a perfect Theist' in his belief 'that everything is governed, ordered, or regulated for the best, by a designing principle or mind, necessarily good and permanent',[33] had pointed to the pagan Jupiter of Strangers as the perfect embodiment of the divine nature, an unjealous and generous God 'benign to mankind, and recommending universal love, mutual kindness and benignity between the remotest and most unlike of human race . . . Such was ancient heathen charity and pious duty towards the whole of mankind, both those of different nations and different worships.'[34] Tindal purported to show that the finest pagans were already the best sort of 'Christians' in their concept of the supreme deity, in their moral and social teachings and in their lives. While undermining revelation, Tindal granted a privileged status to the moral core of Christianity as he defined it, all the while de-historicising it and showing it to be 'as old as the creation'. At all times and in all places it was possible to worship God in a manner acceptable to him.[35] Cicero 'describes our moral Obligations after so beautiful a manner; and by such plain, and irresistable Arguments, shews the necessary Connexion between Virtue and Happiness; Vice and Misery; as can't but make us highly delighted with the One, and create in us a just Aversion to the Other'.[36] Tindal reminds us that the Christian apologist Arnobius (d. *c.* 330) admitted that 'If [Cicero's] Works had been read, as they ought, by the Heathens, there had been no need of Christian Writers.'[37] In fact since true Christianity may be reduced to 'the full Exercise of Piety, and Virtue', advancing 'the Honour of God, and the Happiness of Human Societies',[38] Cicero was evidently writing as a Christian when in the third book of the *De republica* he argued that the divine law is immutable and universal 'and one God is the common Lord, and Governor of all Things. He it is, that has fram'd, propounded, and establish'd this Law; and whosoever obeys not him, abandons even himself, renounces his own Nature; and in so doing, suffers actually in himself the greatest Punishment, tho' he escapes all Things else which are deem'd so.'[39]

Like Tindal, Conyers Middleton, whose two-volume *History of the Life of Marcus Tullius Cicero* (1741) represents the high-water mark of its subject's fortunes in eighteenth-century England, praised the philosopher for his morality, his perceptive analysis of Roman superstition, his belief in a benevolent Creator and general conformity with the central principles of true religion. The author of *The Freeholder's Political Catechism* (1733), probably the deist Lord Bolingbroke, was another defender of 'true religion', pointing out that 'The Decay of the Publick Spirit at this time is much owing to the Decay of Virtue, and that true Religion, which is always free from Bigotry and Superstition, and a persecuting Spirit.'[40]

Tindal implies that, if one can see a Christian in Cicero, a modern Christian might be, like Cicero, a superstition-denouncing philosopher. Without falling into the category of 'infidel', a Middleton or a Bolingbroke could return to the rational piety of an authentically classical disposition.[41] This ability was the legacy of Shaftesbury and Tindal in particular and represents a neglected contribution to English neoclassicism in its ascendancy. Both authors enjoyed a wide readership, Shaftesbury's *Characteristicks* running to eleven editions in English by 1790 besides numerous editions in translation, Tindal's *Christianity as Old as the Creation* to three reprints in its first two years (1730–1), occasioning a second part in *c.* 1732. The atmosphere to which they and others including Locke, Tillotson and Clarke contributed made it possible for the Whig poet James Thomson, a moderate in religious matters, to incorporate in *Liberty* an invocation to a 'RELIGION, rational, and free'.[42]

Whereas Tindal makes good pagans and true Christians interchangeable categories, Anthony Collins, more daring, makes them all freethinkers.[43] His *Discourse of Free-Thinking* (1713), which according to its enemies went beyond deism into atheism,[44] created a sensation. There were at least five editions in the first year including a Dutch edition corrected and annotated by the author.[45] The book provoked at least twenty-one English reactions, most appearing in 1713. The majority of the extended replies were Whiggish, suggesting that this party, widely accused by Tories of encouraging freethinking notions, was engaged in limiting potential damage to itself, afraid of being contaminated by any association with the Whig-sympathising Collins.[46] Collins argues that not only Socrates, Plato, Aristotle, Epicurus, Plutarch, Varro, Cato the Censor, Cicero, Cato of Utica, and Seneca, but also Solomon, a number of the Prophets, Josephus, Origen, Minucius Felix, Synesius, Francis Bacon, Thomas Hobbes, and Archbishop Tillotson were freethinkers.[47] The last was important to his argument because through Tillotson the dominant latitudinarianism of the day could be invoked in support. This was blurring categories with a vengeance.

In 1739 James Harris the philologist and grammarian, author of *Hermes* (1751) and a representative-enough humanist for his day, summarised Shaftesbury's 'theistic' beliefs for the *General Dictionary, Historical and Critical* (1734–41):

> The whole of his Philosophy seems to have been the inculcating its two principles, viz. that *there is a Providence, which administers and consults for the whole, to the absolute exclusion of general evil and disorder*, and that *man is made by that Providence a political or social animal, whose constitution can only find its true and natural end in the pursuit and exercise of the moral and social virtues* . . . they may be proved in every part to be in fact no other than the concurring sentiments of the best writers among the ancients.[48]

The court of appeal is not Christian doctrine (even as loosely defined by Tindal) but simply 'the best writers among the ancients'. It is with them that Shaftesbury stands in conformity and by the standard of their sentiments that a modern philosopher and 'theist' must be judged. In a letter probably to Sir Andrew Mitchell, Whig diplomatist, Harris praised Shaftesbury's comments on the text of Horace (to which Mitchell had referred):

> None, that have commented this elegant Poet, have been Philosophers, and they have rather therefore dwelt upon the Shell, than penetrated into the interior Substance. Philosophy in those [ancient] days was like Religion now: Every Man of every rank profest some Sect or other, tho there was no great mutual Bitterness among the Dissidents. The Sublime Genius loved Plato; the more acute followed Aristotle; the Augustan Courtiers adopted Epicurus, and the old Republicans preferred Zeno. Hence the Necessity of a thorough Knowledge of Philosophy (such as Lord Shaftesbury possesst) to comprehend and explain Horace according to the different Periods of his Life, his Fortunes, and his respective Patrons.[49]

'Philosophy in those days was like Religion now'. In a few words Harris evokes the tolerance of latitudinarian Anglicanism, and also that affinity of spirit between the English cultural present and the classical past embodied in its most influential form in Shaftesbury, for whom correct aesthetics go hand-in-hand with correct ethics and whose theistic philosophy conforms with the sentiments of 'the best writers among the ancients'.

Enlisting the classical past in their campaigns against orthodox Christianity, English freethinkers never paused to consider whether what they treated with contemptuous irony might be reconciled with the best of Roman spirit and culture. Christianity was, after all, the official Roman religion during the last century and a half of the Western Empire. There must have been much that was congenial about it. Plotinus, founder of neo-Platonism, and personally close to two pagan Roman emperors, is never among the philosophers cited by freethinkers, though he was 'classical' enough. His theology was too 'Christian' for their liking. English freethinkers are determined that Christianity be alien to the classical spirit.[50] Perhaps this is why they devote so much ink to Judaism.

Shaftesbury spends page after page on what he sees as the immorality and barbarity of the patriarchs, and Moses in particular.[51] The religion of the Jews and their testament as accepted and revered by Christians are for Shaftesbury discredited out of the mouths of their authors, our humanity affronted by their accounts of the behaviour of 'the chosen seed', and all our natural sympathies engaged by their victims. Anyone of erudition and sensibility, he insists, necessarily becomes pro-pagan in the very reading of 'Holy Writ'. Not surprisingly, where Shaftesbury has a choice he places his trust in pagan as opposed to Jewish sources. On the Exodus he cites the *Histories* of Tacitus, based not on Jewish but on Egyptian sources. The Exodus in this account is not a voluntary departure of the Jews from Egypt against the will of the host country but an expulsion on account of their leprous scabies. Charles Blount had quoted Tacitus at length for a similar purpose. He argued that Tacitus' account had been suppressed, with no English translation of the fifth book of the *Histories* available, Sir Henry Savile's edition of 1591 (several times reprinted) having carefully omitted it.[52] In the 'Miscellaneous Reflections' Shaftesbury quotes Tacitus as well as Justin Martyr, the second-century Christian apologist, who evidently believed Tacitus' version.[53]

Shaftesbury, however, reserves his sharpest barbs for the early Christians. With the triumph of that 'sect' in the west, philosophy and mystery were prostituted to the spirit of bigotry and 'All was reduced to article and proposition.' So alien had this spirit been to Greece and Rome that 'Let anyone who considers distinctly the meaning and force of the word bigotry, endeavour to render it in either of the ancient languages, and he will find how peculiar a passion it implies; and how different from the mere affection of enthusiasm or superstition.'[54] In the face of aggression from 'the new sect', pagan worshippers put up a zealous resistance as at Ephesus, but in distinction to the Christians (and the Jews) 'the zeal of the heathen church . . . was only defensive'.[55] The pagans were essentially tolerant. Hume makes the same point.[56]

The emperor Julian was foremost among pagans admired by freethinkers, not only for what was seen as a brave attempt to disestablish the church but for the classical qualities of character – moral virtue, concern for the commonwealth, restraint, reasonableness, elegance and wit – which he displayed in the effort. Shaftesbury's major note on Julian physically overwhelms the three pages it spills across, on its first two pages leaving just three lines of main text above it in Robertson's edition.[57] With Shaftesbury, as for Gibbon, the notes are not only the formal documentation of textual claims, but also an ironically effective way of highlighting the 'best bits'.[58] Collins follows Shaftesbury in his view of Julian.[59] Gibbon is more balanced, praising the emperor for having 'extended to all the inhabitants of the Roman world, the benefits of a free and equal toleration',[60] while admitting his 'faults and follies', the vanity, the 'superstition' which 'disturbed the peace, and endangered the safety of a mighty empire'.[61] It is partly because his judgements are so careful that Gibbon is still read.

It needs to be stressed that, for most freethinkers, the ancient Roman religion, though tolerant, was in other respects as bad as the 'superstition' which replaced it. They share the perspective of Cicero. One of Conyers Middleton's most interesting works enumerates all the features of Roman Catholicism which derive from pagan Roman religion. Both are roundly mocked.[62]

Only Addison, the Christian author of *Cato*, and the most 'classical' prose stylist of his age, made the bold attempt to see Christianity from a *sympathetic* classical standpoint. His defensive *Of the Christian Religion*, first published in 1721, rests its case largely on pagan sources including Tacitus, the younger Pliny, and the pro-Roman Jewish historian Flavius Josephus, for Addison knew that these were the only ones which held any credibility for the sceptical, since 'generally speaking, a man is not so acceptable and unquestioned as evidence in facts, which make for the advancement of his own party'.[63] In this Addison may have been following Hugo Grotius who, in the *De veritate religionis christianae* (1622), drew much of his evidence for natural theology from other-than-Christian sources.

Addison might justifiably have titled his book *How a Good Pagan Might be Persuaded of the Christian Religion*. For instance, he cites the lost letter of Pontius Pilate to Tiberius and the Senate regarding the trial of Christ, appealed to in the second century by Justin Martyr who, Addison points out, would hardly have laid himself open to exposure by the philosophers he challenges had the letter not then been in existence in the Senate archives.[64] For Addison the historical fact of such a document testifies to the extraordinary impact Christ had upon Judaea, and it is a powerful point. On the historicity of Christ he also cites Tacitus, Suetonius, Pliny the Younger and Celsus. He might also have cited St Paul's conversion on the Damascus road in support of the truth of Christianity, as George Lyttelton was later to do with great effect.[65]

Aware of the class prejudices of his audience, Addison effectively subverts the image of a religion of slaves by stressing the eminent social backgrounds of early converts such as Joseph the Arimathean, a member of the Jewish Sanhedrin; Dionysius of the Athenian Areopagus; and Titus Flavius Clemens, a Roman Senator. Clemens was married to the Christian patrician Flavia Domitilla, granddaughter of the emperor Vespasian, and was in fact consul in 96, the year of his martyrdom under the emperor Domitian, his first cousin. Addison could also have mentioned the Senator Manius Acilius Glabrio, consul in 91 and probably also a Christian martyr. He cites pagan philosophers who converted to the new religion, men 'as learned as any unconverted heathen Authors of the age in which they lived'.[66]

Addison's defence of Christianity is remarkable for being mounted to such an extent from classical ground, the vantage from which its eighteenth-century enemies regularly attacked the faith. The entire document is stimulating in its approach and perfectly judged in its appeal, a testimony to the classical spirit of the age, and appropriately written by an author whose conflicting classical and Christian affinities caused his Cato to voice regret for the act of suicide (and hence, as Bishop Hurd said, 'to violate decorum').[67] The tensions and contradictions which complicate Addison's classicism no doubt tempered the philoromanism of many of those noticed in this book.

Conclusion

Numerous periods and movements, from the Carolingian to the Italian Renaissance, from the sculpture of Louis XIV's Versailles to examples of post-modernist architecture, might claim to be neo-classical, quite aside from the fifty or sixty years of 'official' European neo-classicism from around 1760. However broad or narrow one's definition of this term, however, the British century from 1688 must rank as outstanding in the degree to which its cultural and political elite appropriated and assimilated classical, and particularly Roman, habits of mind. They commonly discussed their recent political history and institutions in terms of classical precepts and principles, with the confidence to claim the superiority of their own accomplishments. They frequently justified their power and privileges by associating themselves analogically with their heroic counterparts in Roman history. An impressive array of flattering parallels was carefully promoted in the print culture and the visual arts, as the twin causes of liberty and civic virtue were proclaimed and defended across the broad spectrum of the nation's politics. It was possible, even at the century's end, for Edmund Burke to conduct a case at law, albeit somewhat incongruously, as though he were Cicero, without a trace of irony.

That Britain had once been a Romanised Britannia, that this Britannia was still there, waiting to be uncovered from beneath the modern surface of things, encouraged those engaged in the essentially classical (and political) Shaftesburian cultural project to enlist archaeology in their service. The physical past was made to re-appear as a result of the collaboration of archaeologists and architects, categories which merge in the persons of Burlington and other members of the cultural elite. In their resurrected Britannia, collectors and connoisseurs filled their houses and gardens with objects shipped from the excavation sites of Rome, from Hadrian's Villa and other classic ground. The world they most admired was made present to them. A tangible reality was given to a classical temper which politics and history had already seemed to make authentically British.

The concept of an 'oligarchy of virtue', though the phrase nowhere occurs in the literature, was actively constructed, rhetorically and visibly, with the collaboration of all the arts and at a time when they were still largely under the patronage of the aristocracy. The cultural project naturally served the political interests of those who were dominant in the nation, but the idealism and enthusiasm with which it was promoted helped close off any criticism by contemporaries regarding the self-interested nature of the entire enterprise. Inevitably there was hypocrisy behind all the professions of civic virtue. No doubt there were thousands of ambivalent sceptics like Horace Walpole and William Hogarth for whom modern Britain, because it was in so many ways so different, could never be more than a caricature of the Roman ideal, which was in any case far less glorious than most wished to believe.[1] More of these sceptics spoke up or struck out in print during the second half of the century. By then, less flattering views of the Roman-republican oligarchy and its heroes had become current, and served to undermine the political value of the Roman analogy at the same time as oligarchy itself was coming under criticism from a growing minority engaged in the promotion of more democratic political and cultural ideals.

In Britain, the appropriation of Roman models was at its strongest in the first half-century following the Glorious Revolution. For as long as that event was a living memory, and its achievement subject to revision at the hands of a potent Jacobite reaction, liberty, classically defined, could be shown to be in the balance. The invasions of 1715 and 1745 were tangible manifestations of a continuing threat not finally vanquished until 1746. Thereafter, whatever urgency and tension there had been in the discourse of liberty and virtue evaporated; even in the 1720s and 1730s it had been cheapened by its promiscuous availability to any political party claiming to have the nation's interests at heart.

Burke could call it up again with dramatic effect in his prosecution of Warren Hastings half a century later, when the *res publica* seemed to be in danger of corruption from the riches of the east. The Foxite Whigs, identifying themselves with the elder and younger Brutuses, could invoke it in their defence of liberty, an ideal suddenly widened in its potential meanings by the fact of the French Revolution. By now, however, British culture was no longer saturated with references to ancient Rome as it had been earlier in the century. This was due partly to a growing sense of cultural autonomy, partly to the fact that Greek taste was gradually supplanting Roman in architecture and sculpture, and partly because in literature and the plastic arts Romanticism was discarding the classical emphasis on order and proportion.

Roman analogies would continue to support the concept of the British Empire throughout the nineteenth and early twentieth centuries, but by then they would be increasingly token, self-confidence born of imperial and industrial power having long since lessened their prestige. The disappearance of compulsory Latin from the school curriculum in the 1960s would make them incomprehensible to most. Henceforth an endless stream of the curious would stare at the Romanised Britons in Westminster Abbey, puzzling over the costumes, attitudes and indecipherable inscriptions, unable to comprehend a period when so much of the nation's culture was harnessed to an oligarchy of virtue.

Appendix. Books on archaeology owned by Burlington: an annotated shelf-list

The following information has been extracted from 'A Catalogue of The Earl of Burlington's Library, At His Lordships Seat at Cheswick; January, 1741/2', in the Burlington Papers at Chatsworth House.

The relevant category in the catalogue is 'Antiquities'. Books on this subject shared shelves 1, 2, 3 and 10 with books on architecture and sculpture, having shelf 9 to themselves. There were a few more on shelves 34 and 35 and within the table marked 'C', as well as odd volumes of relevant works on other shelves and in table 'B'. Note that editions are those given in the catalogue, not the first.

Shelf 1 in the Chiswick library included the *Fragmenta vestigii veteris Romae ex lapidibus farnesianis, cum notis* (Verona, 1732) of Giovanni Pietro Bellori (Queen Christina's librarian in Rome); Giovanni Giacomo de Rossi's *Insignium Romae templorum prospectus* (under 'Iac. de Rubeis'; Rome, 1683); *Il Anfiteatro Flavio*, the *Antiche statue greche e romane nell'Antisala della Libreria di San Marco* in two volumes (Venice, 1740) (no author given for either of these); and Antonio Francesco Gori's *Musaeum etruscum*, the first two volumes (Florence, 1737) but not the third (1743). Gori was the leading Etruscan scholar of the early eighteenth century, and this is a good example of how Burlington kept up-to-date with non-Roman archaeological studies. The final item on this shelf was the *Gemmae antiquae ex thesauro mediceo* in six volumes (Venice, 1733–40).

On shelf 2 was Burlington's own collection of Palladio's reconstructions of ancient *thermae* – the *Fabbriche Antiche* (1730) – as well as various editions of Vitruvius and Italian and French architects.[1] There was also a *Parallele del' architecture antique et moderne* (Paris, 1702), and Antoine Desgodetz's important *Les édifices antiques de Rome dessinés et mesurés très exactement* (Paris, 1682), an especially significant work in the present context because, to an even greater extent than Palladio's *I quattro libri dell'architettura*, the archaeological precision with which it displayed the details of classical Roman buildings could seem to anticipate faithful replication. Finally there were Friderik Ludvig Norden's *Drawings of Some Ruins and Colossal Statues at Thebes in Egypt* (London, 1741), another example of Burlington's widening archaeological and architectural horizons in the early 1740s, and Domenico Fontana's *L'Obeslico Vaticano* (Rome, 1589).

On shelf 3 stood the *Inscrizioni sepolcrali di liberti . . . della Casa di Augusto* (Rome, 1727) by the polymath Francesco Bianchini the Elder; Antonio Francesco Gori's *Columbarium libertorum et servorum Liviae Augustae* (Florence, 1737); and the second part of *Gli antichi sepolcri romani e etrusci* (Rome, 1697) by the painter and engraver Pietro Santi Bartoli, whose prints showed great fidelity to their subjects. Guillaume Du Choul's *Discours de la religion des anciens romains* (Lyons, 1556) was on this shelf too, along with Jean Poldo D'Albenas's *Discours historial de l'antique et l'illustre cité de Nismes* (Lyons, 1560); Hubert Goltz's *Sicilia et Magna Graecia* (Antwerp, 1618); the *Ager Futeolanus* (Rome, 1652) by the painter and engraver Francesco Villamena; and the *De aquaeductibus urbis Romae commentarius* (Patavia, 1722) by Sextus Julius Frontinus, the late first-century *curator aquarum* at Rome. In addition there were the *Praecipua antiquitatis ruinarum monimenta* (Antwerp, 1555); Vincenzo Mirabella e Alagonas's *Dichiarazioni della pianta dell'antiche Siracuse* (Naples, 1613); Guillaume Du Choul's *La castramétation et discipline militaire des Romains* (Lyons, 1595); *Le pitture antiche delle Grotte di Roma, e del Sepolcro di Nasoni* (Rome, 1706); and Bonaventura van Overbeke's three-volume *Les restes de l'ancienne Rome* (Amsterdam, 1709).

Taking up much of shelf 9 were the twelve volumes of Johannes Giorgius Graevius's *Thesaurus antiquitatum romanarum* (presumably the Leyden edition, 1694–9) and, inspired by this great work, the thirteen volumes of Jacobus Gronovius's equally authoritative *Thesaurus antiquitatum graecarum* (Venice, 1732–7). Alongside these were Giovanni Poleni's five volumes of supplements to Graevius and Gronovius (Venice, 1737), and Albert Henri de Sallengre's three-volume *Novus thesaurus antiquitatum romanarum* (Venice, 1735).

On shelf 34 was Famiano Nardini's *Roma antica* (Rome, 1704); the *Galliae antiquitates selectae* (Paris, 1733); and the *Praeneste antiqua* of Joseph Marie Suares (or Suaresius; Rome, 1655).

On shelf 35 were Paulo Alessandro Maffei's *Dell'antica condizione di Verona* (Venice, 1719) and his *De gli amfiteatri e singolarmente del Veronese* (Verona, 1728), as well as *Delle antichita di Roma* (Venice, 1555) by the Renaissance architect and painter Pirro Ligorio.

In table 'C' were two editions of *I vestigi dell'antichita di Roma* (Rome, 1575, 1653), one of the best of the early collections of reproductions of ancient Roman monuments, by the sixteenth-century architect, painter and engraver Etienne du Perac, as well as a Prague edition of the same title (undated in the catalogue). Also in this table was another early edition (Antwerp, 1551) of the *Praecipua antiquitatis ruinarum monimenta* noted on shelf 3.

Palladio's collection of *Antiquitates urbis Romae* (Oxford, 1709) sat on shelf 28, Lucio Fauno's *Delle antichita della Citta di Roma* (Venice, 1548) on shelf 33.

In addition to these mainly continental works on classical archaeology and antiquities, Burlington owned significant British works on Roman and Romano-British antiquity. Robert Castell's *Villas of the Ancients* (1728) was in table 'B', Philemon Holland's 1610 translation of Camden's *Britannia* on shelf 20 and Edmund Gibson's indispensable updated translation and edition of this (1695) on shelf 6. John Horsley's *Britannia romana* (1732) also sat on shelf 6, while Alexander Gordon's *Itinerarium septentrionale* (1726) shared shelf 10 with Francis Drake's *Eboracum: or the History and Antiquities of the City of York* (1736, dedicated to Burlington, with superbly hand-coloured plates in the presentation copy). There were also Inigo Jones's *Stone-Heng, Restored* (1655) and John Webb's *Vindication of Stone Heng Restored* (1665) on shelf 14, and *The Marble Antiquities of the Earl of Pembroke at Wilton* (1731) in table 'C'.

In the early nineteenth century the Chiswick library went to Chatsworth, where many of these books may still be consulted today. They provided the inspiration for Burlington's archaeological activities and constitute an invaluable index to the scholarly archaeological basis of his architecture.

Notes

1 OLIGARCHY OF VIRTUE

For the eighteenth century see Peter Laslett, *The World We Have Lost: English Society Before and After the Coming of Industry* (London, 1965) and *The World We Have Lost Further Explored* (London, 1983), on familial and patriarchal social structures and relationships in the pre-industrial world, as well as Lawrence Stone, *The Family, Sex and Marriage in England 1500–1800* (London, 1977), which traces the transition from 'distance, deference and patriarchy' to 'Affective Individualism' (p. 4) through the diverse materials it examines and concludes that 'the class analysis is wrong' (p. 661); J. G. A. Pocock, *Politics, Language and Time: Essays in Political Thought and History* (New York, 1971), *The Machiavellian Moment: Florentine Political Thought and the Atlantic Republican Tradition* (Princeton, 1975) and *Virtue, Commerce, and History* (Cambridge, 1985) on the recovery of the aristocracy after 1688 within 'a society of masters and servants' (*Virtue, Commerce, and History*, p. 53) and the oligarchy's use of Machiavellian notions of civic humanism and classical ideals generally; John Cannon, *Aristocratic Century: the Peerage of Eighteenth-Century England* (Cambridge, 1984) on the power and relatively closed nature of the elite; J. C. D. Clark, *English Society 1688–1832: Ideology, Social Structure and Political Practice during the Ancien Régime* (Cambridge, 1985) and *Revolution and Rebellion: State and Society in England in the Seventeenth and Eighteenth Centuries* (Cambridge, 1986) on a period of history which is not to be described in terms of 'class conflict, economic revolution or democratic representation' but in terms of 'hierarchy, allegiance and authority' (*Revolution and Rebellion*, p. 23). Clark is one of a number of contemporary historians who are using, modifying and developing certain key insights of Sir Lewis Namier. In his work on the eighteenth century, particularly *The Structure of Politics at the Accession of George III* (London, 1929; 2nd edn, London, 1957) and *England in the Age of the American Revolution* (London, 1930; 2nd edn, London, 1961), Namier described a high politics in the eighteenth century based not on party and even less on class but on 'ins' and 'outs' within a society of patrons and clients.

2 H. T. Dickinson has observed that 'A political agent may well feel the need to disguise his baser motives even from himself. His attempts to explain his behaviour are therefore designed to attain an appropriate self-image and so legitimate his political actions to himself . . . by using ideas and terms which are accepted and approved by others': *Liberty and Property: Political Ideology in Eighteenth-Century Britain* (London, 1977), p. 4.

3 Howard D. Weinbrot, *Britannia's Issue: the Rise of British Literature from Dryden to Ossian* (Cambridge, 1993), pp. 3 and 73.

4 See Pocock, *The Machiavellian Moment* and his 'Machiavelli, Harrington and English Political Ideologies in the Eighteenth Century' (1965) in *Politics, Language and Time*, as well as the earlier studies of Zera S. Fink, *The Classical Republicans* (Evanston, Ill., 1946; 2nd edn, 1962) and Caroline Robbins, *The Eighteenth-Century Commonwealthsman* (Cambridge, Mass., 1959).

5 See Chaim Wirszubski, *Libertas as a Political Idea at Rome during the Late Republic and Early Principate* (Cambridge, 1950); and P. A. Brunt, ch. 6 in *The Fall of the Roman Republic and Related Essays* (Oxford, 1988).

6 On the actual contribution of the Revolution to liberty see the essays in J. R. Jones, ed., *Liberty Secured? Britain Before and After 1688* (Stanford, 1992).

7 Reed Browning, *Political and Constitutional Ideas of the Court Whigs* (Baton Rouge, 1982), p. 9.

8 Ben Jonson, *Sejanus His Fall*, Revels edn, ed. Philip Ayres (Manchester, 1990), introduction, pp. 28–37, for Jonson's attitudes in the context of those of his time.

9 See, *inter alia*, R. E. Smith, *The Failure of the Roman Republic* (New York, 1955), which is generally senatorial in sympathy; Lily Ross Taylor, *Party Politics in the Age of Caesar* (Berkeley, 1968); Ronald Syme, *The Roman Revolution* (Oxford, 1939), which places less emphasis on party divisions (ch. 2); H. H. Scullard, *From the Gracchi to Nero: a History of Rome from 133 BC to AD 68* (London, 1959), chs. 1–9; and Brunt, ch. 1 in *The Fall of the Roman Republic*.

10 On the populist aspects of the rising see Robin Clifton, *The Last Popular Rebellion: the Western Rising of 1685* (London, 1984).

11 Dickinson, *Liberty and Property*, *passim*; and see further on this below. For a more general treatment of the place of property in the thought and temper of the times see Paul Langford, *Public Life and the Propertied Englishman 1689–1798* (Oxford, 1991).

12 'Miscellaneous Reflections', in *Characteristicks of Men, Manners, Opinions, Times*, ed. John M. Robertson, 2 vols. (London, 1900), II, 241ff., and *Advice to an Author*, in *Characteristicks*, I, 143–5.

13 James William Johnson, *The Formation of English Neo-Classical Thought* (Princeton, 1967), p. 91. See also p. 105: 'The extrapolation of certain Roman phenomena into British culture was determined by utilitarian rather than aesthetic criteria. English neo-Romanism, in the main, was more widely disseminated than neo-Hellenism because it was conceived for pragmatic purposes and because its principles were enunciated in such a way as to appeal on nationalistic grounds to as large an audience as possible. Neo-Roman principles were inherently functional, as British unity, strength, and prosperity defined functionalism.'

14 For a recent treatment of the subject see Christine Gerrard, *The Patriot Opposition to Walpole:*

Politics, Poetry, and National Myth, 1725–1742 (Oxford, 1994), pp. 108–49.

15 Fink, *The Classical Republicans,* and Pocock, *The Machiavellian Moment*, both *passim.*

16 Their favourite authority was Robert Filmer's *Patriarcha* (1680) which emphasised kingly authority – tracing this from Adam – not the liberty of the subject.

17 See Julian Martin, *Francis Bacon, the State, and the Reform of Natural Philosophy* (Cambridge, 1992), esp. pp. 129–34.

18 See, most recently, Michael Meehan, *Liberty and Poetics in Eighteenth-Century England* (London, 1986), pp. 76–7.

19 Dickinson, *Liberty and Property*, pp. 201–4.

20 Pocock, *Virtue, Commerce, and History*, p. 235.

21 Browning, *Political and Constitutional Ideas of the Court Whigs*, p. x.

22 Defence of Protestantism, however, might easily be 'Romanised'. Thus, as we shall later see, for bringing in the Bill to exclude Catholics from the throne, Sir Robert Clayton was identified with Cicero as 'Father of the City'.

23 John Oldmixon, *The History of England during the Reigns of the Royal House of Stuart* (1730), pp. iv–v.

24 *Gazetteer*, 29 February 1740.

25 *Reflections on the Rise and Fall of the Antient Republicks Adapted to the Present State of Great Britain* (1759), pp. 362, 365–6.

26 'An Argument against a Standing Army shewing that a Standing Army is inconsistent with a Free Government, and absolutely destructive to the Constitution of the English Monarchy' (1697), in *The Whole Works*, (1727), p. 16.

27 *Poems on Affairs of State: Augustan Satirical Verse, 1660–1714*, vol. v, 1688–1697, ed. William J. Cameron (New Haven, 1971), p. 49.

28 *Ibid.*, v, 235–7.

29 *Ibid.*, vol. vi, 1697–1704, ed. Frank H. Ellis (New Haven, 1970), p. 330.

30 *Ibid.*, vi, 671.

31 Nathaniel Lee, *Lucius Junius Brutus* (1681), p. 72.

32 *Ibid.*, pp. 67–8.

33 Occasionally, analogies are drawn with other periods of Roman history. Gilbert Burnet likened the reigns of Charles II and James II to those of the bad emperors from Tiberius to Domitian, and England's delivery under William to the reign of Marcus Aurelius, when the Romans' 'Ancient Sense of Liberty was revived, which must ever carry with it, all that is Great, or Noble in humane Nature; with it Learning and good Sense, Wit and Eloquence, were again recovered, Frugality and Sobriety were again honoured, and a Modesty and Simplicity of living shined afresh: Truth and Vertue, and Philosophy it self began to reign': *A Sermon Preached at the Coronation of William III and Mary II . . . in the Abby-Church of Westminster, April 11 1689* (1689), pp. 25–6

34 See Duncan Chisholm, 'Handel's *Lucio Cornelio Silla*, its Problems and Context', *Early Music*, 14 (1986), 64–70 and esp. pp. 66–9. The account of Handel's career in the *New Grove Dictionary of Music* will indicate the extent to which *opera seria* relied on classical materials.

35 Joseph Addison in Addison and Steele, *The Spectator*, ed. Donald F. Bond, 5 vols. (Oxford, 1965), III, 19–20 (*Spectator* no. 287, 29 January 1712).

36 Fink, *The Classical Republicans*, p. 183, and ch. 7 generally.

37 *Ibid.*, pp. 183–5. The Swift reference is to the *Discourse of the Contests and Dissentions between the Nobles and Commons in Athens and Rome*, ch. 1.

38 On Sidney's admiration for the Roman Republic and his emphasis on the fact that England under anything but the most tyrannous king is properly a commonwealth, see Jonathan Scott, *Algernon Sidney and the Restoration Crisis 1677–1683* (Cambridge, 1991), pp. 233–6.

39 On Toland's equivocal republicanism see F. H. Heinemann, 'John Toland and the Age of Enlightenment', *RES*, 20 (1944), 138–9, which fails, however, to explore the nature of the Roman analogising here and elsewhere in Toland.

40 John Toland, *The State Anatomy of Great Britain: Containing a Particular Account of its Several Interests and Parties* (1717), pp. 9–10.

41 Jean-Jacques Rousseau, *The Social Contract*, tr. Maurice Cranston (Harmondsworth, 1968), p. 82.

42 Quoted in Caroline Robbins, *The Eighteenth-Century Commonwealthsman*, p. 121.

43 It is the earliest sense recorded by the *OED* which cites – as examples of the word in its meaning of 'The state, the common weal. *Obs.*' – Drayton's *Barons' Wars*, 'Neither yet thinke, by their vnnaturall Fight What the republique suffred them among' (1603); Hobbes's *Government and Society*, v.5.78, 'Those men are of most trouble to the Republique, who haue most leasure to be idle' (1651); and *Scanderbeg redivivus*, III.41, 'The Republick might be highly endangered by an Inter-Regnum' (1684). Predating these is the Latin form as used, for example, in Sir Thomas Smith's *De republica anglorum. The Maner of Gouernement or Policie of the Realme of England* (1583).

44 John Toland, dedication to his edn of James Harrington's *Oceana* (1700), pp. iii–vi.

45 *De la tragédie anglaise*, quoted in Peter Smithers, *The Life of Joseph Addison* (Oxford, 1954), p. 262.

46 Desmond Flower, ed., *Voltaire's England*, (London, 1950), p. 37.

47 The anonymous bust is in the Victoria and Albert Museum, and is illustrated in Margaret Whinney, *English Sculpture 1720–1830* (London, 1971), item 28, p. 95. Cumberland's victory no doubt reminded contemporaries of Agricola's in the same field of battle. He followed it up with the systematic and thorough destruction of the clan culture, a very Roman policy which created a cultural desert that was called peace, to borrow the Caledonian leader Galgacus' words on Agricola as reported by Tacitus. Also apposite is Titus' destruction of the Temple of Jerusalem in AD 70 and his dispersal of the inhabitants. It is worth noting that Titus' actions in Judaea were generally admired in the eighteenth century as in earlier centuries, for he was seen as the instrument of God's punishment upon a God-killing people. Thus Horace Walpole: 'I live in town to hear of mortgages and annuities, and do not wonder that Titus was called the delight of mankind [by Suetonius], for he put *the Jews* to the sword': *HWC*, XXVIII (1955), 92. Walpole jokingly regretted 'that Charles Fox will not, like Titus, though the delight of mankind too, put them to the sword, as they deserve': *HWC*, XXXII (1965), 166.

48 *The Letters of Philip Dormer Stanhope, 4th Earl of Chesterfield*, ed. Bonamy Dobrée, 6 vols. (London, 1932), II, 340.

49 *Ibid.*

50 Chesterfield clearly intends the double negative 'n'était rien' to imply the positive 'was something', forgetting that his French double negative strictly produces a negative.

51 *Ibid.*, II, 343–4.

52 *Ibid.*, II, 349.

53 *Ibid.*, II, 514–16.

54 *The Observator*, 10: 8 (27 January 1711), quoted in M. M. Goldsmith, 'Public Virtue and Private Vices: Bernard Mandeville and English Political Ideologies in the Early Eighteenth Century', *ECS*, 9 (1975–6), p. 489.

55 'Epistle to Mr Addison, Occasioned by his Dialogues on Medals', ll. 53–62, in Pope, *The Poems of Alexander Pope*, Twickenham edn, vol. VI, *Minor Poems*, ed. Norman Ault and John Butt (London, 1954), 204.

56 *HWC*, XXXV (1973), 294.

57 See further in Romney Sedgwick, 'Horace Walpole's Political Articles', in *Horace Walpole, Writer, Politician, and Connoisseur: Essays on the 250th Anniversary of Walpole's Birth*, ed. Warren Hunting Smith (New Haven, 1967), pp. 46ff.

58 See his cartoon caricature of 'Burlington Gate' in *Hogarth: the Complete Engravings*, ed. Joseph Burke and Colin Caldwell (London, 1968), plate 129 and note.

59 *HWC*, XXXVIII (1974), 188.

60 *Ibid.*, 513.

61 *HWC*, XXIII (1967), 401.

62 *HWC*, XXXIII (1965), 158.

63 *Ibid.*, 479; Henry Fielding, *The History of Tom Jones, a Foundling*, XII.xii (see the edn of Martin C. Battestin and Fredson Bowers, 2 vols. (Oxford, 1974), II, 671–2 and 672n.); Gibbon, *The Decline and Fall of the Roman Empire*, Chandos verbatim reprint, 4 vols. (London, 1982), *passim*.

64 Linda Colley, *Britons: Forging the Nation 1707–1837* (New Haven, 1992), p. 168. She adds that 'the classics had a further practical advantage. The societies they celebrated were emphatically dead. Consequently, they could inspire without being in any way threatening': *ibid*. See the section 'The Cultural Reconstruction of an Elite' generally (pp. 164–77).

65 *Decline and Fall*, I, 42–3; *The Miscellaneous Works of Edward Gibbon*, ed. Lord Sheffield, 2 vols. (London, 1814), I, 204; and the discussion in Joseph Ward Swain, *Edward Gibbon the Historian* (London, 1966), p. 130.

66 *Decline and Fall*, II, 368.

67 See, *passim*, *The Structure of Politics at the Accession of George III* and *England in the Age of the American Revolution*. For a concise statement of Namier's arguments and his place in British historiography see Norma Landau, 'Eighteenth-Century England: Tales Historians Tell', *ECS*, 22 (1988–9), 208–18.

68 Carl Philipp Moritz, *Travels, Chiefly on Foot, through Several Parts of England in 1782*, ed. P. E. Matheson (London, 1924), extracted in *English Historical Documents*, vol. X, *1714–1783*, ed. D. B. Horn and Mary Ransome (London, 1969), 191–2.

69 William Blackstone, *Commentaries on the Laws of England*, 7th edn (London, 1775), extracted in *English Historical Documents* vol. X, *1714–1783*, p. 91.

70 John Locke, *Two Treatises of Government*, ed. Peter Laslett (Cambridge, 1960; edn cit. 1963), p. 373 ('Second Treatise', para. 94).

71 J. G. A. Pocock, *Virtue, Commerce, and History*, p. 70.

72 Fink, *The Classical Republicans*, p. 19.

73 Howard D. Weinbrot overstates the animus against Augustus in this period. See his very thorough but adversarial *Augustus Caesar in Augustan England* (Princeton, 1978). Moderating arguments on the issue include Howard Erskine-Hill's in *The Augustan Idea in English Literature*

(London, 1983), *passim*, and Michael Meehan's in *Liberty and Poetics in Eighteenth-Century England*, pp. 64ff.

74 *Julius Caesar Acquitted and his Murderers Condemn'd. In a Letter to a Friend. Shewing that it was not Caesar, who Destroyed the Roman Liberties, but the Corruptions of the Romans Themselves* (1722), p. 10, quoted in Addison Ward, 'The Tory View of Roman History', *SEL*, 4 (1964), 427.

75 Bolingbroke had combined sympathy for the Republic with criticism of the Senatorial party: 'We must not imagine that the freedom of the Romans was lost because one party fought for the maintenance of liberty; another for the establishment of tyranny; and that the latter prevailed. No. The spirit of liberty was dead, and the spirit of faction had taken it's place on both sides': 'Remarks on the History of England', letter 2, in *The Works of the Right Honourable Henry St John, Lord Viscount Bolingbroke*, 8 vols. (London, 1809), II, 132.

76 See Addison Ward, 'The Tory View of Roman History', pp. 443ff.

77 See, e.g., Pocock, *Virtue, Commerce, and History*, p. 241.

78 See Reed Browning, *Political and Constitutional Ideas of the Court Whigs*.

79 Linda Colley quotes the Jacobite John Matthews's *Vox populi, vox dei* (1719) which urged popular insurrection in favour of the Pretender ('Sure you ought to fight with more resolution for liberty than your oppressors do for dominion. Count your numbers.'). She points out that 'In common with many mid-century Jacobite authors, Matthews also espoused contract theory, and this says something about the audience at which these writings were aimed. It was always James Stuart's hope that his cause might attract not only tory but also dissident whig support – hence in part the varied political arguments employed by his apologists': *In Defiance of Oligarchy: the Tory Party 1714–60* (Cambridge, 1982), p. 28. See also her 'Eighteenth-Century English Radicalism before Wilkes', *Transactions of the Royal Historical Society*, 5th ser., 31 (1981), 1–20. Much of pre-Wilkes radicalism came from the Tory party.

80 'Verses on the Death of Dr Swift', ll. 347–50, in *The Poems of Jonathan Swift*, ed. Harold Williams, 3 vols. (1st edn, Oxford, 1937; 2nd edn cit., Oxford, 1958), II, 566. For a good treatment of the subject see Irvin Ehrenpreis, 'Swift on Liberty', *JHI*, 13 (1952), 131–46.

81 *A Discourse of the Contests and Dissensions between the Nobles and Commons in Athens and Rome, with the Consequences they had upon Both those States* (1701), in *The Prose Works of Jonathan Swift*, ed. Herbert Davis, 13 vols. (Oxford, 1939–62), I, 218–19.

82 Nathaniel Hooke, *The Roman History, from the Building of Rome to the Ruin of the Commonwealth*, 4 vols. (London, 1738–71), II, 533–4.

83 James Thomson, for example, in *Liberty*, III.347–8 (quoted below), in *Liberty, The Castle of Indolence and other Poems*, ed. James Sambrook (Oxford, 1986).

84 See the analysis in Isaac Kramnick, *Bolingbroke and his Circle: the Politics of Nostalgia in the Age of Walpole* (Cambridge, Mass., 1968), especially the chapter on 'The Ambivalence of the Augustan Commonwealthman'.

85 See Ward, 'The Tory View of Roman History', pp. 443–56.

86 Velleius Paterculus, *Compendium of Roman*

History, Loeb edn, ed. Frederick W. Shipley (London, 1924), II, XXXV, 2. I quote Jonson's translation of the phrase, *Sejanus*, I.124, where it is used of Germanicus.

87 In the wake of the Second Punic War the elder Cato inveighed against the growth of luxury, which would corrupt virtue. Polybius traced the moral decline of Rome to this period too, seeing it exacerbated by the later victory over Macedon. Scipio Nasica argued against the elder Cato's reiterated advice that 'delenda est Carthago' (advice followed in 146 BC when Carthage was levelled) on the grounds that fear stimulated civic virtue. Sallust, writing during the civil wars following Julius Caesar's assassination, endorsed this view, dating the oligarchy's selfish pursuit of wealth and power at the expense of the *res publica* from the destruction of Carthage. For Livy, religion and morality had declined together, and this was clearly the assumption behind Augustus' moral and religious reforms which were sealed by the Secular Games in 17 BC. See J. H. W. G. Liebeschuetz, *Continuity and Change in Roman Religion* (Oxford, 1979), pp. 56–100. Cremutius Cordus and later Tacitus, writing from the perspective of the mature principate, were in the Sallustian tradition but even more cynical and pessimistic.

88 The best treatment of the influence of civic humanism on eighteenth-century political thought is to be found in three of J. G. A. Pocock's books, *Politics, Language and Time*; *The Machiavellian Moment*; and *Virtue, Commerce, and History*. These works extend and develop material in Zera S. Fink's *The Classical Republicans* and Caroline Robbins's *The Eighteenth-Century Commonwealthsman*.

89 On the character of Cato of Utica as presented in the classical sources see Robert J. Goar, *The Legend of Cato Uticensis from the First Century BC to the Fifth Century AD* (Brussels, 1987).

90 Lucan, *The Civil War (Pharsalia)*, Loeb edn, tr. J. D. Duff (London, 1928), II, 379–80 and 387–8.

91 See D. W. R. Bahlman, *The Moral Revolution of 1689* (New Haven, 1957), pp. 15–17.

92 Jeremy Collier, *A Short View of the Immorality and Profaneness of the English Stage* (London, 1698).

93 As M. M. Goldsmith has stressed, 'Wherever we look during the reigns of William and Mary, of William, or of Anne (or even of George), whether to public life or to private, to the theatre, the press, or the pulpit, we find a campaign against the moral degeneration of Britons': Goldsmith: 'Public Virtue and Private Vices', p. 493.

94 See Liebeschuetz, *Continuity and Change in Roman Religion*, pp. 90–100.

95 That the new moralism was not to everyone's taste was shown by Bernard Mandeville's *Fable of the Bees*, which perversely but brilliantly asserted the public benefit of private vices. On Mandeville's motivation see Goldsmith, 'Public Virtue and Private Vices', p. 493 and *passim*.

96 Joseph Burke, *Oxford History of English Art*, vol IX, *English Art 1714–1800* (Oxford, 1976), p. 261. The Roubiliac bust was commissioned about the same time that Chesterfield purchased a bust of Cicero, referred to on 17 May 1745 in a letter to his son.

97 See Polybius, *Histories*, book VI, 3–4. The most convenient translation is that of W. R. Paton, *The Histories*, Loeb edn, 6 vols. (London, 1922–7).

98 *Ibid.*, book VI, 3 and 10.

99 'A constitution selected and blended from these

types is easier to commend than create; or, if created, its tenure of life is brief': Tacitus, *The Annals*, IV, xxxiii, John Jackson's translation in the Loeb edn of *The Histories and the Annals*, 4 vols. (London, 1925–37), vol. III (London, 1937), p. 57.

100 In *Luxury: the Concept in Western Thought, Eden to Smollett* (Baltimore, 1977), pp. 23–131, Sekora traces the idea of the corruptive effects of luxury from the Old Testament through classical literature and the Church fathers and on to eighteenth-century England, where it became a constant theme.

101 Smithers, *The Life of Joseph Addison*, p. 256.

102 Alexander Pope, 'Prologue to Mr Addison's Tragedy of Cato', ll. 17–18, 37–8, in the Twickenham edn of *The Poems of Alexander Pope*, vol. VI, *Minor Poems*, pp. 96–7.

103 James Welwood, preface to Nicholas Rowe's translation of Lucan's *Pharsalia (The Civil War)* (1718; edn cit. 1722), p. xlvii.

104 *Ibid.*, p. lv.

105 *Advice to an Author*, in *Characteristicks*, pp. 214–15 and 217.

106 See the 'Letter Concerning the Art or Science of Design' printed in some copies of the second edn of the *Characteristicks* (1714) and in all editions from the fifth (1732).

107 For a thoughtful treatment of Cato's ideas see Alan E. Astin, *Cato the Censor* (Oxford, 1978), pp. 78–103, 157–81 and 249–66.

108 Marcus Porcius Cato, *De agri cultura*, Loeb edn, tr. William Davis Hooper and rev. Harrison Boyd Ash (London, 1935), p. 3.

109 See, for example, Machiavelli in the *Discourses*, book III, ch. xxv – Max Lerner, tr., *The Prince and the Discourses* (New York, 1950), pp. 486–8.

110 Recent research suggests that the Court v. Country opposition is largely a matter of 'ins' v. 'outs' and aligns much more closely with the Whig–Tory divide than previously thought. For a summary of some recent positions see Clark, *Revolution and Rebellion*, pp. 113–14. On the Tory party after 1714 see Linda Colley, *In Defiance of Oligarchy*.

111 Machiavelli, however, had distrusted a land-owning nobility, understanding how the flouting of the Licinian Law by the owners of the great *latifundia* of the second century BC had given the Gracchi a just cause and precipitated the first civil bloodshed in centuries: *Discourses*, book I, ch. xxxvii; Lerner tr., pp. 208–12.

112 See *Parl. Hist.*, VII (1714–22), 696–844.

113 See Sekora, *Luxury*, pp. 82–7.

114 See Philip Hicks, 'Bolingbroke, Clarendon, and the Role of Classical Historian', *ECS*, 20 (1987), 445–71.

115 On this theme see Kramnick, *Bolingbroke and his Circle*, pp. 73–5, and Dickinson, *Liberty and Property*, pp. 103ff., 171–3. However, Dickinson's acceptance of a general 'convergence' of Whigs and Tories after 1714 and the development of a distinctly third-force Country ideology (see p. 123, e.g.) underestimates the tenacity of Toryism and is less tenable now than it seemed in 1977 when this work appeared. See Linda Colley, *In Defiance of Oligarchy*.

116 On this see Sekora, *Luxury*, p. 88.

117 See the chapter on 'Virtues, Rights and Manners' in J. G. A. Pocock, *Virtue, Commerce and History*.

118 See John Kenworthy-Browne, 'The Temple of Liberty at Woburn Abbey', *Apollo*, 130 (July 1989), 27–32. The poem is quoted on p. 30.

119 Napoleonic France was another matter. When

Fox visited the emperor in 1802 he was surprised to discover that the man was not after all a Whig. Napoleon would not even accept the basic Whig argument against a standing army. See L. G. Mitchell, *Charles James Fox* (Oxford, 1992), pp. 172–7.

120 National Convention: Robespierre, speech of 17 Pluviôse, Year II of the Republic (5 February 1794). Speech translated by Richard Bienvenu, ed., *The Ninth of Thermidor: the Fall of Robespierre* (Oxford, 1968), pp. 32–9.

121 Adam Smith, *An Inquiry into the Nature and Causes of the Wealth of Nations*, ed. R. H. Campbell, A. S. Skinner and William B. Todd, 2 vols. (Oxford, 1976), II, 794.

122 David Hume, 'Of Civil Liberty', in *Essays Moral, Political, and Literary*, ed. T. H. Green and T. H. Grose, 2 vols. (London, 1882), I, 158–9. Hume did however agree that the arts can only have their first birth in a free state. See 'The Rise of the Arts and Sciences', *Essays*, I, 177.

123 'Of Civil Liberty', p. 159.

124 Hume, 'Of Refinement in the Arts', *Essays*, II, 305.

125 Gibbon, *Decline and Fall*, II, 461.

126 On the connection between military exploits and patriotism, and the place of both in the development of a new British sense of identity, see Linda Colley, *Britons: Forging the Nation 1707–1837*, *passim*. Colley's stress on the congenial nature for Britons of the heroic ideal in classical history, noted in the previous section, is relevant here too.

127 Adam Ferguson, *Essay on the History of Civil Society*, ed. Duncan Forbes (Edinburgh, 1966), p. 14. The best recent analysis of the *Essay* is in Malcom Jack, *Corruption and Progress: the Eighteenth-Century Debate* (New York, 1989), pp. 113–54.

128 Ferguson, *Essay on the History of Civil Society*, p. 223.

129 James Boswell, *The Life of Johnson*, ed R. W. Chapman (Oxford, 1953; edn cit. 1985), p. 615.

130 Samuel Johnson, *Lives of the Poets*, ed. George Birkbeck Hill, 3 vols. (Oxford, 1905), III, 289. Bertrand Goldgar in *Walpole and the Wits* (Lincoln, Nebr., 1976) leaves the point unanswered (p. 142). As he admits, primary motivations of the anti-Walpole wits included indignation at Walpole's indifference to them and his disinclination to dispense patronage. Their interest in politics never descended to real issues such as details of policy. When it suited them they were not averse to currying the Prime Minister's favour. See pp. 19, 218–19 and elsewhere.

131 Pocock, *Virtue, Commerce, and History*, p. 245.

132 J. C. D. Clark, *The Dynamics of Change: the Crisis of the 1750s and English Party Systems* (Cambridge, 1982), p. 2: some modern historians have emphasised and endorsed 'the propaganda of Whig-Patriot or of Tory oppositions as justified critiques of a corrupt regime. In the process, eighteenth-century rhetoric about corruption in high places has been taken literally instead of being interpreted as part of a political strategy.'

133 Quoted in Pocock, *Virtue, Commerce, and History*, p. 149.

134 The literature is extensive. For a recent, balanced survey see Howard Erskine-Hill's *The Augustan Idea in English Literature*, and the chapter 'Augustan, Grecian, Gothic' in Michael Meehan, *Liberty and Poetics in Eighteenth-Century England*. Howard D. Weinbrot in his *Augustus Caesar in Augustan England* devotes considerable space to analysing Augustan and anti-Augustan elements in Alexander Pope. This should be read with

Erskine-Hill and Meehan to hand as correctives, but Weinbrot is incontestably correct to remind us that, for whatever else Augustus may have been admired, it was not for anaesthetising the moribund institutions of the free Republic, for which he was often condemned.

135 See Weinbrot, *Augustus Caesar in Augustan England*, especially the chapter 'Let Horace Blush, and Virgil too.'

136 *First Epistle of the Second Book of Horace* (*Epistle to Augustus*), ll. 1–6, in Pope, *The Poems of Alexander Pope*, Twickenham edn, vol. I, IV, *Imitations of Horace*, ed. John Butt (London, 1939; edn cit. 1961), p. 195.

137 Pope's distaste for the courtly status of both Horace and Virgil is evident from his 'Epitaph on one who would not be buried in Westminster Abbey':

> Heroes, and Kings! your distance keep:
> In peace let one poor Poet sleep,
> Who never flatter'd Folks like you:
> Let Horace blush, and Virgil too.

(Alexander Pope, *Minor Poems*, p. 376.)

138 Quoted from p. 10 of the original, in Frank Stack, *Pope and Horace: Studies in Imitation* (Cambridge, 1985), p. 293.

139 On the relations of Pope and classical satire see Howard Weinbrot, 'The Conventions of Classical Satire and the Practice of Pope', *PQ*, 59 (1980), 317–37. See too his 'Persius, the Opposition to Walpole, and Pope', in *Greene and Centennial Studies: Essays Presented to Donald Greene*, ed. Paul J. Korshin and Robert R. Allen (Charlottesville, 1984), pp. 93–124. Both are reprinted in Weinbrot, *Eighteenth-Century Satire: Essays on Text and Context from Dryden to Peter Pindar* (Cambridge, 1988).

140 Thirty-seven distinct translations of Horace, greatly augmented by multiple editions. The next four most popular were Cicero with thirty-five, Homer with twenty-two, Virgil with twenty-one, and Ovid with nineteen, all of course augmented by multiple editions. For these and the rest see *CBEL*, II, 1487–1502.

141 As opposed to Menippean satire, of which we know little. See Alvin Kernan, *The Cankered Muse* (New Haven, 1959), pp. 12–14; P. K. Elkin, *The Augustan Defence of Satire* (Oxford, 1973), pp. 36–8; and Leon Guilhamet, *Satire and the Transformation of Genre* (Philadelphia, 1987), pp. 5–6 and 170.

142 'Moreover, though the golden bough, gift of the venerated Sibyl, opened merely the infernal regions for Aeneas, frequently the boy whom your magical golden rod has touched sees both heaven and earth, and the deep night.' Swift's text is quoted from *The Poems of Jonathan Swift*, I, 212–14. The humorously equivocal idea of the rod gives the lines a nice tension. For the biographical context of the poem see *Jonathan Swift and Thomas Sheridan: The Intelligencer*, ed. James Woolley (Oxford, 1992), introduction, pp. 16–19.

143 Stack, *Pope and Horace*, pp. xiii and 18. See too p. xv: 'The Horatian text is seen as a dynamic catalyst: not as containing fixed meaning but as creating new meanings within the intertextual field of the parallel poems.'

144 David Foxon, *Pope and the Early Eighteenth-Century Book Trade*, ed. and rev. James McLaverty (Oxford, 1991), p. 67.

145 *Epistle to Arbuthnot*, ll. 115–24, in Pope, *Imitations of Horace*, p. 104.

146 'The Prayer of Brutus', in Pope, *Minor Poems*, p. 192.

147 On Pope's *Brutus* see Miriam Leranbaum, *Alexander Pope's 'Opus Magnum', 1729–1744* (Oxford, 1977), pp. 155–74; and Donald T. Torchiana, 'Brutus: Pope's Last Hero', in *Essential Articles for the Study of Alexander Pope*, ed. Maynard Mack (2nd edn, Hamden, Conn., 1968), pp. 705–23.

148 *The Yale Edition of the Works of Samuel Johnson*, vol. VI, *Poems*, ed. E. L. McAdam, Jr, with George Milne (New Haven, 1964), p. 57, with Johnson's note.

149 Mary Jane W. Scott, *James Thomson, Anglo-Scot* (Athens, Ga., 1988), p. 175.

150 The extensiveness of Virgilian inspiration in *The Seasons* is demonstrated persuasively by John Chalker, *The English Georgic: a Study in the Development of a Form* (Baltimore, 1969), ch. 4 and especially pp. 94ff. Many passages of description are directly modelled on the *Georgics*, especially in 'Spring'. See also Dwight L. Durling, *Georgic Tradition in English Poetry* (New York, 1935), pp. 43–58.

151 As Jane Scott points out, the 'Britannia' passage in 'Summer' (ll. 1438–1619) is nothing less than a project 'to transplant Roman ideals to British soil': *James Thomson, Anglo-Scot*, p. 178.

152 On the sources of *Liberty* see A. D. McKillop, *The Background of Thomson's 'Liberty'*, *Rice Institute Pamphlet*, 38 (July 1951), no. 2.

153 James Thomson, *Liberty, The Castle of Indolence and Other Poems.*

154 Maynard Mack devotes an appendix to the relation of Timon's villa to Walpole's Houghton in *The Garden and the City: Retirement and Politics in the Later Poetry of Pope* (Toronto, 1969).

155 John Dyer, *The Ruins of Rome* (1740), ll. 470, 490 and 536. The comparison of Dyer with Thomson is made by Colin Horne in 'The Classical Temper in Britain: Origins and Components', in *The Classical Temper in Western Europe*, ed. John Hardy and Andrew McCredie (Melbourne, 1983), pp. 69–70.

156 At this time there was a strong presumption among his followers and friends that Burlington would be called upon to design new Houses of Parliament. See, on this, ch. 4 below. Perhaps partly because Burlington had walked out of the government in 1733, the call never came. Ironically, the new Houses of Parliament, when they finally arose, would be in the Gothic revival style.

157 In the *Epistle to Burlington* the Roman character of the engineering works is made more explicit by Pope's identification of Burlington with Vitruvius, whose *De architectura* includes sections on the sorts of projects mentioned by Pope and Thomson. See also ch. 4 below.

158 *Liberty: to George Lyttleton, Esq.*, in Henry Fielding, *Miscellanies by Henry Fielding Esq; Volume I*, ed. Henry Knight Miller (Oxford, 1972), pp. 36–41.

159 Fielding, *Tom Jones*, II, 740.

160 Richard Glover's epic anti-Walpolean *Leonidas* (1737) belongs to the same class of political poetry, as does much of Pope's verse through the mid and late 1730s, telling us little about the political realities of the 1730s but much about the dominant values of the age. See Bertrand Goldgar, *Walpole and the Wits.*

161 On the mid-century decline of party see J. C. D. Clark, *The Dynamics of Change.*

162 See, e.g., Robert H. Murray, *Edmund Burke: a Biography* (Oxford, 1931), pp. 36ff.

163 Joseph Spence, *Observations, Anecdotes, and*

Characters of Books and Men, ed. James M. Osborn, 2 vols. (Oxford, 1966), I, 337–8 (anecdote 836).

164 *Ibid.*, p. 338, Osborn's note to anecdote 836.

165 See J. Holland Rose, 'The Oratory of Pitt', in *Pitt and Napoleon: Essays and Letters* (London, 1912), pp. 1–2.

166 J. Holland Rose, emphasising the Ciceronian training behind the 21-year-old's command of debate, reminds us that 'Lord North pronounced it the best first speech he had ever heard', and quotes others to similar effect: *ibid.*, p. 3. See also p. 17 (paraphrasing Wilberforce): 'The periods of Pitt were like those which Cicero wrote, and such as no contemporary could either speak or write.'

167 *Ibid.*, p. 7.

168 Any analysis of Burke-as-Cicero to Hastings's Verres must be indebted to H. V. Canter, 'The Impeachments of Verres and Hastings: Cicero and Burke', *CJ*, 9 (1914), 199–211. Canter concentrates on the impeachment itself, but (as will be seen) over several preceding years Burke had carefully nurtured and elaborated the Roman analogies in his speeches to the Commons on India. Burke was not the first to play Cicero to another man's Verres: Swift, in *The Examiner*, no. 18 (23–30 November 1710), adopting the style of Cicero's *Verrine Orations*, had conscripted Lord Wharton into the role. I owe this reference to Colin Horne. See his 'The Classical Temper in Britain', p. 68.

169 *Parl. Hist.*, XXIII (1782–3), 798.

170 Speech in Opening, fourth day, 19 February 1788: *The Works of the Right Honourable Edmund Burke*, 12 vols. (London, 1887), X, 145.

171 Speech on the Sixth Article, second day, 25 April 1789: *ibid.*, p. 271.

172 *Ibid.*, p. 270.

173 *Ibid.*, p. 236.

174 *The Writings and Speeches of Edmund Burke*, ed. P. J. Marshall and William B. Todd, V (Oxford, 1981), 402–3.

175 *Ibid.*, p. 416.

176 *Ibid.*, p. 426. Burke used this same Roman analogy of the proscription in his speech on the Sixth Article, first day, 21 April 1789: 'he executes a proscription, and sweeps off the food of hundreds of the nobility and gentry of a great country': *The Works*, X, 237.

177 *Writings and Speeches*, V, 449.

178 *Ibid.*, p. 450.

179 Cicero, *Verrine Orations*, tr. L. H. G. Greenwood, 2 vols. (London, 1928, 1935), I, 113.

180 *The Works*, IX, 331.

181 Speech in Reply, first day, quoted by Canter, 'The Impeachments of Verres and Hastings', p. 207.

182 *Verrine Orations*, II, 603.

183 *The Works*, IX, 342.

184 H. V. Canter, 'The Impeachments of Verres and Hastings', pp. 207–10. Other connections cited include the order and form of the speeches, their conclusions, a twelve-fold anaphora in the perorations, etc.

185 Speech on the Sixth Article, first day, 21 April 1789: *The Works*, X, 156.

186 Speech in Reply, ninth day, 16 September 1794: *The Works*, XII, 350.

187 'The Impeachments of Verres and Hastings', p. 200.

188 *The Institutio Oratoria of Quintilian*, Loeb edn, tr. H. E. Butler, 4 vols. (London, 1920–2), II, 493.

189 Speech in Opening, second day: *The Works*, IX, 483.

190 See Speech in Opening, first day, 15 February 1788: *The Works*, IX, 341.

191 Speech on the Sixth Article, fourth day, 7 May 1789: *The Works*, x, 449–51.

192 On the impeachment generally see P. J. Marshall, *The Impeachment of Warren Hastings* (Oxford, 1965).

2 VIRTUE MADE VISIBLE

1 For Louis XIV, Peter Burke, *The Fabrication of Louis XIV* (New Haven, 1992), treats the subject in detail.

2 See J. W. Atkins, *English Literary Criticism: Seventeenth and Eighteenth Centuries* (London, 1951), chs. 1 and 3.

3 The best general treatment of the topic is still M. L. Clarke's *Classical Education in Britain, 1500–1900* (Cambridge, 1959).

4 *The Works of the Right Honourable Joseph Addison*, ed. Richard Hurd, 6 vols. (London, 1890), I, 167.

5 Flower, ed., *Voltaire's England*, p. 37.

6 'Character' of Sir Robert Walpole, in *The Letters of Philip Dormer Stanhope, Earl of Chesterfield, with the Characters*, ed. John Bradshaw, 3 vols. (London, 1892), III, 1418.

7 *The Freeholder's Political Catechism* (1733), p. 10.

8 *The Works of the late Right Honourable Henry St John, Lord Viscount Bolingbroke*, 8 vols. (London, 1809), IV, 389 ('Some Reflections on the Present State of the Nation'). Cited by Ward, 'The Tory View of Roman History', 430.

9 *The Freeholder's Political Catechism*, p. 13.

10 *Ibid.*, p. 15.

11 For Cicero see 'Remarks on the History of England', *The Works*, II, 132, and 'A Letter on the Spirit of Patriotism', *ibid.*, IV, 217–19, both cited by Ward, 'The Tory View of Roman History', where the connection is succinctly stated: 'The Roman champion of partyless government is Cicero, whose policy of uniting knights and senators is the Roman equivalent of Bolingbroke's own "Patriot" coalition against Walpole.' Cato provided 'a symbol of heroic opposition, and in particular of the good man banned, like Bolingbroke himself after 1714, from political office: it is thus that he appears in the *Reflections Upon Exile*. And the conventional opposition of Cato and Caesar is surely in Bolingbroke's mind as he imagines a man (again, of course, himself) persecuted for his outspoken opposition to Walpole': Ward, p. 429, and Bolingbroke's *Reflections Upon Exile* in *The Works*, I, 163.

12 A good example of Pope in severe classical style is Roubiliac's white marble bust in the Shipley Art Gallery, Gateshead. See William Kurtz Wimsatt, *The Portraits of Alexander Pope* (New Haven, 1965), pp. 241–2, item 60.1.

13 The bust is at Cirencester Park. See James Lees-Milne, *Earls of Creation: Five Great Patrons of Eighteenth-Century Art* (London, 1962), p. 35.

14 *Letters*, v, 2080 (letter no. 1913).

15 On Fox's classical reading see Edward Lascelles, *The Life of Charles James Fox* (Oxford, 1936), pp. 277–81. The analogy with Demosthenes was a Fox cliché. Stanley Ayling points out that at Thomas Coke's Holkham in Norfolk the bust of Fox stood alongside one of Demosthenes: *Fox: the Life of Charles James Fox* (London, 1991), p. 238.

16 See Fielding, *Tom Jones*, XVI.i (Battestin and Bowers edn, II, 740).

17 Thomas Babington Macaulay, essay on Warren Hastings in *Critical and Historical Essays*, 3 vols. (London, 1865), III, 339; *Morning Chronicle*, 14 July 1788.

18 *Edward Gibbon: Memoirs of My Life*, ed. Georges

A. Bonnard (London, 1966), pp. 108, 109, 111.

19 W. B. Carnochan points out that Gibbon's 'irony rests on a sense of paradise as both irrecoverably lost and forever being lost. As he arches his eyebrows at the spectacle of Christianity undermining the empire, Gibbon dreams of lost felicity. The irony is that the empire could not help but have been undermined': *Gibbon's Solitude: the Inward World of the Historian* (Stanford, 1987), p. 81. On Gibbon's irony see pp. 79–100 generally. Though for contemporary readers the most interesting target of the irony was Christianity, pagan superstition is a target too. On the tone of chs. 15 and 16 of vol. I see Patricia B. Craddock, *Edward Gibbon, Luminous Historian 1772–1794*, (Baltimore, 1989), pp. 60ff. See also Martin Price, '"The Dark and Implacable Genius of Superstition": an Aspect of Gibbon's Irony', in *Augustan Worlds: Essays in Honour of A. R. Humphreys*, ed. J. C. Hilson, M. M. B. Jones and J. R. Watson (New York, 1978), pp. 241–78.

20 Chesterfield, *Letters* (1932), IV, 1376: no. 1651, from London, 30 July 1749 OS.

21 *Ibid.*, III, 732: no. 914, from Dublin, 18 February 1746.

22 *Ibid.*, III, 1168: no. 1569, from London, 21 June 1748 OS.

23 *Ibid.*, IV, 1709: no. 1766, from London, 7 April 1751 OS.

24 *Ibid.*, III, 735: no. 916, from Dublin, 26 February 1746.

25 *Ibid.*, IV, 1377: no. 1652, from London, 7 August 1749 OS.

26 *Ibid.*, IV, 1420: no. 1665, from London, 17 October 1749 OS.

27 *Ibid.*, IV, 1466: no. 1678, from London, 16 December 1749 OS.

28 *Ibid.*, III, 1114: no. 1547, from Bath, 9 March 1748 OS.

29 *Ibid.*, III, 1115–16: no. 1547, from Bath, 9 March 1748 OS.

30 William Congreve, *The Double Dealer* (1693), ed. J. C. Ross (London, 1981), I.i.176–7, p. 25.

31 Samuel Johnson, *Lives of the English Poets*, III, 56 (Swift) and 202 (Pope). But see Birkbeck Hill's demurring note to the Swift passage.

32 Bonamy Dobrée's note to the Chesterfield passage in his edition. Chesterfield told his son that 'since I have had the full use of my reason, nobody has ever heard me laugh': *Letters*, III, 1116.

33 Francis Bacon, Essay 30, 'Of Regiment of Health', in *The Essays or Counsels, Civill and Morall*, ed. Michael Kiernan (Oxford, 1985), p. 101.

34 Peter Smithers has noted in his biography that Addison 'consistently sought by criticism and example to prune from contemporary humour all "Gothic" excrescences. Under this epithet he included quaint conceits and artificial turns, puns, rebuses, and other forms of wit not founded in reason, observing that a pun can be neither translated nor engraved. He likewise excluded from true wit all ill nature, and any immoderate quality conducive to laughter as opposed to mirth': *The Life of Joseph Addison*, p. 216. Relevant passages are in *Spectators* 47, 61, 249 and 440, and the 'Dialogues on Medals', II. Bacon's words are from his essay 'Of Regiment of Health'.

35 Letter to William Stukeley, 21 December 1725, quoted by Iain Gordon Brown, 'Sir John Clerk of Penicuik (1676–1755): Aspects of a Virtuoso

Life', doctoral dissertation, University of Cambridge, 1980.

36 W. Lee Ustick, for example, argues that 'No philosophical tendency . . . is so observable in English books on the conduct of life, particularly in the seventeenth century, as Stoicism': 'Changing Ideals of Aristocratic Character and Conduct in Seventeenth-Century England', *MP*, 30 (1932), 149.

37 *Ibid.*, pp. 151ff. For Marcus' influence on Shaftesbury see Robert Voitle, *The Third Earl of Shaftesbury 1671–1713* (Baton Rouge, 1984), pp. 136–45 and 152–63; and more generally, Esther M. Tiffany, 'Shaftesbury as Stoic', *PMLA*, 38 (1923), 642–84.

38 On Shaftesbury's concern with manners and taste, see Lawrence Klein, *Shaftesbury and the Culture of Politeness: Moral Discourse and Cultural Politics in Early Eighteenth-Century England* (Cambridge, 1994).

39 *Characteristicks*, I, 145 (*Advice to an Author*, published separately in 1710 before its inclusion in the *Characteristicks* (1711)).

40 *Ibid.*, I, 146.

41 For the connection between Shaftesbury's project and Burlington's work see Rudolf Wittkower, 'English Neo-Palladianism, the Landscape Garden, China and the Enlightenment', in *Palladio and Palladianism* (New York, 1974), pp. 179–81, summed up on p. 181: 'Just as Shaftesbury had mapped it out, Burlington endeavoured to bring about a national style in the arts, founded upon "right models of Perfection", that is, classical or Italian, because Italy had remained the custodian of the permanent values in ancient art.'

42 *Characteristicks*, I, 214–15 (*Advice to an Author*).

43 *Ibid.*, I, 215–16.

44 *Ibid.*, I, 217–18.

45 *Ibid.*, I, 219–20.

46 *Ibid.*, I, 217.

47 *Ibid.*, I, 222.

48 [James Harris], article on Shaftesbury in J. P. Bernard, Thomas Birch et al. (eds. and trs.), *A General Dictionary, Historical and Critical*, 10 vols. (1734–41), IX (1739), 1[illegible]6. Harris's authorship is established by Clive T. Probyn in *The Sociable Humanist: the Life and Works of James Harris 1709–1780* (Oxford, 1991).

49 Richard Hurd, ed., *The Works of the Right Honourable Joseph Addison*, I, preface.

50 Addison's close inspections of the remains of Roman antiquity, and his aesthetic preference for republican remains over imperial, are detailed in Smithers, *The Life of Joseph Addison*, pp. 64–5.

51 *The Poetical Works of Thomas Tickell* (Edinburgh, 1781), p. 101.

52 On the classical and more immediate sources of Addison's political thought and his 'complex liberalism', see Edward A. Bloom and Lillian D. Bloom, *Joseph Addison's Sociable Animal* (Providence, R.I., 1971), pp. 87–148 *passim*.

53 See Brown, 'Sir John Clerk', p. 162. Brown misses the problem of the pun in *baro*, which Clerk must have noticed.

54 Mary Jane Scott points to the similarity between the Border world of Thomson's youth, 'particularly in summer, and Mantua, the land of Virgil, young Thomson's model and mentor. Virgil was a northern poet, of Gallic, Celtic ancestry; Thomson's identification with Virgil may have been partly to do with the perception that both were provincial, northern poets with certain "Celtic" links.' The wealth of Roman remains in

the region 'reinforced in a concrete way his "Scoto-Roman" ethos – the ideal whereby many Scots identified themselves, in his day, with ancient Roman civilization. Thomson adopted this Roman spirit with enthusiasm': *James Thomson, Anglo-Scot*, pp. 21–2.

55 'An Historical Essay on Chivalry and Modern Honour', printed with an introduction by Ernest Campbell Mossner in *MP*, 45 (1947), 54–60. Extract quoted here from Mossner, *The Life of David Hume* (Edinburgh, 1954), p. 47.

56 'My Own Life', in *The Philosophical Works*, ed. T. H. Green and T. H. Grose, 4 vols. (London, 1882), III (*Essays*, II), p. 2.

57 *The Letters of David Hume*, ed. J. Y. T. Greig, 2 vols. (Oxford, 1932), I, 14.

58 Chesterfield, *Letters* (1932), IV, 1760: no. 1784, from London, 24 June 1751 OS.

59 *HWC*, IX (1961), 3–4, letter of 6 May 1736.

60 See J. A. K. Thomson, *Classical Influences on English Prose* (London, 1956; edn cit. 1962), pp. 136, 144.

61 Gibbon, *Memoirs*, p. 33.

62 *Ibid.*, p. 75.

63 *Ibid.*, p. 76.

64 *Ibid.*, p. 105.

65 See, e.g., the close of part III, section ii.

66 Lord Sheffield in his 1827 edition of Gibbon's *Memoirs* lists its members. Gibbon says nothing of their activities. Sheffield's note is reproduced in George Birkbeck Hill's edition of the *Memoirs* (London, 1900), p. 169.

67 This and the following details of the Society of Dilettanti are from Lionel Cust and Sidney Colvin, *History of the Society of Dilettanti* (London, 1898). On the Society's practices, regulations, etc., see particularly ch. 2.

68 *HWC*, XVIII (1954), 211, letter of 14 April 1743 OS.

69 On the transition to neo-classical architecture in England see Damie Stillman, *English Neo-Classical Architecture*, 2 vols. (London, 1988), I, 27–48, and chapter 4 below.

70 See, e.g., Charles F. Mullett, 'Classical Influences on the American Revolution', *CJ*, 35 (1939–40); Richard M. Grummere, *The American Colonial Mind and the Classical Tradition: Essays in Comparative Culture* (Cambridge, Mass., 1963); and Richard Koebner, *Empire* (Cambridge, 1961).

71 Diana de Marly, 'The Establishment of Roman Dress in Seventeenth-Century Portraiture', *Burl. Mag.*, 117 (1975), 443–4.

72 *Ibid.*, pp. 444–8.

73 Burke, *The Fabrication of Louis XIV*, *passim*.

74 See, e.g., Mignard's portrait of Louis XIV, Lely's of Charles II, and Gascars's of James as Duke of York, reproduced in De Marly, p. 445.

75 See the reproduction of the first in Margaret Whinney, *Sculpture in Britain: 1530–1830* (Harmondsworth, 1964), plate 20.

76 De Marly, 'The Establishment of Roman Dress in Seventeenth-Century Portraiture', p. 450.

77 Linda Colley, *Britons: Forging the Nation 1707–1837*, discusses the cult of heroism in British art depicting contemporary imperial exploits, without exploring the specifically Roman connotations. The section 'Heroes of their Own Epic', pp. 177–93, is pertinent to the present discussion.

78 Margaret Whinney, *Sculpture in Britain*, p. 106.

79 See the *DNB* entries for Archibald Campbell, 9th Earl of Argyll (d. 1685), and John Campbell, 2nd Duke of Argyll and Greenwich.

80 *DNB* entry for John Campbell, 2nd Duke of Argyll and Greenwich.

81 Jonathan Swift, 'Memoirs relating to that Change which happened in the Queen's Ministry in the Year 1710', in *The Prose Works of Jonathan Swift*, vol. VIII, *Political Tracts 1713–1719*, ed. Herbert Davis and Irvin Ehrenpreis (Oxford, 1953), p. 115. See further on this in Winston S. Churchill, *Marlborough, His Life and Times* (London, 1947), vol. II, book IV, p. 642.

82 Pope, *Epilogue to the Satires*, Dialogue II, ll. 86–7, in *The Poems of Alexander Pope*, vol. IV, *Imitations of Horace* (London, 1939), 318.

83 Thomson, *The Seasons*, ed. James Sambrook (Oxford, 1981), 'Autumn', ll. 885–6.

84 The drawing and the terracotta model described here are in the Victoria and Albert Museum.

85 The monument in Westminster Abbey differs in a few minor details from the terracotta model. For an account of the commission, see Katharine A. Esdaile, *The Life and Works of Louis François Roubiliac* (Oxford, 1928), pp. 61–6.

86 Gunnis, p. 309, gives the conception to Plumier.

87 According to Morris R. Brownell, *Alexander Pope and the Arts of Georgian England* (Oxford, 1978), pp. 346–7, the classical motifs on this monument 'ushered in what has been called "the reign of the Roman toga"'.

88 De Marly, p. 450.

89 Thomas Tickell, *Oxford. A Poem. Inscrib'd to the Right Honourable the Lord Lonsdale* (1707), pp. 5–6.

90 Joseph Burke observes of this work that 'The attitude of the hero hesitates between the quarter-deck and the lounge . . . [Wilton] has juxtaposed the two worlds of the eighteenth century and antiquity, and it was this juxtaposition rather than the reconstruction of a wholly Roman image that was his aim': *English Art 1714–1800*, p. 262.

91 See Margaret Whinney, *English Sculpture 1720–1830*, p. 72.

92 This fact is emphasised on the terracotta model of the base, which has trophies of 'War' and 'The Arts' on each side. See Gunnis, p. 15.

93 In addition to Cobham and Westmorland there were the Prince of Wales, the Earl of Chesterfield, the Earl of Marchmont, Lord Gower, Lord Bathurst, Richard Grenville, William Pitt the Elder and George Lyttelton – ten busts on ten pedestals. George Bickham, *The Beauties of Stow* (1750), pp. 53–4, lists them and comments of the Temple, 'It is full of illustrious Busts, but not one Monarch amongst them; perhaps to hint, that this Set of Men does not seem to be formed to love, and much less to be loved' (p. 53).

94 Margaret Whinney comments that it shows Scheemakers's 'first-hand knowledge of good antique busts': *English Sculpture 1720–1830*, p. 60.

95 The best work on Rysbrack is still M. I. Webb, *Michael Rysbrack, Sculptor* (London, 1954), and the following is indebted to it.

96 R. N. Wornum suggests that this is because Walpole lacked biographical material on Scheemakers. See Wornum's edition of Horace Walpole, *Anecdotes of Painting*, 3 vols. (London, 1862), III, 757.

97 Webb, *Michael Rysbrack*, p. 12.

98 See Webb, *Michael Rysbrack*, pp. 21–36 ('Training and Background').

99 *Vertue*, III, 73.

100 Margaret Whinney, *Sculpture in Britain*, pp.

85–6. M. I. Webb notes that Nottingham 'is portrayed by Rysbrack in the guise of a Roman Senator' and that 'It is easy to understand how Rysbrack's bust of Lord Nottingham established his fame, for it combines the two qualities of being a very good portrait and also exceedingly classical, with a genuine Roman air': *Michael Rysbrack*, p. 51.

101 'After about 1720', Margaret Whinney points out, 'almost the only monuments showing men in their own dress are those of lawyers and divines, for gowns are ceremonial dress in their own right and outside changes of fashion. All members of the aristocracy and many professional men now appear on their tombs in Roman dress': *Sculpture in Britain*, p. 68.

102 On this bust, dated 1728, in the National Portrait Gallery, see Malcolm Rogers, 'Michael Rysbrack's Bust of Edmund Waller', *Burl. Mag.*, 119 (1977), 314 and 352. Rogers places the bust 'in the gravely naturalistic tradition of Roman portraiture'.

103 Pope, *Epistle to Augustus*, ll. 263–7, and Pope's note, in *The Poems of Alexander Pope*, vol. IV, *Imitations of Horace*.

104 Reproduced in Webb, *Michael Rysbrack*, p. 40.

105 See Wimsatt, *The Portraits of Alexander Pope*, pp. 227ff. See also Katharine A. Esdaile, *The Life and Works of Louis François Roubiliac*, pp. 47–9. According to M. I. Webb, *Michael Rysbrack*, p. 76, 'It seems to have been more or less understood that if Rysbrack had made a bust of a contemporary in either Roman or contemporary dress then Roubiliac, if he was called upon to make another portrait of the same individual later, adopted the opposite mode, and vice versa.'

106 See Webb, *Michael Rysbrack*, p. 179 and plate 88.

107 *Ibid.*, p. 128.

108 He thought it 'far from a beautiful place', yet remarked to Lady Ossory 'how very fond I am of Houghton, as the object of my father's fondness': *HWC*, XXXII, 140. There is much evidence throughout his correspondence of ambivalence towards the Romans and Roman self-imaging.

109 This monument is discussed by J. Douglas Stewart, 'New Light on Michael Rysbrack: Augustan England's "Classical Baroque" Sculptor', *Burl. Mag.*, 120 (1978), 221–2.

110 See the analysis of these two works in Whinney, *Sculpture in Britain*, p. 111.

111 See, e.g., the bust of the 1st Earl of Yarborough, dated 1808, in the Victoria and Albert Museum, illustrated in John Lord, 'Joseph Nollekens and Lord Yarborough: Documents and Drawings', *Burl. Mag.*, 130 (1988), 918.

112 On the 'deification' of Fox after his death, and the popularity of the busts, see L. G. Mitchell, *Charles James Fox*, pp. 262–3: 'In 1811, the Prince of Wales took the oaths of office as Regent with the bust at his side. His first meeting with the Privy Council was delayed for half an hour while he and his advisers contemplated it.'

113 John Kenworthy-Browne, 'The Temple of Liberty at Woburn Abbey', p. 28.

114 Martin C. Battestin, *The Providence of Wit: Aspects of Form in Augustan Literature and the Arts* (Oxford, 1974). The quotation is from p. 44, but see ch. 1, 'The Idea of Order in Nature and the Arts, 1660–1750' generally, and especially pp. 34–49 on 'Variety'. See also Miles Hadfield, *Gardening in Britain* (London, 1960), pp. 158ff., on the continuing influence of the French style of gardening on less 'fashionable' English gardens

throughout the eighteenth century.

115 In *The Moralists* (1709) Shaftesbury speaks of how 'The genius of the place, and the Great Genius have at last prevailed. I shall no longer resist the passion growing in me for things of a natural kind, where neither art nor the conceit or caprice of man has spoiled their genuine order, by breaking in upon that primitive state. Even the rude rocks, the mossy caverns, the irregular unwrought grottos and broken falls of waters, with all the horrid graces of the wilderness itself, as representing Nature more, will be the more engaging, and appear with a magnificence beyond the formal mockery of princely gardens': *The Moralists*, part III, sect. ii, in the *Characteristicks*, II, 125. Addison, in no. 414 of *The Spectator* (25 June 1712), argues for turning an entire estate into 'a kind of a garden' or 'pretty landskip', rejecting the formal geometry of the typical Queen Anne garden of his day. Pope, in no. 173 of *the Guardian* (29 September 1713), followed Shaftesbury and Addison in advocating the virtues of 'unadorned Nature' and cited classical precedents in Homer and Virgil. He, like Shaftesbury and Addison, was also aware of Pliny the Younger's account of his Tuscan villa (*Letters*, book V, letter 6, to Apollinaris, in *The Letters of Pliny the Consul: with Occasional Remarks*, tr. William Melmeth, 2 vols. (8th edn, corr., London, 1786)) and his villa at Laurentinum (book II, letter 17, to Gallus), both of which were marked by a degree of irregularity in their creative handling of natural landscape. These letters were highly influential on the English landscape garden, and were to be analysed with great care by Robert Castell in his *The Villas of the Ancients Illustrated* (1728).

116 The extensive literature on the subject includes H. F. Clark, *The English Landscape Garden* (London, 1948); Derek Clifford, *A History of Garden Design* (London, 1962); Christopher Hussey, *English Gardens and Landscapes 1700–1750* (London, 1967); Peter Willis, ed., *Furor hortensis: Essays on the History of the English Landscape Garden in Memory of H. F. Clark* (Edinburgh, 1974); Peter Willis, *Charles Bridgeman and the English Landscape Garden* (London, 1977), and John Dixon Hunt, *Garden and Grove* (London, 1986) – see especially ch. 11, '"Palladian" Gardening', which questions the 'Englishness' of the English landscape garden. For a fine, concise discussion of the poetic–classical elements in the gardens of Castle Howard, Stowe, Rousham and Stourhead see Ronald Paulson's *Emblem and Expression: Meaning in English Art of the Eighteenth Century* (Cambridge, Mass., 1975), ch. 2, pp. 19–34.

117 See further on this below; and Battestin, *The Providence of Wit*, pp. 38–40.

118 See, e.g., H. F. Clark, 'Eighteenth Century Elysiums: the Role of "Association" in the Landscape Movement', *JWCI*, 6 (1943), 165–89, and Kenneth Woodbridge, *Landscape and Antiquity: Aspects of English Culture at Stourhead 1718 to 1838* (Oxford, 1970). George Clarke's 'Grecian Taste and Gothic Virtue: Lord Cobham's Gardening Programme and its Iconography', *Apollo*, 97 (June 1973), 566–71, usefully highlights the older Whig identification, evident at Stowe, of English political liberty with 'Gothic' institutions and Anglo-Saxon virtue, a traditional association never entirely displaced by the English 'classical republicans', whose identification of English political liberty

with Greece and Rome is perhaps even more strongly enshrined at Stowe than the Gothic. On the use of the Gothic in landscape gardens of the time see also Alistair Rowan, 'Batty Langley's Gothic', in *Studies in Memory of David Talbot Rice*, ed. Giles Robertson and George Henderson (Edinburgh, 1975), pp. 197–215.

119 In his five acres on the bank of the Thames at Twickenham.

120 James Thomson, *Liberty*, v.683, 696–700, in *Liberty, the Castle of Indolence and Other Poems*.

121 On Stowe's gardens and temples see Laurence Whistler, 'The Authorship of the Stowe Temples', *Stoic*, 14: 4 (December 1950), and Michael Gibbon, 'Stowe, Buckinghamshire: the House and Garden Buildings and their Designers', *AH*, 20 (1977), 31–44. On the aesthetic and political dimension of the gardens see George Clarke's articles, 'Grecian Taste and Gothic Virtue'; 'Moral Gardening', *Stoic*, 24 (July 1970); and 'The Gardens of Stowe', *Apollo*, 97 (June 1973), 558–65. A history of Stowe by George Clarke and Michael Gibbon appeared in instalments in *Stoic* to July 1977.

122 Pope, *Epistle to Burlington*, l. 70, *Epistles to Several Persons*, ed. Bateson. On Pope's interest and involvement in the gardening movement see Maynard Mack, *The Garden and the City*; Brownell, *Alexander Pope and the Arts of Georgian England*; and Peter Martin, *'Pursuing Innocent Pleasures': the Gardening World of Alexander Pope* (Hamden, Conn., 1984).

123 Pope imagines his last words as 'Oh, save my Country, Heaven!': *Epistle to Sir Richard Temple, Lord Cobham*, l. 265.

124 Walpole noted that 'Those dear friends have hated one another, till some of them are forced to love one another again – and as the cracks are soldered by hatred, perhaps that cement may hold them together': *HWC*, LI (1980), 6, letter of 6 March 1766. Earlier, on 26 May 1765, he told a correspondent that 'The edifices and inscriptions at Stowe should be a lesson not to erect monuments to the living': *ibid.*, n. 19.

125 William Gilpin, *A Dialogue upon the Gardens of . . . Stow* (1748), p. 49.

126 Some treatment of inscriptions, though not of their specifically Romano-British analogues, is provided by George Clarke, 'Grecian Taste and Gothic Virtue'.

127 Thus the classical entrance pavilions and the pyramid-topped Boycott Pavilions by Gibbs at the opening to the park, one of them housing statues of Cicero, Marcus Aurelius, his wife Faustina, and Livia, wife of Augustus; the Temple of Venus, by Kent; an Egyptian pyramid, a Temple of Bacchus, a 'Tuscan' (really Ionic) Rotunda, and Dido's Cave, housing Aeneas and Dido, all these by Vanbrugh; the Saxon Temple and the Temple of Diana by Gibbs; the Shell Bridge, the Witch House, the Chinese House, and so on. Gilpin appreciated neither the Chinese House nor Chinese art: 'Their Ingenuity lies chiefly in the knick-knack Way', he made Callophilus observe, a comment Bickham obviously liked, since he plagiarised it. Gilpin: *A Dialogue upon the Gardens of . . . Stow*, p. 28; Bickham, *The Beauties of Stow*, p. 36.

128 George Bickham, *The Beauties of Stow*, p. 18.

129 *Ibid.*, p. 19.

130 *Ibid.*, p. 21. Nikolaus Pevsner, *The Buildings of England: Buckinghamshire* (Harmondsworth, 1960), p. 261, gives the statue to Rysbrack. It is not listed in Webb, *Michael Rysbrack*, appendix

2, 'Alphabetical Catalogue'.

131 See Whistler, 'The Authorship of the Stowe Temples'; Gibbon, 'Stowe, Buckinghamshire: the House and Garden Buildings and their Designers', p. 40; and Christopher Hussey, *English Gardens and Landscapes 1700–1750*, p. 101.

132 See the analysis of this temple and its relation to the surrounding landscape and architectural elements in Paulson, *Emblem and Expression*, pp. 25–6.

133 Bickham, *The Beauties of Stow*, p. 25.

134 See Clarke, 'Grecian Taste and Gothic Virtue', p. 568; and Gibbon, 'Stowe, Buckinghamshire: the House and Garden Buildings and their Designers', p. 40.

135 Nikolaus Pevsner remains neutral in the dispute over whether the other eight are by Rysbrack or Scheemakers: *The Buildings of England: Buckinghamshire*, p. 258. Those definitely by Rysbrack are Queen Elizabeth, Shakespeare, Bacon, Milton, Hampden, Newton, Locke and William III.

136 From the left as the spectator saw them they were Pope (initially without any inscription), Sir Thomas Gresham (who built the Royal Exchange), Inigo (Romanised to 'Ignatius') Jones (for his introduction of Palladian principles to English architecture), Milton, Shakespeare, Locke, Newton, and Bacon; then Mercury; and on the other side those whose contribution was more in the world of action: King Alfred (whose inscription referred to him as 'the Founder of the English Constitution'), the Black Prince, Queen Elizabeth, King William III in Roman dress, Sir Walter Ralegh, Sir Francis Drake, John Hampden and John Barnard (no inscription, but he was Lord Mayor of London and MP for London, frequently leading attacks on Walpole in Parliament).

137 Also called the Gothic Temple, and attributed to James Gibbs by Whistler and Gibbon.

138 Unattributed in Gibbon, 'Stowe, Buckinghamshire: the House and Garden Buildings and their Designers', p. 43.

139 Gilpin, *A Dialogue upon the Gardens of ... Stow*, p. 56.

140 For instance by Michael Gibbon, 'The First Neo-Classical Building?', *CL*, 11 April 1974, pp. 852–3. On more minor sources for particular elements (though not Palladio) see also Stillman, *English Neo-Classical Architecture*, II, 539, n. 7.

141 *The Four Books of Andrea Palladio's Architecture*, ed. Isaac Ware (1738) (the best eighteenth-century English edition), fourth book, ch. 30, p. 109 and plates 92–4. Compare these with plates 81–6 (Maison Carrée).

142 Designed by James Gibbs and dated 1739. As Christopher Hussey has pointed out, 'The high central room, with decorations by [Francesco] Sleter of which some traces remain, has cellars beneath for the Patriots' refreshments, and on either side of it arched loggias, reminiscent of those in the pavilions at Mereworth, for their gatherings on summer evenings': *English Gardens and Landscapes 1700–1750*, p. 103. The connection with Mereworth is not surprising, as one of the friends who met in the Temple of Friendship was the Earl of Westmorland, who built Mereworth.

143 *HWC*, XXXIX (1974), 127, letter of 12 July 1770.

144 See the discussion of Castle Howard in Hussey, *English Gardens and Landscapes 1700–1750*, pp. 114–31, and in ch. 4 below.

145 *Spectator*, no. 414 (25 June 1712).

146 James Turner, 'The Structure of Henry Hoare's Stourhead', *Art Bulletin*, 61 (1979), 77.

147 See Battestin, *The Providence of Wit*, pp. 39–40, and his caveat, p. 38, against Pevsner's description of the English garden as 'the garden of liberalism'. Later in the century the idea of landscape was to become intimately bound up with agricultural improvement, though here the farmers concerned were generally not aristocratic – see John Barrell, *The Idea of Landscape and the Sense of Place 1730–1840* (Cambridge, 1972), ch. 2, 'The Landscape of Agricultural Improvement', and more generally ch. 1, 'The Idea of Landscape in the Eighteenth Century'.

148 James Lees-Milne, *Earls of Creation*, p. 213.

149 For example, Goldgar devotes 13 pages to the 'Patriot' literary circle, but has to admit their lack of organisation and planning (pp. 139–40). Their impact on Walpole was insignificant, though of course they were answered in kind by the government's hack writers. On the dubious motivation of much anti-Walpole writing see Goldgar, *Walpole and the Wits*, pp. 218–19. Even Maynard Mack, who gives over 40 pages of *The Garden and the City* to Pope and Walpole as 'Mighty Opposites' (ch. 6), generally accepts the positive assessment of Walpole's administration by modern historians and has to admit that the worlds of the poet and the Prime Minister never in fact touched: 'Walpole broke his political opponents because they threatened his power; Pope of course had no such interest for him, was merely a gnat to be brushed aside' (p. 206).

150 I am indebted here to the only detailed analysis of the Temple of Liberty yet published, John Kenworthy-Browne's 'The Temple of Liberty at Woburn Abbey'.

151 'Its overall character', John Kenworthy-Browne notes, 'and plain classicism recall the supposed republican virtues of ancient Rome': *ibid.*, p. 32.

152 Charles James Fox and the 5th and 6th Dukes of Bedford, all draped; Lord Robert Spencer, General Richard Fitzpatrick, James Hare, Charles (later Earl) Grey, Lord Holland and the 6th Earl of Lauderdale, all (like the two Brutuses) undraped in severe republican style.

3 BRITANNIA ROMANA

1 This was in marked contrast to an overall decline in the prestige of other antiquarian studies. See Stuart Piggott, *Ancient Britons and the Antiquarian Imagination* (London, 1989), pp. 18–21 and 26–7. Piggott's focus in this book is on pre-Roman Britain, and his remarks on the decline of antiquarianism in the early eighteenth century are misleading if referred to Romano-British studies.

2 On this interesting question see Joseph M. Levine, *The Battle of the Books: History and Literature in the Augustan Age* (Ithaca, N.Y., 1991), especially pp. 374–413. Elsewhere (p. 336) he describes Camden's *Britannia* as 'in nearly every respect the perfect embodiment of the modernist commitment to the collaborative advancement of learning'.

3 On Bentley's advanced methods of scholarship see C. O. Brink, *English Classical Scholarship: Historical Reflections on Bentley, Porson, and Housman* (Cambridge, 1986), pp. 1–83.

4 Bentley was the first Boyle Lecturer, speaking on the *Evidences of Natural and Revealed Religion* (1692).

5 Camden spreads it over 'about 476 years' –

Edmund Gibson's edition and translation of *Camden's Britannia, Newly Translated into English: with Large Additions and Improvements* (1695), p. lxxxvii.

6 See Stephen Johnson, *The Roman Forts of the Saxon Shore* (London, 1976; edn cit. 1979), ch. 8, 'Breakdown of the Command', especially pp. 146–54.

7 The date of this appeal is known from the sixth-century ecclesiastic Gildas who, in the *De excidio et conquestu britanniae*, places it in the third consulship of Aetius.

8 William Camden, *Britannia sive florentissimorum regnorum, angliae, scotiae, hiberniae chorographica descriptio* (1586).

9 *The Laboryouse Iourney and Serche of Johan Leylande, for Englandes Antiquitees* was edited by Thomas Hearne in 1710.

10 On the history of the *Britannia* in its various forms see Stuart Piggott, 'William Camden and the *Britannia*', Reckitt Archaeological Lecture, 21 November 1951, in *PBA*, 37 (1951), 199–217.

11 Edmund Gibson's translation, from his enlarged edition of *Camden's Britannia*, section on 'The Romans in Britain', p. lxxxvii.

12 See Kevin Sharpe, *Sir Robert Cotton, 1586–1631: History and Politics in Early Modern England* (Oxford, 1979), *passim*.

13 William Burton, *A Commentary on Antoninus his Itinerary or Journies of the Romane Empire, so far as it concerneth Britain* (1658).

14 It used to be thought that the work had been authorised by Antoninus Pius, but (Antoninus) Caracalla is now thought a better candidate, if in fact the name in the title refers to an emperor.

15 Burton, *A Commentary on Antoninus his Itinerary*, p. 45.

16 On this subject see the essays in T. F. C. Blagg and A. C. King, eds., *Military and Civilian in Roman Britain: Cultural Relations in a Frontier Province*, BAR, 136 (1984).

17 David C. Douglas, *English Scholars 1660–1730* (London, 1939; rev. edn 1951), p. 59.

18 See Douglas, *English Scholars*, pp. 105–6.

19 On Stukeley see Stuart Piggott, *William Stukeley, an Eighteenth-Century Antiquary* (Oxford, 1950; rev. edn, 1985). On Roger and Samuel Gale see their entries in the *DNB*.

20 *The Family Memoirs of the Reverend William Stukeley*, 3 vols. (Durham, 1882–7), I, 71.

21 *Ibid.*, I, 60.

22 *Ibid.*, I, 59. This and other references clearly show the familiar terms of Stukeley's friendship with Lord Harley.

23 *Ibid.*, I, 77.

24 *Camden's Britannia, Newly Translated into English: with Large Additions and Improvements.*

25 Piggot, *William Stukeley*, p. 7. Elsewhere, Piggott calls the 1695 edition 'one of the key works in the formation of the eighteenth-century mind': *Ancient Britons and the Antiquarian Imagination*, p. 11.

26 Later translated and abridged as *The Antiquities of Richborough and Reculver* (1774).

27 See particularly the chapter 'Roman London' in Joseph M. Levine, *Dr Woodward's Shield: History, Science, and Satire in Augustan England* (Berkeley, 1977), pp. 133–50

28 The main primary source on the 'Equites Romani', the Society of Roman Knights, is Bodl. MS. Eng. Misc. c. 401, to which the following discussion is principally indebted. The Society was discussed by Piggott in *William Stukeley*, pp. 53–6; more material is provided by Iain Gordon

Brown, 'Chyndonax to Galgacus: New Letters of William Stukeley to Alexander Gordon', *AJ*, 67 (1987), 111–28, who points out (citing Bodl. MS. Eng. Misc. e. 121, fol. 31) that Stukeley's co-founders were Gerard Vandergucht and John Pine (see below).

29 Gordon's comments on the need to extirpate 'Gothicism' from the Society of Antiquaries are quoted below; Clerk complained to Roger Gale in 1736 of the degree to which 'Gothicism' still prevailed in the Society although it was 'only the degeneracy of Greek and Roman Arts and Sciences', mere 'Dullness and Stupidity'. Quoted from the Clerk Papers in Piggott, *William Stukeley*, p. 56.

30 See Pope's *Epistle to Burlington*, l. 9. Pope articulates the response of the classical spirit to Anglo-Saxon and medieval studies, seen to be the epitome of dullness. In the *Dunciad* (1728), Hearne is caricatured as Wormius. Hearne was of course also interested in Roman antiquities.

31 On this aspect see Piggott, *William Stukeley*, *passim*.

32 Brown, 'Chyndonax to Galgacus', p. 115 and n. 24.

33 'John Warburton bears an evil name as the Vandal who openly boasts of having prompted the scheme under which Hadrian's Wall was destroyed for many miles, in order to facilitate the building of the Newcastle–Carlisle road': Sir George Macdonald, 'John Horsley, Scholar and Gentleman', *AA*, 4th ser., 10 (1933), p. 41. For more unflattering details about Warburton see the following pages of this article.

34 A few of these names are subsequently recorded as having been 'admitted' at later meetings, e.g. on Bodl. MS Eng. Misc. c. 401, fol. 9, where Roger Gale, Maurice Johnson and Alexander Gordon 'were admitted Members of the Society', but Stukeley may simply have meant that they were admitted to the *praetorium* as old members, rather than that their membership was in some way renewed.

Other members with amateur interests in the field or marital association who came in during the first year included William Hulet ('Brennus', a Gallic general, appropriate for one with a French background); Gerard Vandergucht, Stukeley's close friend, accompanying him on archaeological excursions and engraving frontispieces for him ('Indutiomarus', a chief of the Treveri, father-in-law and rival of Cingetorix at the time of Caesar's second invasion of Britain); John Pine, friend of his fellow-engraver Hogarth, and fellow-traveller with Stukeley on field excursions; Thomas Bawtree ('Scribonius'); Nicola Haym, composer, librettist to Handel, and compiler of a catalogue of antique medals in British collections ('Varro', a Roman author who, like Haym, produced numerous volumes, or perhaps a Gallic poet, Varro Atacinus); and Frances Stukeley ('Cartismandua', queen of the Brigantes and ally of the Romans). Most of these were early members, listed immediately above a poem on the Society by Michael Mattaire dated 12 December 1722. See Bodl. MS. Eng. Misc. c. 401, fol. 7.

35 New candidates included Jonathan Sisson, perhaps the eminent scientific instrument maker of that name, from whom Burlington bought the mathematical and drawing instruments with which he designed his buildings – see E. G. R. Taylor, *The Mathematical Practitioners of*

Hanoverian England (Cambridge, 1966), pp. 143–4, and the Graham and Collier accounts book, Burlington Papers, Chatsworth; Robert Stephens (probably the historiographer-royal and one of the founders of the Society of Antiquaries); Samuel Buck (probably the draughtsman and engraver who produced views of ruins, country seats, towns, etc.); and Henry Johnson (perhaps the translator and traveller of that name, FSA 1720, who in 1724 translated La Motte's tragedy *Romulus*). Stukeley's records of the Society list each member with his Roman name and also the Roman name for his place of residence: Bodleian MS. Eng. Misc. c. 401, fol. 8, a list of *Candidati* for 1723.

36 Bodl. MS. Eng. Misc. c. 401, fol. 9, meeting for 11 November 1724.

37 Bodl. MS. Eng. Misc. c. 401, fols. 22–3, the complete speech occupying fols. 19–23.

38 *Itinerarium curiosum: or, an Account of the Antiquities, and Remarkable Curiosities in Nature or Art, Observed in Travels through Great Britain* ('Centuria I', 1725; republished with 'Centuria II', 1776, the edition cited here), 'Iter I', p. 3.

39 *Ibid.*, 'Centuria II', 'Iter boreale', p. 67.

40 *Ibid.*

41 *Ibid.*, p. 61.

42 *Ibid.*, p. 67.

43 *Ibid.*

44 *Ibid.*, 'Centuria I', 'Iter romanum', p. 76.

45 *Ibid.*, 'Centuria II', 'Iter V', p. 77. Italics mine.

46 *Ibid.*, 'Centuria '', 'Iter VI', pp. 135–6.

47 Letter to Alexander Gordon, 30 November 1723, printed in Brown, 'Chyndonax to Galgacus', p. 119.

48 *Itinerarium curiosum*, 'Centuria I', 'Iter VI', p. 137.

49 Letter of 24 October 1724 to Alexander Gordon, printed in Brown, 'Chyndonax to Galgacus', p. 122.

50 On Clerk's archaeological work see Stuart Piggott, 'The Ancestors of Jonathan Oldbuck', *Antiquity*, 29 (1955), 150–6; and *William Stukeley*, *passim*.

51 On his life in Carolina see Anna Wells Rutledge, 'A Cosmopolitan in Carolina', *William and Mary Quarterly*, 6 (1949), 637–43.

52 Clerk to Roger Gale, 2 June 1726, *The Family Memoirs of the Reverend William Stukeley*, I, 184.

53 *Ibid.*

54 Roger Gale to Sir John Clerk, London, 24 June 1726, *ibid.*, III, 87–8.

55 *Itinerarium septentrionale: or, a Journey thro' Most of the Counties of Scotland, and Those in the North of England* (1726), preface, sig. C1.

56 *Ibid.*

57 *Ibid.*

58 *Itinerarium curiosum*, 'Centuria I', 'Iter V', p. 77.

59 *Itinerarium septentrionale*, preface, sig. C1v.

60 The Earl of Hertford (six books), the Earl of Pembroke, the Earl of Winchilsea (two), Sir John Clerk (five), Roger and Samuel Gale.

61 These included Sir James Dalrymple (author of a supplement to Camden, on Scotland); Smart Lethieullier; Richard Ellys (or Ellis), dedicatee of John Horsley's *Britannia romana* (1732); and John Ward, whose work on Roman Britain is frequently cited by Horsley and whose essay on Peutinger's Table is printed by him: Horsley, *Britannia romana*, pp. 505–20.

62 See Joseph M. Levine, *Dr Woodward's Shield*.

63 On John Horsley see Sir George Macdonald, 'John Horsley, Scholar and Gentleman', 1–57; R. C. Bosanquet, 'John Horsley and His Times', *ibid.*, 58–81; R. G. Collingwood, 'John Horsley

and Hadrian's Wall', *AA*, 4th ser., 15 (1938), 1–42; Eric Birley, 'John Horsley and John Hodgson', *AA*, 4th ser., 36 (1958), 1–46; and Joseph M. Levine, *The Battle of the Books*, pp. 389–402.

64 Lecture of 1907, published in Haverfield's posthumous *The Roman Occupation of Britain* (London, 1924), p. 75. In many ways Horsley's book is far more thorough than R. G. Collingwood's *The Archaeology of Roman Britain* (London, 1930; updated by Ian Richmond for the revised edition, London, 1969) or Sheppard Frere's *Britannia: a History of Roman Britain* (London, 1967; rev. edn, 1987).

65 George Macdonald, 'John Horsley, Scholar and Gentleman', pp. 1–2.

66 R. G. Collingwood and J. N. L. Myres, *Oxford History of England*, 15 vols., vol. 1, *Roman Britain and the English Settlements* (Oxford, 1936), p. 466.

67 Though Horsley, to a lesser extent, disguises his own indebtedness to Gordon. See Eric Birley, 'John Horsley and John Hodgson', pp. 9ff.

68 George Macdonald, 'John Horsley, Scholar and Gentleman', p. 21. On Horsley's 'passion for accuracy' see p. 23.

69 This significant feature of the *Britannia romana* has been noted by Joseph M. Levine in *The Battle of the Books*, p. 398.

70 Letter from Horsley to Oxford, 11 February 1730/1, printed in R. C. Bosanquet, 'John Horsley and His Times', pp. 74–5.

71 Copy inspected in the Library at Chatsworth.

72 Bosanquet, 'John Horsley and His Times', p. 78.

73 Horsley, dedication 'To Sir Richard Ellys Bart.', *Britannia romana*, sigs. A1v, A2r.

74 *Ibid.*, sig. A2r.

75 On this building see John Summerson, 'Inigo Jones', *PBA*, 50 (1964), 170–82 and plates.

76 Inigo Jones, *The Most Notable Antiquity of Great Britain called Stone-Heng, Restored*, ed. John Webb (1655). Jones's study had been carried out in 1620 at the request of James I.

77 Walter Charleton, *Chorea gigantum* (1663); John Webb, *A Vindication of Stone Heng Restored* (1665).

78 Letter of 24 October 1724 to Alexander Gordon, printed in Brown, 'Chyndonax to Galgacus', p. 122. Brown notes Stukeley's undiplomatic timing – the new edition of Jones and Webb came out in 1725.

79 *The Designs of Inigo Jones, Consisting of Plans and Elevations for . . . Buildings, Published by W. Kent, with Some Additional Designs*, 2 vols. (1727).

80 Fiske Kimball, 'Burlington Architectus', *RIBA Journal*, 34 (15 October 1927), 691.

81 Colen Campbell, *Vitruvius britannicus, or the British Architect*, vol. II (1717), plate 27. The implications of these plans, historically important for Britain and Europe as a whole, are further considered in the next chapter.

82 On this building see Rudolph Wittkower, 'Burlington and his Work in York', *Studies in Architectural History*, 1 (1954), 47–66, reprinted in Wittkower, *Palladio and Palladianism*, ch. 9.

83 Damie Stillman points to other aspects of the York Assembly Rooms 'inspired by antique examples – ranging from the rectangular lobby with two apsed ends and the flanking rooms with one projecting exedra to the circular card room with corner alcoves' which 'seem to come from the [Palladio] drawings owned by Burlington. The exterior, too, as originally built, reflected

this influence, featuring a segmented portico with three arched openings, each forming a column screen topped by the mullioned semi-circular openings found on the Baths of Diocletian': Damie Stillman, *English Neo-Classical Architecture*, I, 36. See also Wittkower, *Palladio and Palladianism*, p. 138.

84 'The Letters and Drawings of Nicholas Hawksmoor relating to the Building of the Mausoleum at Castle Howard', *Wal. Soc.*, 19 (1931), 111–64 and plates.

85 Christopher Hussey, *English Gardens and Landscapes 1700–1750*, p. 101.

86 On the architectural evocation of classical antiquity at Stourhead see Kenneth Woodbridge, *Landscape and Antiquity: Aspects of English Culture at Stourhead 1718–1838*; and elsewhere in the present work.

87 There is no detailed work on the subject for Burlington's period, but for the connection between architecture and archaeology in the mid and later eighteenth century see Stillman, *English Neo-Classical Architecture*, especially ch. I, 'The Emergence of Neo-Classicism and the English Context', I, 27–48.

88 *Fabbriche Antiche Disegnate da Andrea Palladio Vicentino e Date in Luce da Riccardo Conte di Burlington* (London, 1730).

89 Robert Castell, *Villas of the Ancients*. This is dedicated to Burlington, of whose patronage Castell hopes to 'be thought worthy', as if he were not yet in Burlington's pay. Burlington had a copy, now at Chatsworth. Lees-Milne states that the work was published 'at [Burlington's] entire expense' (*Earls of Creation*, p. 144). I have not seen evidence for this in the Burlington Papers at Chatsworth, and Timothy Connor's paper on Burlingtonian publications, delivered to the Georgian Group Symposium in 1982, rightly emphasises that dedications by themselves mean nothing.

90 For an analysis of this library as a whole see my article, 'Burlington's Library at Chiswick', *SB*, 45 (1992), 113–27.

91 The connection between Romano-British archaeology and English Palladianism, explored below, has been briefly remarked by Giles Worsley in his article 'Rokeby Park, Yorkshire', part I, *CL* (19 March 1987), pp. 74–9 and esp. pp. 75–6. See also my article, 'Pope's *Epistle to Burlington*: the Vitruvian Analogies', *SEL*, 30 (1990), 429–44 and esp. 437–41.

92 Journal, 1714–15 tour, Burlington Papers, Chatsworth.

93 On Burlington's second Italian tour see Lees-Milne, *Earls of Creation*, pp. 122–5.

94 This and many of the books from the Library at Chiswick are now at Chatsworth and I am most grateful to His Grace the Duke of Devonshire for permission to consult these in the Chatsworth Library.

95 The enthusiasm is comprehensively described in Francis Haskell and Nicholas Penny, *Taste and the Antique: the Lure of Classical Sculpture 1500–1900* (London, 1981). Many of the works noticed by Haskell and Penny were in Burlington's Library, which also included significant works not listed in their extensive bibliography.

96 For example, his copy of Newton's *Opticks* (1704) and a book by Roger Long on astronomy are clearly related in their interests to his purchase of a Newtonian telescope from the maker Eccleston in 1747; another book on the principles of

mathematical instruments relates to his use of the silver-cased mathematical and drawing instruments he purchased from Jonathan Sisson and with which he designed his buildings; the books on architecture and archaeology supply him with motifs for his own designs. See my article, 'Burlington's Library at Chiswick', *passim*, but esp. pp. 119–20.

97 Plate 57.

98 Thomas Gale, *Antonini iter britanniarum*, ed. Roger Gale (1709).

99 Francis Drake, *Eboracum: or, the History and Antiquities of the City of York* (1736), p. 31.

100 See John Burton, 'A Dissertation on the Situation of the Ancient Roman Station of Delgovitia in Yorkshire', *Royal Society: Philosophical Transactions*, 44 (1747), 541–52; and Francis Drake, 'An Appendix to the Foregoing Paper', *ibid.*, pp. 553–6.

101 *The Family Memoirs of the Reverend William Stukeley*, III, 355. George Vertue, whose practice as an engraver did not generally descend to topographical works, evidently contracted the engraving to J. Mynde, who signed the engraving printed with Burton's and Drake's articles in the Royal Society's *Philosophical Transactions* (previous note). See *Vertue*, VI (1950), 197, for George Vertue's list of London engravers in 1743. This includes 'Mynde' (for 'etching').

102 *The Family Memoirs of the Reverend William Stukeley*, III, 356.

103 *Ibid.*, pp. 359–60.

104 Drake, *Eboracum*, p. 60.

105 The new pavement is illustrated on the plate to p. 519 of *Eboracum*.

106 Drake, *Eboracum*, dedication.

107 *Ibid.*, book I, p. 338.

108 'Jones and Palladio to themselves restore, / And be whate'er Vitruvius was before': *Epistle to Burlington*, ll. 193–4.

109 'Returned from Italy after inspecting the remains of ancient buildings, he transferred the Roman arts into his own country, and among the chief men who had begun to revive and perfect architecture in England, he shone forth as almost the first.' On Phillipps see Mark Girouard, 'Ambrose Phillipps of Garendon', *AH*, 8 (1965), 25–38; and *DBA*, pp. 632–3.

4 BRITANNIA ROMANA REVIVED

1 Damie Stillman, *English Neo-Classical Architecture*, I, 28.

2 The best single book on Palladianism is still Rudolf Wittkower, *Palladio and Palladianism*, a collection of earlier lectures and articles on the subject. Stillman rightly emphasises that 'it was the new [continental] archaeological zeal and the new attitude toward antiquity permeating Rome' which in the second half of the century inspired neo-classicism proper – *English Neo-Classical Architecture*, I, 38 – but his statement that 'in the hands of the Burlingtonians and their contemporaries antique elements were relatively restricted and employed as seen in Palladio and similar works' (*ibid.*) blurs the important distinction between their borrowings from Palladio's own buildings (as at Chiswick and Mereworth, for example) and their borrowings from his paper reconstructions of Roman temples, basilicas and other buildings (as in the case of the Assembly Rooms at York and some of the English neo-Palladian garden temples by Burlington and others). Palladio's paper reconstructions, though inevitably hypothetical

to a greater or lesser extent, were of course archaeologically based on his on-site examinations and measurement of the Roman remains. Stillman also seems here to underrate the practical influence on Burlington and his followers of the archaeologically based and minutely precise drawings in the work of Desgodetz and others.

3 Stimulated by the expeditions of Robert Wood and James Dawkins (*The Ruins of Palmyra, otherwise Tedmore, in the Desert* 1753), James Stuart and Nicholas Revett (*Antiquities of Athens*, from 1762), Robert Adam (*Ruins of the Palace of the Emperor Diocletian at Spalatro in Dalmatia*, 1764), and Richard Chandler, Nicholas Revett and William Pars (*The Antiquities of Ionia*, from 1769). For a survey see Stillman, *English Neo-Classical Architecture*, I, 29–30.

4 'A Letter concerning the Art or Science of Design', in *Characteristicks* (1732), III, 402–3.

5 *Ibid.*, pp. 400–1. Inigo Jones had drawn up magnificent designs for a royal palace for Charles I, and these were dramatically featured in the second volume of *Vitruvius britannicus*, a clear but unsuccessful temptation to George I.

6 Colen Campbell, *Vitruvius britannicus*, vol. I (1715). A second volume followed in 1717, a third in 1725, all published by subscription. On Campbell see *DBA*, pp. 182–5; and H. E. Stutchbury, *The Architecture of Colen Campbell* (Manchester, 1967).

7 This is not noticed by Stutchbury, *The Architecture of Colen Campbell*, who notes on p. 24, however, that Campbell's patrons were by no means exclusively Whig.

8 Jane Clark, 'The Mysterious Mr Buck: Patronage and Politics 1688–1745', *Apollo*, 129 (May 1989), 317–22 and 371.

9 For an overview of English Palladianism in its relation to Burlington see John Harris, *The Palladian Revival: Lord Burlington, his Villa and Garden at Chiswick* (London 1994).

10 For a detailed account of the progress of Palladians through the King's Works see H. M. Colvin, *The History of the King's Works*, 5 vols., vol. V, *1660–1782* (London, 1976), *passim*.

11 John Woolfe and James Gandon, *Vitruvius britannicus, or the British Architect*, vol. IV (1767) – the continuation of J. Badeslade and J. Rocque's vol. IV (1739) – introduction p. 1.

12 Inigo Jones had been appointed Surveyor of the King's Works in 1615, and until the outbreak of the Civil War in 1642 had been continuously occupied with the supervision of architectural works in the service of James I and Charles I, much of it on royal residences. Among the legacies of this period are the Queen's House at Greenwich – the first properly classical building in Britain – and the Banqueting House at Whitehall. Lost legacies include Jones's restoration of St Paul's Cathedral, and projects frustrated by the outbreak of civil war include his designs for Whitehall Palace. During the period 1660–1702 royal building projects, most of them completed, included the New Gallery at Somerset House, Chelsea Hospital, Winchester Palace, the substantial reconstruction of Windsor Castle, Wren's rebuilding at Whitehall Palace and his work at Hampton Court, his City churches and pre-eminently his continuing work on St Paul's, as well as the initial development of Greenwich Hospital. For a detailed discussion of the Restoration period and after, see Colvin, *The History of the King's Works*, V; and John Summerson, *Architecture in Britain 1530–1830*

(London, 1953) – ch. 8, 'The Surveyorship of Inigo Jones', pp. 74–85; ch. 15, 'The Royal Works 1660–1702', pp. 146–53; and ch. 18, 'The Royal Works 1702–1726', pp. 179–83.

13 Colvin notes that 'After Wren there ensued sixty years during which his post was treated as a political sinecure': *The History of the King's Works*, v, ix. Summerson is scathing: 'From Vanbrugh's time all the places in the Works rapidly take on the character of plums, to be distributed to the clients of the oligarchy in power, irrespective of professional merit. Not only the senior offices, but the clerkships and the places of the Patent Artisans become a prey to nonentities with good connexions; and the prestige of the Office steadily disintegrates. Behind this tendency, and one of its undoubted causes, lies the shift of patronage from the Court to the two great political parties. William and Mary were the last sovereigns to conduct palace-building in the Stuart tradition, and after Mary's death in 1694 it was on Whig aristocrats rather than on the Sovereign at Whitehall or St James's that architecture depended for encouragement and opportunity': *Architecture in Britain 1530–1830*, p. 179.

14 Summerson is not overstating the case when he says that 'The importance of the Office of the Works may be said to cease with Vanbrugh's death in 1726': *The History of the King's Works*, v, 183.

15 Although Martin Battestin correctly points to the implicit criticism of George II's 'dereliction, as churches sink on their foundations, the Thames overflows its banks, highways become impassable, and the building of Westminster Bridge is given to an incompetent carpenter' (*The Providence of Wit*, p. 87, and also p. 40), the standard modern reading sees the lines as wide-eyed nationalism: Peter Dixon, *The World of Pope's Satires* (London, 1968), p. 61; Avril Henry and Peter Dixon, 'Pope and the Architects: a Note on the *Epistle to Burlington*, *ES*, 51 (1970), 437–41, esp. p. 441; and William A. Gibson, 'Three Principles of Renaissance Architectural Theory in Pope's *Epistle to Burlington*', *SEL*, 11 (1971), 487–505.

16 Alexander Pope, *Epistle to Burlington*, ll. 191–204, *Epistles to Several Persons*, ed. F. W. Bateson (London, 1951; edn cit., 1961), pp. 155–6.

17 Horace, *Odes*, IV, ii, 49; and Virgil, *Aeneid* VI, 851–2, as translated by Dryden, 'These are imperial arts and worthy thee'.

18 Though they fail to see the complexity of the Vitruvian aspects of the *Epistle*, Morris Brownell and Howard Erskine-Hill have pointed to the variety of Pope's allusions to Vitruvius, showing how the poet, in Erskine-Hill's words, 'was not just an enthusiastic onlooker, but a real participant' in Burlington's Palladian programme, with a facility for referring to Vitruvius in his correspondence. See Brownell, *Alexander Pope and the Arts of Georgian England*, pp. 276–93; and Erskine-Hill, 'Heirs of Vitruvius: Pope and the Idea of Architecture', in *The Art of Alexander Pope*, ed. Howard Erskine-Hill and Anne Smith (London, 1979), pp. 144–56. See also Charles Beaumont, 'Pope and the Palladians', *TSLL*, 17 (1975), 462–79.

19 Vitruvius, *De architectura*, book V. Also directly relevant to the concluding lines of Pope's *Epistle* is Vitruvius' preface, in which he reviews his tasks in the surveyorship of the Augustan Works.

For a translation of this see Frank Granger's translation of Vitruvius, *On Architecture*, 2 vols. (London, 1931–4), I: book I, preface, sections 1–3, pp. 3–5. For a more extended discussion of the Vitruvian parallels here, see my article, 'Pope's *Epistle to Burlington*: the Vitruvian Analogies.

20 Francis Drake, *Eboracum*, book I, p. 338.

21 Treated in detail in my article, 'Pope's *Epistle to Burlington*: the Vitruvian Analogies'.

22 *Fabbriche Antiche Disegnate da Andrea Palladio Vicentino*.

23 *I Dieci Libri dell'Architettura di M. Vitruvio* (Venice, 1556). Burlington had copies of three editions of Barbaro's Vitruvius including a 1567 edition with manuscript notes by Inigo Jones.

24 *The Diary of Humfrey Wanley, 1715–1726*, ed. C. E. and Ruth C. Wright, 2 vols. (London, 1966), II, 302–3 (p. 59, fol. 33a, in Wanley's diary).

25 See the section 'The History of the Manuscripts of Vitruvius' in Frank Granger's introduction to his Loeb edition of Vitruvius, *On Architecture*, 2 vols., I (London, 1931), pp. xvi–xxi.

26 According to James Lees-Milne's biography of Oxford, 'Lord Oxford's three most intimate friends were the three most distinguished poets of their day, namely Swift, Pope and Prior': Lees-Milne, *Earls of Creation*, p. 187. In the 1720s, of course, Swift was in Ireland, but he had known Oxford since the latter's childhood.

27 James Ralph, *A Critical Review of the Publick Buildings, Statues and Ornaments in, and about London and Westminster* (1734), p. 2.

28 *Ibid.*, pp. 18–19.

29 *Ibid.*, pp. 56–7.

30 Battestin, *The Providence of Wit*, p. 87.

31 Battestin, *The Providence of Wit*, pp. 22–7, with the references.

32 See, e.g., his prefatory remarks in *Rural Architecture, Consisting of Regular Designs of Plans and Elevations for Buildings in the Country* (1750).

33 *Epistle to Burlington*, ll. 23–38.

34 Colen Campbell, *Vitruvius britannicus*, vol. II (1717), plate 27, described on p. 1.

35 See Stutchbury, *The Architecture of Colen Campbell*, p. 78.

36 Joseph Burke, *English Art 1714–1800*, p. 30.

37 See John Summerson's three-part article, 'The Classical Country House in Eighteenth-Century England', *Journal of the Royal Society of Arts*, 107 (July 1959), I: 'Patronage and Performance', 551–2, and III: 'The Idea of the Villa', 570–87.

38 Palladio had used the word in reference to the entire estate including the house, and Campbell employs it in this sense on the one occasion he uses it in the *Vitruvius britannicus*. See Summerson, 'The Classical Country House', p. 570. The term was used in Scotland before it was common in England – see below. Summerson does not deal with Scotland. Damie Stillman, *English Neo-Classical Architecture*, I, 153 appears to understate the use of 'villa' before the mid-century.

39 See, e.g., Pliny the Younger's description of life at his Tuscan villa: *The Letters of Pliny the Consul: with Occasional Remarks*, tr. William Melmoth, 2 vols. (8th edn) (London 1786), I, 254–70 (book V, letter VI, to Apollinaris). The large number of editions of Melmoth's translation is indicative of Pliny's popularity in eighteenth-century England.

40 Giles Worsley, 'Taking the Ancients Literally: Archaeological Neoclassicism in Mid-

Eighteenth-Century Britain', typescript provided by Giles Worsley to the author, p. 1. This paper was delivered to the Georgian Group Symposium on 'New Light on English Palladianism', 13 October 1988.

41 Worsley, 'Taking the Ancients Literally', p. 3, mentions also John Webb's unpublished plans for a Roman house. For an analysis of these see E. Eisenthal, 'John Webb's Reconstruction of the Ancient House', *AH*, 28 (1985), 7–31.

42 In *The Plans, Elevations, and Sections of Holkham in Norfolk, the Seat of the Earl of Leicester* (1761), Brettingham implies that he was the architect. Belated acknowledgement of Burlington's contribution is made in the posthumous second edition, *The Plans and Elevations of the Late Earl of Leicester's House at Holkham* (1773). Kent's drawings survive and attest his important role, but the history of Holkham's construction is not yet clear. See *DBA*, under the heads of the relevant architects.

43 Worsley, 'Taking the Ancients Literally', p. 8; Vitruvius, *De architectura*, p. 216; Rudolf Wittkower, 'Lord Burlington and William Kent', in *Palladio and Palladianism*, p. 127.

44 On this and other Roman elements at West Wycombe see Giles Worsley's article on this house in *CL* (6 September 1990), pp. 112–17.

45 On some of these aspects see James Lees-Milne's biography of Leicester in *Earls of Creation*, pp. 250–1.

46 'An original and highly effective composition that had no precedent among English country houses', in the view of *DBA*, p. 703. Its twin towers are 'almost certainly a deliberate reference to Pliny's Tuscum villa, one of the key features of which was its twin towers': Worsley, 'Taking the Ancients Literally', p. 12. For other Roman aspects of Rokeby Park see Worsley's articles on this house in *CL* for 19 and 26 March and 2 April 1987, pp. 74–9, 176–9, 116–17 respectively.

47 Worsley, 'Taking the Ancients Literally', pp. 1, 15.

48 On Sir John Clerk's contributions to Scottish Palladianism and his influence on the early work of the Adams, see John Fleming, *Robert Adam and his Circle in Edinburgh and Rome* (London, 1962), pp. 15–44; A. A. Tait, 'William Adam and Sir John Clerk: Arniston and "The Country Seat"', *Burl. Mag.*, 111 (March 1969), 132–40; Stuart Piggott, 'Sir John Clerk and "The Country Seat"', in *The Country Seat*, ed. Howard M. Colvin and John Harris (London, 1970); William Spink, 'Sir John Clerk of Penicuik: Landowner as Designer', in *Furor Hortensis: Essays on the History of the English Landscape Garden in Memory of H. F. Clark*, ed. Peter Willis (Edinburgh, 1974), pp. 31–40; and *DBA*, pp. 219–21.

49 Roger Gale to William Stukeley, 26 August 1739, *The Family Memoirs of the Reverend William Stukeley*, I, 317.

50 An expansion of his *The Nobleman, Gentleman, and Gardener's Recreation* (1715). On Switzer see William Alvis Brogden, 'Stephen Switzer: "*La Grand Manier*"', in *Furor Hortensis*, ed. Willis, pp. 21–30.

51 See *Memoirs of the Life of Sir John Clerk of Penicuik, Baronet, ... Extracted by Himself from his own Journals, 1676–1755*, ed. John M. Gray, Publications of the Scottish Historical Society, 13 (Edinburgh, 1892), pp. 236–40; and Iain Gordon Brown, 'Sir John Clerk', pp. 179ff. Clerk

drank goats' milk as though he lived in Arcadia and took up bee-keeping through the inspiration of Virgil's *Georgics*. He advocated the provision in British constitutional law of a dictatorial power, available in the case of national emergency, just like that of the Romans. In his Latin correspondence he compared his retired life at Penicuik to Pliny's life at his Laurentine and Tuscan villas, and he designed decorative inscriptions from Horace and Pliny expressing his own thoughts and situation, to be placed at appropriate sites around Penicuik: *Memoirs*, *passim*, and Brown, 'Sir John Clark', pp. 163, 171–2, 195–6.

52 James Thomson, *The Seasons*, 'Summer', ll. 1453–6.

53 *Ibid.*, ll. 1442–5.

54 Compare the plan of the Chiswick gardens by Rocque done in 1736 (reproduced in Bladesdale and Rocque, *Vitruvius britannicus*, IV (1739), plates 82–3) with Castell's plan of Pliny's estate at Laurentinum in *Villas of the Ancients* (1728). The fashion in the 1730s for gardens combining, as Pliny's did, formality near the house with naturalistic features further away is evidenced throughout the Rocque and Bladesdale volume. See for example Rocque's plans of the gardens of Claremont (plates 19–23) and Wrest (plates 30–3), and compare their general layout and garden architecture – pavilions, temples in the antique style, etc. – with Burlington's.

55 On the Chiswick gardens see H. F. Clark, 'Lord Burlington's Bijou, or Sharawaggi at Chiswick', *Architectural Review*, 95 (1944), 125–9; Jacques Carre, 'Lord Burlington's Garden at Chiswick', *Garden History*, 1 (1973), 23–30; and Cinzia M. Sicca, 'Lord Burlington at Chiswick: Architecture and Landscape', *Garden History*, 10 (1982), 36–69, which explores Burlington's modern as well as classical borrowings at Chiswick.

56 See Marie P. G. Draper, *Marble Hill House, Twickenham: a Short Account of its History and Architecture* (London, 1966), p. 11.

57 A convenient summary of borrowings is given by Lees-Milne, *Earls of Creation*, pp. 256–9.

58 *DBA*, p. 909. For Kedleston see the plans in John Woolfe and James Gandon, *Vitruvius Britannicus* (London, 1767), plates 45–51; and on both Kedleston and the Circus see Joseph Burke, 'The Grand Tour and the Rule of Taste', in *Studies in the Eighteenth Century: Papers Presented at the David Nichol Smith Memorial Seminar, Canberra 1966* (Canberra, 1968), pp. 243–4. How closely the saloon at Kedleston recalls the interior of the Pantheon is strikingly revealed in the north–south sectional plan of the house given by Woolfe and Gandon on plate 51 of their work (see plate 27). In his *English Art 1714–1800*, p. 31, Burke notes of the Circus in relation to the Colosseum, 'The three orders, Roman Doric, Ionic, and Corinthian, were identically superimposed and the spaces in between filled with windows and doors, a change drastic enough to disguise the borrowing from many modern eyes, but immediately detected at the time' – for instance by Smollett's Matthew Bramble in *Humphrey Clinker* (1771): the Circus is 'like Vespasian's amphitheatre turned outside in'.

59 *DBA*, p. 909.

60 Morris R. Brownell observes that 'In the tradition of Vitruvius and Palladio [Pope] looks on architecture as a manifestation of virtu, an index

of the moral character of the builders, the architect, or the entire nation; and his judgements of builders, buildings, and architects depend as much on ethical as aesthetic principles': *Alexander Pope and the Arts of Georgian England*, p. 294. In this Pope is at one with Thomson, and speaks not only for the Burlington circle but the entire cultural enterprise first outlined by Shaftesbury. The conception of the arts as reflecting the standard of civic virtue in the nation is still strong at mid-century. In the dedication of his poem *Public Virtue* (1753), in which he intended to consider in three books the progress of agriculture, commerce and the arts, Robert Dodsley speaks of his work as 'this attempt to delineate such objects of public virtue': *Minor English Poets 1660–1780*, ed. David P. French, 10 vols. (New York, 1967), IV, 608–9.

61 *Guardian*, no. 173.

62 For a good survey of the classical elements in Pope's ideas on garden design, their antique models and their application at Twickenham, see chs. 4 and 5, 'Pope's Concept of Garden Design' and 'Twickenham, Paradigm of the Picturesque Garden' in Brownell, *Alexander Pope and the Arts of Georgian England*, pp. 102–45; Maynard Mack, *The Garden and the City*; and Peter Martin, *'Pursuing Innocent Pleasures': the Gardening World of Alexander Pope*, ch. 2, 'Chiswick and Twickenham', pp. 19–61.

63 Brownell has shown in detail how at Twickenham 'The classical ideal in the garden is apparent in the garden architecture, ornament, statuary, and inscriptions. The Twickenham Inventory lists various "Deities" and "Antike busttos" ... The ornament of sculpture and architecture Pope was planning to erect on the riverside in his garden the year before he died was an elaborate composition of classical iconography': *Alexander Pope and the Arts of Georgian England*, p. 123 and ch. 5 generally.

64 Joseph Spence, *Observations, Anecdotes, and Characters of Books and Men*, I, anecdote 619, pp. 256–7.

65 Most of the following are noticed, and several illustrated, in Hussey, *English Gardens and Landscapes 1700–1750*.

66 Chambers's friend Robert Wood had illustrated the Baalbek temple in his *The Ruins of Balbec, otherwise Heliopolis, in Coelosyria* (1757). See John Harris, *Sir William Chambers, Knight of the Polar Star* (London, 1970), pp. 36–7 and plates 38 and 30. See plates 28–9 illustrating other temples by Chambers in Kew Gardens after Roman models.

67 Christopher Hussey points out that the amateur architect Sir Thomas Robinson 'claimed to have made a particular study of round temples in connection with the Mausoleum; Hawksmoor and he had "look'd into all the designs of the Ancients of this kind of Building"': Hussey, *English Gardens and Landscapes 1700–1750*, p. 146 with the references.

68 See Geoffrey Beard, 'Magnificent Landscape Garden', *CL*, 130 (10 August 1961), 284–7.

69 Hussey, *English Gardens and Landscapes 1700–1750*, pp. 144 and 146, suggests the Mausoleum at Castle Howard as their inspiration, but if (as Hussey thinks likely) Sir Thomas Robinson was their architect, it would have been logical for him to adapt them from the round temples he had studied with Hawksmoor for the Mausoleum.

70 See Michael J. McCarthy, 'The Rebuilding of Stowe House 1770–1777', *HLQ*, 36 (1973), 279–80.

71 See Harris, *Sir William Chambers*, pp. 251–2 and plate 47.

72 The continuing strength of the Roman element in the English artistic imagination in the second half of the eighteenth century can be gauged by looking at what Damie Stillman calls the 'Roman fantasies' of the most prominent English neo-classical architects, projected works of an often startling grandeur owing their inspiration to Rome in its imperial phase and to Britain's own imperial glory in the decades before her forced recognition of the independence of the United States in 1782. These include Sir William Chambers's 1751 design for a mausoleum for Frederick, Prince of Wales; Robert Adam's 1757 design for a palace; James Adam's designs of *c.* 1761–2 for a Parliament house; Sir John Soane's 1776 design for a triumphal bridge, his 1778 design for a British senate house and his 1779 design for a triangular palace; James Paine II's design of *c.* 1781 for a national monument to the Earl of Chatham; and others. See Stillman, *English Neo-Classical Architecture*, I, 49–78, with plates for these.

73 On this, and particularly Fontainebleau, see ch. 1, 'A New Rome', in Haskell and Penny, *Taste and the Antique*.

74 See chapter 1 of the present volume.

75 Before Winckelmann pointed out the distinguishing characteristics which, it was said, made Greek art superior to Roman, it was generally thought that Greek and Roman art together constituted a universal standard. This is exemplified for literature by Pope's *Essay on Criticism* (1711) and for painting by Jonathan Richardson the Elder's *Theory of Painting* (1715) and *Two Discourses on the Art of Criticism in so far as it Relates to Painting and the Science of a Connoisseur* (1719).

76 John Northall, *Travels through Italy, Containing New and Curious Observations on that Country* (1766), p. 362, cited in Haskell and Penny, *Taste and the Antique*, p. 50.

77 See Adolf Michaelis, *Ancient Marbles in Great Britain* (Cambridge, 1882), pp. 42–3.

78 As suspicion of the value of the collection increased, its reputation declined. By 1810 the Pembroke marbles were no longer so prized. A visitor described 'floors . . . half-rotten, and the poor antiques, thrown about higgledy-piggledy, sans nose, sans fingers, sans every other prominent member, form a marble field of battle, half melancholy, half ridiculous': quoted by John Bold, *Wilton House and English Palladianism* (London, 1988), p. 69.

79 Stukeley's descriptive catalogue was never completed owing to Pembroke's constant interference, but a convenient list for the collection as it was *c.* 1724 is provided in the *Itinerarium curiosum* (1725; 2nd edn cited, 1776), 'Centuria I', 'Iter VII', pp. 185–7. See also *The Marble Antiquities of the Earl of Pembroke at Wilton* (1731); Richard Cowdrie, *A Description of the Pictures, Statues, &c., at Wilton House* (1751); James Kennedy, *A Description of the Antiquities and Curiosities in Wilton-House* (1769); and Adolf Michaelis, *Ancient Marbles in Great Britain*, pp. 665–715.

80 See Michaelis, *Ancient Marbles in Great Britain*, pp. 6–27; and for the fate of the marbles in the collection, and the Pembroke purchases, pp. 32–8.

81 On the development of the idea of virtuosity through the seventeenth century see Walter E. Houghton, Jr, 'The English Virtuoso in the Seventeenth Century', parts I and 2, *JHI*, 3 (1942), 51–73 and 190–219.

82 The 8th Earl of Pembroke 'was liberal in bestowing great names upon busts impossible to identify': Michaelis, *Ancient Marbles in Great Britain*, p. 43.

83 Julius, Augustus, Tiberius, Caligula, Claudius, Nero, Galba, Otho, Vitellius, Vespasian, Titus, Domitian (the 'twelve Caesars'), Nerva, Trajan, Hadrian, Antoninus Pius, Marcus Aurelius, Commodus, Pertinax, even the two-month emperor Didius Julianus, and Septimius Severus.

84 Stukeley, *Itinerarium curiosum*, 'Centuria I', 'Iter VII', p. 185.

85 *Ibid.*, 'Centuria I', 'Iter VI', p. 135.

86 *Ibid.*

87 Colen Campbell, *Vitruvius britannicus*, I, plates 98–100.

88 George Vertue, *A Description of Easton Neston in Northamptonshire, the Seat of the Right Hon. the Earl of Pomfret*, appendix to *Catalogue of the Collection of the Duke of Buckingham* (1758), pp. 53–9. See too *Vertue*, III, 73–4; IV, 40; V, 103–4.

89 *HWC*, XX (1960), 390. Walpole refers to the statues as 'famous, but few good. The Cicero is fine and celebrated, the Marius I think still finer. The rest are Scipios, Cincinnatuses and the Lord knows who, which have lost more of their little value than of their false pretensions, by living out of doors.' See also *HWC*, IX (1941), 5.

90 Michaelis, *Ancient Marbles in Great Britain*, pp. 36–40.

91 William Stukeley, *Itinerarium curiosum*, 'Centuria I', 'Iter II', p. 39.

92 *Ibid.*

93 Cornelius Vermeule, 'Graeco-Roman Statues: Purpose and Setting', parts I and 2, *Burl. Mag.*, 110 (October 1968), 545–58, 607–13.

94 Cicero, *Letters to Atticus*, Loeb edn, ed. E. O. Winstedt, 3 vols. (London, 1912–18), vol. I, I, iv.

95 *Ibid.*, I, viii.

96 *Ibid.*, I, x.

97 Vermeule, 'Graeco-Roman Statues: Purpose and Setting', I, 546–9. He calls this passion for collecting 'a Roman state of mind regarding the arts that would persist throughout antiquity, into the church facades of the Middle Ages, and to the formal pavilions and gardens of the High Renaissance': *ibid.*, p. 546.

98 Pliny the Elder, *Natural History*, XXXVI, iv, 22–9, Loeb edn, tr. H. Rackham, W. H. S. Jones and D. E. Eicholz, 10 vols. (London, 1938–62).

99 *Ibid.*, XXXVI, iv, 33ff.

100 *Ibid.*, XXXV, ii, 9–10.

101 Chesterfield, *Letters*, I, introduction, 173.

102 Isaac Ware, *A Complete Body of Architecture* (1756), plates 60, 61, 81–3, 85, 88; Wolfe and Gandon, *Vitruvius britannicus*, IV, plates 67–70.

103 Chesterfield, *Letters*, IV, 1549 (letter 1707, from London).

104 The latter two with heads by, respectively, Rusconi and (it was said) Bernini. See Haskell and Penny, *Taste and the Antique*, p. 62.

105 Matthew Brettingham, 'Accounts of Works of Art Bought in Rome', Holkham MS. 744.

106 For this suggestion see Joseph Burke, *English Art 1714–1800*, pp. 52–3.

107 Haskell and Penny, *Taste and the Antique*.

108 *Ibid.*, p. 67.

109 See Wolfgang Helbig, *Führer durch die öffentlichen Sammlungen klassicher Altertümer in*

Rom, 4 vols. (4th edn, Tubingen, 1963–72).

110 They include a copy of the *Belvedere Antinous* in the ante-room before the Hall at Syon House in Middlesex; a plaster cast of the *Apollo Belvedere* in the Hall at the same place; a copy in white enamelled lead by John Cheere of the Belvedere *Cleopatra* for Henry Hoare at Stourhead in Wiltshire, noticed again below; Soldani's 1710 bronze copy of the celebrated *Dancing Faun* for the Duke of Marlborough at Blenheim, and Simon Vierpyl's 1751 copy of the same in marble for Wentworth Woodhouse (the vast Palladian edifice designed by Burlington's disciple Henry Flitcroft) in Yorkshire; Chatsworth's reversed copy in lead of the *Faun with Kid*, and a plaster cast in the Duke of Richmond's gallery at Whitehall, opened in 1758; Filippo della Valle's full-scale marble copy of the *Capitoline Flora* for Wentworth Woodhouse, Matthew Brettingham the Younger's cast of the same statue at Burlington House and another at Holkham Hall, John Cheere's cast supplied in 1767 to Croome Court in Worcestershire, and another in the Duke of Richmond's gallery at Whitehall; Rysbrack's reduction (*c.* 1759–62) of the large *Farnese Flora* to life size for the Pantheon at Stourhead; the copies of the *Borghese Gladiator* noted above; Scheemakers's 1743 copy in stone of the *Dying Gladiator* for the garden at Rousham in Oxfordshire, Simon Vierpyl's copy of some twenty years later, in marble, for Wilton, and Luigi Valadier's 1773 bronze cast for the Hall at Syon House; a bronze of the *Laocoon*, from a cast made by the Kellers in France, in the Great Hall at Sir Robert Walpole's Houghton; Scheemakers's full-size stone copy of the *Lion attacking a Horse* for the garden at Rousham; a full-size, early replica in bronze of the equestrian *Marcus Aurelius at* Wilton, and adaptations with the emperor's place taken by a heavily Romanised William III (by Rysbrack, in Bristol) or later by George III, who in 1761 ordered that his figure on the Great Seal be taken from the Roman statue (see *Horace Walpole's Journals of Visits to Country Seats, &c.*, *Wal. Soc.*, 16 (1928), p. 24); Filippo della Valle's 1740–1 copy of the *Pudicity* (or *Livia Mattei*) for Horace Walpole, who commissioned it to commemorate his mother in Westminster Abbey; a *Borghese Silenus* in bronze by Valadier in the ante-room at Syon House; the Duke of Marlborough's bronze copy of the *Venus de' Medici* and also, as with others above, countless copies of this in lead for the gardens of Georgian England. Several of these are illustrated in Haskell and Penny, *Taste and the Antique*.

111 For John Cheere see Terry Friedman and Timothy Clifford, *The Man at Hyde Park Corner: Sculpture by John Cheere 1709–1787* (London, 1974), catalogue for the exhibition at Marble Hill House and Temple Newsam, Leeds.

112 Pope, *Epistle to Burlington*, ll. 123–4.

113 *Horace Walpole's Journals of Visits to Country Seats, &c.*, 72–3.

114 On this see Christopher Hussey, *English Gardens and Landscapes 1700–1750*, pp. 114ff.

115 *Continence of Scipio*, measuring 59 x 79.5 inches, by Giuseppe Chiari, was sold at auction by Christies of London on 31 October 1975 (lot 6), to an Italian who was using a pseudonym. Information from T. B. Ronnay, Administrator, Holkham Estate Office. I am grateful to Mr Ronnay for providing me with a photocopy of William Kent's drawing of the Leicester Chiari.

116 *The Journal of the Rev. John Wesley, AM*, ed. N. Curnock, 8 vols. (London, 1909–16), VI, 128, entry of 12 September 1776. From the earliest times Christians had considered the pagan deities to be demons.

117 On the evocation of the numinous at Stourhead see especially Kenneth Woodbridge, 'The Sacred Landscape: Painters and the Lake-Garden of Stourhead', *Apollo*, 88 (September 1968), 210–14; the same author's *Landscape and Antiquity*, pp. 2, 3–4 (on Wesley), 31, and generally ch. 2, 'The Genius of the Place'; and his *The Stourhead Landscape* (London, 1982), esp. pp. 18–20. See also Christopher Hussey, *English Gardens and Landscapes 1700–1750*, pp. 158–64. The idea of a programmatic classical iconography at Stourhead is taken further in Ronald Paulson, *Emblem and Expression*, ch. 2. For a counter-view see Malcolm Kelsall, 'The Iconography of Stourhead', *JWCI*, 46 (1983), 133–43. Kelsall points to Christian elements outside the garden itself.

118 *Letters*, ed. Melmoth, II, 85–7 (book VIII, letter viii). Melmoth's translation was first published in 1746. Georgina Masson, in *Italian Gardens* (London, 1961), proposed the connection with Stourhead, and both Woodbridge and Hussey follow her. Kelsall, within the constraints of his argument, also accepts the connection.

119 There are numerous allusions in the Stourhead landscape to Virgil, a favourite author of Henry Hoare. See Woodbridge, *The Stourhead Landscape*, esp. pp. 19–21.

120 On this, and on Pope's verse below, see Otto Kurz, 'Huius Nympha loci', *JWCI*, 21 (1953), 171.

121 *Landscape and Antiquity*, p. 2.

122 Letter of December 1755, quoted in Woodbridge, *Landscape and Antiquity*, p. 23.

123 See Kelsall, 'The Iconography of Stourhead', esp. pp. 140ff. Kelsall's suggestion that Hoare used classical iconography to lead the spectator subtly towards an awareness of the superiority of revealed Christianity, represented outside the garden in the church and (implicitly) in Alfred's Tower, is to read the Stourhead landscape as programmatically as the critics Kelsall attacks, and much is construed on the basis of less than overwhelming evidence. Kelsall also implies that Hoare was a Whig (p. 142). He was of course a Tory.

124 See above, ch. 2, and James Turner, 'The Structure of Henry Hoare's Stourhead', *passim*.

125 On the wider concerns of *Polymetis* see Austin Wright, *Joseph Spence: a Critical Biography* (Chicago, 1950), *passim* and esp. pp. 84–112.

126 *Polymetis: or, an Enquiry Concerning the Agreement between the Works of the Roman Poets, and the Remains of the Ancient Artists* (1747), pp. 2–3.

127 *Ibid.*, pp. 217, 226, 228 and 236.

128 *English Gardens and Landscapes 1700–1750*, p. 115.

129 *Ibid.*

130 'For the Augustan Age [of England] the classical deities were as vividly and individually symbolic as had been particular saints to the Medieval': *ibid.*, p. 125.

131 Kerry Downes, *Vanbrugh* (London, 1977), p. 113; and see plates 129 and 132.

132 *Polymetis*, p. 201.

133 Isabel Chase, *Horace Walpole: Gardenist* (Princeton, 1943), p. 29. On Kent's Praeneste Terrace see John Dixon Hunt, *William Kent, Landscape Garden Designer* (London, 1987), pp. 84–5.

134 As John Dixon Hunt has pointed out, Kent knew that modern Italian gardens 'revived the lost gardens of antiquity, and their role in passing on those Roman traditions to modern England is what is acknowledged in this valley, if only unconsciously; aptly, the presiding genius of the place is Venus, the Roman goddess of gardens': *Garden and Grove: the Italian Renaissance Garden in the English Imagination, 1600–1750*, p. 215.

135 *The Buildings of England: Buckinghamshire*, p.258.

136 *Travels Through France and Italy* (1766), p. 263 in the edn of Frank Felsenstein (Oxford, 1979).

137 *Memoirs*, pp. 236–40; the parallels are noted also by Dixon Hunt, *Garden and Grove*, pp. 218–19.

138 Sir John Clerk, 'The Country Seat', unpublished poem, quoted in William Spink, 'Sir John Clerk of Penicuik: Landowner as Designer', in Willis, ed., *Furor Hortensis*, p. 38.

139 Robert Lloyd, 'The Cit's Country Box, 1757', in *The Poetical Works of Robert Lloyd, AM*, 2 vols. (1774), I, 46.

140 Walpole to Conway, Thursday 12 July 1770, *HWC*, XXXIX (1974), 127.

141 Among numerous other examples, all cited by Mavis Batey, are the removal of the fishing village of East Lulworth 'to allow the lawn to sweep uninterruptedly down from the castle to the cove', the demolition of the riverside hamlet of Ladsome near Warwick Castle 'so that Capability Brown could landscape both sides of the River Avon', the removal of cottages from the line of vision at Edgcote in Northamptonshire, and the scattering of a village at Lilford in Northamptonshire to make way for the pleasure grounds of Sir Thomas Powys. Lord Scarsdale, after building his imposing house at Kedleston, 'found himself surrounded by the Domesday village of Chetlestone and proceeded to cast out every vestige of habitation, including the corn mill and the inn for the accommodation of those who came to drink of a medicinal well. A new estate village was built outside the park limits, but the villagers lost their green fields and chalybeate spring for ever': Mavis Batey, 'Oliver Goldsmith: An Indictment of Landscape Gardening', in Willis, ed., *Furor Hortensis*, p. 58.

142 'A parliament of landed gentry put no difficulties in the way of enclosing a village green or diverting a highway; while county concerns, such as the blocking of a local road or the demolition of a bridge, were easily handled when some member of the improving family was Lord Lieutenant of the county or Chairman of Quarter Sessions': *ibid.*, p. 60.

143 *Ibid.*, p. 61.

144 See G. R. Hibbard, 'The Country House Poem of the Seventeenth Century', *JWCI*, 19 (1956), 159–74, repr. in Maynard Mack, ed., *Essential Articles for the Study of Alexander Pope* (Hamden, Conn., 1964); and Virginia Kenny, *The Country House Ethos in English Literature 1688–1750* (New York, 1984). It is not surprising that Kenny finds the theme of retreat so dominant. See also Peter Laslett, *The World We Have Lost Further Explored*, pp. 22[illegible]–8.

145 See Webb, *Michael Rysbrack*, ch. 6, and appendix 2, pp. 227–8.

146 See Margaret Jourdain, *The Work of William Kent, Artist, Painter, Designer and Landscape Gardener* (London, 1948), p. 53 and fig. 11.

147 See *Reynolds*, ed. Nicholas Penny (London, 1986), pp. 224–6; and Joseph Burke, 'Romney's

"Leigh Family" (1768): a Link between the Conversation Piece and the Neo-Classical Portrait Group', in *Annual Bulletin of the National Gallery of Victoria*, vol. II (Melbourne, 1960), 10–11 with plates.

148 E. H. Gombrich, 'Reynolds's Theory and Practice of Imitation', *Burl. Mag.*, 80 (1942), 40–5; and *Reynolds*, pp. 262–3.

149 *The Yale Edition of the Works of Samuel Johnson*, vol. VI, *Poems*, p. 302. The poem can be dated *c.* 1779, and the portrait was published by T. Wright in 1776.

5 BEYOND THE MAINSTREAM: CLASSICAL NOSTALGIA AND FREETHINKING

1 The most powerful recent statement of the position is J. C. D. Clark, *English Society 1688–1832: Ideology, Social Structure and Political Practice during the Ancien Régime*, *passim*, but especially chapters 3, 4 and 5. The term 'confessional State' is his. 'Too little weight is often given to the immense continuity, the vast inertia, of popular and rural sentiment, especially in the case of England. Not least has this reflected the polemical denigration, within the "Whig interpretation", of the Church as somehow at once both somnolent or ineffectual, and the advance guard of modern rationalism': p. 165.

2 Information supplied by Martin Battestin, reporting recent research by David Vander Meulen on the *Eighteenth-Century Short Title Catalogue*.

3 On heterodoxy in seventeenth- and eighteenth-century Anglicanism see J. Hay Colligan, *The Arian Movement in England* (Manchester, 1913); H. McLachlan, *Socinianism in Seventeenth-Century England* (Oxford, 1951); and John Redwood, *Reason, Ridicule and Religion: the Age of Enlightenment in England 1660–1750* (London, 1976).

4 Clark speaks perhaps too sweepingly of 'Whig aristocratic *hauteur* and religious indifference . . . the party of Fox and Grey could as often dismiss Orthodox Anglicanism as "speculative nonsense"': *English Society 1688–1832*, p. 358.

5 As is the case with John Toland in *Christianity not Mysterious* (1696), Anthony Collins in *A Discourse of Freethinking Occasion'd by the Rise and Growth of a Sect call'd free-thinkers* (1713) and Matthew Tindal in *Christianity as Old as the Creation: or, the Gospel a Republication of the Religion of Nature* (1730). John Locke's *The Reasonableness of Christianity as Delivered in the Scriptures* (1695) was also generally regarded as a deistic tract, though Locke denied he was a deist.

6 On Joseph Butler's apologetic see Ernest Campbell Mossner, *Bishop Butler and the Age of Reason: a Study in the History of Thought* (New York, 1936); and Terence Penelhum, *Butler* (London, 1985), pp. 89–112.

7 Mossner, *Bishop Butler and the Age of Reason*, pp. 152–5.

8 Elisha Smith, *The Cure of Deism . . . In Answer to . . . the Author of Christianity as Old as the Creation, and the Author of the Characteristicks* (1736), title-page.

9 *Tom Jones* was 'Shaftesbury vulgarised', according to the *County Magazine* (March 1787), 235, 'Novels and Romances, with Characters and Anecdotes of Writers', which took the idea from *The Works of Samuel Johnson*, ed. John Hawkins (1787), I, 214–15.

10 Cicero respected the public religion but thought freely on religious matters. In some respects he

foreshadows the 'natural theology' of the seventeenth and eighteenth centuries. See *De natura deorum*, tr. H. Rackham, Loeb edn (London, 1933), at the end of which Cicero declares himself most in accord with the position put by the Stoic Balbus, who has argued for God's existence, goodness and providence; *De divinatione*, in *De senectute, De amicitia, De divinatione*, Loeb edn, tr. W. A. Falconer (London, 1923); and *De finibus bonorum et malorum*, Loeb edn, tr. H. Rackham (London, 1914; 2nd edn, 1931); and elsewhere.

11 As an example of how an extreme Whig emphasis on liberty and civic virtue could reject Christianity and seek in Islam a socially regulatory body of religious practice, see J. R. Jacobs, *Henry Stubbe, Radical Protestantism, and the Early Enlightenment* (Cambridge, 1983).

12 Compare Cicero's distinction between ignorant superstition, which he rejects, and true religion: *De divinatione*, II, lxxii, 148–50.

13 *The Christian Hero*, ed. Rae Blanchard (Oxford, 1932), dedication to Lord Cutts.

14 *Ibid.*, p. 15.

15 *Ibid.*, pp. 14–15.

16 For a recent assessment of Toland and his work see Stephen H. Daniel, *John Toland, his Methods, Manners, and Mind* (Kingston, Ont., 1984).

17 Michael Maittaire to Dr Charlett, 23 May 1718. Ballard MS. 17, f. 110, quoted in Piggott, *William Stukeley*, p. 118.

18 *Philosophical Essays Concerning Human Understanding* (1748), essay 21, 'Of National Characters', in David Hume, *The Philosophical Works*, III, 251.

19 *Philosophical Essays Concerning Human Understanding*, essay 7, 'Whether the British Government inclines more to Absolute Monarchy, or to a Republic', *ibid.*, p. 125.

20 *Philosophical Essays Concerning Human Understanding*, essay 10, 'Of Miracles', *ibid.*, p. 150.

21 For Hume's position on religion see J. C. A. Gaskin, *Hume's Philosophy of Religion* (London, 1978; 2nd edn, 1988); and for a recent Christian apologetic countering Hume, Timothy A. Mitchell, *David Hume's Anti-Theistic Views: a Critical Appraisal* (Lanham, Md., 1986).

22 This anticipation, which is largely a matter of tone and vocabulary, has received little analysis. On the relation of Hume and Gibbon generally see R. W. Winks, 'Hume and Gibbon: a View from a Vantage', *Dalhousie Review*, 41 (1962), 496–504.

23 John Witherspoon, *Ecclesiastical Characteristics: or, the Arcana of Church Policy* (4th edn, 1755), pp. 26–7 and 64.

24 In 1765 Diderot wrote to Sophie Volland that 'La religion chrétienne est presque éteinte dans toute l'Angleterre. Les déistes y sont sans nombre.' This is the wildest exaggeration of them all, even given that the phrase 'presque éteinte', like 'tout le monde', refers only to the social elite: Diderot, *Lettres à Sophie Volland*, ed. André Babelon, 2 vols. (Paris, 1938), II, 77.

25 *Edward Gibbon: Memoirs of My Life*, pp. 157, 159.

26 Swain, *Edward Gibbon the Historian*, p. 64.

27 As E. L. Cloyd puts it, 'Lord Monboddo makes a single system of Platonism, Christianity, and the Great Chain of Being', and, one might add, of natural religion: *James Burnett Lord Monboddo* (Oxford, 1972), 175.

28 On the poem's development through several versions, and the general consistency of its views

throughout this process (despite some Christian concessions), see Robert W. Rogers, 'Alexander Pope's *Universal Prayer*', *JEGP*, 54 (1955), 612–24.

29 'The Universal Prayer' in Pope, *The Poems of Alexander Pope*, vol. VI, *Minor Poems*, pp. 145–50.

30 First developed by Ficino; taken up by Bacon in the *De sapientia veterum* (1610), and by Ralph Cudworth, leader of the Cambridge Platonists, in *The True Intellectual System of the Universe* (1678).

31 Joseph Spence, *Polymetis*, p. 47.

32 Wharton as quoted in Tindal, *Christianity as Old as the Creation*, (2nd edn, 1732), p. 372.

33 'An Inquiry Concerning Virtue or Merit', in *Characteristicks*, I, 240.

34 Shaftesbury, notes to 'Miscellaneous Reflections', III.i, in *Characteristicks*, II, 251.

35 Tindal, *Christianity as Old as the Creation*, p. 356.

36 *Ibid.*

37 *Ibid.*, p. 360.

38 *Ibid.*, p. 381.

39 *Ibid.*, p. 388. Tindal is quoting Cicero.

40 *The Freeholder's Political Catechism* (1733), p. 14.

41 There is no study of the predisposition of freethinkers in England and France to reject, on *aesthetic* grounds, unclassical intrusions upon the classical frame of mind such as Judaism and its derivative, doctrinal Christianity. The anti-Jewish animus in much Enlightenment writing might more fruitfully be referred to aesthetic, rather than racial and instinctual, causes.

42 James Thomson, *Liberty*, IV, 561, in *Liberty, The Castle of Indolence and Other Poems*, p. 106. Mary Jane W. Scott, *James Thomson, Anglo-Scot*, p. 222, commenting on *Liberty*, III, 49–54, claims that Thomson's benevolent deity 'clearly reflects optimistic Moderate views, but at the same time the poet affirms God's providential omnipotence and omnipresence, His orthodox, nondeistical attributes.' This is somewhat misleading. Though deism in its later development tended to discard belief in divine Providence, seeing God as analogous to a watchmaker who made and wound the clock but takes no part in its subsequent going, many earlier deists, including the second and fourth categories of deists identified in Samuel Clarke's *A Demonstration of the Being and Attributes of God* (1705–6), taught a divine Providence. The God of *Liberty* is worshipped

> not from servile Fear,
> By Rites for some weak Tyrant Incense fit,
> . . . but from a Heart
> Effusing Gladness

in the person who 'lives Devotion' (IV.564–7, 570). This is consistent not only with the eighteenth-century Anglican and Scottish Moderate emphasis upon virtuous works, but also with (for example) the 'theism' of Shaftesbury.

43 For a general study of Collins in the context of his times see James O'Higgins SJ, *Anthony Collins, the Man and his Works* (The Hague, 1970).

44 For instance Collins quotes Bacon prominently in his text without comment or contradiction: 'Atheism leaves a Man to Sense, to Philosophy, to natural Piety, to Laws, to Reputation; all which may be Guides to an outward moral Virtue, tho Religion were not: But Superstition dismounts all these, and erecteth an absolute Monarchy in the Minds of Men. Therefore Atheism did never perturb States; for it maketh Men wary of themselves, as looking no further: and we see the Times inclin'd to Atheism (as the Times of

AUGUSTUS CAESAR) were civil Times': *Discourse of Free-Thinking*, p. 106.

45 O'Higgins, *Anthony Collins*, p. 80.

46 Robert Phiddian, 'The Reaction to Collins's *A Discourse on Free-Thinking* "Not Politicks"?', *Swift Studies*, 4 (1989), 63–76. A concise expression of Whiggish principles of religious toleration at around this time can be found in Viscount Molesworth's 'The Principles of a Real Whig', the preface to Francis Hotman, *Franco-Gallia* (1711): 'Whiggism is not circumscribed and confined to any one or two of the religions now professed in the world, but diffuses itself among all. We have known Jews, Turks, nay, some Papists, (which I own to be a great rarity) very great lovers of our constitution and liberty . . . I must have charity for those that differ from me in religious opinions, whether pagans, Turks, Jews, Papists, Quakers, Socinians, Presbyterians, or others . . . We ought no more to expect to be all of one opinion, as to the worship of the Deity, than to be all of one colour or stature.' See H. T. Dickinson, ed., *Politics and Literature in the Eighteenth Century* (London, 1974), p. 25.

47 Anthony Collins, *Discourse of Free-Thinking*, pp. 123–76.

48 Harris's notes to the entry on Shaftesbury in Bernard, Birch, *et al.*, eds. and trs., *A General Dictionary, Historical and Critical*, IX (1739), note R, p. 186. The *Dictionary* is an English version of Pierre Bayle's *Dictionnaire historique et critique*, (1695–7; 2nd edn, enlarged, 1702). Harris's authorship of the notes to the Shaftesbury article can be deduced from the fact that he had access to the Shaftesbury letters quoted therein, some of which were unpublished at the time. He probably also revised the text proper for Birch. On this see Clive T. Probyn, *The Sociable Humanist*, pp. 61ff. With Harris's treatment of Shaftesbury's 'theism' compare Chesterfield's sympathetic comment on Bolingbroke: 'He professed himself a Deist, believing in a general Providence, but doubting of, though by no means rejecting (as is commonly supposed) the immortality of the soul, and a future state': Chesterfield, *Letters*, IV, 1464.

49 BM Add. MS. 6858 (Mitchell Papers, vol. LV), p. 22.

50 Gibbon's controversial chapters on the rise of Christianity were scarcely the novel and revolutionary documents which, from their noisy reception, one might deduce them to have been. They were the culmination of a minority tradition going back to Shaftesbury, in which early Christians were viewed from a Roman-philosophical perspective. The question of Shaftesbury's influence on Gibbon has generally been ignored. Patricia B. Craddock does not have a single reference on the subject in her annotated bibliography, *Edward Gibbon: a Reference Guide* (Boston, 1987).

51 See, e.g., *Advice to an Author*, in *Characteristicks*, I, 230–1.

52 Charles Blount, *The Oracles of Reason* (1693), in *The Miscellaneous Works of Charles Blount*, ed. Charles Gildon (1695), pp. 128–36.

53 'Miscellaneous Reflections', in *Characteristicks*, II, 190, extended footnote to the observation that even as the expelled people were being 'conducted by visible Divinity, supplied and fed from heaven, and supported by continual miracles . . . it was with the utmost difficulty they could be withheld from returning again' to the gods and customs of Egypt.

54 *Ibid.*, II, 206–7.

55 *Ibid.*, II, 208–9.

56 *The Philosophical Works*, IV, 337–8.

57 'Miscellaneous Reflections', in *Characteristicks*, II, 210–12.

58 For the sensitive reader the note at the foot of the page, typographically distinctive, quickly becomes a sign and a lure – a technique pioneered by Pierre Bayle in his *Dictionnaire historique et critique*. There is a temptation, especially with Gibbon, to read the notes of a page before one reads the text above.

59 Collins, *Discourse of Free-Thinking*, p. 118.

60 *Decline and Fall*, Chandos verbatim reprint, II, 49 (ch. 23).

61 *Ibid.*, II, 110 (ch. 24).

62 Conyers Middleton, *A Letter from Rome, Shewing an Exact Conformity between Popery and Paganism: or, the Religion of the Present Romans to be Derived Entirely from That of their Heathen Ancestors* (1729).

63 *The Miscellaneous Works of Joseph Addison*, ed. A. C. Guthkelch, 2 vols. (London, 1914), II, 418.

64 This lost document is almost certainly distinct from the document now referred to as the Acts of Pilate, which appears to be a fourth-century fabrication.

65 George Lyttelton, *Observations on the Conversion and Apostleship of St Paul* (1747). Lyttelton's most telling point is that an illusionary enthusiastical experience of a Christian kind could not logically happen to a disbeliever and persecutor, and that therefore the experience was not the product of natural causes but genuinely miraculous. Like Addison, Lyttelton knows that most sceptics can only be won over by logic and historical fact.

66 *The Miscellaneous Works of Joseph Addison*, p. 422.

67 And yet methinks a beam of light breaks in
On my departing soul. Alas! I fear
I've been too hasty. O ye powers that search
The heart of man, and weigh his inmost thoughts,
If I have done amiss, impute it not! –
The best may err, but you are good, and – oh! [*Dies.*

The Works of the Right Honourable Joseph Addison, I, 225 and note.

CONCLUSION

1 It is worth recalling, however, that when Byron defended Walpole's literary reputation he fixed on 'Ultimus Romanorum' as an especially apt term of praise: preface to *Marino Faliero Doge of Venice* (1821). As noted in the present book, Walpole could occasionally use Roman analogies with a perfectly straight face.

APPENDIX. BOOKS ON ARCHAEOLOGY OWNED BY BURLINGTON: AN ANNOTATED SHELF-LIST

1 For a detailed account of books on architecture in this library see Ayres, 'Burlington's Library at Chiswick'.

Bibliography

BIBLIOGRAPHIES AND DICTIONARIES

Bernard, J. P., Birch, Thomas *et al.*, eds. and trs., *A General Dictionary, Historical and Critical*, 10 vols., 1734–41 (an English version of Pierre Bayle's *Dictionnaire historique et critique*, 1695–7; 2nd edn enlarged 1702).

Colvin, H. M., *A Biographical Dictionary of British Architects 1600–1840*, London, 1978.

Gunnis, Rupert, *A Dictionary of British Sculptors 1660–1851*, London, 1953.

MANUSCRIPT SOURCES

BM Add. MS. 6858 (Mitchell Papers, vol. LV).

Bodl. MS. Eng. Misc. c. 401: papers of the Society of Roman Knights.

Bodl. MS. Eng. Misc. e. 121.

Burlington Papers, Chatsworth:

accounts books;

journal of 1714–15 tour;

'A Catalogue of The Earl of Burlington's Library, At His Lordships Seat at Cheswick; January, 1741/2'.

Holkham MS. 744: Matthew Brettingham, 'Accounts of Works of Art Bought in Rome'.

CONTEMPORARY AND EARLY SOURCES

Adam, Robert, *Ruins of the Palace of the Emperor Diocletian at Spalatro in Dalmatia*, 1764.

Addison, Joseph, *The Works of the Right Honourable Joseph Addison*, ed. Richard Hurd, 6 vols., London, 1890.

The Miscellaneous Works of Joseph Addison, ed. A. C Guthkelch, 2 vols., London, 1914.

Addison, Joseph and Steele, Richard, *The Spectator*, ed. Donald F. Bond, 5 vols., Oxford, 1965.

The Tatler, ed. Donald F. Bond, 3 vols., Oxford, 1987.

Bacon, Francis, *De sapientia veterum*, 1610.

The Essays or Counsels, Civill and Morall, ed. Michael Kiernan, Oxford, 1985.

Battely, John, *Antiquitates rutupinae*, Oxford, 1711.

Bentley, Richard, *Evidences of Natural and Revealed Religion*, Boyle Lectures, 1692.

Bickham, George, *The Beauties of Stow*, 1750.

Blackstone, William, *Commentaries on the Laws of England*, 7th edn, London, 1775.

Bladesdale, J. and Rocque, J., *Vitruvius britannicus, or the British Architect*, vol. IV, 1739.

Blount, Charles, *The Miscellaneous Works of Charles Blount*, ed. Charles Gildon, 1695.

Bolingbroke, Henry St John, Viscount, *The Works of the late Right Honourable Henry St John, Lord Viscount Bolingbroke*, 8 vols., London, 1809.

Boswell, James, *The Life of Johnson*, ed. R. W. Chapman, Oxford, 1953; edn cit. 1985.

Bramston, John, *The Autobiography of Sir John Bramston*, ed. P. Braybrooke, Camden Soc., OS, 32, 1845.

Brettingham, Matthew, *The Plans, Elevations, and Sections of Holkham in Norfolk, the Seat of the Earl of Leicester*, 1761; 2nd edn as *The Plans and Elevations of the late Earl of Leicester's House at Holkham*, 1773.

Burke, Edmund, *The Works of the Right Honourable Edmund Burke*, 12 vols., London, 1887.

The Correspondence of Edmund Burke, ed. Thomas W. Copeland *et al.*, Cambridge, 1958–78.

The Writings and Speeches of Edmund Burke, ed. P. J. Marshall and William B. Todd, Oxford, 1981– .

Burlington, Richard Boyle, 3rd Earl of, *Fabbriche antiche . . .*, see Palladio, Andrea.

Burnet, Gilbert, *A Sermon Preached at the Coronation of William III and Mary II . . . in the Abby-Church of Westminster, April 11 1689*, 1689.

Burton, John, 'A Dissertation on the Situation of the Ancient Roman Station of Delgovitia in Yorkshire', *Royal Society: Philosophical Transactions*, 44 (1747), 541–52.

Burton, William, *A Commentary on Antoninus his Itinerary or Journies of the Romane Empire, so far as it concerneth Britain*, 1658.

Butler, Joseph, *The Analogy of Religion, Natural and Revealed, to the Constitution and Course of Nature*, 1736.

Camden, William, *Britannia sive florentissimorum regnorum, angliae, scotiae, hiberniae chorographica descriptio*, 1586.

Camden's Britannia, Newly Translated into English. with Large Additions and Improvements, tr. and ed. Edmund Gibson, 1695.

Campbell, Colen, *Vitruvius britannicus, or the British Architect*, vol.I, 1715; vol. II, 1717; vol. III, 1725.

Castell, Robert, *The Villas of the Ancients Illustrated*, 1728.

Cato, Marcus Porcius, *De agri cultura*, tr. William Davis Hooper and rev. Harrison Boyd Ash, Loeb edn, London, 1935.

Chandler, Richard, Revett, Nicholas and Pars, William, *The Antiquities of Ionia*, 1769.

Charleton, Walter, *Chorea gigantum*, 1663.

Chesterfield, Philip Dormer Stanhope, 4th Earl of, *The Letters of Philip Dormer Stanhope, Earl of Chesterfield, with the Characters*, ed. John Bradshaw, 3 vols., London, 1892.

The Letters of Philip Dormer Stanhope, 4th Earl of Chesterfield, ed. Bonamy Dobrée, 6 vols., London, 1932.

Cicero, Marcus Tullius, *Letters to Atticus*, tr. E. O. Winstedt, Loeb edn, 3 vols., London, 1912–18.

De finibus bonorum et malorum, tr. H. Rackham, Loeb edn, London, 1914; 2nd edn 1931.

De senectute, de amicitia, de divinatione, tr. W. A. Falconer, Loeb edn, London, 1923.

Verrine Orations, tr. L. H. G. Greenwood, 2 vols., London, 1928, 1935.

De natura deorum, tr. H. Rackham, Loeb edn, London, 1933.

Clarke, Samuel, *A Demonstration of the Being and Attributes of God*, Boyle Lectures of 1704–5, pub. 1705–6.

Clerk, Sir John, of Penicuik, *Memoirs of the Life of Sir John Clerk of Penicuik, Baronet, . . . Extracted by Himself from his own Journals, 1676–1755*, ed. John M. Gray, Publications of the Scottish Historical Society, 13, Edinburgh, 1892.

Collier, Jeremy, *A Short View of the Immorality and Profaneness of the English Stage*, London, 1698.

Collins, Anthony, *A Discourse of Free-Thinking, Occasion'd by the Rise and Growth of a Sect call'd Free-Thinkers*, 1713.

Congreve, William, *The Double Dealer* (1693), ed. J. C. Ross, London, 1981.

Country Magazine

Cowdrie, Richard, *A Description of the Pictures, Statues, &c., at Wilton House*, 1751.
Cudworth, Ralph, *The True Intellectual System of the Universe*, 1678.
Dennis, John and Hill, Aaron, *Julius Caesar Acquitted and his Murderers Condemn'd. In a letter to a friend. Showing that it was not Caesar, who Destroyed the Roman Liberties, but the Corruptions of the Romans themselves*, 1722.
Desgodetz, Antoine, *Les édifices antiques de Rome dessinés et mesurés très exactement*, Paris, 1682.
Diderot, Denis, *Lettres à Sophie Volland*, ed. André Babelon, 2 vols., Paris, 1938.
Dodsley, Robert, *Public Virtue*, 1753, in *Minor English Poets 1660–1780*, ed. David P. French, 10 vols., New York, 1967, vol. IV.
Drake, Francis, *Eboracum: or, the History and Antiquities of the City of York*, 1736.
'An Appendix to the Foregoing Paper' [John Burton, 'A Dissertation on the Situation of the Ancient Roman Station of Delgovitia in Yorkshire'], *Royal Society: Philosophical Transactions*, 44 (1747), 553–6.
Dyer, John, *The Ruins of Rome*, 1740.
Examiner
Ferguson, Adam, *Essay on the History of Civil Society* (1765), ed. Duncan Forbes, Edinburgh, 1966.
History of the Progress and Termination of the Roman Republic, 1782.
Fielding, Henry, *Miscellanies by Henry Fielding Esq; Volume I*, ed. Henry Knight Miller, Oxford, 1972.
The History of Tom Jones, a Foundling, ed. Martin C. Battestin and Fredson Bowers, 2 vols., Oxford, 1974.
Filmer, Robert, *Patriarcha*, 1680.
The Freeholder's Political Catechism, 1733.
Gale, Thomas, *Antonini iter britanniarum*, ed. Roger Gale, 1709.
Gazetteer
Gibbon, Edward, *The Decline and Fall of the Roman Empire*, 1776–88; Chandos verbatim reprint of the first edn, 4 vols., London, 1892.
The Miscellaneous Works of Edward Gibbon, ed. Lord Sheffield, 2 vols., London, 1814.
Memoirs, ed. George Birkbeck Hill, London, 1900.
Edward Gibbon: Memoirs of My Life, ed. Georges A. Bonnard, London, 1966.
Gilpin, William, *A Dialogue upon the Gardens of the Right Honourable the Lord Viscount Cobham at Stow in Buckinghamshire*, 1748.
Glover, Richard, *Leonidas*, 1737.
Goldsmith, Oliver, *The Deserted Village*, 1770.
Gordon, Alexander, *Itinerarium septentrionale: or, a Journey thro' Most of the Counties of Scotland, and Those in the North of England*, 1726.

Guardian

Hawksmoor, Nicholas, 'The Letters and Drawings of Nicholas Hawksmoor Relating to the Building of the Mausoleum at Castle Howard', *Wal. Soc.*, 19 (1931), 111–64 and plates.

Hogarth, William, *Hogarth: the Complete Engravings*, ed. Joseph Burke and Colin Caldwell, London, 1968.

Hooke, Nathaniel, *The Roman History, from the Building of Rome to the Ruin of the Commonwealth*, 4 vols., London, 1738–71.

Horn, D. B. and Ransome, Mary, *English Historical Documents*, vol. x, *1714–83*, London, 1969.

Horsley, John, *Britannia romana: or the Roman Antiquities of Britain*, 1732.

Hume, David, *Essays Moral, Political, and Literary*, ed. T. H. Green and T. H. Grose, 2 vols., London, 1882.

The Philosophical Works, ed. T. H. Green and T. H. Grose, 4 vols., London, 1882 (includes the *Essays* above).

The Letters of David Hume, ed. J. Y. T. Greig, 2 vols., Oxford, 1932.

'An Historical Essay on Chivalry and Modern Honour', printed with intro. by Ernest C. Mossner in *MP*, 45 (1947), 54–60.

New Letters of David Hume, ed. Raymond Klibansky and Ernest C. Mossner, Oxford, 1954.

Johnson, Samuel, *The Works of Samuel Johnson*, ed. Sir John Hawkins *et al.*, 15 vols., 1787–9.

Lives of the English Poets, ed. George Birkbeck Hill, 3 vols., Oxford, 1905.

The Yale Edition of the Works of Samuel Johnson, vol. VI, *Poems*, ed. E. L. McAdam, Jr, with George Milne, New Haven, 1964.

Jones, Inigo, *The Most Notable Antiquity of Great Britain called Stone-Heng, Restored*, ed. John Webb, 1655.

The Designs of Inigo Jones, Consisting of Plans and Elevations for . . . Buildings, Published by W. Kent, with Some Additional Designs, 2 vols., 1727.

Kennedy, James, *A Description of the Antiquities and Curiosities in Wilton-House*, 1769.

King, William, *An Historical Account of the Heathen Gods and Heroes; Necessary for the Understanding of the Ancient Poets*, 1710.

Lee, Nathaniel, *Lucius Junius Brutus*, 1681.

Leland, John, *The Laboryouse Iourney and Serche of Johan Leylande, for Englandes Antiquitees* (1549), ed. Thomas Hearne, 1710.

Lloyd, Robert, *The Poetical Works of Robert Lloyd, AM*, 2 vols., 1774.

Locke, John, *The Reasonableness of Christianity as Delivered in the Scriptures*, 1695.

Two Treatises of Government, ed. Peter Laslett, Cambridge, 1960; edn cit. 1963.

London Journal
Lucan, Marcus Annaeus, *Pharsalia (The Civil War)*, tr. Nicholas Rowe, 1718; edn cit. 1722.
The Civil War (Pharsalia), tr. J. D. Duff, Loeb edn, London, 1928.
Lyttelton, George, *Observations on the Conversion and Apostleship of St Paul* (1747).
Machiavelli, Niccolò, *Discourses on the First Ten Books of Livy*, in *The Prince and the Discourses*, tr. Max Lerner, New York, 1950.
The Marble Antiquities of the Earl of Pembroke at Wilton, 1731.
Matthews, John, *Vox populi, vox dei*, 1719.
Middleton, Conyers, *A Letter from Rome, Shewing an Exact Conformity between Popery and Paganism: or, the Religion of the Present Romans to be Derived Entirely from That of their Heathen Ancestors*, 1729.
The History of the Life of Marcus Tullius Cicero, 2 vols., 1741.
Molesworth, Robert, 1st Viscount, 'The Principles of a Real Whig', preface to Francis Hotman, *Franco-Gallia*, 1711.
Montagu, Edward Wortley, *Reflections on the Rise and Fall of the Antient Republicks Adapted to the Present State of Great Britain*, 1759.
Montfaucon, Bernard de, *L'antiquité expliquée et représentée en figures*, 5 vols. and 5 supp. vols., Paris, 1719–24.
Moritz, Carl Philipp, *Travels, Chiefly on Foot, through Several Parts of England in 1782*, ed. P. E. Matheson, London, 1924.
Morning Chronicle
Morris, Robert, *Essay in Defence of Ancient Architecture*, 1728.
Lectures on Architecture, Consisting of Rules Founded upon Harmonick and Arithmetical Proportion in Building, 1734–6.
Rural Architecture, Consisting of Regular Designs of Plans and Elevations for Buildings in the Country, 1750.
Moyle, Walter, *The Whole Works*, 1727.
Northall, John, *Travels through Italy, Containing New and Curious Observations on that Country*, 1766.
Observator
Oldmixon, John, *The History of England during the Reigns of the Royal House of Stuart*, 1730.
Palladio, Andrea, *I quattro libri dell'architettura*, Venice, 1570.
Fabbriche antiche disegnate da Andrea Palladio Vicentino e date in luce da Riccardo Conte di Burlington, London, 1730.
The Four Books of Andrea Palladio's Architecture, ed. Isaac Ware, 1738.
Parliamentary History of England, ed. William Cobbett, London, 1808–20.
Pliny the Elder, *Natural History*, tr. H. Rackham, W. H. S. Jones and D. E.

Eichholz, Loeb edn, 10 vols., London, 1938–62.
Pliny the Younger, *The Letters of Pliny the Consul: with Occasional Remarks*, tr. William Melmoth, 2 vols., 8th edn corr., London, 1786.
Poems on Affairs of State: Augustan Satirical Verse, 1660–1714, vol. v, ed. William J. Cameron, New Haven, 1971, and vol. vi, ed. Frank H. Ellis, New Haven, 1970.
Polybius, *The Histories*, tr. W. R. Paton, 6 vols., Loeb edn, London, 1922–7.
Pope, Alexander, *The Poems of Alexander Pope*, Twickenham edn, 6 vols. in 7, Oxford, 1939–61.
Quintilian, Marcus Fabius, *The Institutio Oratoria of Quintilian*, tr. H. E. Butler, Loeb edn, 4 vols., London, 1920–2.
Ralph, James, *A Critical Review of the Publick Buildings, Statues and Ornaments in, and about London and Westminster*, 1734.
Reynolds, Joshua, *Reynolds*, ed. Nicholas Penny, London, 1986.
Richardson, Jonathan, the Elder, *The Theory of Painting*, 1715.
Two Discourses on the Art of Criticism in so far as it Relates to Painting and the Science of a Connoisseur, 1719.
Robespierre, Maximilien, speech of 17 Pluviôse, Year II of the Republic (5 February 1794), tr. Richard Bienvenu, in Bienvenu, ed., *The Ninth of Thermidor: the Fall of Robespierre*, Oxford, 1968, pp. 32–9.
Rousseau, Jean-Jacques, *The Social Contract*, tr. Maurice Cranston, Harmondsworth, 1968.
Shaftesbury, Anthony Ashley Cooper, 3rd Earl of, *Characteristicks of Men, Manners, Opinions, Times* (3vols., 1711; 5th edn 1932), ed. John M. Robertson, 2 vols., London, 1900.
Sibbald, Robert, *Historical Inquiries, Concerning the Roman Monuments and Antiquities in the North-Part of Britain called Scotland*, Edinburgh, 1707.
Miscellanea quaedam eruditiae antiquitatis quae ad borealem britanniae majoris partem pertinent, Edinburgh, 1710.
Smith, Adam, *An Inquiry into the Nature and Causes of the Wealth of Nations*, ed. R. H. Campbell, A. S. Skinner and William B. Todd, 2 vols., Oxford, 1976.
Smith, Elisha, *The Cure of Deism . . . In Answer to . . . the Author of Christianity as Old as the Creation, and the Author of the Characteristicks*, 1736.
Smollett, Tobias, *Travels through France and Italy* (1766), ed. Frank Felsenstein, Oxford, 1979.
Somner, William, *A Treatise of the Roman Ports and Forts in Kent*, ed. Edmund Gibson, 1693.
Spence, Joseph, *Polymetis: or, an Enquiry Concerning the Agreement between the Works of the Roman Poets, and the Remains of the Ancient Artists*, 1747.

Observations, Anecdotes, and Characters of Books and Men, ed. James M. Osborn, 2 vols., Oxford, 1966.

Steele, Richard, *The Christian Hero* (1701), ed. Rae Blanchard, Oxford, 1932.

Stuart, James and Revett, Nicholas, *The Antiquities of Athens*, 1762.

Stukeley, William, *Itinerarium curiosum: or, an Account of the Antiquities, and Remarkable Curiosities in Nature or Art, Observed in Travels through Great Britain*, 'Centuria I', 1725; repub. with 'Centuria II', 1776 (edn cit.).

The Family Memoirs of the Reverend William Stukeley, 3 vols., Durham, 1882–7.

Swift, Jonathan, *The Poems of Jonathan Swift*, ed. Harold Williams, 3 vols., Oxford, 1937; 2nd edn cit. 1958.

The Prose Works of Jonathan Swift, ed. Herbert Davis, 13 vols., Oxford, 1939–62.

Swift, Jonathan and Sheridan, Thomas, *Jonathan Swift and Thomas Sheridan: The Intelligencer*, ed. James Woolley, Oxford, 1992.

Switzer, Stephen, *The Nobleman, Gentleman, and Gardener's Recreation*, 1715.

Ichnographia rustica, 3 vols., 1718.

Tacitus, Publius (or Gaius) Cornelius, *The Histories and the Annals*, tr. John Jackson, Loeb edn, 4 vols, London, 1925–37.

Thomson, James, *The Seasons*, ed. James Sambrook, Oxford, 1981.

Liberty, The Castle of Indolence and Other Poems, ed. James Sambrook, Oxford, 1986.

Tickell, Thomas, *Oxford. A Poem. Inscrib'd to the Right Honourable the Lord Lonsdale*, 1707.

The Poetical Works of Thomas Tickell, Edinburgh, 1781.

Tindal, Matthew, *Christianity as Old as the Creation: or, the Gospel a Republication of the Religion of Nature*, 1730; 2nd edn 1732.

Toland, John, *Christianity not Mysterious*, 1696.

Dedication to his edn of James Harrington, *Oceana*, 1700.

The State Anatomy of Great Britain: Containing a Particular Account of its Several Interests and Parties, 1717.

Trenchard, John and Gordon, Thomas, *Cato's Letters*, 1724.

Velleius Paterculus, Marcus or Caius, *Compendium of Roman History*, ed. Frederick W. Shipley, Loeb edn, London, 1924.

Vertue, George, *A Description of Easton Neston in Northamptonshire, the Seat of the Right Hon. the Earl of Pomfret*, appendix to *Catalogue of the Collection of the Duke of Buckingham*, 1758.

The Notebooks of George Vertue, *Wal. Soc.*, I (18, 1930), II (20, 1932), III (22, 1934), IV (24, 1936), V (26, 1938), Index (29, 1947), VI (30, 1950).

Vitruvius Pollio, Marcus, *De architectura*, tr. Daniele Barbaro, Venice, 1567.
On Architecture, tr. Frank Granger, Loeb edn, 2 vols., London, 1931–4.
Voltaire, Jean François Marie Arouet de, *Oeuvres complètes*, ed. L. Molland, 32 vols., Paris, 1877–85.
Walpole, Horace, *Anecdotes of Painting*, ed. R. N. Wornum, 3 vols., London, 1862.
Horace Walpole's Journals of Visits to Country Seats, &c., *Wal. Soc.*, 16 (1928), 9–80.
Correspondence, ed. Wilmarth S. Lewis, Yale edn., 48 vols., New Haven, 1937–83.
Wanley, Humfrey, *The Diary of Humfrey Wanley, 1715–1726*, ed. C. E. Wright and Ruth C. Wright, 2 vols., London, 1966.
Ware, Isaac, *A Complete Body of Architecture*, 1756.
Webb, John, *A Vindication of Stone Heng Restored*, 1665.
Welwood, James, preface to Nicholas Rowe's trans. of Lucan's *Pharsalia*, 1718.
Wesley, John, *The Journal of the Rev. John Wesley, AM*, ed. N. Curnock, 8 vols., London, 1909–16.
Witherspoon, John, *Ecclesiastical Characteristics: or, the Arcana of Church Polity*, 1753; 4th edn 1755.
Wood, Robert, *The Ruins of Balbec, otherwise Heliopolis, in Coelosyria*, 1757.
Wood, Robert and Dawkins, James, *The Ruins of Palmyra, otherwise Tedmor, in the Desert*, 1753.
Woolfe, John and Gandon, James, *Vitruvius britannicus, or the British Architect*, London, 1767.

SECONDARY SOURCES: BOOKS

Astin, Alan E., *Cato the Censor*, Oxford, 1978.
Atkins, J. W., *English Literary Criticism: Seventeenth and Eighteenth Centuries*, London, 1951.
Ayling, Stanley, *Fox: the Life of Charles James Fox*, London, 1991.
Bahlman, D. W. R., *The Moral Revolution of 1689*, New Haven, 1957.
Barrell, John, *The Idea of Landscape and the Sense of Place 1730–1840*, Cambridge, 1972.
Battestin, Martin C., *The Providence of Wit: Aspects of Form in Augustan Literature and the Arts*, Oxford, 1974.
Blagg, T. F. C. and King, A. C., eds., *Military and Civilian in Roman Britain: Cultural Relations in a Frontier Province*, BAR, 136, 1984.
Bloom, Edward A. and Bloom, Lillian D., *Joseph Addison's Sociable Animal*, Providence, R.I., 1971.
Bold, John, *Wilton House and English Palladianism*, London, 1988.
Brink, C. O., *English Classical Scholarship: Historical Reflections on Bentley,*

Porson, and Housman, Cambridge, 1986.

Brown, Iain Gordon, 'Sir John Clerk of Penicuik (1676–1755): Aspects of a Virtuoso Life', doctoral dissertation, University of Cambridge, 1980.

Brownell, Morris R., *Alexander Pope and the Arts of Georgian England*, Oxford, 1978.

Browning, Reed, *Political and Constitutional Ideas of the Court Whigs*, Baton Rouge, 1982.

Brunt, P. A., *The Fall of the Roman Empire and Related Essays*, Oxford, 1988.

Burke, Joseph, *Oxford History of English Art*, vol. IX, *English Art 1714–1800*, Oxford, 1976.

Burke, Peter, *The Fabrication of Louis XIV*, New Haven, 1992.

Cannon, John, *Aristocratic Century: the Peerage of Eighteenth-Century England*, Cambridge, 1984.

Carey, John, *John Donne: Life, Mind and Art*, London, 1981.

Carnochan, W. B., *Gibbon's Solitude: the Inward World of the Historian*, Stanford, 1987.

Chalker, John, *The English Georgic: a Study in the Development of a Form*, Baltimore, 1969.

Chase, Isabel, *Horace Walpole: Gardenist*, Princeton, 1943.

Churchill, Winston S., *Marlborough, His Life and Times*, 4 'books' in 2 vols., London, 1947.

Clark, H. F., *The English Landscape Garden*, London, 1948.

Clark, J. C. D., *The Dynamics of Change: the Crisis of the 1750s and English Party Systems*, Cambridge, 1982.

English Society 1688–1832: Ideology, Social Structure and Political Practice during the Ancien Régime, Cambridge, 1985.

Revolution and Rebellion: State and Society in England in the Seventeenth and Eighteenth Centuries, Cambridge, 1986.

Clarke, M. L., *Classical Education in Britain 1500–1900*, Cambridge, 1959.

Clifford, Derek, *A History of Garden Design*, London, 1962.

Clifton, Robin, *The Last Popular Rebellion: the Western Rising of 1685*, London, 1984.

Cloyd, E. L., *James Burnett Lord Monboddo*, Oxford, 1972.

Colley, Linda, *In Defiance of Oligarchy: the Tory Party 1714–60*, Cambridge, 1982.

Britons: Forging the Nation 1707–1837, New Haven, 1992.

Colligan, J. Hay, *The Arian Movement in England*, Manchester, 1913.

Collingwood, R. G., *The Archaeology of Roman Britain*, London, 1930.; rev. edn., updated by Ian Richmond, London, 1969.

Collingwood, R. G. and Myres, J. N. L., *Oxford History of England*, vol. I,

Roman Britain and the English Settlements, Oxford, 1936.

Colvin, H. M., *The History of the King's Works*, 5 vols., vol. v, *1660–1782*, London, 1976.

Craddock, Patricia B., *Edward Gibbon: a Reference Guide*, Boston, 1987.

Edward Gibbon, Luminous Historian 1772–1794, Baltimore, 1989.

Cust, Lionel and Colvin, Sidney, *History of the Society of Dilettanti*, London, 1898.

Daniel, Stephen H., *John Toland, his Methods, Manners, and Mind*, Kingston, Ont., 1984.

Dickinson, H. T., *Liberty and Property: Political Ideology in Eighteenth-Century Britain*, London, 1977.

Dickinson, H. T. ed., *Politics and Literature in the Eighteenth Century*, London, 1974.

Dixon, Peter, *The World of Pope's Satires*, London, 1968.

Dixon Hunt, John, *Garden and Grove*, London, 1986.

William Kent, Landscape Garden Designer, London, 1987.

Douglas, David C., *English Scholars 1660–1730*, London, 1939; rev. edn 1951.

Downes, Kerry, *Vanbrugh*, London, 1977.

Draper, Marie P. G., *Marble Hill House, Twickenham: a Short Account of its History and Architecture*, London, 1966.

Durling, Dwight L., *Georgic Tradition in English Poetry*, New York, 1935.

Elkin, P. K., *The Augustan Defence of Satire*, Oxford, 1973.

Erskine-Hill, Howard, *The Augustan Idea in English Literature*, London, 1983.

Esdaile, Katharine A., *The Life and Works of Louis François Roubiliac*, Oxford, 1928.

Fink, Zera S., *The Classical Republicans*, Evanston, Ill., 1946; 2nd edn 1962.

Fleming, John, *Robert Adam and his Circle in Edinburgh and Rome*, London, 1962.

Flower, Desmond, *Voltaire's England*, London, 1950.

Foxon, David, *Pope and the Early Eighteenth-Century Book Trade*, rev. and ed. James McLaverty, Oxford, 1991.

Frere, Sheppard, *Britannia: a History of Roman Britain*, London, 1967; rev. edn 1987.

Friedman, Terry and Clifford, Timothy, *The Man at Hyde Park Corner: Sculpture by John Cheere 1709–1787*, London, 1974, catalogue for the exhibition at Marble Hill House and Temple Newsam, Leeds.

Gaskin, J. C. A., *Hume's Philosophy of Religion*, London, 1978; 2nd edn 1988.

Gerrard, Christine, *The Patriot Opposition to Walpole: Politics, Poetry, and National Myth, 1725–1742*, Oxford, 1994.

Goar, Robert J., *The Legend of Cato Uticensis from the First Century BC to the Fifth Century AD*, Brussels, 1987.

Goldgar, Bertrand, *Walpole and the Wits*, Lincoln, Nebr., 1976.

Gray, James, *Johnson's Sermons, a Study*, Oxford, 1972.

Grummere, Richard M., *The American Colonial Mind and the Classical Tradition: Essays in Comparative Culture*, Cambridge, Mass., 1963.

Guilhamet, Leon, *Satire and the Transformation of Genre*, Philadelphia, 1987.

Hadfield, Miles, *Gardening in Britain*, London, 1960.

Harris, John, *Sir William Chambers, Knight of the Polar Star*, London, 1970.

The Palladian Revival: Lord Burlington, his Villa and Garden at Chiswick, London, 1994.

Haskell, Francis and Penny, Nicholas, *Taste and the Antique: the Lure of Classical Sculpture 1500–1900*, London, 1981.

Haverfield, Francis, *The Roman Occupation of Britain*, London, 1924.

Helbig, Wolfgang, *Führer durch die öffentlichen Sammlungen klassicher Altertümer in Rom*, 4 vols., 4th edn, Tübingen, 1963–72.

Hussey, Christopher, *English Gardens and Landscapes 1700–1750*, London, 1967.

Jack, Malcolm, *Corruption and Progress: the Eighteenth-Century Debate*, New York, 1989.

Jacobs, J. R., *Henry Stubbe, Radical Protestantism, and the Early Enlightenment*, Cambridge, 1983.

Johnson, James William, *The Formation of English Neo-Classical Thought*, Princeton, 1967.

Johnson, Stephen, *The Roman Forts of the Saxon Shore*, London, 1976; 2nd edn cit. 1979.

Jones, J. R., ed., *Liberty Secured? Britain Before and After 1688*, Stanford, 1992.

Jourdain, Margaret, *The Work of William Kent, Artist, Painter, Designer and Landscape Gardener*, London, 1948.

Kenny, Virginia, *The Country House Ethos in English Literature 1688–1750*, New York, 1984.

Kernan, Alvin, *The Cankered Muse: Satire of the English Renaissance*, New Haven, 1959.

Klein, Lawrence E., *Shaftesbury and the Culture of Politeness: Moral Discourse and Cultural Politics in Early Eighteenth-Century England*, Cambridge, 1994.

Koebner, Richard, *Empire*, Cambridge, 1961.

Kramnick, Isaac, *Bolingbroke and his Circle: the Politics of Nostalgia in the Age of Walpole*, Cambridge, Mass., 1968.

Langford, Paul, *Public Life and the Propertied Englishman 1689–1798*, Oxford, 1991.

Lascelles, Edward, *The Life of Charles James Fox*, Oxford, 1936.

Laslett, Peter, *The World We Have Lost: English Society Before and After the Coming of Industry*, London, 1965.

The World We Have Lost Further Explored, London, 1983.

Lees-Milne, James, *Earls of Creation: Five Great Patrons of Eighteenth-Century*

Art, London, 1962.
Leranbaum, Miriam, *Alexander Pope's 'Opus Magnum', 1729–1744*, Oxford, 1977.
Levine, Joseph M., *Dr Woodward's Shield: History, Science, and Satire in Augustan England*, Berkeley, 1977.
The Battle of the Books: History and Literature in the Augustan Age, Ithaca, N.Y., 1991.
Liebeschuetz, J. H. W. G., *Continuity and Change in Roman Religion*, Oxford, 1979.
Macaulay, Thomas Babington, *Critical and Historical Essays*, 3 vols., London, 1865.
Mack, Maynard, *The Garden and the City: Retirement and Politics in the Later Poetry of Pope*, Toronto, 1969.
Marshall, P. J., *The Impeachment of Warren Hastings*, Oxford, 1965.
Martin, Julian, *Francis Bacon, the State, and the Reform of Natural Philosophy*, Cambridge, 1992.
Martin, Peter, *'Pursuing Innocent Pleasures': the Gardening World of Alexander Pope*, Hamden, Conn., 1984.
Masson, Georgina, *Italian Gardens*, London, 1961.
McLachlan, H., *Socinianism in Seventeenth-Century England*, Oxford, 1951.
Meehan, Michael, *Liberty and Poetics in Eighteenth-Century England*, London, 1986.
Michaelis, Adolf, *Ancient Marbles in Great Britain*, Cambridge, 1882.
Mitchell, L. G., *Charles James Fox*, Oxford, 1992.
Mitchell, Timothy A., *David Hume's Anti-Theistic Views: a Critical Appraisal*, Lanham, Md., 1986.
Mossner, Ernest Campbell, *Bishop Butler and the Age of Reason: a Study in the History of Thought*, New York, 1936.
The Life of David Hume, Edinburgh, 1954.
Murray, Robert H., *Edmund Burke: a Biography*, Oxford, 1931.
Namier, Lewis, *The Structure of Politics at the Accession of George III*, London, 1929; 2nd edn, London, 1957.
England in the Age of the American Revolution, London, 1930; 2nd edn, London, 1961.
O'Higgins, James, *Anthony Collins, the Man and his Works*, The Hague, 1970.
Paulson, Ronald, *Emblem and Expression: Meaning in English Art of the Eighteenth Century*, Cambridge, Mass., 1975.
Penelhum, Terence, *Butler*, London, 1985.
Pevsner, Nikolaus, *The Buildings of England: Buckinghamshire*, Harmondsworth, 1960.
Piggott, Stuart, *William Stukeley, an Eighteenth-Century Antiquary*, Oxford, 1950, rev. edn 1986.
Ancient Britons and the Antiquarian Imagination, London, 1989.

Pocock, J. G. A., *Politics, Language and Time: Essays in Political Thought and History*, New York, 1971.

The Machiavellian Moment: Florentine Political Thought and the Atlantic Republican Tradition, Princeton, 1975.

Virtue, Commerce, and History, Cambridge, 1985.

Probyn, Clive T., *The Sociable Humanist: the Life and Works of James Harris 1709–1780*, Oxford, 1991.

Redwood, John, *Reason, Ridicule and Religion: the Age of Enlightenment in England 1660–1750*, London, 1976.

Robbins, Caroline, *The Eighteenth-Century Commonwealthsman*, Cambridge, Mass., 1959.

Sambrook, James, *The Eighteenth Century: the Intellectual and Cultural Context of English Literature, 1700–1789*, London, 1986.

Scott, Jonathan, *Algernon Sidney and the Restoration Crisis 1677–1683*, Cambridge, 1991.

Scott, Mary Jane W., *James Thomson, Anglo-Scot*, Athens, Ga., 1988.

Scullard, H. H., *From the Gracchi to Nero: a History of Rome from 133 BC to AD 68*, London, 1959.

Sekora, John, *Luxury: the Concept in Western Thought, Eden to Smollett*, Baltimore, 1977.

Sharpe, Kevin, *Sir Robert Cotton, 1586–1631: History and Politics in Early Modern England*, Oxford, 1979.

Smith, R. E., *The Failure of the Roman Republic*, New York, 1955.

Smithers, Peter, *The Life of Joseph Addison*, Oxford, 1954.

Stack, Frank, *Pope and Horace: Studies in Imitation*, Cambridge, 1985.

Stillman, Damie, *English Neo-Classical Architecture*, 2 vols., London, 1988.

Stone, Lawrence, *The Family, Sex and Marriage in England 1500–1800*, London, 1977.

Stutchbury, H. E., *The Architecture of Colen Campbell*, Manchester, 1967.

Summerson, John, *Architecture in Britain 1530–1830*, London, 1953.

Swain, Joseph Ward, *Edward Gibbon the Historian*, London, 1966.

Syme, Ronald, *The Roman Revolution*, Oxford, 1939.

Taylor, E. G. R., *The Mathematical Practitioners of Hanoverian England*, Cambridge, 1966.

Taylor, Lily Ross, *Party Politics in the Age of Caesar*, Berkeley, 1968.

Temmer, Mark J., *Samuel Johnson and Three Infidels: Rousseau, Voltaire, Diderot*, Athens, Ga, 1988.

Thomson, J. A. K., *Classical Influences on English Prose*, London, 1956; 2nd edn cit. 1962.

Voitle, Robert, *The Third Earl of Shaftesbury 1671–1713*, Baton Rouge, 1984.
Webb, M. I., *Michael Rysbrack, Sculptor*, London, 1954.
Weinbrot, Howard D., *Augustus Caesar in Augustan England*, Princeton, 1978.
Eighteenth-Century Satire: Essays on Text and Context from Dryden to Peter Pindar, Cambridge, 1988.
Britannia's Issue: the Rise of British Literature from Dryden to Ossian, Cambridge, 1993.
Whinney, Margaret, *Sculpture in Britain 1530–1830*, Harmondsworth, 1964.
English Sculpture 1720–1830, London, 1971.
Willis, Peter, *Charles Bridgeman and the English Landscape Garden*, London, 1977.
Willis, Peter, ed., *Furor Hortensis: Essays on the History of the English Landscape Garden in Memory of H. F. Clark*, Edinburgh, 1974.
Wimsatt, William Kurtz, *The Portraits of Alexander Pope*, New Haven, 1965.
Wirszubski, Chaim, *Libertas as a Political Idea at Rome during the Late Republic and Early Principate*, Cambridge, 1950.
Wittkower, Rudolf, *Palladio and Palladianism*, New York, 1974.
Woodbridge, Kenneth, *Landscape and Antiquity: Aspects of English Culture at Stourhead 1718–1838*, Oxford, 1970.
The Stourhead Landscape, London, 1982.
Wright, Austin, *Joseph Spence: a Critical Biography*, Chicago, 1950.

SECONDARY SOURCES: ARTICLES AND PARTS OF BOOKS

Ayres, Philip, 'Pope's *Epistle to Burlington*: the Vitruvian Analogies', *SEL*, 30 (1990), 429–44.
'Burlington's Library at Chiswick', *SB*, 45 (1992), 113–27.
Batey, Mavis, 'Oliver Goldsmith: an Indictment of Landscape Gardening', in Willis, ed., *Furor Hortensis*, pp. 57–71.
Beard, Geoffrey, 'Magnificent Landscape Garden', *CL*, 130 (10 August 1961), 284–7.
Beaumont, Charles, 'Pope and the Palladians', *TSLL*, 17 (1975), 462–79.
Birley, Eric, 'John Horsley and John Hodgson', *AA*, 4th ser., 36 (1958), 1–46.
Bosanquet, R. C., 'John Horsley and His Times', *AA*, 4th ser., 10 (1933), 58–81.
Brogden, William Alvis, 'Stephen Switzer: "*La Grand Manier*"', in Willis, ed., *Furor Hortensis*, pp. 21–30.
Brown, Iain Gordon, 'Chyndonax to Galgacus: New Letters of William Stukeley to Alexander Gordon', *AJ*, 67 (1987), 111–28.
Burke, Joseph, 'Romney's "Leigh Family" (1768): a Link between the Conversation Piece and the Neo-Classical Portrait Group', *Annual Bulletin of the National Gallery of Victoria*, II (Melbourne, 1960), 5–14.
'The Grand Tour and the Rule of Taste', in *Studies in the Eighteenth Century:*

Papers Presented at the David Nichol Smith Memorial Seminar, Canberra 1966, ed. R. F. Brissenden, Canberra, 1968.
Canter, H. V., 'The Impeachments of Verres and Hastings: Cicero and Burke', *CJ*, 9 (1914), 199–211.
Carre, Jacques, 'Lord Burlington's Garden at Chiswick', *Garden History*, 1 (1973), 23–30.
Chisholm, Duncan, 'Handel's *Lucio Cornelio Silla*, its Problems and Context', *Early Music*, 14 (1986), 64–70.
Clark, H. F., 'Eighteenth-Century Elysiums: the Role of "Association" in the Landscape Movement', *JWCI*, 6 (1943), 165–89.
'Lord Burlington's Bijou, or Sharawaggi at Chiswick', *Architectural Review*, 95 (1944), 125–9.
Clark, Jane, 'The Mysterious Mr Buck: Patronage and Politics 1688–1745', *Apollo*, 129 (May 1989), 317–22 and 371.
Clarke, George, 'Moral Gardening', *Stoic*, 24 (July 1970), 113–21.
'The Gardens of Stowe', *Apollo*, 97 (June 1973), 558–65.
'Grecian Taste and Gothic Virtue: Lord Cobham's Gardening Programme and its Iconography', *Apollo*, 97 (June 1973), 566–71.
Colley, Linda, 'Eighteenth-Century English Radicalism before Wilkes', *Transactions of the Royal Historical Society*, 5th ser., 31 (1981), 1–20.
Collingwood, R. G., 'John Horsley and Hadrian's Wall', *AA*, 4th ser., 15 (1938), 1–42.
De Marly, Diana, 'The Establishment of Roman Dress in Seventeenth-Century Portraiture', *Burl. Mag.*, 117 (1975), 443–51.
Ehrenpreis, Irvin, 'Swift on Liberty', *JHI*, 13 (1952), 131–46.
Eisenthal, E., 'John Webb's Reconstruction of the Ancient House', *AH*, 28 (1985), 7–31.
Erskine-Hill, Howard, 'Heirs of Vitruvius: Pope and the Idea of Architecture', in *The Art of Alexander Pope*, ed. Howard Erskine-Hill and Anne Smith, London, 1979, pp. 144–56.
Gibbon, Michael, 'The First Neo-Classical Building?', *CL* (11 April 1974), 852–3.
'Stowe, Buckinghamshire: the House and Garden Buildings and their Designers', *AH*, 20 (1977), 31–44.
Gibson, William A., 'Three Principles of Renaissance Architectural Theory in Pope's *Epistle to Burlington*', *SEL*, 11 (1971), 487–505.
Girouard, Mark, 'Ambrose Phillipps of Garendon', *AH*, 8 (1965), 25–38.
Goldsmith, M. M., 'Public Virtue and Private Vices: Bernard Mandeville and English Political Ideologies in the Early Eighteenth Century', *ECS*, 9 (1975–6), 477–510.

Gombrich, E. H., 'Reynolds's Theory and Practice of Imitation', *Burl. Mag.*, 80 (1942), 40–5.
Greene, Donald, 'Johnson, Stoicism, and the Good Life', in *The Unknown Samuel Johnson*, ed. John J. Burke, Jr, and Donald Kay, Madison, Wis., 1983.
Heinemann, F. H., 'John Toland and the Age of Enlightenment', *RES*, 20 (1944), 125–46.
Henry, Avril and Dixon, Peter, 'Pope and the Architects: a Note on the *Epistle to Burlington*', *ES*, 51 (1970), 437–41.
Hibbard, G. R., 'The Country House Poem of the Seventeenth Century', *JWCI*, 19 (1956), 159–74, repr. in *Essential Articles for the Study of Alexander Pope*, ed. Maynard Mack, Hamden, Conn., 1964.
Hicks, Philip, 'Bolingbroke, Clarendon, and the Role of Classical Historian', *ECS*, 20 (1987), 445–71.
Horne, Colin, 'The Classical Temper in Britain: Origins and Components', in *The Classical Temper in Western Europe*, ed. John Hardy and Andrew McCredie, Melbourne, 1983.
Houghton, Walter E., Jr, 'The English Virtuoso in the Seventeenth Century', parts 1 and 2, *JHI*, 3 (1942), 51–73, 190–219.
Kelsall, Malcolm, 'The Iconography of Stourhead', *JWCI*, 46 (1983), 133–43.
Kenworthy-Browne, John, 'The Temple of Liberty at Woburn Abbey', *Apollo*, 130 (July 1989), 27–32.
Kimball, Fiske, 'Burlington architectus', *RIBA Journal*, 34 (15 October and 12 November 1927).
Kurz, Otto, 'Huius Nympha loci', *JWCI*, 21 (1953), 171.
Landau, Norma, 'Eighteenth-Century England: Tales Historians Tell', *ECS*, 22 (1988–9), 208–18.
Lord, John, 'Joseph Nollekens and Lord Yarborough: Documents and Drawings', *Burl. Mag.*, 130 (1988), 915–19.
Macdonald, George, 'John Horsley, Scholar and Gentleman', *AA*, 4th ser., 10 (1933), 1–57.
McCarthy, Michael J., 'The Rebuilding of Stowe House 1770–1777', *HLQ*, 36 (1972–3), 267–98.
McKillop, A. D., *The Background of Thomson's Liberty*, *Rice Institute Pamphlet*, 38 (July 1951), no. 2.
Mullett, Charles F., 'Classical Influences on the American Revolution', *CJ*, 35 (1939–40), 92–104.
New, Melvyn, 'Gibbon, Middleton, and the "Barefooted Fryars"', *N&Q*, 223 (1978), 51–2.
Phiddian, Robert, 'The Reaction to Collins's *A Discourse on Free-Thinking* "Not

Politicks"?', *Swift Studies*, 4 (1989), 63–76.

Piggott, Stuart, 'William Camden and the *Britannia*', Reckitt Archaeological Lecture, 21 November 1951, in *PBA*, 37 (1951), 199–217.

'The Ancestors of Jonathan Oldbuck', *Antiquity*, 29 (1955), 150–6.

'Sir John Clerk and "The Country Seat"', in *The Country Seat*, ed. Howard M. Colvin and John Harris, London, 1970.

Price, Martin, '"The Dark and Implacable Genius of Superstition": an Aspect of Gibbon's Irony', in *Augustan Worlds: Essays in Honour of A. R. Humphreys*, ed. J. C. Hilson, M. M. B. Jones and J. R. Watson, New York, 1978, pp. 241–78.

Rogers, Malcolm, 'Michael Rysbrack's Bust of Edmund Waller', *Burl. Mag.*, 119 (1977), 314, 352.

Rogers, Robert W., 'Alexander Pope's *Universal Prayer*', *JEGP*, 54 (1955), 612–24.

Rose, J. Holland, 'The Oratory of Pitt', in *Pitt and Napoleon: Essays and Letters*, London, 1912, pp. 1–19.

Rowan, Alistair, 'Batty Langley's Gothic', in *Studies in Memory of David Talbot Rice*, ed. Giles Robertson and George Henderson, Edinburgh, 1975, pp. 197–215.

Rutledge, Anna Wells, 'A Cosmopolitian in Carolina', *William and Mary Quarterly*, 6 (1949), 637–43.

Scholtz, Gregory F., 'Anglicanism in the Age of Johnson: the Doctrine of Conditional Salvation', *ECS*, 20 (1988–9), 182–207.

Sedgwick, Romney, 'Horace Walpole's Political Articles', in *Horace Walpole, Writer, Politician, and Connoisseur: Essays on the 250th Anniversary of Walpole's Birth*, ed. Warren Hunting Smith, New Haven, 1967.

Sicca, Cinzia M., 'Lord Burlington at Chiswick: Architecture and Landscape', *Garden History*, 10 (1982), 36–69.

Spink, William, 'Sir John Clerk of Penicuik: Landowner as Designer', in Willis, ed., *Furor Hortensis*, pp. 31–40.

Stewart, J. Douglas, 'New Light on Michael Rysbrack: Augustan England's "Classical Baroque" Sculptor', *Burl. Mag.*, 120 (1978), 215–22.

Summerson, John, 'The Classical Country House in Eighteenth-Century England', three Cantor Lectures, *Journal of the Royal Society of Arts*, 107 (July 1959), 539–87.

'Inigo Jones', *PBA*, 50 (1964), 170–82.

Tait, A. A., 'William Adam and Sir John Clerk: Arniston and "The Country Seat"', *Burl. Mag.*, 111 (March 1969), 132–40.

Tiffany, Esther M., 'Shaftesbury as Stoic', *PMLA*, 38 (1923), 642–84.

Torchiana, Donald T., 'Brutus: Pope's Last Hero', in *Essential Articles for the Study of Alexander Pope*, ed. Maynard Mack, 2nd edn, Hamden, Conn., 1968, pp. 705–23.

Turner, James, 'The Structure of Henry Hoare's Stourhead', *Art Bulletin*, 61 (1979), 68–77.

Ustick, W. Lee, 'Changing Ideals of Aristocratic Character and Conduct in Seventeenth-Century England', *MP*, 30 (1932), 147–66.

Vermeule, Cornelius, 'Graeco-Roman Statues: Purpose and Setting', parts 1 and 2, *Burl. Mag.*, 110 (October 1968), 545–58, 607–13.

Ward, Addison, 'The Tory View of Roman History', *SEL*, 4 (1964), 413–56.

Weinbrot, Howard, 'The Conventions of Classical Satire and the Practice of Pope', *PQ*, 59 (1980), 317–37.

'Persius, the Opposition to Walpole, and Pope', in *Greene and Centennial Studies: Essays Presented to Donald Greene*, ed. Paul J. Korshin and Robert R. Allen, Charlottesville, 1984, pp. 93–124.

Whistler, Laurence, 'The Authorship of the Stowe Temples', *Stoic*, 14.4 (December 1950).

Winks, R. W., 'Hume and Gibbon: a View from a Vantage', *Dalhousie Review*, 41 (1962), 496–504.

Woodbridge, Kenneth, 'The Sacred Landscape: Painters and the Lake-Garden of Stourhead', *Apollo*, 88 (September 1968), 210–14.

Wootton, David, 'Hume's "Of Miracles": Probability and Irreligion', in *Oxford Studies in the History of Philosophy*, vol. 1, *Studies in the Philosophy of the Scottish Enlightenment*, ed. M. A. Stewart, Oxford, 1990.

Worsley, Giles, 'Rokeby Park, Yorkshire', *CL* part I (19 March 1987), pp. 74–9; part II (26 March 1987), pp. 176–9; part III (2 April 1987), pp. 116–17.

'Taking the Ancients Literally: Archaeological Neoclassicism in Mid-Eighteenth-Century Britain', paper delivered to the Georgian Group Symposium on 'New Light on English Palladianism', 13 October 1988.

'West Wycombe Park, Bucks', *CL* (6 September 1990), pp. 112–17.

Index

Lightning Source UK Ltd.
Milton Keynes UK
09 February 2011

167213UK00004B/28/P

9 780521 105798